C000054035

CONTENTS

COVERING PUBLIC ISSUES

Coverage of public issues is a traditional criterion of the quality of American journalism, demonstrated in part by journalism's highest awards being earmarked to honor outstanding reporting about government.

JAMES K. VANLEUVEN and GARRETT W. RAY. 1988. Communication Stages and Public Issue Coverage. *Newspaper Research Journal* 9(4):71–83.

ADVICE FOR REPORTERS ASPIRING TO COVER PUBLIC ISSUES

I'd want them to know how to write well, I'd want them to know history. I'd want them to be infinitely curious about the human condition. And I'd want them to have the sensitivity of a safe-cracker's fingers.

JOHN PATRICK HUNTER, Associate Editor, Madison (WI) *Capital Times,* 13 Aug. 1983, in the *Wisconsin Journalist.*

INTERPRETING PUBLIC ISSUES

INTERPRETING PUBLIC ISSUES

by **Robert J. Griffin,
Dayle H. Molen,
Clay Schoenfeld,** and
James F. Scotton

with **David Cassady, Bruce Garrison,
Thomas Heuterman, Freda McVay,
Robert Meier,** and **Kenneth Rystrom**

IOWA STATE UNIVERSITY PRESS / AMES

Manufactured in the United States of America
∞ This book is printed on acid-free paper.

First edition, 1991

Library of Congress Cataloging-in-Publication Data
Interpreting public issues / by Robert J. Griffin . . . [et al.]. — 1st ed.
    p. cm.
    Includes index.
    ISBN 0-8138-0994-0 (alk. paper) — ISBN 0-8138-0992-4 (pbk. alk. paper)
    1. Journalism — United States. 2. Journalism — Social aspects.
    I. Griffin, Robert J.
    PN4832.I57 1991
    071'.3 — dc20   90-40080

TO **DION HENDERSON**

Consummate professional,
Compelling writer,
Friend

PREFACE

"What does it all mean?"

"What's the news behind the news?"

"What's the connection?"

Questions like these we journalists are increasingly being asked to answer for our readers and viewers. No longer can we be content only to provide spot news coverage. Today is the day—in both print and electronic media—of what is variously called "interpretive reporting," "in-depth reporting," "backgrounding," or "news analysis."

We are not talking about the free-swinging commentaries or "think pieces" on the editorial page. Interpreting public issues is rooted in solid front-page reporting, but it is reporting that goes beyond the "who," "what," "where," and "when" to emphasize the "how," the "why," and the "so what"—issue-centered journalism.

This book is a guide to issue-centered journalism. It explains how you go about identifying issues, collecting and collating information, and then interpreting the story comprehensively yet clearly. The emphasis is on how this type of reporting can be practiced on the small-city media where most journalism school graduates begin their careers. The book is the work of a team of professors, each with specialties, and thus, it illustrates the increasing use of team reporting in developing in-depth series. The public issues we have selected as the subjects of chapters stem from an analysis of the current tables of contents of newspapers and newsmagazines and from a content study of current network news programs, again with an emphasis in the immediate environment of small-city media.

You will find five main features in this book: (1) a discussion of the broad public issues on the agenda of small-city media today; (2) a scenario that assumes you may be reporting for radio, television, or a magazine, as well as for a daily newspaper; (3) practical "how to" examples of reporting and interpreting; (4) summaries of relevant communication research; and (5) a running emphasis on covering issues as opposed to just covering events.

The case histories, including many prize winners, illustrate problems and possibilities inherent in analyzing and interpreting the news. They will show you how to go beyond just reporting the news and get into the analysis and interpretation that are demanded of the modern journalist.

AUTHORS

DAVID CASSADY is Associate Professor of Journalism at Pacific University, Forest Grove, Oregon. A graduate of the University of Iowa, where he received his M.A. and Ph.D. degrees, he has a varied professional background with a stint on papers ranging from a Washington state weekly to a major metropolitan daily in Arizona. Although involved in a variety of courses and programs, his primary interests lie in community journalism. He is particularly interested in increasing the dialogue between the newspaper and its readers and increasing the newspaper's sense of involvement in and responsibility for its community.

BRUCE GARRISON is Professor in the School of Communication at the University of Miami, Florida. He received his Ph.D. degree from Southern Illinois University, his M.S. degree from the University of Tennessee, and his B.S. degree from the University of Southern Mississippi. He has worked for daily newspapers in Florida, Kentucky, Massachusetts, Mississippi, Tennessee, Texas, and Wisconsin and for the news department of WTMJ-TV in Milwaukee. Garrison has directed survey research projects for city governments and television and radio stations, and he has served as manager of the News Election Service and as an election supervisor for Associated Press in Miami. Garrison is author of *Sports Reporting, Professional Feature Writing, Professional News Writing,* and of articles in several journals. He taught public affairs reporting at Marquette University before redesigning the course at Miami.

ROBERT J. GRIFFIN is Associate Professor in the College of Communication, Journalism and Performing Arts at Marquette University in Milwaukee, Director of the Center for Mass Media Research, and former Director of the Graduate Program in Journalism. He earned his Ph.D. degree in mass communications (specializing in theory and research methodology) and his M.A. degree in journalism (with emphasis in environmental communications) from the University of Wisconsin-Madison. His research interests include surveys of news audiences, mental processing of news by journalists and by audiences, and science and environmental communication. Griffin has been a guest on a number of radio and television public affairs shows and has varied media experience.

THOMAS H. HEUTERMAN is Professor and former Chair, School of Communication, Washington State University, Pullman, where he has been teaching an advanced reporting course for twenty-five years. He is a veteran of eight years on the *Yakima* (Washington) *Herald-Republic* government beat. He is active in the History Division of the Association for Education in Journalism and Mass Communication. Heuterman was a Visiting Professor at the School Voor De Journalistick at Utrecht and at the Academie Voor De Journalistick at Tilburg in 1983, and at Sichuan University in Chengdu in 1989.

FREDA McVAY is Assistant Professor of Journalism at Texas Tech University, Lubbock, from which she holds two degrees. With more than fifteen years experience in both semiweekly and daily newspaper reporting and editing, she has also worked in college public relations, and has served as director of Tech's summer publications workshops. She has worked as campaign strategist and media adviser for numerous local and state political campaigns during the past twenty-five years. Her first book is a biography of pioneer Southwest newspaper editor, the late Charles A. Guy of the *Lubbock Avalanche-Journal*.

ROBERT F. MEIER is Professor of Sociology and Chair of the Department of Sociology and Anthropology at Iowa State University. He received his Ph.D. from the University of Wisconsin and has taught at the University of California at Irvine and Washington State University before joining the faculty at Iowa State. He is the author of *Crime and Society* (1989), coauthor of *Sociology of Deviant Behavior* (seventh edition, 1989), and editor of several books on criminology. His interests include processes of deviance and social control.

DAYLE H. MOLEN is Professor of Journalism at California State University-Fresno, and a past department chair. He holds a B.A. degree in political science from the University of Idaho and an M.S. degree in journalism from the University of Oregon. He joined the Cal State U.-Fresno faculty in 1965. His field experience covers more than fifteen years as a reporter, editor, and copyreader on Rocky Mountain and West Coast daily newspapers. He has written numerous articles for journalism trade publications and historical publications.

KENNETH RYSTROM is Professor of Communication Studies at Virginia Polytechnic Institute and State University in Blacksburg. He formerly taught at the University of Redlands in southern California and has been visiting professor at the University of Montana and Washington State University. During twenty years in newspaper work, he was an editorial writer for the *Des Moines* (Iowa) *Register* and reporter, editorial page editor, and managing editor of the *Vancouver* (Washington) *Columbian*. He holds a B.A. degree in journalism from the University of Nebraska-Lincoln, an M.A. degree in political science from the University of California-Berkeley, and an M.A. degree in journalism and a Ph.D. in political science from the University of Southern California. He is the author of *The Why, Who, and How of the Editorial Page*.

CLAY SCHOENFELD is Emeritus Professor of Journalism and Mass Communication, Emeritus Affiliated Professor of Environmental Studies, Emeritus Chair of the Center for Environmental Communication and Education Studies, and Emeritus Dean of Inter-College Programs at the University of Wisconsin-Madison, from which he holds two degrees. With experience on both weekly and daily newspapers and in public relations, Schoenfeld is best known as the author of twenty-six books and over two-hundred national magazine and journal articles. A retired Army Reserve Colonel, he is past president of three national associations in the fields of university administration and environmental education. In 1982 he was named Conservation Educator of the Year by the National Wildlife Federation. Schoenfeld is now president of the Wisconsin Public Relations Institute, Madison.

JAMES F. SCOTTON is Associate Professor in the College of Communication, Journalism and Performing Arts at Marquette University in Milwaukee. He has taught at South Dakota State, Pennsylvania State, Temple, Michigan State, and the City University of New York in this country. He has also taught at Makerere University in Uganda, Lagos University in Nigeria, and the University of Nairobi in Kenya. He has ten years of experience as a reporter and editor with daily newspapers, the Associated Press, and as a correspondent in Washington, D.C. He holds a Ph.D. degree from the University of Wisconsin.

PART 1

Your environment as a public issues reporter

In this section we lay out the broad background needed for reporting and interpreting all the public issues that are discussed in the balance of the book.

Chapter 1, "Getting Oriented," explores such key issues as the nature of news and public issues, the real meanings of reporting and interpreting, and the way to approach issue-centered reporting.

Chapter 2, "Getting Started," reviews the professional skills of the practiced public issues reporter. Topics discussed include doing background reading, searching records, interviewing, adapting social science research methods to reporting, planning strategy, identifying the audience, striving for effective writing, becoming familiar with computerized media operations, and coordinating tools and techniques. Many of these skills are already somewhat familiar to you, but they are worth reviewing, at least briefly.

Chapter 3, "Law and Ethics," discusses the laws, such as freedom of information acts, that aid you in covering public issues. It also reviews those laws and court decisions that constrain you in covering public issues — largely by protecting individuals from libel or invasion of privacy. Chapter 3 also discusses the formal and informal codes of journalistic ethics that are the hallmarks of professional reporting and editing.

The broad working philosophy, professional tools, legal knowledge, and ethical considerations discussed in this section are applied in later sections to reporting and interpreting particular public issues.

CHAPTER 1

Getting oriented

CORVALLIS, OREGON, located a hundred miles south of Portland, is representative of many small American cities today. Its population is 42,500; its economy is a mixture of business and diversified farming; and it is the site of a university. Its daily newspaper, the *Gazette-Times,* has a circulation of 15,000. A current overriding public issue in Corvallis is the economy and its many tangents.

One of those tangents in early 1983 was the proposed development of a research park. To report and interpret ramifications of that proposal, editor Rod Deckert, city editor Kay Black, and reporter Pat Kight outlined a five-part series to be developed by Kight and Russ Mitchell.

The two reporters identified pertinent angles and tied them together into a coherent series aimed at Corvallis readers (Kight and Mitchell 1983a). Here are the beginning and ending of the first article of the series:

Research park posed as cure for economy

(*First in a series*)

Research and development. High technology. Science parks.

Those are the buzz words of 1983, to judge from conversations heard all over Corvallis.

Many people believe a research park — as proposed by a local council of governments report last summer — could immunize Benton County from the economic ills plaguing the rest of Oregon.

Others wonder whether the research park will merely be the latest version of Corvallis's downtown redevelopment plan: planned and discussed for years, but ultimately abandoned.

If testimony at several hearings last fall is any clue, many Corvallis residents have more questions than answers about the research-park concept. . . .

The discussion originated early last year with a committee of business, government and university leaders who continue to meet about once a month.

Out of those discussions emerged an idea and a report: "A Research-Technology Park in the Corvallis Area—An Examination of Feasibility and Options."

The eighty-one-page report, released in July, said such a park could create jobs for 2500 people within a dozen years.

Next: What does Oregon State University have to offer?

The *Gazette-Times* reporters then went on in four articles to consider (1) the relationship of Oregon State University, a major Corvallis industry in itself, to the proposed high technology research park (Kight and Mitchell 1983b); (2) how Corvallis stacks up against other communities trying to attract high technology industry (Kight and Mitchell 1983c); (3) what Oregon and Corvallis have that could be attractive to high technology industry (Kight and Mitchell 1983d); and (4) what Corvallis should do—and should not do—to ready itself for rapid growth (Kight and Mitchell 1983e).

The new reporter: opportunities and rewards

As Corvallis reporters Pat Kight and Russ Mitchell can testify, an institutional truth in journalism is that few new graduates step directly from campus to big-city reporting jobs, and those who do often find the experience frustrating.

This fact of life led Garrett Ray, a former editor of the Littleton, Colorado, *Independent,* to urge more exposure for journalism students to the fascinating complexity of small cities and rural areas. In a column in *Publishers' Auxiliary* on June 13, 1983, Ray put the prospects for first jobs into perspective by noting that "the reality facing most graduates of most journalism schools is this: You may picture yourself as the Paris bureau chief for Associated Press or the Beirut correspondent for CBS News. But you are going to start your career in Aransas Pass or Hoopeston" (Ray 1983).

This is hardly catastrophic in terms of career goals. You may find advantages in the small-city news environment with the premium it places on versatility and the consequent wide variety of reporting experiences that it offers. A small community also inevitably brings you closer to the people who make up your audience. For example, Pat Kight stepped from college to the Associated Press bureau in Detroit, and Russ Mitchell started in Ft. Lauderdale; however, both made a conscious decision to switch to small-city journalism. "My experience," says Kight (1983), "has been that only a tiny few of those coveted big-city jobs are the plums so many J-grads seem to think they are. A relatively young reporter for a progressive small-city paper has many more opportunities to tackle important stories than he or she would working at, say, the *Chicago Tribune.*"

Because many rewarding jobs can be found with small-city media, this book places an emphasis upon situations you will encounter there. Size does not always equate with quality in journalism, and many small-city media are big-league performers. For instance, the list of Pulitzer Prize winners over the years includes smaller publications such as the *Hutchinson News* in Kansas, the weekly *Point Reyes Light* in California, the weekly *Hungry Horse News* in Columbia Falls, Montana, and the *Zenia Daily Gazette* in Ohio. Still, the big-city media generally are better able to spring reporters free to concentrate on special assignments and investigations, so some of our examples come from metropolitan publications and broadcast stations. Regardless of the size of the medium, the examples are intended to acquaint you with excellence in public affairs reporting and to help you avoid the mistakes of the not-so-excellent.

News: what is it?

Obviously, this is a book about how to report *news*. Yet there is no completely satisfactory definition of what news is. Much the same thing can be said about news as St. Augustine said about time: we know perfectly well what it is — until someone asks us (Ryan 1960).

A conventional definition of news would probably go something like this: an interesting, unusual, or significant event occurring in the past twenty-four hours (Hall 1973). For example, author Stephen Hess has noted that for most Washington, D.C., reporters, news is "a tangible activity — a Congressional vote, a Supreme Court decision, a Presidential speech — that occurs in the current 24-hour period" (Hess 1983).

But is "a current event" a sufficient definition of "news"? Pollster George Gallup does not think so. He calls for "more reporting of social, economic, and political problems — covering ideas: the new field of journalism. Our press services do a good job of covering events, but have yet to make a systematic effort to cover ideas" (Gallup 1980). Michael Schudson, a sociologist who has written about the news and advertising professions, also insists that news is more than just presentation of information and includes explanation. "Readers want not just to know but to understand," Schudson (1986) says.

Issue-centered news

In this book we employ Gallup's more encompassing concept of news. We are not denigrating events; after all, they supply valuable news pegs. We are simply pointing out that the world is not made up of discrete events; everything is connected to everything else.

Not only are single events never isolated but each event also has a past, a present, and a future. Some events and their interrelationships are obviously more important than others at any given time. They cannot be interpreted in the absence of sensitivity to their larger context and significance.

Even the most sustained coverage of an event and its aftermath begins with a spot news incident. Issue-centered reporting, on the other hand, starts with questions: what is going on, what does it mean, what and where is its impact?

The question the *East Side Community News* started with in its investigation of area property taxes was simple, direct, and in its page one headline: "Why Are the Assessments Up on the East Side?" Reporter Michael Zeidler (1988) then went on in his story to ask, "But why such a jump in assessments now?" and "What does it all mean?"

Diedre Carmody (1982) of the *New York Times* used the questions parents asked school drug counselors to help focus and structure her article on the threat of drugs to high school students. The parents asked:

"How do I know if my child is involved in drugs?"
"What do I do if the parents of my child's best friend smoke marijuana at home themselves?"
"When my child says there is no difference between my having a drink when I come home at night and his or her having a joint or marijuana, what do I answer?"
"How can I prevent my child from using drugs?"

Both Zeidler and Carmody used an event as a news peg to lend currency to their reports. Property values and taxes had been going up sharply on Milwaukee's East Side for a decade, but Zeidler tied his article to new city reassessments. Drug problems in New York schools were not a new story, but Carmody tied her story to a new drug-counseling program. The actual events, however, were incidental to their investigations into ongoing public issues in their communities.

While the Kight-Mitchell *Gazette-Times* series revived a couple of news pegs—an old council of governments committee report and a more recent city council decision—the series really was based on four basic questions, questions the reporters worked right into their first story: What is a research park? What would it take to build one here? What kind of industry would it attract? Who would benefit, and who would pay?

The series represented deep digging for answers to those questions. It reported and interpreted the possible relationship of a new research park to Corvallis's faltering economy. Kight and Mitchell provided the answers for their Corvallis readers in the background of a national public issue.

Public issues: what are they?

Like news, a public issue is difficult to define. Overlapping terms are involved. Sociologists typically speak of "social problems," journalists of "public issues" or "public affairs." We do not equate public issues only with the activities of government. While public issues or public affairs may indeed represent the concerns of the various echelons of government, public issues or public affairs are not necessarily covered exclusively by governmental reporters. As the following prize-winning examples (Journalism's Best 1988) show, a public issue can appear on any beat.

• In Tucson, Arizona, three reporters of the *Arizona Republic* found sexual abuse, inadequate housing, and poor health care for Native Americans who were also victims of an oil-lease fraud. "Fraud in Indian Country: A Billion Dollar Betrayal," won reporters Mike Masterson, Chuck Cook and Mark N. Trahant a Heywood Broun Award from the Newspaper Guild.

• In Jacksonville, Florida, the news staff of WJXT-TV decided to look into their own constant reports of rush-hour traffic accidents. "The Deadly Drive Home," a one-hour documentary, pointed to the traditional after-work stop at a bar plus poorly constructed and overcrowded area roads as the causes of many accidents. The program won a duPont-Columbia University Award for public service broadcasting.

• In Lawrence, Massachusetts, editors of the *Eagle-Tribune* spotted a brief wire story about a violent Maryland crime that started them on a major investigation. The accused man had killed a Lawrence gas station attendant and had been given a life sentence. Reporters Susan Forrest and Barbara Walsh spent months checking records, tracking down elusive state officials and interviewing prison authorities across the country. They found that only in Massachusetts were prisoners with such violent backgrounds given weekend furloughs with little supervision. The paper's investigation brought it one of the two 1987 Pulitzer Prizes for reporting.

• In Charleston, West Virginia, reporter Paul J. Nyden and his paper, the *Charleston Gazette,* kept after a story for more than four years. After a

Freedom of Information Act lawsuit, Nyden finally got access to West Virginia Board of Medicine records of malpractice complaints. He found that doctors charged with malpractice rarely suffered serious discipline. Records also showed insurance companies were making high profits from malpractice insurance. His series won a Distinguished Service Award from the Society of Professional Journalists, Sigma Delta Chi.

• In Montgomery, Alabama, Managing Editor Jim Tharpe of the *Alabama Journal* (a circulation of twenty thousand) was appalled to discover that the state had the highest rate of infant mortality in the nation. His small staff dug through state records and talked with poverty-stricken rural families to find out why. The resulting series, "A Death in the Family," shocked the state and brought the paper the 1987 Pulitzer Prize for Public Service.

• In Lexington, Kentucky, Reporter Craig Cheetham of radio station WLAP examined how sexual abuse can devastate individuals. His thirty-minute documentary, "Passing on the Secret of Sexual Abuse," won a National Press Club Award and a duPont-Columbia University Award.

These stories all involved public issues. Public laws and government agencies were involved, either directly or because of overriding public interest. And all of these stories went beyond the framework of official regulations to show the impact or potential impact upon people.

This role of keeping watch on the community is an important, perhaps the most important, function of the media in our society. The public is often critical of the media and grants press freedom only grudgingly. A *Los Angeles Times-Mirror* survey found, however, that the public strongly supports the press in its watchdog function, particularly when it is keeping watch over politicians and government (*The People & The Press* 1986).

Characterizing public issues

Public issues are both stable and transitory. Of the seventeen major topics proposed in the original 1922 prospectus for *Time* magazine, fourteen are still in use today. On the other hand, in recent years *Time* has introduced sections on "Environment" and "The Sexes," and *Newsweek* has created a "Cities" department — all in response to changing perceptions of major public issues.

While new public issues appear, some disappear. One journalist, categorizing the issues of the 1960s, included the Vietnam War and student unrest (Funkhouser 1973). Later, two other journalists, listing the principal public issues of the 1970s, included no such categories (Ryan and Owen 1976).

Invariably, each era will be characterized by one transcendent issue.

Certainly, in 1983 in Corvallis, Oregon—and throughout the country—an overriding issue was that which was variously called "the economy," "the recession," "unemployment," and the "slump." The prominence of the economic issue is one reason why the *Gazette-Times* series on the possible relationships of a proposed research park to economic recovery was so significant and so timely.

Public issues are frequently marked by controversy. Thus, some groups, in attempting to persuade others, often develop antagonistic relationships. In many public issues, rival groups compete for public attention and support. Gun control, the Equal Rights Amendment (ERA), marijuana

SOME KEY PUBLIC ISSUES FOR THE '90s

U.S. News and World Report ran a special double issue called "Outlook 1990s" to kick off the decade. Key public issues they addressed included:

The Economy, Business, Labor
    Yankee ingenuity in industry
    Tokyo's challenge
    Family-friendly employers
    Jobs to the rescue
Social Issues
    Retiree numbers
    Housing costs
Science and Health
    Health costs
    Fewer hospital stays
    Genetic cures
The Environment
    A whole-earth agenda
    The greenhouse effect
    A new garbage ethic
The Electoral Process
    The leadership gap
    Power to the people: building a new world
    Age of indifference: the dulling of American politics

U.S. News and World Report. Dec. 25, 1989/Jan. 1, 1990. 107(25):3.

control, abortion, the federal government's role in education and civil rights, crime control, and birth control are only a sampling of such issues. In each instance, some group has defined a condition as a problem and another group (and in some cases more than one group) has disagreed either with the initial group's definition of the problem or with its suggestion for a solution. Conflict among these groups ensues—and makes issue-centered news.

Identifying public issues

Two criteria may be useful in identifying public issues: (1) the extent to which large numbers of persons are affected or will be affected; and (2) the extent to which the implications or consequences of the issue go beyond the parties immediately involved. Thus, Joe Smith's loss of his job affects his family and, perhaps indirectly, his neighbors, but usually not someone, say, in a nearby town. If many persons, however, lose their jobs, the impact on other people could be quite significant. Or when steelworkers are on strike, auto manufacturers cannot make cars; low production in the steel industry is associated with high unemployment in the auto industry.

You can detect public issues in part by employing what sociologist C. Wright Mills (1959) called "sociological imagination." That is, by recognizing troubles that are bothering you and your associates, you may be alerted to problems that may, in fact, be widespread. To change such awareness of personal problems into an understanding of social issues, however, will require a basic knowledge of how society is organized and how it works. You cannot simply generalize from a single case or even several cases to society at large.

You also can detect public issues by examining the relationships among events and attempting to gain a broader perspective on those events. A single burglary is one event, but several burglaries that produce increased public sentiment about community safety are a public issue; a child's low marks in school can be a source of personal discomfort, but a community's low scores on a national academic achievement test can become a public issue.

Do audiences like issue-centered news? In San Diego, at least, viewers of television newscasts do. In a recent survey, they ranked "issues" ahead of "unexpected events," "entertainment," "weather," and "sports" in audience preference. Among issues, interest was highest in stories about the economy and about how to be a wise consumer (Wulfemeyer 1983). Chapters 4 and 9 of this book discuss reporting on the economy and consumer affairs.

Substantive beats

This book addresses public issues in the broadest sense of the term. A good reporter does not merely hold up a mirror to events. A good reporter actively helps to construct social reality for readers or viewers by digging into public issues that span conventional beats. What sociologist Herbert Gans (1980) called "substantive beat reporters," as opposed to what might be called "geographic beat reporters," are responsible for a wide range of subject matter, since issues such as the environment or education include many disciplines, agencies, and institutions.

Traditionally, reporters cover beats that reflect the organization of a community and the sites where news events habitually break. Typical beats include a city hall beat, a courthouse beat, a police station beat, a federal building beat, and so forth. This geographic division of labor—the assignment of reporters to buildings—divides the work load into manageable proportions, minimizes jurisdictional disputes among reporters, and assures that key sources will be covered. Yet news often does not conform to community organization. The government in Washington, D.C., for example, is a web of interconnected officials, agencies, and policies. Farm policy is not the exclusive province of the Department of Agriculture nor economic policy that of the Treasury Department. So news organizations increasingly are defining beats by substance, not by the location of buildings. There is a diplomacy beat rather than a State Department beat, an economics beat rather than a Treasury Department beat, and so on. Substantive beats give reporters more control over what is news and increase their ability to interpret events and issues.

The substantive beat approach is employed, for example, by the Corvallis *Gazette-Times*. Instead of a city hall reporter, there is a government issues reporter whose beat includes local government, some aspects of state government, land use planning, and facets of economic development. The *Gazette-Times* counterpart of the standard business reporter covers forestry, agriculture, economics, and the like, in keeping with the Corvallis environment. A science and technology beat focuses on high technology industries, research at Oregon State University, and so on. "Although we sometimes spin our wheels a bit trying to decide whose beat covers what," Pat Kight (1983) says, "we find that the approach works well and leads to lots of team projects. Thus the research park series was a natural for Russ, on the science and technology beat, and me, the government issues reporter. We could have pulled our business person into it, too, if we'd needed to."

Reporting: what does it mean?

Public issues reporting is, in many ways, a state of mind that you strive to maintain throughout your daily work. Occasions will arise when time, budget, and the nature of an issue allow for a special effort — either a comprehensive article or a series providing an in-depth analysis. Numerous examples of such efforts are provided throughout this book. While such reports may be the public affairs reporter's showpieces, he or she can practice on a daily basis the investigative and analytical techniques necessary for good public affairs reporting.

We use the term "reporting" in this book in the most sophisticated sense. The best reporters are persevering searchers for truth in the public service, pursuers of facts, not juicy angles. They constantly fret over quality and perfection in their work. Above all, they dig out the facts on their own; they do not merely report what somebody happens to say or do. The true reporter may have help, but he or she is the main force that uncovers the information (Dygert 1976).

For example, Corvallis reporters Kight and Mitchell were not content merely to warm over old committee reports, speeches by officials, and city council actions; they dug out facts and interpretations on their own:

• For Story No. 1 they interviewed the mayor, local developers, the city community development director, and a state representative.

• For Story No. 2 they interviewed a New Jersey research park director, the dean and associate dean of research and a botany professor at Oregon State University (OSU), and the head of a Denver agribusiness; and they dug into OSU's history as a land grant institution.

• For Story No. 3 they did an extensive interview with an Oregon graduate school administrator who had made a study of North Carolina's famed research park; and they talked again to the mayor.

• For Story No. 4 they did background reading in various reports, interviewed a California industrialist, a Stanford research director, and five Oregon businessmen; and researched the business climate in Massachusetts and California.

• For wrap-up Story No. 5 they did a detailed study of a California electronics industry boomtown, comparing its before- and after-development situation with that of Corvallis.

In short, Kight and Mitchell literally made things happen. They did not invent a public issue; the public issue was there. They gave it form and substance through sensitive reporting and interpreting.

Good, solid, in-depth reporting can be applied to any public issue. We believe an attitude of fairness is still the ideal attitude for a journalist. You do not have to play an adversarial role to make your points.

For example, you cannot tell from the Kight-Mitchell stories in Corvallis whether the reporters are for or against development, whether they think a research park concept in Oregon is realistic, or whether they think Oregon State University has been grievously hurt by budget cuts. They do editorialize a bit by conveying the opinion that the Corvallis thrust toward a research park lacks coordination and leadership, but their factual comparisons with similar events in other cities make that obvious anyway. Furthermore, as Kight (1983) says, "we wouldn't have included the conclusion that the research park thrust lacked leadership had we not heard it again and again from multiple sources." In other words, if Kight and Mitchell are motivated by any particular fixation, they do not deliberately expose it. They leave that to publisher Tom Jenks and the editorial page. Meanwhile they cover their story from a 360-degree perspective.

Some reporters may be energized only by a personal sense of outrage over an issue, and some editors may identify public issues reporting only with uncovering some kind of malfeasance in high public office. That, however, is not the kind of reporting we are talking about in this book. You can report and interpret public issues without expecting to uncover crooks at every turn and without pandering to your own predilections.

Do newspaper readers like interpretive, in-depth, research-oriented reporting? According to a study by researchers Virginia Fielder and David Weaver, they certainly do. When readers of the *Chicago Sun-Times* were asked if they felt it was important for a newspaper to do such reporting, 96.5 percent said it was (Fielder and Weaver 1982).

Of course, reporters will always encounter pockets of resistance. Readers in small communities, for instance, are sometimes unhappy with the media for investigating and printing "bad news."

As a matter of fact, aspiring public issues reporters may occasionally be stymied in their own newsrooms. Media rightfully recognize that interpretive reporting can be expensive. To assign a reporter to spend weeks digging into public records or traveling to interview sources who hold information about an issue is expensive enough, but to create a task force of reporters to uncover a scandal of major proportion is beyond the financial means of most daily newspapers and local television stations. Moreover, some editors or news directors, familiar with straight news coverage, may find the style and methods of public issues reporting difficult to accept.

So take a reasoned, sensible approach to public issues reporting. After all, covering public issues may not be your only assignment. Considerable general assignment, feature, and spot news coverage is likely to be mixed in. A public issues reporter need not be brash and showy. The philosophy of this book, properly applied, does not lead necessarily to expensive extravaganzas. It can lead to a style of reporting that is thoughtful, alert,

---

MUDD ON REPORTING

In the great quest for supreme position in the ratings, the main reason for our calling—which is to get close to the truth—competes with other factors. . . . The best chore we can perform is to provide a believable service of disseminating news and information. If reporters allow their sense of outrage, or lack of patience, or frustration to get into their reporting, then they destroy their credibility.

ROGER MUDD of NBC's "Nightly News," 1982. *TV Guide* Vol. 30, No. 50 (December 11–18), 32.

---

curious, and intelligent. It would be difficult to find an editor who would not approve of that.

Interpreting: what does it mean?

The concept of interpretive reporting, as opposed to straight news reporting, has existed at least since Curtis MacDougall wrote a text by that name more than fifty years ago. Interpretive reporting, Professor Mac-Dougall explained, meets "a demand on the part of the intelligent reader to know not only what is happening, but why it is happening, and how what transpires fits into the general political and social pattern." MacDougall was careful to draw a distinction between interpretive writing and opinionated or editorial writing: "Never is it good policy to make categorical statements of evaluation; rather, facts should be generated to speak for themselves" (MacDougall 1938).

Remember that the interpretive "why" does not stem from what the reporter thinks or feels. It stems from facts. We use the term "interpreting" in that context. For example, if you are writing an editorial on the problems minority students continue to face on some American college campuses, you can pontificate freely without citing facts to support your general statements, and you can propose whatever solution your editorial board has agreed upon. When it comes to doing an interpretive background article on the same subject, however, any general statement you make should be documented with quotes from an authoritative source, statistics, representative anecdotes, and so on. Any proposed solutions should be backed up by reports of what remedial action seems to be working — where, when, how, and why.

Without background information, you have an adequate story but not a complete story. By interpreting, rather than merely by reporting, you supply your audience with a frame as well as with a picture. The more specialized you become in covering a particular public issue, the easier it will be for you to add dimensions of interpretation that flesh out skeletons of bare facts.

"Interpretation," agrees Hugh Culbertson, a professor of journalism at Ohio State University, "involves defining implications and causes, not simply reporting facts which 'reveal themselves naturally from events.'" The interpretive journalist "reports news in context, sifting through available information to find meaning." He or she sees "a distinction between supporting or opposing a cause or person and seeking truth" (Culbertson 1983).

Corvallis reporters Kight and Mitchell supplied their readers with background and related information that explained the crucial "why." In Story No. 2, (Kight and Mitchell 1983b), their theme was: If Corvallis is to be a contender in attracting high technology industries to a research park, Oregon State University's research programs will be crucial to success. They explained *why* this was so.

> Already, OSU is the largest research center in the state. Last year outside sources contributed more than $50 million in research grants and contracts. The majority was spent on research into agriculture, forestry, and the oceans — unquestionably OSU's strengths. . . . "I don't know of any university that has strengths in all these areas — agriculture, forestry, and oceanography."

Then they explained how it came to be so:

> OSU's base in agriculture goes back to its creation as a land-grant college in 1868. The partnership between government and land-grant colleges helped the United States become the world leader in agriculture. The 1980s mark the beginning of a new partnership, this time between the universities and business.

and to what end:

> A strong technology transfer program gives a university a solid working relationship with business, says William Lovell, the University's patent manager. That may give OSU an advantage in attracting companies to a

research park, according to Princeton's Robert Wolfe: "I think they are focusing on a key issue—the ability to translate research into the private sector, and thus into jobs."

The long-term effort required to develop a successful industrial park was the theme of Story No. 3 (Kight and Mitchell 1983c). The *Gazette-Times* reporters pointed out that developers of a similar "science park" in Beaverton, Oregon, had been at work for three years on the project.

Not a single building was up yet in the Beaverton project. The three years had been devoted to assembling land, winning a zoning change, financial planning, and "drafting plan after plan."

"The time spent planning, getting capable people on board—it's an enormously big task," warned F. Paul Carlson, developer of the Beaverton science park.

In Story No. 4, Kight and Mitchell (1983d) checked out the competition and faced up to this theme. Now the reporters could have dropped that point right there, but they went on to supply the "why," and its upshot:

> The companies remember the outcry in Corvallis 10 years ago, when sectors of the community tried to block Hewlett-Packard Co.'s attempts to build here.
>
> "That scared a lot of people," said HP's Verley. "Our experience was highly publicized."
>
> Companies "see no reason to swim upstream and try to force themselves on Oregon," said Steve Cottrell of California's Stanford Research Institute. His sentiments were echoed by several other California business executives.
>
> Whether Oregon deserves a no-growth reputation in 1984 may be beside the point. It's got it. And if it wants high-tech industry, it must deal with it.
>
> According to Verley: "If the state shakes the image, it's got at least as good a chance as anyone else of attracting high-tech industry." . . .
>
> Oregon's attitude toward higher education is perceived as yet another hindrance to high-technology development. High-tech industry feeds on engineers and scientists and the kinds of research and training opportunities that a high-quality technical university offers. However, the state government's lack of support is hurting its reputation. Oregon's financial support of higher education was among the highest in the country 10 years ago and is now one of the lowest, and that fact does not escape high-tech executives.
>
> "The attitude from the Legislature detracts from [OSU's] ability to maintain good programs," said Jon Birck of Northwest Instruments in Portland. "I don't want to sound negative, but I never saw a high-technology center grow up except around widely recognized highly technical universities."

In Story No. 5, Kight and Mitchell (1983e) wonder how a flourishing high technology research park might change Corvallis, for good or ill. Instead of speculating or quoting someone, they acquired strongly related background data by looking at Roseville, California. This electronics industry boomtown, sixteen miles northeast of Sacramento, had a research park which included a branch of the same company (Hewlett-Packard) that has a plant in Corvallis:

> A decade ago, Roseville was a sleepy community of about 13,000, best known as a major West Coast railroad junction and, in incessant TV ads, as "the used-car capital of Northern California."
>
> Today, 27,000 people live there, many brought in by the electronics and computer companies that came to Roseville during the late 1970s and early '80s.
>
> Hewlett-Packard has 1,000 workers in Roseville, in what the company says is just the first phase of an electronics complex that eventually will employ 22,000.
>
> The plant is in Roseville's high-technology industrial park, the largest piece of vacant, industrially zoned land in California.
>
> Other companies followed HP to Roseville: Shugart Associates, a Zerox subsidiary; Electronic Arrays, an offshoot of Nippon Electronics; a Palo Alto-based company called OMTAC.
>
> The rapid growth has brought problems.
>
> Roseville's schools are near capacity. The average house, available for $35,000 a decade ago, now costs $115,000.
>
> And the city's downtown area, never a strong retail center, has been devastated by heavy traffic from Highway 65, which runs past the industrial park and through downtown.
>
> Belatedly, Roseville is learning to deal with the side-effects of its electronics boom.
>
> The city recently began charging new industries in advance for everything from sewer and water lines to schools and electricity.

Fortunately, Kight and Mitchell could go on to say that "Corvallis is better equipped to handle a high-technology influx than Roseville was," thanks to a farsighted land use plan and "a longstanding systems development charge." Anticipating the readers' question about what a long-standing systems development charge is, Kight and Mitchell explain:

> — The developer pays in full for all services inside his project's boundaries.
> — The developer also pays a share — usually the lion's share — of improvements outside the boundaries (such as trunk-lines to link the property with distant city sewers).
> — Nearby property owners who directly benefit from the services are charged a proportional share of the costs.

— City money, from systems development charges or sometimes bond proceeds, pay for "oversized improvements — an extra-wide street, for instance, or a water main designed to serve an area beyond the immediate development."

Actually, Kight and Mitchell did not travel to Roseville, because the paper could not afford such a jaunt. Kight (1983) explains: "I went to high school in Roseville and my mother still lives there. I drew my account of the changes from recent vacations I've spent there and from many, many telephone calls. This is a point that needs to be made: Even on small news media like the *Gazette-Times* you can delve economically outside your audience area for comparisons. For example, a year ago I did a series on various downtown redevelopment projects in similarly sized cities by phoning incessantly and by gaining cooperation from other newspapers."

All in all, reporters Kight and Mitchell did a nice job of applying Professor MacDougall's definition of interpreting: covering not only what is happening but why it is happening and how it fits into the general political and social pattern. They do not, however, become so wordy that the main thrust of their series is submerged (Pitts 1982). (Incidentally, soon after the high technology series Pat Kight was promoted to features and special assignments writer-editor for a Sunday magazine launched by the Corvallis *Gazette-Times,* and Russ Mitchell went to the Massachusetts Institute of Technology on a science-writing fellowship.)

Issue-centered reporting: how?

As in the case of the Corvallis research park stories by *Gazette-Times* reporters Kight and Mitchell, reporting and interpreting public issues can involve a team of reporters working on special assignment to develop a series. But issue-oriented reporting does not necessarily involve a special series of articles or an hour-long documentary. Often, it involves continuing coverage as developments occur and as time allows you to delve into the ramifications of an issue. In fact, if you are reporting for a small weekly or daily newspaper or are doing double duty at a radio station as reporter and disc jockey, you rarely will have the time to concentrate on a single story to the exclusion of all else that is happening in the community. Eventually, however, the opportunity should arise to put the parts of an issue together so that the audience can see the whole issue, and not just its separate elements.

For example, Bob Anderson of the *Morning Advocate* of Baton Rouge, Louisiana, had been covering stories ranging from asbestos dangers in elementary school construction to the disappearance of the state's marshes under a cover of oil waste. His reporting on a controversial plan to site a toxic waste disposal plant near the city made page one sixteen days in a row in 1984 as he doggedly followed the issue until the key public hearing (Anderson 1984).

Although the application for the disposal plant was withdrawn after the hearing, Anderson was convinced that the paper's readers still did not understand the continuing threat to their community and environment. Anderson, along with reporters Mike Dunne and Sonny Albarado, developed a forty-page tabloid report on the chemical threat to Louisiana. "Prosperity in Paradise? Louisiana's Chemical Legacy" (Anderson 1985a) tried to cover every aspect of the problem. In summary of the situation, the special section told its readers:

> Air pollution—Baton Rouge companies put thousands of tons of pollutants into the air each year. The city's air quality does not meet federal standards for ozone and contains cancer-causing agents. The state's laws and enforcement program have been called deficient.
>
> Surface water pollution—The Mississippi River is among the problem sites, which a researcher says may be bad news for health in communities that are drinking water from it.
>
> Plant dangers—Eight of the top ten chemicals produced in Louisiana are hazardous. Officials say a Bhopal-type accident could happen here but is not likely because of safety precautions.
>
> Pipelines—Aging pipelines and inadequate inspection programs are turning one of the safest modes of moving hazardous materials into a potential time bomb.
>
> Money—Most states spend more for environmental protection than Louisiana. Meanwhile, the state gives big tax exemptions to companies with major environmental violations.
>
> Cancer—The state leads the nation in lung cancer death rate, but there is debate, even among cancer researchers, on the role of the petrochemicals industry.

The report tried to put the problem in human terms. Reporters interviewed people who lived near hazardous waste sites, workers suffering from illnesses related to air pollution, and residents fearful for their water supplies. Others who were forced to flee their homes because of hazardous fumes told their stories.

Anderson and his colleagues tried to be fair. State officials who were working hard on the problem were interviewed. Some progress was noted. While the *Morning Advocate* reported "an immense groundwater pollution problem" was beginning to appear in Louisiana, it carefully told readers that Baton Rouge's water supply was still safe to drink (Anderson 1985a). As Anderson wrote, "I hope as you read these stories you will notice the attempt to be fair to all sides. This more than anything else has given our newspaper credibility. Oddly enough, my work has been honored by both environmental and industrial groups" (Anderson 1985b).

Day-to-day reporting will challenge your ability to perceive the interactions of events and the issues that extend beyond a single event. In a small news operation, you may be occupied with a variety of spot news that leaves little time for series or special reports such as Anderson's. You still should be able to accumulate the information you need for a similar overview through your daily coverage of a developing public affairs story.

A series should not represent a be-all and end-all to coverage of the issue concerned. "The point is," says Pat Kight (1983), "to try not to drop the ball after taking an in-depth look at something. Since our series ran we've stuck to the research-park issue like glue. We cover the routine stuff: the zoning hearing, the annexations, the announcements of tenants. And then again we try to pause periodically and look at the cumulative effect of those decisions: What does this mean? Are things going as planned?"

An interpretive strategy

Like Kight, as a public affairs reporter you can place the news to be covered on two mental spectrums. One spectrum ranges from the specific to the general, and the other from the descriptive to the analytical. These two spectrums cross one another to produce an *interpretive matrix*. This matrix is not meant to be a formula for writing a story, but rather to be a guide for formulating questions in your investigative and interpretive efforts.

For example, as a police beat reporter examining arrest records or meeting dispatchers, detectives, or administrators, your first task is to record the *basic facts* of specific happenings — the spot news. This news usually stems from events — traffic accidents, assaults, burglaries, robberies, and human interest incidents — and the stories can be classified as descriptive of those specific events. A basic auto accident story, for example, might contain little more than information about who the drivers were, what happened in the accident, when and where it occurred. Doing some probing would get you into questions of process — the why and how of the accident, and its outcomes. Was a driver intoxicated? Was visibility poor? If anyone was killed, was there a family left without a father or a mother? Such questions of cause and effect, homely as they may seem, are at the heart of interpretation and analysis. Such *basic analysis* fleshes out a spot news story by providing analytical information about the specific event.

Your interpretive strategy can also take you from describing a specific event to describing for your readers the general context of events in which the spot news happened. For example, has there been a rash of accidents at this intersection lately? Is this intersection unusually unsafe? Are there accident "hot spots" in other parts of town? This *descriptive context* can provide evidence of trends that you can use to take both you and your audience into the realm of evaluation that we term *interpretive context*. At this level of reporting, you deal analytically with the issues facing your community that are based and manifest in discrete happenings but that usually transcend any specific event. One way to approach interpretive

INTERPRETIVE MATRIX APPLIED TO AN ACCIDENT STORY

	DESCRIPTIVE	ANALYTICAL
SPECIFIC	*Basic Facts* The details of this accident (especially who? what? when? where?)	*Basic Analysis* What caused this accident? What effects did it have?
GENERAL	*Descriptive Context* How many accidents like this recently?	*Interpretive Context* What is causing these accidents? What effects are they having? What can be done?

INTERPRETIVE MATRIX APPLIED TO CORVALLIS *GAZETTE-TIMES* SERIES

	DESCRIPTIVE	ANALYTICAL
SPECIFIC	*Basic Facts* The details about the research park (What? Where? When? How?)	*Basic Analysis* Who will benefit? Who will pay?
GENERAL	*Descriptive Context* What does industry want?	*Interpretive Context* How does Corvallis stack up against the competition?

context is to ask some of the process-type questions — from your basic analysis — of the information you gathered in providing descriptive context.

In other words, you are looking for cause and effect relationships in the general trends you have found. What is causing the rash of accidents of which the latest crash is an example? If alcohol was a factor in the spot news accident, how widespread generally is drinking as a cause of traffic accidents in your community? How does your town compare to other communities in that regard? What leads people to drink and then to drive? How are the police handling the problem? The legislature? The courts? What are the effects of a driving while intoxicated (DWI) conviction on the driver? What are other communities doing to solve the problem of intoxicated drivers? Are their programs working? What is likely to work in your community?

An effective reporter is equally at home when operating in any part of the interpretive matrix. In this sense, interpretive reporting is a continuing analytical state of mind. For example, Roberta Heiman covers the busy health, welfare, and social issues beat for the *Evansville* (Indiana) *Press*. Her beat leaves little time for special projects, but she made time for a ten-part series, "Children of Neglect," which examined the state's failure to reach youngsters in trouble.

"It was one of those topics I'd written about on a fragmented basis," Heiman (1983) says. "I wanted to pull it together for readers." So she began to squeeze interviews on the topic into her daily routine. Finally, she took three weeks from her beat to finish the research and report her findings. "I looked at the nine notebooks I'd filled plus the stacks of other papers I'd collected and I wanted to cry or quit." she recalls. Instead she retyped her notes to refresh her memory and categorize the information. When she was finished writing, the *Press* featured her work for five consecutive days. Each story that identified a problem was accompanied by another one about solutions.

The series was reprinted in tabloid form and circulated among the state's legislators and others who deal with youth. Response was immediate and positive. A group of Evansville civic leaders has already started working on local problems. For her efforts, Scripps-Howard's judges named Heiman Reporter of the Month for February 1983. They called her work "a critical weapon in a reform program."

The beginning of Heiman's series had all of the suspense elements of a novel and all of the interpretive elements of analytical reporting. It was reproduced in the May 1983 *Scripps-Howard News:*

> October 6, 1971: Evansville police have their first encounter with Tommy.
> It's 3:20 in the morning and they're called to a near-downtown gas

station to check out a report that three little kids are hiding out in the restroom there.

They find Tommy, 7, described as a cute kid with curly blond hair, blue eyes and freckles. He's hiding with his brother, 10, and a friend, 8. The youngsters refuse to tell police their names so they're taken to a foster home until the next morning, then returned to their parents.

An officer who assisted in the case later submitted a report to Vanderburgh Juvenile Court. He noted that Tommy's mother "said she had wondered where they were but she didn't seem concerned.

"The home was filthy and smelled so badly of urine that we nearly gagged before getting out of there.

"We talked with the neighbors and apartment manager and they said the parents are both heavy drinkers and never take care of their (six) children. There have been a lot of complaints about the kids running wild and throwing rocks through windows.

"Neighbors said when the parents get their food stamps they sell them for booze and the kids never get enough to eat.

"They said these children have been seen eating food out of garbage cans in the neighborhood."

It was the officer's opinion that "these children are at an age where they could be helped, but if they go on like this any longer, they will be beyond help. Hope the court can find an answer, and soon." . . .

May 27, 1981: A man at the Towne Motel is robbed of $4000 and beaten. His assailants are two youths, one armed with a knife and the other with a gun.

The one with the knife is Tommy.

He has helped juvenile court find an answer, at last, to the question of what to do with him.

Because of the seriousness of his crime, Tommy is waived to adult court. He is 17 years old.

He is now serving a four-year term in prison. . . .

Tommy didn't become a hardened criminal overnight. He went from eating food out of garbage cans at age 7 to snatching purses from old women at age 12.

He grew up in the so-called child protection system—removed from his parents because of neglect, made a ward of the county welfare department, overseen by juvenile court—at a public cost of thousands of dollars.

The system's responsibility was to protect him. Instead, it lost him. . . .

Tommy's story is not an isolated case. It's one of many examples of a system that's not working—even in the opinion of the people who run it.

Indiana's juvenile justice and child welfare system "seems almost programmed for failure," says Howard County Circuit Judge Robert J. Kinsey of Kokomo, president last year of the Indiana Juvenile Judges Association.

"It is time," he added, "that we stopped fooling around and misleading the public about the situation."

Dealing with community values

When reporters realize that serious examination of community issues should supplement basic reporting, they may be confronted by the *Jaws* Syndrome. Community forces depicted in the movie *Jaws* objected to steps that would have made the beaches safe from sharks, because by taking the steps community income would have been reduced during the tourist season. Likewise, reporters may be told their investigations will drive potential businesspeople away from town, force industry to close, create divisions in communities where all had been "normal," and so on. The reporter, of course, believes that issues hidden from the public are not normal.

A perception among citizens of the press as a booster of the local community is quite common in both large and small communities. A study of newspapers in New England, however, suggests that readers in both large and small towns seem to prefer a paper that performs well journalistically. "Good papers were published as often in small communities as large ones, in growing as well as declining or stagnant ones, in wealthy communities and not-so-wealthy ones," say Professors Maxwell McCombs and Lee Becker. "Editors frequently say, for example, that they would like to do more investigative pieces or write or air more strident editorials, but the community won't tolerate it," McCombs and Becker state. While to some extent it is true that the community sets boundaries on the behavior of its news media, they say, "the evidence, however, is that editors overstate the case" (McCombs and Becker 1979).

Gazette-Times reporters Kight and Mitchell undoubtedly were aware that some Corvallis entrepreneurs would really have liked them simply to beat the drums for the city and the state as an ideal site for a research park, but their series exposed the cons as well as the pros, avoiding raw boosterism.

Getting beneath the surface

Suppose you are a reporter in Corvallis, where a developer has asked city approval to build a high-rise building near the OSU campus. The proposal has been greeted by rumblings of public opposition as well as by divided opinion among professional planners. You already have reported that the city's comprehensive plan prohibits high-rise structures in that area, and that the developer has asked for a zoning change or a variance that would allow the project. The issue is now before the city council for a decision, and you know enough about the controversy to anticipate a stormy session. The meeting is long and tumultuous, with many voices heard, pro and con, before the council votes approval of the project by a 5 to 2 margin. Because the meeting ends shortly before your deadline, you can only report the major points, but you should know the direction you need to take in the following days.

If the 5 to 2 vote signals that this council has declared an open season on the city's comprehensive plan, the public should be so advised. Approval of too many rezoning applications or individual variances can destroy a city's general plan and change the way a city looks, how it grows, and where its residents live and shop. You will need to inform your audience of the role of the community power structure in the high-rise decision: Who owns Corvallis? Who really plans its growth — commercial and industrial interests, governmental boards and agencies, or citizen organizations? What is the role of labor unions in community development? Has the developer an unhealthy influence on council members because of financial contributions to their campaigns? What are the motives of the people who testified for and against it? Is there a silent majority that was not represented at the meeting?

You should also look anew at the effects of the high rise. Will it create jobs, bring shoppers to the district, and vitalize the area? Or will traffic congestion and increasing crime result, compounding the demands on city services and budget?

This particular investigation was prompted by an event: the request for rezoning or a variance for the high-rise development. As a reporter, you may be handicapped until something "happens," but you also can learn to routinely recognize and define developing issues by maintaining a community inventory. This lists the resources and problems that affect the life of the community.

A COMMUNITY INVENTORY. Who are Corvallis's leaders, and from what sectors of the community do they come? Are leaders being developed for the decade ahead? Will they represent all citizens? What is the quality of life in Corvallis? Are recreational and arts facilities adequate? Is crime under control? What is the air and water quality? Are traffic problems alienating citizens and precluding commercial development? Indeed, is commercial development adequate, or do citizens have to leave town to find a satisfactory range of goods and services? Is an opportunity for employment developing? Do citizens, business, and labor sectors work together to provide a satisfactory industrial base from which all elements benefit?

By examining such substantive issues, you are undertaking a community inventory. When the findings are presented to the public, the community as a whole may be surprised that it has been immersed in day-to-day problems and has not made decisions from the perspective of comprehensive community priorities and development.

Getting the big picture

As thorough as such community reporting may be, it is provincial to dwell on local issues without seeing residents as part of the national or international community. Certainly, oil prices, grain embargoes, valuation of the dollar, and national defense prompt people today to follow stories they might have avoided in a simpler time. Likewise, a news medium that ignores the issues that are staple fare for the League of Women Voters, members of Common Cause, or the Moral Majority will simply be dismissed as insignificant in the course of community affairs.

Professor Richard T. Stout of the American University School of Communication states that "it does little good to tell a student how to cover a school board meeting, or even send him or her to one, unless he or she understands the issues facing education at local, state, and national levels, and how those issues intermingle among the three levels. That is what is wrong with too much public affairs reporting: it is ill-informed about ramifications beyond single communities" (Stout 1980).

Examination of national trends at the local level should involve far more analysis than that used by a wire editor who merely localizes an Associated Press story by putting a Corvallis angle in the lead. National social currents can be interpreted in light of local movements and opinions, and the comparison between these two levels may indeed make lively copy.

EXAMPLES. Reporter Laura Coleman and Girard Steichen of the Streator, Illinois, *Times-Press* picked up from their surveillance reading that the nation was losing its arable farmland. Despite the conventional image of the United States as a land of agricultural surpluses, the supply of America's arable farmland may be in peril with thousands of acres after thousands of acres lost annually to urban sprawl, soil erosion, highway construction, and recreational developments. Was it true in the area of Streator, Illinois? Their *Times-Press* editor thought it would be a good idea to find out.

An eleven-part series later, Coleman and Steichen (1983) had produced an Inland Daily Press Association prize-winning analysis of the local problem in the context of the national issue. Eleven segments could have been too much coverage for the average reader, but the issue turned out to be complex and significant. To help, the series was attractively packaged, with a graphic symbol by Ken Stark and action photographs.

Another example of linking the national and local situations in a series of stories was the Corvallis *Gazette-Times* series on the community's search for a research park. Reporters Kight and Mitchell astutely wove into their series the fact that Corvallis was not the only community seeking such a research park. Other cities seeking to strengthen their economic base were doing the same thing.

Even a single report on a social issue should present the local situation in its broader setting. For a Labor Day report on the employment situation in Rock County, Wisconsin, Mike Dupre (1988a) of the *Janesville Gazette* did the normal interviewing of area workers. He found that the major problem was not unemployment but workers who said they could not find jobs utilizing the education and skills they had. A college graduate was working as a janitor while a trained electrical technician was selling snacks in a bowling alley.

Dupre decided that the real labor problem in the area was underemployment. He called the Wisconsin Labor Department and asked how widespread underemployment was in the state. State labor analyst August Cibarich told him there was no "hard definition" of underemployment so there was no accurate measure of how many underemployed people there were in Wisconsin. Dupre did, however, learn that Wisconsin had lost more than sixty thousand manufacturing jobs in the past decade. The jobs lost averaged 33 percent above the average salary for Wisconsin workers. Wisconsin had gained one hundred and eighty thousand new jobs in the same period, mostly in service industries. These new jobs averaged 16 percent below the average state worker salary. Dupre had, in fact, found his "hard definition" of underemployment and presented it in a separate story (Dupre 1988b). In each of the forthcoming chapters, we summarize for you the big pictures that impinge on or even precipitate local issues everywhere.

Exploring ideas

Having moved from spot news to in-depth coverage, and having examined community value systems and power structures, performed a community inventory, and assessed social currents, can a beleaguered reporter also find time to cover ideas?

The answer is yes. By stepping back from spot news reporting to cover the changing ideas and attitudes that motivate people, you can become an even more perceptive observer—intellectually curious, not just curious.

For role models you have some distinguished reporters on national television. For example, on ABC, David Brinkley's Sunday morning "This Week" may contrast French and West German socialism; on CBS, Charles Kuralt's "Sunday Morning" may examine the ethos of a racetrack tout; or on his weekday show Bill Moyers may speculate on the Apostle Paul's views of the Palestine Liberation Organization (PLO); on NBC, a John Chancellor documentary has focused on "America in Search of Itself"; and on PBS, the inimitable MacNeil and Lehrer devote a solid program every weeknight to unraveling the snarls of two conflicting ideologies—the fundamental pros and cons of the ERA, for example.

Covering ideas is also a strength of national magazines such as *The Atlantic, New York Times Magazine, Commonweal,* and even *Time* and *Newsweek,* on occasion. One issue of *Chicago* magazine discussed the city's buildings designed by architect Louis Sullivan and tried to show how he was trying to create a city for a "new man and a new culture of faith" (Newman 1985).

National newspapers, especially in their huge Sunday editions, also cover ideas. Don Colburn looked at "The New Definition of 'Old' " in the *Washington Post* (June 10, 1985). Russell Chandler, *Los Angeles Times* religion writer, explored new ideas that are creating uncertainty within the Catholic Church (May 19–20, 1985).

But covering ideas is not confined to the national media; strong small-city media do it, too. In just one Sunday issue of a Midwest daily (*Wisconsin State Journal,* October 24, 1982), these localized "idea" stories appeared:

New ideas link animal infanticide, child abuse

'Kangaroo' apartments: A new housing idea

Low voltage energy ideas

Do-it-yourself house building idea catches on

New ideas coming from the Vatican

A cheap idea? Inexpensive dates

Idea of Japanese productivity called a myth

The Kight-Mitchell Corvallis *Gazette-Times* series was a prime example of exploring an idea—the concept of a research park: "Just what is a research park? What will it take to build one here? What kind of industry would it attract? Who will benefit—and who will pay?"

Nearly every reporter in even a fairly large newsroom will have a piece of the public issues action. Covering a public issue beat may not be your sole assignment. You are likely to be assigned considerable feature and general assignment reporting as well. But reporting and interpreting public issues will be a bread-and-butter challenge to you at least some of the time, calling for the professional skills and techniques outlined in Chapter 2.

References

Anderson, Bob. 1984. Rollins Violations Exceed 100. *Sunday Advocate* (Baton Rouge, LA), Dec. 9, 1.
_____. 1985a. Prosperity in Paradise? Louisiana's Chemical Legacy. *Morning Advocate* (Baton Rouge, LA), April 25.
Anderson, Bob. 1985b. Personal correspondence in authors' files, July 12.
Carmody, Deidre. 1982. Helping Young Students Avoid Drugs. *New York Times,* Jan. 7, III:1.
Chandler, Russell. 1985. A Church Still Changing. *Los Angeles Times,* May 19–20, 1A.
Colburn, Don. 1985. The New Definition of Old. *Washington Post* (National Weekly Edition), June 10, 4.
Coleman, Laura and Steichen, Girard. 1983. Disappearing Farms. *Times-Press* (Streator, IL), April 10–20.
Culbertson, Hugh M. 1983. Three Perspectives on American Journalism. *Journalism Monographs* 83 (June).
Dupre, Mike. 1988a. More Working at Lesser Jobs. *Sunday Gazette* (Janesville, WI), Sept. 4, 1A.
_____. 1988b. Underemployment Is Hard to Measure. *Sunday Gazette* (Janesville, WI), Sept. 4, 12A.
Dygert, James H. 1976. *The Investigative Journalist.* Englewood Cliffs, NJ: Prentice-Hall.
Fielder, Virginia Dodge and Weaver, David H. 1982. Public Opinion on Investigative Reporting. *Newspaper Research Journal* 3(2):54–62.
Funkhouser, G. Ray. 1973. Trends in Media Coverage of Issues of the '60s. *Journalism Quarterly* 50(2):533–38.
Gallup, George. 1980. Commentary. *Newspaper Research Journal* 2(3):94–97.
Gans, Herbert J. 1980. *Deciding What's News.* New York: Vintage Books, 131–32.
Hall, Stuart. 1973. A World at One with Itself. In *The Manufacture of News,* edited by Stanley Cohen and Jock Young, 85–94. Beverly Hills, CA: Sage.
Heiman, Roberta. 1983. Pacesetters. *Scripps Howard News* (May):9–11.
Hess, Stephen. 1983. *The Washington Reporters.* Washington, DC: Brookings Institute.
Journalism's Best. 1988. *The Quill* 76(6)17–44.
Kight, Pat. 1983. Personal correspondence in authors' files, July 7.
Kight, Pat, and Mitchell, Russ. 1983a. Research Park Posed as Cure for Economy. *Gazette-Times* (Corvallis, OR), Mar. 15, A1.
_____. 1983b. OSU Crucial to Success of Park. *Gazette-Times* (Corvallis, OR), Mar. 16, B1.
_____. 1983c. Fishing for Research Companies Requires the Right Bait. *Gazette-Times* (Corvallis OR), Mar. 17, B1.
_____. 1983d. Can State Get Bite of High-Tech Pie? *Gazette-Times* (Corvallis, OR), Mar. 18, B1.
_____. 1983e. Will City Be Ready for Rapid Growth? *Gazette-Times* (Corvallis, OR), Mar. 19, A1.
McCombs, Maxwell and Becker, Lee B. 1979. *Using Mass Communication Theory.* Englewood Cliffs, NJ: Prentice-Hall.
MacDougall, Curtis D. 1938. *Interpretive Reporting.* New York: Macmillan.

Mills, C. Wright. 1959. *The Sociological Imagination.* New York: Oxford Univ. Press.

Newman, M.W. 1985. The Dreamer. *Chicago* 34(3):24.

Pitts, Beverly J. 1982. Protocol Analysis of the Newswriting Process. *Newspaper Research Journal* 4(1):12–21.

Ray, Garrett. 1983. *Publishers Auxiliary* 119(25):11. June 13.

Ryan, John K. (ed.) 1960. *The Confessions of St. Augustine.* Vol. 11, no. 14. New York: Doubleday.

Ryan, Michael and Owen, Dorothea. 1976. A Content Analysis of Metropolitan Newspaper Coverage of Social Issues. *Journalism Quarterly* 53(4):634–40.

Schudson, Michael. 1986. *What Time Means in a News Story.* New York: Gannett Center for Media Studies, 10.

Stout, Richard T. 1980. Personal correspondence in authors' files, Aug. 6.

The People & The Press. 1986. Los Angeles: Times-Mirror Corp. 41–42.

Wisconsin State Journal. 1982. Oct. 24.

Wulfemeyer, K. Tim. 1983. The Interests and Preferences of Audiences for Local Television News. *Journalism Quarterly* 60(2):322–28.

Zeidler, Michael. 1988. Why Are the Assessments Up on the East Side? *East Side Community News,* June 1988, 1.

This chapter was initiated by Heuterman. Collaborators were Griffin, Molen, Schoenfeld, and Scotton.

CHAPTER 2

Getting started

ASKED RECENTLY to describe the caliber of local news coverage he would like to see in the news media in his mid-size, Midwestern city, the editor of a national magazine said that he wished the media would "tell me why the subject matter is significant. Tell me how decisions are made here, who exercises power, and who benefits from the outcome. Provide me with the background information necessary to sort out issues and arrive at an informed opinion. Do in-depth, behind-the-scenes digging. Don't be content to offer only bulletin-board, event-oriented spot news reporting. Identify and interpret public issues" (Rothschild 1983).

That is the type of public issues reporting we are talking about in this book. Preparing to be a good public issues reporter means starting to assimilate the professional skills and techniques outlined in this chapter, many of which you are already somewhat familiar with from earlier courses in newswriting and reporting.

Doing background reading

Indiana University journalism professor Owen V. Johnson notes that in recent years news media executives have frequently lamented the fact that young reporters have a general unfamiliarity with the background on public issues (Johnson 1983).

One thing that distinguished the reporting job of Corvallis *Gazette-Times* staffers Pat Kight and Russ Mitchell on their research park series was the clear evidence that they had done their homework. Take Story No. 3, for instance. They quote from a report by the District 4 Council of Governments, a body which coordinates the activities of local governments in the Corvallis area. Such evidence lends a great deal of credibility to any story.

Reporting begins not with writing but with reading—lots of it. You may think that when you get out of journalism school you will be through with cramming. Forget it. Your days and nights in libraries are just beginning. No self-respecting reporter today tackles a public issues assignment without first educating himself or herself with all the background information time permits to be mustered; and the more-specialized pros maintain their own reference files. For example, the late Dion Henderson, a Wisconsin Associated Press bureau chief, had a whole room in his home set aside as a library stacked with historical and current material on his personal beat—covering state environmental issues. Nor did Henderson just file Wisconsin clips; he kept in touch with national and international developments. So knowledgeable was Henderson in his field that he was recognized as an authority himself (Schoenfeld 1985). To improve public issues reporting, says columnist Joseph Kraft, the news media must "find and promote more intelligent people" (Kraft 1980). To be marked as an intelligent reporter, do your background reading.

Searching records

To list an inventory of the different public records in the United States would require a volume much larger than this book. Probably no individual is aware of all of these documentary sources, but you will use some of them with reasonable regularity, and you will find others invaluable occasionally. In any case, you will profit by remembering to ask yourself a

---

DOING HOMEWORK

I set out on a course of self-study on the issues we were writing about. Just as when I was assigned to cover the Supreme Court back in the 1930s I had prepared by reading up on constitutional history and past court decisions, so I tried to educate myself on economics, having at Chapel Hill taken only an introductory course. . . . In the same way as other issues arose, whether in foreign affairs or whatever, I tried to come to grips with them by reading extensively. I gradually built up a personal reference library which has stood me in good stead over the years.

VERMONT ROYSTER, editor of the *Wall Street Journal*. 1983.
My Own, My Country's Time. New York: Algonquin Press.

question whenever you are digging for information: Is there a public record I should check?

Some records are almost matter-of-fact sources. These include minutes of government meetings, building permits, arrest records, planning commission records, election campaign finance reports, property transfers, births, deaths, and divorce actions. Others may not be available locally or, in some instances, may not be open to the public. As you cover various assignments, you should automatically acquire more knowledge of such source material, where to write or call for it, and what information it will provide. The Freedom of Information Service Center, operated jointly in Washington, D.C., by the Society of Professional Journalists (Sigma Delta Chi) and the Reporters Committee for Freedom of the Press, can provide helpful information on public records. If your state has a Freedom of Information Committee, contact it for assistance.

Public documents are especially useful in sensitive stories because they can provide accurate detail that may be lacking in some source's account from memory. Public records also lend authority to news stories because they are "on the record."

When reporters from the Gannett News Service and Gannett's KOCO-TV in Oklahoma City were investigating reports of widespread abuse of children in Oklahoma institutions, they relied extensively on public records. Note how the public record lends authenticity to the findings in this excerpt from the Gannett News Service series, "Oklahoma Shame" (*Gannetteer* 1982):

> OKLAHOMA CITY—Several mentally retarded children have died in Oklahoma institutions this year, some under circumstances considered by experts to be suspicious or questionable.
>
> Six deaths at Enid State School within 23 days during January are listed, in documents on file with the state registrar of vital statistics here, as attributable in all but one case to causes that three medical experts told Gannett News Service are "perplexing" and "appalling" or "inexcusable."

The records listed the cause of the deaths, and the Gannett reporting team then turned to doctors in three other states to evaluate the official explanations.

Checking the records was an essential step in developing this Oklahoma story on child abuse. Without such checks, a misleading story can develop from the apparent facts. After looking at representative television and radio newscasts on child abuse, Laura Green (1984) pointed out the hazard of building reports around what could be isolated incidents in the absence of documentary records.

Searching records can provide a mass of information for public issues

TYPICAL PUBLIC RECORDS

Criminal court files and trial transcripts; prosecutor's case records; arrest records; criminal records; complaint reports and other police records; coroner's records;

Civil lawsuit files, transcripts of testimony, exhibits, depositions, pleadings; probate court records on estates and appointments; divorce court pleadings, transcripts, financial statements;

Minutes of meetings by government bodies;

Contracts awarded by government agencies for materials and services;

Rezoning applications; planning commission records; building department and housing inspection records;

Government payrolls, budgets, purchase vouchers; travel expense vouchers;

Election records and campaign finance reports;

Records, reports, and hearing transcripts of state and federal government regulatory agencies and commissions (such as those regulating utilities, insurance, or atomic energy); files and hearing transcripts of state legislative and congressional committees;

Property records, including transfers, deeds, mortgages, and land contracts; chattel mortgages;

Tax assessments, tax payment records, tax liens; U.S. Tax Court cases; state tax department records;

Corporation charters, reports, and franchise tax statements filed with the state; partnership and business name records, usually filed with the county; Securities and Exchange Commission records;

County and state auditor's office records;

Health department records;

Federal grant applications and records of applicant agencies;

Some records of federal agencies and programs;

Licensing records, especially for liquor sales and horse racing;

Reports filed by lobbyists;

Vital statistics of births, marriages, divorces, deaths;

Automobile and drivers' licenses;

TYPICAL PUBLIC RECORDS *(continued)*

Veterans' records;

Labor union reports filed with the government;

Environmental impact statements;

Minutes of faculty meetings.

TYPICAL NONPUBLIC RECORDS

Some government records are not public:

Police intelligence files; criminal records in some jurisdictions; police investigation reports; parole and probation records; juvenile court files in some jurisdictions; Federal Bureau of Investigation (FBI) and other federal law enforcement agency records;

Income tax returns in some states; income tax investigation reports; internal memoranda and letters;

Welfare case records; state hospital patient records.

Some other records are also clearly not public: Credit bureau reports; telephone call records; bank records; insurance investigation reports; private investigators' files; business records; employment records; student grade reports; hospital records; union records; real estate development plans; personal finance records. Since you have no inherent right to such records, they can only be reached through sources willing to pass the information or provide copies.

JAMES H. DYGERT. 1976. *The Investigative Journalist.*
Englewood Cliffs, N.J. Prentice-Hall.

reporters, because it is frequently in the offices of public agencies that corporations and private developers must file documents reflecting their activity. For example, as a part of Corvallis Story No. 1, reporters Kight and Mitchell brought readers up-to-date on property sites zoned for development under the city's new research-park category. Five of these had been recommended by a committee of business, government, and university leaders. A sixth site, Sunset Park, had been added to the list by the city council itself.

Suppose Kight and Mitchell had asked themselves if there could be a conflict of interest between a city council member or members and the ownership of Sunset Park. How could they find out? A visit to the county register of deeds could tell them in whose name or names the property was held. Suppose the ownership was in a "Sunset Park Corporation." How could they identify the corporation's directors? The articles of incorporation would be on file in a state office, usually in the office of the secretary of state. How could they determine Sunset Park's worth on the commercial market? The city assessor's records would indicate the value at which the property was assessed last year. The assessor could estimate the relationship of assessed valuation to the going market price, and his or her figures could be checked against comparable current transactions.

Interviewing

Along with pursuing public records, interviewing is your stock-in-trade. Some journalists attack interviews like confident prizefighters; others stumble into them with fear and insecurity. Almost anything works if journalists act like themselves — shy or aggressive, stiff or informal, candid or cagey. Good interviewing is personal, unpredictable, and spontaneous. The interview is not an isolated exercise that adheres to sets of rules and guidelines. Rather, the interview is an intimate expression of your whole thinking, researching, and writing processes (Ross 1983).

In short, interviewing is not an exact science and the techniques you use will vary according to your personality, the topic being discussed, and the type of person being interviewed. Experience will help you to develop a style for particular situations, but you can get a head start by learning from experts.

Interviewing does not begin as you step through a door or pick up a phone. It begins when you do your homework. Experienced interviewers are in universal agreement on this point. "I always seek maximum knowledge of the person I am questioning and the subjects we are talking about," says Edwin Newman, longtime NBC newscaster. "When I was conducting the 'Speaking Freely' series for nine seasons, roughly 250 unedited one-hour interviews, the program required so much reading that I read little else. How, after all, do you prepare for interviewees without going through their books and going through what has been written about them?" (Newman 1977). Noted investigative reporter James H. Dygert advises interviewers to "learn as much as possible beforehand about the subject matter and the interviewee" (Dygert 1976). Magazine writer Dennis Chaptman puts his advice very pungently: "Thou shalt research. You will rise or fall on what you know about your interview subject. You have to know his shoe size before climbing into his Florsheims" (Chaptman 1982).

Lack of preparation can bring disaster. Consider the case of a reporter who was assigned to the premier of the movie classic, *Gone With the Wind,* when it was rereleased for the first time in many years. His first question of actress Vivien Leigh was "What role do you have in the movie?" End of interview (Schoenfeld and Diegmueller 1982). Leigh had won international acclaim for her performance in the female lead as the tempestuous southern belle, Scarlett O'Hara. Her negative reaction to the woefully unprepared reporter is understandable.

Another reporter's interview with a nationally known poet came to an abrupt end after his first question: what had the poet written? The poet's response was to "go back and read one or two of my books and then come and talk with me" (Schoenfeld and Diegmueller 1982).

Some tolerant interviewees will overlook the failure to prepare and patiently will help a young reporter through an interview. Even so, your ability to ask perceptive questions will be limited if you have not done your preliminary research.

Many of your interviews will be with people experienced in dealing with reporters. Such persons can recognize quickly a lack of preparation and can brush you off with generalities or exploit your ignorance in almost any way they wish. The interviewee winds up in control of the conversation. You will win more respect from the news source when you demonstrate a reasonable knowledge of the subject.

Sound preparation will not be effective, however, if you do not listen carefully to the answers. Your question format should be flexible enough that some unexpected revelation should prompt you to alter the direction of the interview. You cannot do this very well if you do not listen.

In the interview itself, what approach do you use? Breezy? Amiable? Down-to-earth? Hard-hitting? Merciless? Edwin Newman says that "the best interviewer will alter his or her approach according to the needs of the interview being conducted. For example, there are occasions when the cross-examiner's attitude is justified; certainly with most politicians in most circumstances, it may be the only way to get a straight answer" (Loh 1982).

Interviewing people who are not experienced in talking with reporters may require more initial explanation than is necessary for the skilled news source. Jules Loh, a veteran Associated Press reporter, explains how he tries to establish a rapport with people who are strangers to news interviews:

> These people are scared to death when a reporter comes along so you've got to get over that and get them comfortable with you. The subject has

read all this stuff about how reporters pry and they see people on TV asking, "How did you feel when your boy's body with both legs cut off came up from the surf?"

And they think that all reporters are going to talk to them like that. Well, you really have to give them confidence in you. The way I do it is talk to these people and tell them why I'm there, what I want to write about. . . . (Loh 1982).

Once you have allayed the interviewee's apprehensions about talking with a reporter, a new problem arises. How do you decide whether to take notes or to tape? You will have to play it by ear. Some interviewees will clam up at the first sight of a pad and pencil or a recorder, no matter how unobtrusive. Others will be frustrated if you give no evidence that you are capturing accurately and completely what is being said.

Loh approaches the problem this way: "Now, how do you get the notebook out? . . . We get to talking about what we're going to talk about — and then comes the time when I say, 'When did you say you graduated from high school?' A *fact*. Now that does two things: it gets the notebook out on a subject that is not their opinion or anything controversial. It is just a matter of fact. Now you have it out. The second thing, it tells them you want to be accurate" (Loh 1982).

You also want to include some direct quotations in your story, if possible. Getting direct quotes down accurately during note taking is difficult, but with practice you can fix in mind a speaker's key words and use notes to jog that memory. Whatever technique you employ, go to a typewriter as fast as you can after the interview and write a rough draft of the conversation while all the nuances are fresh in your mind. If typewriters have been replaced by video display terminals in your office, use pencil and pad initially to flesh out your notes.

Weighing evidence

Do the quotes from a single interview constitute compelling "evidence?" It depends on the authenticity of the interviewee, the volatility of the topic, and, to some extent, the stature of the reporter. In unraveling the Watergate saga, reporters Bob Woodward and Carl Bernstein never introduced new charges from one source unless the claims had been corroborated by at least one other source. In investigating controversial public issues, you may often find that the two "sides" do not agree on what constitutes valid evidence. For example, in covering chemical-related stories, some reporters are willing to accept as compelling evidence the self-reports of individuals who feel they have been affected by chemicals. The chemical industry, on the other hand, insists that the only valid evidence would be scientific data that would help to clarify for viewers and readers whether a problem really exists and, if so, to what extent (Dunwoody 1982). Answering the questions of what will constitute "evidence" is an essential part of every investigative reporter's plan.

How usable are quotes from interviewees who insist on remaining anonymous? The major elements of most press policies regarding the use of anonymous sources are that editors must be told the names of the sources; the sources are used as a last resort; the information is verified before it is printed; the source is described as fully as possible to allow the audience to assess credibility; and personal attacks by anonymous sources are prohibited (Wulfemeyer 1983).

Applying social science research methods to reporting

Research methods of the social and behavioral sciences have rapidly been adopted by journalists during the past two decades. Polls, surveys, systematic uses of records, various techniques of observation, and even field experiments have found their way into the news-gathering toolbox. These techniques provide ways of gathering valid and reliable evidence firsthand and reduce reliance on authorities, anecdotes, and traditional assumptions about the way things are.

In *Precision Journalism,* Philip Meyer notes how journalistic intuition, even when well-informed, can lead you astray. For instance, during the period of urban racial disorders of the late 1960s, news stories overwhelmingly assumed that race relations were getting worse. Attitude surveys, however, showed just the opposite. Over the years of the major riots, blacks and whites were actually growing more tolerant. "As reporters," Meyer observes, "we failed to notice. We tend to have our heads geared to reinforce the conventional wisdom. The effect is multiplied because we tend to imitate and reinforce each other" (Meyer 1979).

Use of anecdotes is often a journalist's trap. Anecdotes may be good examples, but they are poor evidence. In other words, case studies can add spice and interest to a story, but it is misleading to generalize from them, as we too often do. Cases of persons committing sexual assaults after reading or viewing pornography do not prove that pornography causes sexual misconduct. Instances of rehabilitation after a new drug treatment program do not mean that the program works. Ninety out of a hundred people you interview on the street corner may favor a change in the local zoning ordinance, but no matter how many you interview and how good the quotations are these people do not represent "public opinion" — in fact, they do not represent anyone but themselves.

Knowledge of the methods of social science can help you sort true claims from false ones and cut through the confines of intuition, conventional wisdom, and journalistic "groupthink." These techniques can help you get a better picture of the changing feelings, knowledge and behavior of local residents, and to conduct your own investigations into the events in your community. These are powerful tools for a reporter to have. While a complete introduction to these methods is beyond the scope of this book, we can offer some general guidelines.

Surveys

Surveys (sometimes called polls) can help you find out how members of the public feel about some issue at some point in time. They can also help you tap into the dynamics of the processes that influence the way people think and behave. Surveys rely on techniques of probability sampling to make sure that the views of the people you interview represent the views of the larger population. Use of probability sampling usually spells the biggest difference between a valid and representative picture of community opinion and the usually misleading efforts of the traditional journalistic street corner interviews.

The first step in conducting a valid survey is to specify explicitly the group — usually referred to as the "population" or "universe" — you will study. If you say you will study community opinion about some issue, does that include preschool children? Adults only? Eligible voters? Does that include persons outside the city limits but within the circulation area of the paper, or just persons living within the city itself? The population must be defined clearly, because a basic rule in sampling is that you can generalize the results of a sample survey only to the group from which the sample was drawn.

For example, the *Milwaukee Journal* (1979), which is usually very careful when reporting on polls, erred in a story headlined "Survey Says Most Oppose Double-Bottom Trucks." The story was based on a study conducted by a state agency that purported to show that most Wisconsin residents were not in favor of allowing these large vehicles on state highways. The survey was not based on a scientific sample of Wisconsin residents, however. It was based on letters received by the agency and on a mail survey of Wisconsin newspaper editors. The editors simply gave their impressions of what local residents thought. Unfortunately, letter writers usually are those who feel most strongly about an issue and therefore do not constitute a valid representation of the public. The survey of editors was just that — a survey of what editors think. And the editors were no doubt basing their impressions partly on letters they had received, some probably from the same letter writers.

In drawing a probability sample, the person doing the research must ensure that each member of the population being studied – adult residents of a community, for example – has an equal chance of being included in the sample. There are a number of ways to do this, including what are known as simple random sampling (like drawing numbers from a drum), and systematic probability sampling (like taking every seventh name on a list or stopping at every twelfth house after starting at a randomly selected point). The high cost of conducting personal interviews in people's homes is making telephone surveys more popular for researchers. Because nearly all homes in the United States have telephones, potential bias in the sample due to persons not having phones is minimal.

An accepted technique for getting around the problem of unlisted phone numbers is to "add a digit" (or add 1) to each of a sample of phone numbers from the city telephone directory. For example, if the number is 493–9386 in the phone directory, the survey interviewer dials 493–9387. This will thus include unlisted phone numbers. Other methods are often used to select randomly the specific person to be interviewed ("respondent") in multi-resident dwellings, or to find out whether the person qualifies as a respondent. So-called screening questions at the beginning of an interview, for example, might sort out eligible or likely voters for a preelection poll. Any valid political poll must take into account in some way whether the respondent is likely to vote in the election if the poll is to have any value in predicting election results.

No matter how good your survey, it will not be perfect. That is, like every survey it will have a margin of error. The true community opinion will probably differ from what the survey shows. The difference, however, is likely to be small and you can estimate it if you have conducted a valid sample survey. Based on the size of your sample, you can calculate the margin of error (or sampling error) that you must allow. A useful sample size is usually around four hundred people, because this will give you a margin of error of plus or minus 5 percent. The size of this error margin decreases as the size of the sample increases (See Meyer 1979 for a complete explanation). Many journalists ignore the margin of error and come up with survey stories that are misleading.

For example, suppose you had a sample of four hundred likely voters in your community. Your survey shows that 42 percent of them favor candidate Smith, 38 percent favor candidate Jones, and the rest are undecided. You might be tempted to report that Smith is ahead of Jones. You would be wrong. By including the 5 percent margin of error, you would know that the proportion of likely voters favoring Smith is somewhere between 37 percent and 47 percent (which is 42 percent plus or minus 5 percent). The proportion favoring Jones is some percentage between 33 and 43 percent. Thus, Jones could actually be ahead of Smith. Because the error margins overlap, you must say that it is a dead heat or too close to call. Reporting the margin of error in a sample survey is a hallmark of responsible journalism.

As any reporter knows, interview questions must not be biased or "leading." This is certainly true of surveys as well. For a survey to be valid, every respondent must be asked the same straightforward questions and have his or her responses recorded in the same way. There are many sources, such as Meyer (1979) or Frey (1989), which can help you craft questionnaires so that the survey responses you get are reliable (that is, comparable from person to person) and valid (that is, they truly represent what you expect them to measure—a person's preference for a candidate, for example). Most survey questions are closed-ended, like those you would get in a multiple-choice test, and can get you information about the public's

REPORTING THE MARGIN OF ERROR

Explaining the margin of error to readers and audiences takes relatively little air time or news space. One newspaper commonly adds the following to the survey stories they run:

The *Journal* poll was based on interviews conducted Monday with 400 Milwaukee County adults selected from a computer-generated random sample of telephone numbers.

In theory, in 19 out of 20 cases, the results should vary by no more than 5 percentage points from the results that would have been obtained by interviewing every adult in the county who could be interviewed by telephone.

The practical difficulties of conducting any public opinion survey may introduce additional sources of error.

Poll Indicates Growing Support for County Sales Tax.
The Milwaukee Journal, July 12, 1990, A1, A8.

knowledge, attitudes, perceptions, and behaviors. Survey interviewers, like good journalists, need to develop some rapport with the people they interview without injecting their own ideas or influencing the responses they get. Survey interviewers need some training in order to to this. Many colleges offer courses in survey research that help journalism students and working professionals learn how to design and conduct polls and interpret the results responsibly.

In the *Handbook of Reporting Methods,* Cleveland Wilhoit and Maxwell McCombs (1976) have identified a set of questions that should be answered for your readers, viewers, or listeners whenever you are reporting the results of polls or surveys:

- Who sponsored the survey?
- Who was interviewed (that is, what population was being described)?
- How were the persons selected for interviews (that is, how was the sample designed)?
- How many persons were interviewed?
- How accurate were the results (that is, what is the estimated size of the sampling error)?
- Who were the interviewers?
- How were the interviews conducted (for example, by phone)?
- When were the interviews conducted?
- What were the actual questions asked?
- By whom were the data tabulated and analyzed?

Answering these questions will put you well within the guidelines for reporting surveys as established by the American Association for Public Opinion Research (AAPOR).

A FEW CAUTIONS. First, be wary of any survey conducted by special interest groups or anyone with a stake in the outcome of the survey. Second, be very skeptical of any "survey" done by asking listeners to call in or readers to write in. Such "self-selection" invalidates the survey but occurs rather often. Finally, find out and report the survey-response rate—that is, the percentage of persons in the sample who actually were interviewed. Good response rates are usually 70 percent or higher; when you have more than half of those contacted refusing to be interviewed, you have problems.

A television station went on the air with a story based on a survey with only an 18 percent rate of response at the time. After broadcasting these results, the station than encouraged the rest of the sample to send in their replies. More respondents did reply. Not only was the response rate too low, but the new respondents were now influenced by hearing what the early respondents had said. Unfortunately, the station reported these later results as well.

Some other techniques

Many other methods from the social sciences are adaptable to reporting and interpreting public issues. Field experiments are designed to determine cause and effect relationships which answer the journalist's question of *how* things happen. Participant-observation in which the reporter assumes the role of some other member of society (for example, a medicare patient, an indigent, or a bus driver) allows the reporter to observe human behavior without making his or her presence known. Another technique, content analysis of documents and records, can reveal patterns otherwise hidden or speculated about. For example, content analysis could be used to determine if there is really more violence on television now than there was ten years ago. (See McCombs et al. 1976 for more explanation of how reporters can use these methods.)

Statistical techniques of analysis, as we have seen, are very useful tools for journalists, especially in an age when quantification and the use of computers are increasing in many aspects of American life. In fact, columnist James Kilpatrick suggests that if he were teaching journalism, he would require students to take a year of statistics for every semester they study newswriting, and that this would produce better reporters (Kilpatrick 1982).

Reporters educated in the social sciences are learning means to apply "precision journalism" techniques to their reporting to achieve greater accuracy and efficiency in analyzing data. With the growing use of the computer, large amounts of data are becoming easier to handle. Some newsrooms have invested in small computers that can tabulate survey results, and the local college or university might also lend a hand. The computer is useful in reviewing financial documents, performing content analysis, researching public opinion polls and surveys, and doing secondary research of data gathered by agencies. Reporters and editors are learning to use the computer as a predictive tool as well, using data they have collected to project trends and developments in their communities.

Special ethical considerations

Your responsibilities in using social science techniques are twofold. You have responsibilities to the persons being observed, and to your readers, listeners, or viewers. The ethics of social science research require that persons involved are not harmed physically or psychologically, do not suffer a loss of dignity, and are not made to do things they would not otherwise do. Veteran reporter James H. Dygert offers these guidelines in his book, *The Investigative Journalist* (1976):

> Tailing a politician to see whom he meets with is seldom appropriate. Impersonation can be effective if there's no false representation that may produce false information. Posing as a medical patient, for example, or a waiter or sales clerk, is not pretending to be something a reporter isn't qualified to be. But information received by a reporter posing as a mechanic or a lawyer might be distorted because the person giving it assumes the recipient has specialized knowledge which he or she in fact doesn't have. Posing as some sort of official to solicit information by phone violates no law but many news media organizations prohibit this tactic as unethical. Getting a job in a place or institution to be investigated usually requires some falsification of background. It may border on invasion of privacy in cases involving private businesses, groups, or individuals rather than government. Many news media organizations consider such undercover tactics unethical or al least improper. Responsible investigative journalists and news gathering organizations don't break the law. Surreptitious wiretapping, for instance, is not done. If the news media are to monitor the ethics of government and business, they must see to the impeccability of their own.

Planning strategy

The task of reporting and interpreting public issues requires special planning. Investigations may originate in many ways—for example, in a decision to look into long-standing social problems; in recurrent rumors; in a desire to delve behind a current story; in letters to the editor; in tips from reliable sources or even from anonymous callers; in your own experiences; in the discovery of something unusual in a public record; in background reading; and in current events.

Dygert suggests that once a project is chosen you perform "a 'smell' or 'sniff'—a quick scrutiny of published materials and a preliminary survey of records and sources—to help evaluate potential results and costs, to plan strategy, and to pinpoint possible 'fallback' stars short of the maximum goal" (Dygert 1976). For example, when Charles Pluckhahn of the *Dubuque* (Iowa) *Telegraph Herald* went about investigating the strange case of the city's one passenger train, which never ran on time but drew a government subsidy just the same, he "drew up a 2000-word summary of the issues involved and an idea of the questions [he] wanted to ask" (Pluckhahn 1984). He took the summary to his city editor for evaluation and guidance.

When a project has reached this stage, a city editor must decide whether a team or a lone reporter should be assigned to the story. The answer will usually depend on the scope of the investigation, the people available, and how quickly the job must be done.

After such decisions have been made, Dygert recommends mapping out a tentative plan for the entire project, specifying the techniques to be used, the individuals to be interviewed, the records to be examined, the polls to be taken, and so on, and the order in which it is all to be done. Do you start by gaining a thorough background in the subject matter, by searching through a stack of records, or by beating the bushes for sources? It all depends. Usually, it is helpful to check records and files before conducting interviews, but some cases require early interviews to determine which records should be checked.

Alert reporters discover public issues

Although public issues reporting requires background research, the story may start anywhere. Every successful reporter keeps his or her eyes and ears open and looks for trends even in routine events. Reporter Scott Wright of the *Burlington* (VT) *Free Press* turned a routine Fourth of July holiday feature assignment into a report on the state's new citizens. Vermont has traditionally attracted immigrants from Canada, but Wright (1987) found a new trend. Like other states Vermont was now getting more immigrants from Korea, India, Cambodia, and other Asian countries.

Some places where alert reporters found public issues stories include:

A COMPLAINT. Complaints from airline passengers about late flights and lost baggage are routine, but *Pittsburgh Press* public health reporter Andrew Schneider heard a different kind of complaint from doctors and nurses at Pittsburgh hospitals. They said they were treating pilots and other flight crew members for cocaine overdoses (Schneider 1986). The hospitals were forbidden by law from reporting these drug patients and potential safety hazards. With that as a start, Schneider and *Press* general assignment reporter Matthew Brelis dug up enough information for a twelve-part series. The series brought major changes in airline and federal regulations. It also brought the reporters a 1987 Pulitzer Prize for Public Service.

AN OBSERVATION. Andy Young, a reporter and runner, was pursuing his hobby when he literally ran into a story that developed into a prize-winning series. While running through the Eastern Heights area of Elyria, Ohio, he noticed that black families had moved in. Young's research into a "changing neighborhood" introduced him to the mysteries of mortgages and bank lending practices. Using the federal Home Mortgage Disclosure Act, Young

CRITERIA USED IN JUDGING LOCAL PUBLIC AFFAIRS
REPORTING (SERIES) IN THE 1985 INLAND DAILY PRESS
ASSOCIATION NEWS CONTEST

- *Enterprise in uncovering subject, developing sources, pursuing leads, and coordinating information*
- *Persistence in the face of indifference, hostility, or technical difficulties*
- *Clarity and effectiveness of design and art*
- *Overall quality of writing and reporting*
- *Impact measured by ensuing action*

Inland Daily Press Association Contests. Chicago: Inland Daily Press Association. Pages 2,3.

was able to gather information on hundreds of home loans to show how bank lending policies can hinder or promote housing integration. How did he get on the trail of these lenders? He just went to the yellow pages of the Elyria telephone book and looked under "Banks" and "Savings and Loans." "The New Neighbors" series by Young (1982) won an Inland Daily Press Award.

A LETTER TO THE EDITOR. An editorial sent to the *Lawrence* (Kansas) *Journal-World* led Reporter Jeff Collins to dig through the intricacies of state and federal rulings with such vigor that, eventually, the state changed its rules, and the federal government notified all states that its regulations could be misunderstood. The process originated when a new welfare rule in Kansas required that the value of tools a worker used to earn a living had to be included in figuring his or her eligibility for welfare. A letter to the editor initiated the first related story, about a handyman, injured in a fall, who needed temporary financial assistance. That story brought to light similar cases. Reporter Collins searched across state borders and found that other states interpreted the same federal regulations differently. His reports prompted the federal government to "clarify" its regulations and the state government to exclude a worker's tools from considerations of welfare eligibility (Collins 1984). In this case, careful reporting and clear and considerate writing illustrated the effectiveness of the watchdog role of the press in a situation involving not criminal or even unethical behavior by public officeholders, but merely confusion.

One-shot or series?

Once the strategic decision is made to investigate a story, sooner or later the reporter or reportorial team is faced with the tactical decision of whether to try to wrap up the story in one long "take" or to deliberately construct a series. Increasingly, the series approach is becoming a common mode for reporting and interpreting public issues.

A series is not simply a long story snipped into several parts with scissors. Each increment is carefully constructed to stand on its own feet, as well as to make clear its relationship to the rest of the series. Typically, the lead increment will outline the main points of the series, and each successive increment will both recap what has gone before and foreshadow what is coming. The final increment performs a news wrap-up and, perhaps, alludes to an editorial-page comment. Frequently, a staff artist will provide a running set of artwork for the series.

Corvallis *Gazette-Times* reporters Kight and Mitchell made sure their series had a rational organization; and then they made that organization pop out at their readers by ending each increment with a foreshadowing of what would happen next. For example, at the close of Story No. 1 (Kight and Mitchell 1983a) came the line, "Next: What Does Oregon State University Have to Offer?; at the close of Story No. 2 (Kight and Mitchell 1983b), "Next: Checking Out the Competition," and so on.

Intermediate between the comprehensive single story and the series is the multiple-story approach, in which related stories on the same issue appear simultaneously. For example, when a major industry announced it was closing its Sheboygan, Wisconsin, plant, the *Sheboygan Press* (1983) gave the news top play on the front page under this 72-point headline: "Armira to Close Plant, Idling 320." Then, on pages 3 and 15, the *Press* included additional stories under these headlines: "The Loneliest Man in Town" (about a boiler tender at the idle plant); "Sorrow and Dismay Expressed at Armira Loss" (based on interviews with representative citizens); and "Armira Firm was in the Forefront of Industrial Development of Sheboygan" (about the firm's 125 years in the city). The next day, the *Press* followed up on the story with editorial comment.

Another example of the increasingly popular multiple-story techniques was given when, in the beginning of 1987, the (Madison) *Wisconsin State Journal* editors took an in-depth look at an adjoining small city. On page one of the Sunday issue of January 11 was a lead-in article headlined

"Middleton Struggles to Keep Its Identity." A box called attention to follow-on stories on pages six and seven: "Growth Puts Squeeze on Middleton," "Middleton's History Colorful," "Restraints in Place to Prevent Madison Sprawl," and "Other Communities Face Growth Battle." The stories could have run as a series over a week's time, but the editors wanted the impact of a single-issue display.

Striving for effective writing

Suppose your reporting job is done and you are set to write your story, or stories. You have had years of instruction and practice in writing, so here we will just remind you of two key attributes of effective writing that you have been hearing about since your tenth grade English composition course. These two attributes are coherence and unity, except that we are going to give them more utilitarian names: outline and focus.

Outline

Unless you are working against an imminent deadline, it is often a good idea to make an outline of your story before you begin to write. The outline need not be fancy, just so it is clear enough to help you get from beginning to end in logical fashion. Next, translate that outline directly into the flow of your story, leading the audience by the hand, so to speak, from key point to key point by supplying abundant connectives.

To see how this might be done, we will use a story from the *Clarion-Ledger* of Jackson, Mississippi. The Jim Walter Corporation, which got its start in 1946 building shell houses (houses unfinished on the interior) for low and middle income families, has grown into one of the nation's largest corporations. But in March 1981, the *Clarion-Ledger* began looking into complaints from poor, rural residents of Jefferson Davis County that the corporation's practices were deceptive and its product shoddy.

It soon became obvious that the story was not confined to southern Mississippi. Eventually, it took the *Clarion-Ledger* from Appalachia to the Rio Grande, from Florida to Indiana. A twenty-four-page special report prepared by reporters Maria Halkias and W. Stevens Ricks and picture editor David Frank told the story.

After organizing their notes, the reporters developed an outline that went something like this:

Theme
Legal Results in Summary

Summary of Corporation Practices
History of State Investigation
History of Civil Lawsuits
Sampling of Home Buyers' Experiences

Following are excerpts from the first article (Halkias and Ricks 1981), illustrating the outline principle in practice:

> CORPUS CHRISTI, Texas—The Jim Walter Corp's sales pitches promise that those who buy the company's houses will soon be living on "Easy Street."
>
> But for hundreds of low-income Mexican-Americans who have bought Jim Walter houses, there's no such address in south Texas.
>
> Hundreds of Jim Walter customers in south Texas have filed suits in state courts alleging that the houses they bought were poorly built, structurally defective, and/or that the firm engaged in deceptive and excessive sales and financing practices.

The first three paragraphs set the theme, stressing the difference between the corporation's promises and performance. Then come two paragraphs giving added detail on the legal issues:

> About 600 lawsuits, filed mainly by one small-town lawyer in south Texas, have resulted in Jim Walter and its subsidiaries paying millions of dollars in out-of-court settlements.
>
> The home builder's legal woes in Texas also include a recent out-of-court agreement, between the company and Texas Attorney General Mark White, which prevented a possible indictment of the corporation by a Duval County, Texas, grand jury on theft charges. The settlement resulted in a round of rebates for Jim Walter home buyers, who signed sales contract supplements that included charges listed as "electrical code," "plumbing code" and "building code," but never specified on the documents what those charges represented.

At this point the reader has been exposed to the theme and a general summary of the legal results of buyer complaints. Now the writers provide a three-point summary specifying the nature of the complaints:

> • After advertising that the firm's houses would meet "prevailing building codes," Jim Walter salesmen in south Texas added hundreds of dollars to sales contracts in itemized charges for meeting building, plumbing and electrical codes that didn't even exist in most of the rural areas where the houses were built.
>
> • Jim Walter executives in Texas frequently used a person's willingness to work cheaply as one of the company's few standards for hiring carpen-

ters. As a result, many of those hired were inexperienced workers or un-documented aliens.

• Hundreds of Jim Walter clients were left with houses that weren't completed to the specifications in the sales contracts—and the company either refused to make adjustments or delayed doing so, the *Clarion-Ledger* found.

The major points have been established but more explanation is needed. Thus the article backtracks to 1974, when Texas authorities began investigating complaints against the corporation, and traces the results of the state investigation and the individual lawsuits. Experiences of individual home buyers are used to illustrate the specific complaints.

A second example of the proper way to use an outline involves two Scripps-Howard Reporters of the Month for June 1983, Connie Remlinger and Gary Webb (1983) of the (Covington) *Kentucky Post*. Remlinger and Webb made sure their readers knew the outline of their whole series by including it in the lead story:

In the streets outside your front door, time eats away at the sanctity of your home.

Someday, somewhere, time will take one bite too many—perhaps in Covington, in Newport, or perhaps in Edgewood.

When it does, your home could become uninhabitable. Your neighborhood school could be closed. Business and jobs could be driven out of town. An epidemic could start.

Time is eating away ever so slowly, ever so continually at northern Kentucky's sewer system.

The cure is not simple, not quick and certainly not cheap. A major sewer collapse could cost millions of dollars and no one is prepared to pay the bill.

The *Kentucky Post* has spent several months looking at northern Kentucky's sewer systems. During the seven-part series that begins today, we'll explore these main findings:

• More of the urban population is served by large municipal sewer plants. But not one of them works as it should. Federal inspectors haven't rated one of them as acceptable.

• A great deal of the area served by the sanitation district has obsolete, pollution-causing combined sewers, built in the day when no one worried about dumping untreated sewage into the Ohio and Licking rivers.

• Not worrying about its sewage problems can be a costly mistake for a community hoping to lure new industry into the area. When businessmen begin considering where to locate a new plant, a community's public works are often a prime factor.

• Where sewer lines or septic tanks don't exist, homes and businesses are hooked to privately owned package treatment plants, many of which are prime sources of water pollution.

   • Solving our sewer problems is a costly proposition. But money isn't the only hurdle.

Focus

"Focus" is our word for unity. By focus, we mean that you should reduce your subject to a lowest common denominator that your audience can grasp and identify with — a representative situation or character. For example, if you are analyzing changing trends in campus life-styles in your area, you report hard data, of course, but you also zero in on the life of at least one student on one campus in one week, making the data come to life.

The following story is an example of multilevel focus. Bob Eure (1983), reporting in the *Roanoke Times and World News* on the problem of hundreds of failing septic systems in southwest Virginia, zeros in on a typical subdivision, and then zooms in even closer to an individual homeowner:

Septic fields raising stench

On hot, humid summer afternoons, the stench outside Sam Angle's house can get unbearable.

When the wind blows across the small subdivision where Angle lives, it carries the rank odor of human sewage from the failing septic fields of several of his neighbors.

"There's really no way to describe the smell," said Angle, who recently retired from an Army civil service career.

The septic fields of all 15 homes in the Dudley Village Development along Virginia 114 near the Radford Army Ammunition Plant are failing, said Angle, who last week had his septic tank pumped out for the third time since he bought his home 15 years ago.

The homeowners have taken their plight to the Montgomery County Public Service Authority in hopes the development could hook onto a sewerline serving the nearby Belview Elementary School.

"We got a petition signed by everyone granting absolute right of way for a sewer line," said Angle. "The PSA told us we would have to pay for the line ourselves and that it would cost $50,000 or more.

"They are asking for something that's impossible."

The problem faced by Angle and his neighbors could threaten literally hundreds of homes in Southwest Virginia that were built on areas where large deposits of clay, shale or limestone lie just beneath the surface, said C. C. Hartley, district sanitarian supervisor with the New River Health District.

"It's a problem I'm afraid we are going to see more and more of in the future with many of these small subdivisions built 15 to 20 years ago," said Hartley.

Hartley said the homes were built under old Health Department codes that allowed smaller drainage fields for septic systems. Because of poor soil conditions, many of the systems are failing, leaving basements or back yards flooded with sewage.

"Within the next few years, these old septic systems are going to start popping out of the ground," said Hartley.

Angle said, "It's so bad that some of my neighbors can't walk on the grass or cut it because they sink into the ground. It's a serious health problem."

Another example of how to focus your story comes from an "Economics Report '82" news analysis by Chuck Martin, economics reporter for the (Madison) *Wisconsin State Journal* (Martin 1982):

Last month, 220,000 Wisconsin workers were unemployed — a record since data-keeping began in 1954. The economist in charge of state unemployment statistics, August Cibarich, says he expects unemployment to be greater when data for this month are processed.

Interest rates for consumer loans and mortgages remain in double digits, discouraging families from major purchases. Many of the state's employers are struggling with declining sales, and asking workers to take pay cuts or freezes.

The result for Wisconsin families has been hardship. Dreams of new homes, cars, and vacations have been dashed for many. Finding a place to sleep and enough to eat has become a daily challenge for a few.

Yet despite the recession, some Wisconsin people refuse to be beaten. They are taking their futures in their hands, facing difficult times and marching forward as best they can.

First we will examine the context of Martin's story. Then we will see how he focuses his writing to make it fit the context. The subject of Martin's story is hard times and how you can cope. The audience is Sunday morning newspaper readers in the Midwest. The medium is the *Wisconsin State Journal*. The purpose is to attract interest and to inform. The story is the lead in the annual special section on the state of the economy.

To tailor his writing to his story's context, Martin breathes human interest into his facts. What are his readers interested in? They ordinarily seem to be interested in people doing things that are appealing and/or significant. So Martin leads off his story with information about real people:

For Jamie Ylvisaker, 900 miles was not too far to travel to find a job.
Left jobless when the Dana Corp. plant closed in Edgerton in 1979, Ylvi-

saker, 24, is now making $8.48 an hour in Oklahoma City.

Doug Diehl, 26, was "emotionally drained" and deep in debt after his Madison home building and remodeling business failed in 1980. He picked himself up, found another job, and expects to have most of his debts paid later this year.

Julie Ziech, 43, didn't want welfare; she wanted a job. In the midst of the highest unemployment rate in Wisconsin's post-Depression history, she sold herself as a good worker and got a job. Though the pay is low, she is "making do," raising two children in Baraboo.

In other words, Martin made his theme come alive and achieved unity by focusing on three real people whose situations were illustrative of the general condition on which he was reporting. Keep in mind, though, that as you deal with more people and more facts in any story the reader is more likely to become confused. You cannot just stack up sentences, but must logically link them together with transitional words and phrases. The use of these is what journalism professor Barbara Straus Reed (1985) identifies as "a distinguishing mark of a good writer."

Another example of the invaluable "focus" technique is illustrated in that to the readers of the *Seattle Post-Intelligencer,* the huge Boeing Company, the area's largest employer, is big news. The key to Boeing's success is its strong move into the high technology that is revolutionizing its aircraft manufacturing processes. How do you make such an arcane subject come alive for your readers? On a page fittingly titled "Focus," you zoom in on a fascinating woman scientist who heads Boeing's High Tech Center. Reporter Carol Smith Monkman (1986) makes Boeing's Dr. Edith Martin, the highest-ranking woman executive at the plant, come alive. The carefully crafted story shows Martin as a "boat rocker" who's determined to "take risks, do things, push people, cause growth." Readers may not understand high technology, but they can identify with its personification in Edith Martin.

As you learned in the section on adapting the methods of social science research to public issues reporting, you cannot casually interview a few people and draw sweeping generalizations from a pseudosurvey. But once you have dug deeply and acquired a solid set of facts, you can illuminate your data by finding real people doing things that graphically illustrate your main points. Do they have to be real people? Yes. What if they do not want to be identified? Use pseudonyms, but be prepared to level with your editor if he or she asks for full disclosure. When a careless reporter constructs a fictitious character, disaster looms (Anderson 1982).

Four key perspectives

Immediately before you put one word after another on paper, think for a moment about the following four key perspectives which your story should reflect.

HUMAN INTEREST. Do not get so bogged down in the mechanics of note taking, lead construction, and so on that you forget the overwhelming importance of being interesting — of writing for people about people.

SIGNIFICANCE. "That's for me!" is what you want your audience to say. They will not, unless you make the significance — the relevance — of your story abundantly clear.

GEOGRAPHY. Time and space are important factors to include in reporting and interpreting public issues. Your audience wants to know the depth and breadth of the subject. The perspective of geography lends such a dimension to your story. Make clear that "this is a local story," or that "this story has national aspects," or both, as the case may be.

HISTORY. Just as the perspective of geography relates your story to space, so the perspective of history relates it to time. Does your subject have a past? Tell your audience what it is. Does your subject have a future? Tell the audience what it is. Give your story depth.

Perspective in action

Here is *Chicago Tribune* staffer Pam Sebastian's beginning to the first in a two-part series on Illinois farmers and their political involvement (Sebastian 1984). Note her human interest focus on farmer Don Horton; the significance of a new radical rural-urban alliance; the geography of a story that is both local and national; and the distinct history and uncertain future of the subject.

Farmers sowing seeds of political power

Farmer Don Horton figures it's tough to be a breadwinner these days whether the family dinner table is in a farmhouse or a city apartment.

The Illinois coordinator of the American Agriculture Movement (AAM), Horton is part of a small but active farmer group allying itself with organized labor, citizen-action and church groups nationwide on common bread and butter issues.

Sitting around his own dinner table near this Down-state town, Horton explains why he feels he has more in common with the assembly-line worker than "those boys who inherited 6,000 acres or so."

Horton began getting riled a few years ago when he realized his sons had no chance to get started in farming.

At 57, Horton farms 450 acres in corn and soybeans but owns only the land around his house. His debt for operating loans goes back four years. His children have left the farm.

"I considered myself at one time a middle-class person," Horton said. But he believes he was shoved down the economic ladder by two years of record crops and low prices, political moves that slashed export markets and soaring interest rates.

Dissatisfied with the middle-of-the-road approach of the National Farmers Union (NFU), and philosophically opposed to the conservative American Farm Bureau Federation, Horton turned to the AAM and its willingness to join forces with nonfarm groups.

"This country wasn't built by just farmers," Horton said. "The people have got to buy our product, and we've got to buy their product in town."

Politically left-of-center, the AAM sprang up in the 1970s with tractorcades and demonstrations. More recently it won notoriety when AAM farmer Wayne Cryts became a folk hero for "ransoming" his soybeans from a bankrupt elevator.

The AAM and the National Farmers Organization (NFO), a group formed in the 1950s around the concept of collective bargaining, have joined forces with the Illinois Farm Alliance. In April, the North American Farm Alliance was formed through the coalition of some 50 farm, labor and community groups in the U.S. and Canada.

The rural-urban alliances have sprouted around the country, mustering grass-roots support for stopping home and farm foreclosures, easing world hunger and embargoes and developing cheaper fuels, among other common goals.

It suggests a rekindling of the Populist movement of the 1800s, when labor and rural groups united against the bigness of business and government.

Farmers have been seeking urban support for radical changes in farm policy, including guaranteed farm prices at 90 percent of parity (or their cost to produce), higher government price supports, and a moratorium on farm-loan payments.

They are seen up against formidable odds.

Corvallis *Gazette-Times* reporters Kight and Mitchell injected human interest into their research-park series by profiling the developer of an Oregon science park. They gave the series significance by suggesting a possible tie between infusion of high technology and economic recovery. They lent geographic perspective by relating Corvallis events to national trends, and they recalled the history of the city's downtown redevelopment plans.

Implementing skills and techniques

In the series leadoff that follows, see how a (Madison) *Wisconsin State Journal* team applied various reporting and interpreting strategies (Balousek 1983).

A running head that lends cohesion

Madison Blacks: their struggle continues

In the summer of 1963, the *Wisconsin State Journal* examined the status of "The Negro in Madison." This series, by Marvin Balousek, Doug Mell and Dianne Paley, under the direction of City Editor Cliff Behnke, updates the gains blacks have made and obstacles that remain.

Big-picture perspectives: history and geography

It was the summer of 1963. A youthful President Kennedy, symbol of the country's high ideals and unflagging optimism, surveyed the growing discontent among the nation's blacks and issued a dire warning:

"The fires of frustration and discontent are burning in every city."

It was a portentous, prophetic statement.

Before the decade was out, violence and hatred would rock the nation as blacks demanded their rights as equal citizens under the law.

It was a long, tumultuous summer, a time when the impact of protests and demonstrations in such Southern cities as Montgomery, Ala., and Jackson, Miss., sent shock waves far into the North.

In June 1963, *The Wisconsin State Journal* dispatched a team of reporters to investigate the condition of blacks in Madison.

Their findings, published in July and August 1963, were stark testimony that discrimination was occurring in every arena: housing, employment and social practice.

In 1963, an estimated 80 percent of the city's homes and apartments were unavailable to blacks.

Many jobs were closed—some because of prejudice, others because blacks were not trained or experienced enough to meet job standards.

There were holes in state and city laws that allowed discrimination and prejudice to slip through.

The series outline: significance

How much has changed in the two decades since 1963, since the summer which now stands as a watershed in the history of civil rights in this country?

Are blacks in Madison—backed by a spate of equal housing and employment laws, affirmative-action plans and other efforts—on equal footing with whites?

In an investigation that began last January, *The State Journal* has attempted to find answers to those questions.

Interviewing: human interest

During the past six months, reporters spoke with dozens of the city's 4,600 black residents—professionals, blue-collar workers and the unemployed. In interviews and a meeting scheduled by *The State Journal,* black leaders talked about their perceptions of Madison, their experiences with discrimination and racial prejudice.

Reporters walked the streets of South Madison, where many black families have settled. They talked to the longtime neighborhood residents and those who recently moved to the area.

Social science research methods

They made hundreds of phone calls, conducting a survey of Madison-area residents to measure the prevalence of racial stereotypes and prejudices.

Searching records

They poured over records and documents, physical testimony that racial discrimination in Madison has had much to do with housing patterns and the development of neighborhoods.

A focus: human interest

They followed two couples—one black and one white—through the process of apartment hunting to determine whether there are differences in approach and reaction.

Straightforward tone

> Throughout the investigation, blacks in Madison repeatedly expressed a single opinion: The city has come a long way in two decades, since the time when discrimination against "Negroes" was legal and socially acceptable.
>
> But racism and discrimination—albeit in less obvious forms—still plagues Madison. . . .
>
> Following six months of investigation, the *Wisconsin State Journal* begins today to present its report on the status of blacks in Madison. Without exception, Madison blacks concurred on a single point: For them, as for blacks in all parts of the country, the struggle for equality continues.

Behind the scenes

Behnke, Balousek, Mell, and Paley take us behind the scenes of their *Wisconsin State Journal* series to reveal the nitty-gritty of reporting and interpreting the subject of progress and perversion in discrimination (Schoenfeld 1984). The editor and three reporters involved in the project are proud of their efforts. Mell, who first proposed an article on Madison blacks in November 1982, says the series went far beyond superficial reports of prejudice in the community. "Everybody's heard stories like that already," Mell notes. "But with this series, particularly with the survey, our readers for the first time had empirical, factual, irrefutable data."

To get to that point, Mell recalls, "the whole series underwent considerable genesis." Behnke liked Mell's idea, and told him to collaborate with Paley, who was working on a story on the school system in south Madison, where a large proportion of the city's blacks reside. Shortly thereafter, police reporter Marvin Balousek, who had recently taken a university course dealing with the construction of surveys, was asked to join the effort.

Interestingly, the series got its biggest boost when the *Capital Times,* the city's rival afternoon daily, came out with its own series on blacks in February 1983. "That is what brought us all together," Mell says. "It made our series 1000 percent better. The meetings went on and on—How can we make our series different? How can we make it better?"

The team naturally thinks the *Capital Times* was tipped off about the *Journal's* developing series. "Maybe they thought when they ran their stories, we would abandon our series," Mell speculates. "We never for an instant considered that. It had already taken up four months of my life—there's no way we were going to abandon it at that point." The series in the *Times* was based largely on interviews with black community leaders. The

Journal team, which had already spoken to those same leaders, renewed efforts to interview as many everyday citizens, both black and white, as it could manage, and to turn its survey into a significant and important piece of research. Behnke, who agrees that the series was rejuvenated and improved because of the other paper's series, says, "This is one example of why it's good to have news media competition in a city. I think that's critical."

Mell, the city hall reporter, Paley, the education reporter, and Balousek were all pulled off their regular beats for about six weeks each in order to give greater attention to the special project. The newspaper, in other words, was willing to run the risk of missing some stories on the reporters' regular beats. "You have to assume you give something up when you do something like this," Behnke admits. "But by and large we got by all right." "I missed a big story once," Paley recalls. "But Cliff said that with our involvement in the project, this is going to happen. When he said that to me, I thought 'OK, they're really committed to this series.' "

It was not until the team was months into the project that the connection was made with the report from twenty years earlier. "Someone just happened to remember we did that earlier series," Paley said. "That gave us a peg. That's what we needed. We went back and talked to people who had been interviewed twenty years ago." The "anniversary" connection provided the series with coherence, direction, and its powerful lead.

In order that each reporter could contribute something to each of the stories without feeling he or she was infringing on another's territory, individual bylines were eschewed in favor of a logo and an explanation of the series that ran each day. The reporters found that condensing the massive amount of information they had gathered and actually writing their stories was the hardest part of the project. "We'd finish one article, and feel a sense of relief," Paley smiles. "Then Behnke would come back and say, 'It doesn't make it,' I remember getting discouraged at the beginning." What finally emerged from all this effort was a comprehensive series that ran for eight straight days, two or more articles each day, except Saturday, when a picture page was featured.

Balousek notes that in addition to the obvious benefits for the paper's readers, the series gave each of the reporters an opportunity for personal growth. Balousek says he benefited from the chance to put his survey-making skills to work, and enjoyed getting away from the routine of the police beat and working closely with other staff members. The cooperation made for a bigger, and probably a better, series. "Those two are complete opposites," says Paley of her cowriters. "Doug tends to say, 'Let's write this sucker and get it in the paper.' Marv is more deliberate. I'm somewhere in between. For some of the articles, it was a very good balance."

What did the team conclude about the situation for blacks in Madison? As their lead indicates, while things have improved considerably in the past twenty years, racism still exists in forms more subtle than in years before. Despite a reputation as a mid state "liberal bastion," the reporters say, the city seems to have many of the same problems of racism and prejudice that exist in the country's larger cities.

"You feel frustration, doing a series like this," Mell observes. "I kept looking for some kind of panacea, and there isn't one." Yet the team believes that bringing the matter clearly into the open by frankly and honestly reporting and interpreting a pervasive public issue is an important step in stimulating community efforts toward improvement.

In summary

Reporting and interpreting any public issue requires much preliminary work so you understand the background of the issue. Unfortunately, reporters do not always develop this understanding and thus cannot explain the issues to the public. Analyzing the coverage of Black Americans since 1950 in five representative dailies, Carolyn Martindale (1985) concludes all five papers failed to provide readers with adequate background needed to understand continuing civil rights concern.

But attitudes and priorities of journalists may be changing. Even small publications and broadcast stations are investing time and money in substantial investigations and reports on community issues. The *Columbia* (Maryland) *Flier*, a weekly with a circulation of twenty-six thousand, surveyed the state of its community eighteen years after its founding as a racially integrated community. With the help of the University of Maryland Survey Research Laboratory, the newspaper looked into the thoughts and emotions of a sample of nearly four hundred of the community's residents. Three pages of its June 13, 1985, edition reported its initial findings. The writer of the articles, John Murchison (1985a), effectively wove together the survey results and background material which gave the report national as well as local significance.

A month later, in a second set of articles based on the survey, the *Flier* (Murchison 1985b) focused on Columbia's black minority. While it found much support for the integrated neighborhoods and multiracial community goals on which Columbia had been founded, the survey also found newer residents less interested and less involved in working for those goals. Using quotations from individual Columbia residents, Murchison was able to add human interest to a series built on social science research method. The series was an example of a journalist putting his skills to work to report fully on social issues in the community.

References

Anderson, Douglas A. 1982. How Newspaper Editors Reacted to *Post's* Pulitzer Prize Hoax. *Journalism Quarterly* 59(3):363–66.

Balousek, Marvin, Mell, Doug, and Paley, Dianne. 1983. Madison Blacks: Their Struggle Continues. (Madison) *Wisconsin State Journal* July 10–14, 1.

Chaptman, Dennis. 1982. Getting the Most Out of a Short Interview. *Writer's Digest.* (July):32.

Collins, Jim. 1984. Awards Honor Public Service. *Inland Daily Press Newsletter* (May):16.

Dunwoody, Sharon. 1982. Using Dow in the Classroom. *Sciphers* 3:5.

Dygert, James H. 1976. *The Investigative Journalist.* Englewood Cliffs, NJ: Prentice-Hall.

Eure, Bob. 1983. Septic Fields Raising Stench. *Roanoke* (VA) *Times and World News,* June 26, 1.

Frey, James H. 1989. *Survey Research by Telephone.* Newbury Park, California: Sage.

Gannetteer. 1982. Child Abuse–Oklahoma Style. (November):9–11.

Green, Laura. 1984. Amelia in Medialand. *The Quill* (October):16–22.

Halkias, Maria and Ricks, W. Stevens. 1981. Low-Cost Housing Comes With High Cost Problems. *Clarion-Ledger* (Jackson, MS), May 18, 1.

Johnson, Owen V. 1983. Reporting Students Analyze Selected Newspapers. *Journalism Educator* 38(1):51.

Kight, Pat, and Mitchell, Russ. 1983a. Research Park Posed as Cure for Economy. *Gazette-Times* (Corvallis, OR), Mar. 15, A1.

_____. 1983b. What Does Oregon State University Have to Offer? *Gazette-Times* (Corvallis, OR.) Mar. 16, B1.

Kilpatrick, James J. 1982. Cigaret-Cancer Link Still Falls Short of Proof. *Milwaukee Journal,* Feb. 28, 19.

Kraft, Joseph. 1980. (Madison) *Wisconsin State Journal,* Dec. 22, 12.

Loh, Jules. 1982. What Writers Think About Writing. *AP World* 18(2):7–8.

McCombs, Maxwell, Shaw, Donald, and Grey, David, eds. 1976. *Handbook of Reporting Methods.* Boston: Houghton Mifflin.

Martin, Chuck. 1982. Three Who Cope with Hard Times. (Madison) *Wisconsin State Journal,* Jan. 31, 1,2.

Martindale, Carolyn. 1985. Coverage of Black Americans in Five Newspapers Since 1950. *Journalism Quarterly* 62(2):321–28, 436.

Meyer, Philip. 1979. *Precision Journalism.* Bloomington: Indiana Univ. Press. 1,2.

Milwaukee Journal. 1979. Survey Says Most Oppose Double-Bottom Trucks. Mar. 26, 9.

Monkman, Carol Smith. 1986. Flying Into the Future with Boeing's Lofty Heights–Edith Martin Maps the Course for Technology. *Seattle Post-Intelligencer,* Dec. 28, E4.

Murchison, John. 1985a. Columbia: How Does It Compare With Its Image? *Columbia* (Maryland) *Flier,* June 13, 16–18.

_____. 1985b. Columbia Survey: Part II. The *Columbia* (Maryland) *Flier.* July 18, 20–23.

Pluckhahn, Charles. 1984. Personal correspondence in author's files.

Reed, Barbara Straus. 1985. 'Sacred Sheet' Makes Transitions a Snap to Write. *Journalism Educator* 40(1):29–31.

Remlinger, Connie and Webb, Gary. 1983. Pacesetters. *Scripps-Howard News* (September):27–28.

Ross, James R. 1983. Book Review. *Newspaper Research Journal* 4(3):65–66.

Rothschild, Matthew. 1983. Tracking the Daily Double. *Isthmus,* July 1–7, 1, 16.

Schneider, Andrew. 1986. Pilots on Drugs—Doctors Can't Report Them. *Pittsburgh Press,* Sept. 21, 1.

Schoenfeld, Clay. 1984. Interviews. Madison, WI. March 11.

_____. 1985. *Ribbands of Blue.* Barneveld, WI: WPRI Press. 58.

Schoenfeld, Clay, and Diegmueller, Karen. 1982. *Effective Feature Writing.* New York: Holt, Rinehart, and Winston. 89.

Scripps-Howard Newsletter 1983 (June):6.

Sebastian, Pam. 1984. Farmers Sowing Seeds of Political Power. *Chicago Tribune,* June 10, 11, 3:1.

Sheboygan Press. 1983. Armira to Close Plant, Idling 320. July 15, 1.

Wilhoit, G. Cleveland, and McCombs, Maxwell. 1976. Reporting Surveys and Polls. In *Handbook of Reporting Methods,* edited by Maxwell McCombs, Donald Shaw, and David Grey, 81–95. Boston: Houghton Mifflin.

Wright, Scott. 1987. Opening the Borders. *Burlington Free Press,* July 4, 1.

Wulfemeyer, Tim K. 1983. Use of Anonymous Sources in Journalism. *Newspaper Research Journal* 4(2):43–50.

Young, Andy. 1982. The New Neighbors. *Elyria Chronicle-Telegram,* July 11, F6.

This chapter was initiated by Schoenfeld. Collaborators were Garrison, Griffin, Heuterman, Molen, and Scotton.

CHAPTER 3

Law and ethics

QUESTIONS of law and ethics are a nettlesome aspect of media life, particularly in public issues reporting. Ethical problems are always present in the newsroom, whether they involve an agonizing decision on whether to run a story that may harm innocent individuals or a relatively uncomplicated question of whether to accept a free pass to a circus performance. Legal issues are almost as omnipresent. Despite the unequivocal statement of the First Amendment that Congress shall make no law abridging freedom of speech and press, innumerable laws still constrain journalists. The dissemination of information always carries some risk of legal entanglement. A misspelled name, a distorted bit of information, an erroneous headline — all can mean a trip to the courts to defend against a lawsuit.

Law and ethics are interrelated. A person can commit both ethical and legal offenses in one instance of carelessness or thoughtless pursuit of a story. One can also, however, operate legally and still violate standards of journalistic ethics. Unethical conduct entails legal peril, as Louis B. Hodges, a professor of applied ethics has noted. "It is a fact of life," he has said, "that the courts stand as an instrument to protect those who are injured or who think they are. And we are a litigious society. Thus when our conduct becomes sufficiently unacceptable, law and government come into the picture. When ethics fails us, law steps in. And that is always, under every condition, a threat to press freedom" (Hodges 1981).

Journalists and the law

On the job, the journalist deals with many statutes and various court decisions that are pertinent to mass communication. The legal issues involved include libel, invasion of privacy, confidentiality of sources, prior restraint, and restrictive judicial orders. Some laws, such as those calling for open meetings of public bodies, will help you to do your job. Other laws, such as those restricting access to information, will make your work more difficult. Some laws encourage litigation, which can be both expensive and time consuming.

Financial consequences of legal problems

Mistakes are costly. A breach of law not only has a negative impact on public perceptions of media credibility, but it can also be financially disastrous. In 1981, the *Alton* (Illinois) *Telegraph* filed a voluntary bankruptcy petition so that it could appeal a $9.2 million libel judgment. The suit was not even the result of a *Telegraph* story. It was based upon a confidential memo from two reporters to a federal attorney investigating organized crime in the area. The memo eventually wound up in the federal bureaucracy in Washington, D.C., and figured in an investigation of loans made to an Alton-area businessman. He sued the *Telegraph* for libel on grounds that the memo had damaged his credit rating and his business. The case eventually was settled out of court for $1.4 million (Reporters Committee 1982).

One legal suit can be all that is needed to jeopardize a news organization's existence or lead it into stringent self-censorship to avoid additional financial losses. United States Circuit Court Judge Robert Bork warned of that danger in a 1984 libel decision, noting that "remarkable upsurge in libel actions, accompanied by a startling inflation in damage awards, has threatened to impose a self-censorship on the rest, which can effectively inhibit debate and criticism as would overt governmental regulation that the First Amendment certainly would not permit" (*Ollman v. Evans and Novak* 1984).

Even when a news staff is wholly justified in what it has done, it may still have to defend its actions in court. Henry Kaufman, head of the Libel Defense Resource Center in New York, said some insurers estimate the average cost of defending a media libel suit to be as much as $150,000. The defense costs in some major media cases have gone into the millions of dollars. "So win or lose, media companies pay out huge sums when they're sued for libel; for small companies such costs can be crippling, even life threatening," Kaufman said (The Cost of Libel 1986).

If the precautions that are taken to avoid such costs become unduly restrictive, self-censorship can transform the media from watchdogs against abuses of the public interest into paper tigers that report only what will not drag them into legal proceedings.

The courts as friends

Judicial leaders often contend, with justification, that the media forget that support of the First Amendment by the courts has been a mainstay of freedom. Although judges sometimes rule against the media in cases involving conflicts of rights, they still generally have provided strong backing for the First Amendment. Traditionally, the courts have rejected efforts to impose licensing and prior restraint as forms of media censorship.

U.S. Circuit Court Judge Alfred Goodwin sees the judiciary-media relationship as one that is not always amicable, but is nevertheless essential. "The relationship between the press and the judiciary in this country," he has stated, "is sometimes strained, often misunderstood, yet, like a shotgun marriage, the relationship is there, and necessary. Looking back over the years that have produced a free press and a federal republic, the courts, more often than not, have been the guardians of whatever liberty the press enjoys" (Associated Press 1980).

The libel problem

For years libel probably has been the most common legal problem for the media. Libel is written defamation, a word derived from the verb "to defame." Slander is oral defamation. Whether broadcast defamation is libel or slander varies from state to state, but the legal consequences for the media are the same, whatever the labels.

Definitions of defamation may differ slightly, but this summary from a New York legal handbook is typical: "Defamation is a statement which is false and which tends to discredit or disgrace the person to whom it refers. It may expose the person to public hatred, contempt or ridicule, or injure the person in his business or profession" (New York State Newspapers Foundation 1980). When individuals do not approve of something that has been written about them in the press, they are quick to talk about suing, even if they are ignorant of the exact meaning of libel. It is one thing, however, for someone to threaten to sue, and another thing for them to follow through on the threat. Many threatened complaints are never filed. Many that are filed are pressed no further or are dismissed when a judge reviews the complaints. A study by the Libel Defense Resource Center (1984) for the period from 1982 through 1984 showed that about three of every four libel cases were dismissed summarily without the necessity for a full trial.

Nevertheless, an article about one person filing a libel suit may stimulate other persons to do the same, regardless of the legal merits of their cases. To respond to any libel suit, whether inane or worthy, requires time and money. If the case goes to the appellate courts, the outcome may be pending for years. For example, a Chicago lawyer, Elmer Gertz, waited fourteen years to receive a $482,000 libel judgment awarded to him against *American Opinion* magazine. He had filed the suit in 1969 after the magazine had labeled him a "Communist fronter" (Reporters Committee 1982a).

The public attention given to major libel trials can obscure the fact that most libel suits can be avoided without resorting to unreasonable self-censorship, provided that you have a basic knowledge of communication law. Knowledge provides an early warning system but you must keep your knowledge up to date if it is to be useful. As the Associated Press warns its reporters and editors, "As is the case in other fields of the law, the law of libel is not static. We have seen dramatic changes in the past 20 years — not always in the same direction" (Associated Press 1986).

Libel defenses

TRUTH AND PROOF. Truth is an all-purpose and complete defense if the proof is available. Libel by definition involves false statements. If there is no falsity, there is no libel. Truth is a defense in virtually any type of libelous situation, although some states qualify it by requiring that the truth be published with good motives and justifiable ends.

In practice, truth is not always a reliable defense because it is not necessarily easy to prove. If some of the evidence is ruled inadmissible in court or if a key witness wavers from his original story, the evidence needed to convince a judge or jury may be lacking. In some instances, the witnesses who have provided the information needed to establish truth may have been promised confidentiality. You have pledged not to reveal their identity so you cannot call them to testify. Without their evidence your defense of truth may not stand up.

PRIVILEGE. This defense provides the media with a qualified immunity in libel suits. The American philosophy of democratic government and freedom of press encourages a relatively unhampered flow of information and debate on public issues. It is in the public interest that the media be able to report otherwise defamatory statements from public meetings or court proceedings without fear of libel.

Legislators and government executives in official public proceedings have an absolute privilege or protection from libel. They may make defamatory statements about someone but they are immune from libel suits. In turn reporters are granted a qualified privilege to report those proceedings, provided the account of the event is fair and true. Public proceedings, particularly court hearings, often produce statements damaging to an individual's reputation. For example, charges and countercharges voiced at a heated city council meeting may defame someone. But any libel suit filed against the media because of a reporter's article about those damaging charges and countercharges will not succeed unless the story is inaccurate or unfair.

Although state laws are not uniform, they generally provide reporters with this qualified privilege in reporting meetings of public legislative bodies and court proceedings. The same type of privilege covers use of material from governmental reports. However, the privilege does not apply when the documents or sessions are required by law to be sealed or secret. Reporters may have the qualified privilege in covering nonofficial public meetings provided matters of public concern are discussed, but state policies in this area may differ. You should make a point of learning the policy in your state as expressed in state laws and court decisions.

FAIR COMMENT AND CRITICISMS. This defense is somewhat akin to qualified privilege because it is intended to encourage discussion of matters of public interest. A writer can express opinions about the performances of people who voluntarily offer their talents for public consumption — politicians, actors, writers, sports figures, singers, and others. The comments may be harsh and damaging, but fair comment will be a valid defense if the opinion has a factual basis and deals with the public activities of the individual rather than the private life. In public affairs reporting, the defense of fair comment is most likely in reviews or news analysis pieces.

Other legal defenses are available to the media, but they are usually matters for attorneys to explore after a complaint has been received. It is more important for you to concentrate on minimizing the libel dangers before a story is published than on defending yourself after a lawsuit has been initiated.

Types of libel plaintiffs

Jurisdiction over libel is the province of the states and each state has its own laws, as well as its own collection of state court decisions. Nevertheless, the United States Supreme Court in recent years has attempted to provide some consistency to the states' applications of libel laws. Decisions since 1964 have created particular standards for three types of libel plaintiffs.

THE PUBLIC OFFICIAL. This category includes elected public officials and appointed officers with decision-making power in matters of public policy. To win a libel suit, the public officials in this category must prove that the defamatory statements were published with the knowledge that they were false or with reckless disregard of their truth or falsity.

THE PUBLIC FIGURE. This group includes individuals who have voluntarily thrust themselves into matters of significant public interest. In a few states, anyone involved in a public issue falls into this category. The public figure must meet the same requirement as the public official (that is, he or she must prove that the defamation was published with the knowledge that it was false or with reckless disregard of truth or falsity).

THE PRIVATE FIGURE. These people are neither public officials nor public figures within the context of the disputed news story. To win a libel suit, they must prove some fault on the part of the media, the degree of fault to be established by each state. The fault standards may range from simple negligence to reckless disregard of truth. In weighing the risk of libel, you should consider the individual's potential legal classification. For example, a college professor who publicly has called for protest demonstrations against the opening of a nuclear power plant would be a public figure in stories about the protest. The professor probably would be a private figure in stories about protests of other issues, provided he or she were a disinterested party who involuntarily had been drawn into the controversy.

Whatever the category, a blatant defamation will find little protection in law. Presumably, few reporters and editors will abandon ethical propriety to deliberately publish lies about someone, so the greater danger of libel lies in the unintentional defamation that originates through carelessness or ignorance of the law.

Hints on how to reduce risks of libel

Because few news operations can afford the luxury of a legal staff to scrutinize every potentially dangerous item, the responsibility for preventive action falls first upon the reporter and next upon the copyreader and editor.

Knowing where the libel dangers lie simplifies the task of eliminating them. Steps you should take to reduce the risk of libel include:

• Knowing the state libel law and keeping abreast of court decisions that may signal changes in legal interpretation, particularly rulings by the United States Supreme Court and your state's highest court;

- Contacting the subject of an unfavorable news report for his or her reaction to give the story better balance and negate charges of one-sided reporting;
  - Reading your copy carefully for omitted words or misspellings that might turn an innocent construction into a defamatory one;
  - Being alert to gaps or contradictions in a source's statement that may raise questions of credibility; and
  - Seeking other sources for confirmation of statements from one individual.

Occasionally, an investigative story or expose requires a slightly different approach. Sometimes a publication takes a calculated risk of legal backlash by publishing a story that it believes is too important to kill. Reporters, editors, and lawyers all may have a hand in analyzing the story to locate any defamatory pitfalls. Often you can change the wording to eliminate needless libel danger without deleting the key information. Libelous material can be deleted if it does not contribute materially to the story, or it can be withheld for use after further investigation and confirmation.

Invasion of privacy

The same careful techniques that can minimize the danger of libel can also minimize the danger of invasion of privacy, but new state and federal statutes and recent court decisions intended to protect an individual's right to privacy have complicated the reporter's task. Four basic categories of privacy law are still the primary concern of the media, but some new laws have sealed off information about individuals that formerly was available to journalists.

APPROPRIATION. The first basic category of privacy, the appropriation tort, seldom involves the public issues reporter. A tort is a wrongful act for which a civil suit can be brought. Since appropriation involves the use of someone's name or likeness for commercial purposes without consent, it is more often an issue for advertising or promotions personnel. If there is doubt about such appropriation in news coverage, the subject's signature on a consent form should be obtained. The form should be worded broadly enough to cover whatever uses are planned for the material.

INTRUSION. A second category, intrusion, raises a warning against using an assumed identity or eavesdropping illegally to gain access to a story. Such

WHAT TO DO IF YOU ARE ACCUSED OF LIBEL

The New York State Newspapers Foundation (1980) offers these suggestions in dealing with complaints of libel:

• Be courteous and polite. Harsh replies or lack of patience may make a potentially difficult situation even worse. The complainant's position may well become firmer if you fail to show interest.

• Never admit error or agreement with the complainant's argument at this stage. The law is sufficiently complex so that what you believe to be error may not be sufficient to sustain a libel suit. There is no doubt, however, that any admission you make can be "used against you" in court.

• Do agree to look into the matter. It is easy to tell a caller that you will do so, and should mollify the caller, at least temporarily.

• When a lawyer is inquiring about a libel and is speaking to you, you are in danger. Libel law is played with a lawyer's rules and he or she is at a distinct advantage. Lawyers should speak to other lawyers; refer any phones calls from a lawyer to your attorney.

• Notify your editor or attorney immediately of any complaint you receive. The liability for libel runs not only against the reporter, but also against the editor, the publisher, and the newspaper itself. Generally, libel complaints can be resolved without litigation. But they often require sensitive handling and a full awareness of applicable legal principles. An attempt to resolve the problem without adequate consultation may make a problem more serious.

action can lead to an invasion of privacy suit. It can also involve trespassing and result in prosecution of the reporter. Either way, it spells legal trouble. Even if the material is not published, intrusion can produce damages. Whether operating under false pretenses is justified to obtain a story is a question with both legal and ethical aspects. You should check with news supervisors in advance to determine if subterfuge is warranted.

In 1963 a *Life* magazine reporting team, armed with hidden tape recorder and camera, used a ruse to gain entry to the home office of a medical-quackery suspect. Although the suspect later was convicted of practicing medicine without a license, he won a $1000 judgment in a separate privacy action against *Life*. The magazine's contention that the First Amendment protected the reporters' actions was dealt with rudely by U.S. Circuit Judge Shirley Hufstedler (*Dietemann* v. *Time* 1971):

We agree that newsgathering is an integral part of news dissemination. We strongly disagree, however, that the hidden mechanical contrivances are 'indispensable tools' of newsgathering. Investigative reporting is an ancient art; its successful practice long antecedes the invention of miniature cameras and electronic devices. The First Amendment has never been construed to accord newsmen immunity from torts or crimes committed during the course of newsgathering. The First Amendment is not a license to trespass, to steal, or to intrude by electronic means into the precincts of another's home or office. It does not become such a license simply because the person subjected to the intrusion is reasonably suspected of committing a crime.

A tape recorder, however, is a valuable tool in reporting, and its use need not involve intrusion. One ethical consideration is whether a source should be advised that a telephone interview is being recorded. As a general rule, courtesy and ethics dictate that the source be informed. Whether some circumstances justify secret recording is debatable. In any case, you should know the applicable laws. State statutes governing the recording of telephone calls are not uniform, so familiarity with provisions of your state's laws is essential.

FALSE LIGHT. A much more hazardous form of privacy for the media is the false light tort, in which a person is portrayed in a false, but not necessarily defamatory, manner. A false light account commonly includes exaggeration or fictional material. The portrayal may even be favorable but still can be damaging if it causes extreme embarrassment or would be offensive to a person of ordinary feelings.

If the reporting is accurate and fair, false light will not be a problem. If the story is only partly true, the inaccurate portion may be the basis for the false light action. A reporter who falsifies an interview risks legal troubles — a libel suit if the material is defamatory or a false light invasion of privacy suit if the material is not defamatory but distorts the individual's character.

EMBARRASSING FACTS. The fourth basic category of privacy law, publication of embarrassing facts, surfaces most often in stories recounting events of the past, going back ten or more years. Court decisions are mixed, but the risk is minimal if the information comes from public records and is reported correctly. Factual errors can overcome the defense of privilege in reporting on public records.

If an individual's name is not essential to the news, it may be wise to eliminate it. This point is especially relevant in general stories about crime when the subject of a case illustration is going through rehabilitation and has been out of the public eye for several years. Court rulings on invasions of privacy in this type of situation have been narrow and have usually involved references to individuals linked to crimes that took place years earlier. Using precaution does not mean, however, that identification should be eliminated when a name or identity is necessary as in more current stories.

Even accurate reporting can lead to courtroom problems if a jury finds sympathy for someone who has had an embarrassing event of the past resurrected. If the account is newsworthy and accurate, the publication probably will be secure from suit. Unfortunately, sometimes a resort to the appellate courts is required to establish that defense, especially if the trial judge shares the jury's sympathy and lets his or her judgment be swayed from generally accepted legal principles.

Government and privacy

Invasion of privacy cases in which the aggrieved party files a civil suit to seek redress for a private wrong have been given another dimension by relatively new federal and state laws that regulate government information policies.

The Federal Privacy Act

The Federal Privacy Act of 1974 (U.S. Code, Title 5, Section 552a) originated from the general public concern about the vast quantity of personal data collected by the government and the potential it created for abuse of private rights. Passage of the act was seen as a means of allaying public concerns. The act allows individuals to review files pertaining to them and to correct any errors. It limits the collection of data by federal agencies and prohibits agencies from releasing "private" information to others without the consent of the person involved. The law does specify that records considered public under the federal Freedom of Information Act (FOI) are not subject to restrictions by the privacy act.

Although the privacy act is directed to the government, not the media, it complicates the reporter's access to information. One restrictive factor is a provision that penalizes any agency that illegally releases information covered by the privacy act. While the objective may be meritorious, it exacerbates a common problem in government decision making: government officials often would rather err on the side of caution than release some legitimate public information and risk penalties for making an error.

State privacy laws

Most states have followed the federal example and have adopted laws governing privacy of information to protect citizens from needless government exposure of personal information. In general, the state laws allow individuals access to state records containing personal information about them and establish guidelines for state agencies in collection and dissemination of data.

In many states, criminal-records laws limit access to public records, especially those that pertain to individuals who have been arrested but not convicted of a criminal offense. Few states have identical statutes, however, and in almost every state the prescribed practices have been affected to some extent by court rulings, attorney general opinions, and local traditions.

In some instances, poorly drafted laws or overly arbitrary interpretations by agency officials have created confusion and, at times, have placed a higher priority on individual rights than on the public interest.

TOO MUCH PRIVACY. Excessive caution in releasing information may sometimes cover up abuses of power by law enforcement agencies. Occasionally, it may even protect privacy more than the affected individual would like. One such case involved an unforeseen side effect of Oregon's first criminal records law. During the Pendleton Roundup, a major western rodeo, authorities arrested numerous people and held them on minor charges related to celebrating too enthusiastically. The new law prohibited disclosure of criminal records, including notice of arrest and detention, so although most of those held could have been released on bail, officers could not notify friends and relatives that the people were in jail. Pendleton authorities were left with a jail full of people. Oregon hastily called a special legislative session to repeal the law, four days after it had taken effect.

At the other extreme are instances where lack of knowledge of the law has created problems. An Iowa study found that many reporters and peace officers in that state were either not familiar with or misread the Iowa code that deals with disclosure of law enforcement records (Hvistendahl and Blinn 1982).

FINDING A BALANCE. The balance between a person's right to privacy and the public interest is sometimes difficult to achieve. For the legislator, the task of drawing up laws that govern information practices and separating records into public, private, and confidential is complex. For the agency official, administering freedom of information and privacy laws that are supposed to safeguard individual and public rights is also complicated. And for the news media, weighing the public's need to know against an individual's right to privacy is a sensitive matter. You need to keep these some-times-conflicting rights in mind, approach them with fairness, and be alert to side effects of laws that may damage First Amendment rights and lead to abuses of power.

Fair trial and free press

A battle over the Bill of Rights has been running at high intensity since 1966, and in covering crime and the courts you may find yourself caught up in the dispute. The issue boils down to the sometimes-conflicting First and Sixth Amendments to the Constitution, and the question of whether extensive news coverage of a crime hampers the courts' responsibility to find an unbiased jury.

Discussions of the degree to which news stories affect potential jurors have been around for many years, but conflict over the answers has become more heated in the past two decades. In 1966, the United States Supreme Court ruled that an Ohio doctor, Samuel Sheppard, had been deprived of a fair trial in a sensational murder case. The court blamed the injustice upon the press for its excessive and often inflammatory stories and upon the trial judge for failing to take proper steps to offset the prejudicial publicity (*Sheppard* v. *Maxwell* 1966).

The Sheppard ruling set off a struggle between the legal and journalistic professions that is still going on. The courts and attorneys began a campaign to control juror exposure to potentially contaminating information about a criminal defendant. One effect was to restrict media access to such information. The media fought to maintain a right of access to courtrooms and information of public record. The struggle has been waged principally on the home grounds of lawyers and judges, the nation's courtrooms. Generally, the result has been a subordination of the First Amendment to the competing values of the Sixth Amendment and its guarantee of a speedy and public trial before an impartial jury.

Although potentially virulent publicity appears inevitable about crimes that shock the nation, the effects of the dispute have been felt in criminal trials of far less importance. Reporters have been confronted by two different barriers to effective coverage: restrictive orders shutting off information at the source, and closed courtrooms or secret proceedings.

RESTRICTIVE ORDERS. These orders prohibit parties directly involved in a case (the prosecutor, defense attorney, witnesses, bailiffs, and other officers of the court) from commenting on the case outside the courtroom. When a judge extends the restrictions to reporters, telling them what they can or cannot report, the restrictions are known as gag orders. When the court extends its authority that far, a question is raised as to whether a court legally can impose such prior restraint on the press. The United States Supreme Court finally broke its silence on the matter in a 1975 Nebraska case, ruling that such prior restraints are illegal except in the most extreme circumstances (*Nebraska Press Association* v. *Stuart* 1976). But Chief Justice Warren Burger's opinion engendered a new media problem when he said that judges might consider closing preliminary hearings to the public if extensive publicity would make it difficult to empanel an impartial jury. The media then found its battlefront shifted from gag orders to closed courtroom doors.

CLOSED COURTROOMS. In 1980, the United States Supreme Court formally upheld a judge's right to bar the public from preliminary court procedures, but the opinions were so confusing that the nation was treated to the unusual spectacle of individual justices publicly explaining what they thought they had decided (*Gannett* v. *DePasquale* 1979). A year later, in a different case, the court ruled clearly that final trials could not be closed except in the rarest of circumstances, but that judges could close preliminary proceedings (*Richmond Newspapers* v. *Virginia* 1980).

In response to a surge in the number of closed preliminary hearings, some press representatives began preparing statements for presentation to a trial judge, asking that a closure order be delayed until the media arguments for an open hearing could be made. Other news organizations simply advised reporters to ask a judge for time to consult with editorial executives before taking action. The Associated Press provides its reporters with an eight-paragraph statement to read in court when they are confronted with an attempt to close the proceedings (Associated Press 1986). The statement sets out the legal arguments against closed courtrooms and asks for a hearing to consider the arguments. In most cases, the reporter's best course is to ask the court for a delay until the editors can be consulted.

A 1980 United States Supreme Court decision brightened the situation somewhat for the media. The Court specified that there is a qualified First Amendment right of access to preliminary hearings in criminal cases. It said that such hearings can be closed only when it is demonstrated clearly that there is "a substantial probability" that the defendant's right to fair trial will be prejudiced by publicity (*Richmond Newspapers* v. *Virginia* 1980).

Voluntary guidelines

One progressive step to ease tensions between journalists and the courts has been the formation of state and regional bench-bar-press committees, which bring together judges, attorneys, and reporters to consider how to protect the interests of defendants and the free press. In about half the states, cooperative efforts have led to establishment of voluntary fair trial–free press agreements. Most of the agreements represent an attempt to balance needs, advising what types of information should be available to press and public, and cautioning reporters about what pretrial information probably should not be reported in the interest of a fair trial. Generally, the agreements recommend against pretrial publication of items considered most likely to contaminate a jury panel, including:

• Existence of a confession or an admission that implies guilt

• Statements about what a prospective witness is expected to relate in court

• Refusal of a defendant to take a lie detector test, or results of specialized investigative procedures such as ballistics tests

• Opinions as to the guilt or innocence of a defendant

• References to prior criminal records if the previous offenses are not linked in a pattern with the case in question. (However, a parole violation or a prior offense related to the current crime may be justifiably used if it seems in the public interest. For example, an arrest after a series of particularly brutal crimes may justify publication of a prior record simply to ease public fears.)

The legal profession is leery of pretrial publication of such items because they may not be admissible as evidence and a decision on admissibility may not be made until trial proceedings begin.

Adherence to the voluntary guidelines can eliminate some sources of bench-bar-press antagonism, but only if the parties involved are aware that the guidelines exist. A study in a state with such agreements revealed that 71 percent of the attorneys, 10 percent of the newspaper editors, and 43 percent of the television news directors were unaware that the voluntary agreements even had been made (American Bar Association 1981).

A recent Washington state court decision created some doubt as to the value of voluntary agreements. The Washington State Supreme Court upheld a trial judge's right to make the voluntary guidelines mandatory. The judge had ruled that reporters would be banned from pretrial proceedings in a murder case unless they agreed in writing to abide by the voluntary guidelines. Despite press contentions that the ruling was an unconstitutional form of prior restraint, the United States Supreme Court in 1982 refused to review the case (Reporters Committee 1981). As a result, some news organizations have withdrawn support from the agreements. In other cases, permanent bench-bar-press committees have been working to ensure that the agreements remain voluntary. Should the voluntary agreements be abandoned, the guidelines still can be useful to you as an informal indicator of the rights of both defendant and press.

Shield laws

In about twenty-five states, reporters are given special protection against having to disclose confidential sources. These shield laws, so called because they shield the sources from identification and the reporter from having to perform a dual role as reporter and witness, provide varying degrees of coverage. Some flatly give reporters the right to refuse to disclose sources and confidential information in any type of legal proceeding; others offer only partial protection. Even in states with "absolute" shield laws, the courts have taken a narrow view of the reporter's privilege and have found ways to require his or her testimony.

The United States Supreme Court has ruled that the press has no First Amendment privilege to refuse to testify before a grand jury investigating the commission of crime (*Branzburg* v. *Hayes* 1972). Lower court decisions on state shield laws and on First Amendment claims in the absence of shield laws have been mixed. Reporters probably should not rely too heavily upon even "absolute" shield laws. If a reporter's testimony is essential to achieving justice in criminal cases, the courts usually will rule that Sixth Amendment principles override shield-law protections. In civil suits, where journalists are involved only as third parties, the chances are good that First Amendment protection will be granted, unless the information or source identification is crucial to the case.

Courts and confidentiality

Traditionally, reporters have felt honor-bound to keep secret the identity of a confidential news source. It is an ethical principle: if you make a promise, you should keep it. But it also has a practical side. Insiders' leaks of information often lead to stories of great significance. If a reporter grants a pledge of confidentiality, then later reveals the identity of the secret source, other potential sources will not volunteer information in the future for fear that the promises will not be kept. The result would be a crimp in the flow of information, particularly in sensitive areas in which information is difficult to obtain through regular sources. The journalist should keep in mind one dilemma involved here. There is a perceived professional obligation to identify the source when disclosure is required to set the record straight (Langley 1988).

This journalistic ethic and the laws were in conflict in 1974 when Judge William Davis of the Los Angeles County Superior Court listened to three nationally known newsmen testify eloquently that an unwritten ethic in journalism requires a reporter to keep a promise of confidentiality to a secret news source. The issue before the court was whether more time in the Los Angeles County Jail would coerce reporter William Farr of the *Los Angeles Times* to reveal who gave him copies of a prospective witness's statement during the trial in California of mass-murderer Charles Manson and his "family" of disaffected young followers (Associated Press 1980). Farr already had served forty-six days of an indeterminate sentence for contempt of court, but remained adamant in his refusal to identify the source or sources. Supporting the argument that his position was underwritten by a journalistic ethic were Jack Nelson, Washington, D.C., bureau chief for the *Los Angeles Times;* Walter Cronkite, anchorman for CBS, and Tom Brokaw, Washington correspondent for NBC.

At the conclusion of the hearing, Judge Davis ruled that there is an unwritten journalistic ethic that governed Farr's refusal to divulge his sources, and that additional jail time would not coerce him to talk (California District Court 1974).

Virtually every journalist in the United States could have advised that court of the existence of the ethical principle. A pledge of secrecy to a confidential source should be adhered to, even if it does send the reporter to jail. But this ethic in which reporters and editors believe so intensely can lead to decision-making dilemmas. If, as Justice Oliver Wendell Holmes once wrote, "the character of every act depends upon the circumstances in which it is done" (*Schenck* v. *United States* 1919), then different contexts can leave a reporter torn between the ethic of a pledge of confidentiality and the ethic of a citizen's responsibility to prevent an injustice that the pledge might cause.

One answer for the journalist is to exercise extreme care in promising confidentiality, and to anticipate the most extreme circumstances under which the pledge might bring different ethics into conflict.

Access to information

If some laws work to restrict the information you can relay to the public, other laws serve to expand your ability to obtain information about the government. In recent years, a number of federal and state statutes have been enacted to help bring public business into the open through limitations on government secrecy and through procedures to grant access to public records and meetings.

The demand for open public records and meetings is embedded in traditional American democratic philosophy as expressed in the slogan of Scripps-Howard Newspapers: "Give light and the people will find their own way." Although at times, the information acts have elicited only lip service from government officials, their net effect has been to make more information available to the public.

Federal public records laws

The federal Public Records Act (U.S. Code, Title 5, Section 552) was adopted in 1966 and strengthened in 1974. Known generally as the Freedom of Information Act, it is designed to bring more government information to the people. It is constantly the subject of a legislative tug-of-war between those who would narrow its application and those who want it left intact. The law, which applies to federal government agencies, opens public records and prescribes a legal procedure people can use to obtain access to agency documents. The act is based on a positive note, stressing that "disclosure be the general rule, not the exception; that all individuals have equal rights of access; that the burden be on the agency to justify the withholding of a document and not the person who requests it; that individuals improperly denied access to the documents have the right to seek injunctive relief in the courts."

A psychological goal of the act's backers was to undercut a dictum common among agency employees: when in doubt, classify documents as secret, confidential, or restricted. Whether that goal has been reached is open to dispute, but the law does emphasize an open-records philosophy. A key element is the right of a person to petition the courts to resolve a disagreement over availability of documents. The act does contain nine categories of exceptions to the general rule of disclosure. Exceptions include such matters as national security, law enforcement investigatory records, trade secrets, personnel and medical files, geological data, and some internal agency memoranda.

Media use of the act has not been extensive; lawyers for business and industry have been more active in seeking information through the process for their clients. In part, the media reluctance to rely too heavily upon the act reflects reporters' ability to dig out the information from other sources, some of them government employees willing to leak data on a confidential basis. In addition, a request for information from a reporter may be enough to bring release of information without the need for formal court action.

The media have produced a number of public services stories through Freedom of Information action. One such story brought the *Detroit News* a citation from the Associated Press Managing Editors Association. The *News* used the federal act to obtain government records that revealed that dozens of Medicaid recipients had died after receiving drugs in unlimited quantities from doctors and pharmacies. In Salt Lake City, KSL-TV used the act to help obtain information for a series exposing poor conditions in Utah nursing homes.

State public records acts

Using the federal law as a model, many states have developed their own public records acts. Generally, they contain similar exceptions to disclosure and establish a procedure to seek court action, if necessary, to obtain public records. In public affairs reporting, knowledge of such procedures is essential on both state and federal levels. An awareness of the exemptions that exist in all public records laws is important because you then can recognize whether an agency's refusal to release information has any probable basis in law.

The process for obtaining records generally calls for submitting a written request for information, with a description of what is wanted in as specific detail as possible. If the request is denied, you should then file an appeal with the agency administrator, asking that the decision to withhold be reversed. If that fails, you can file a formal complaint in court, asking that the agency be ordered to produce the requested documents for inspection and duplication.

Information on public records problems and processes can be obtained from journalistic organizations such as publishers' associations, state Freedom of Information groups, and the Freedom of Information (FOI) Service Center in Washington, D.C., a joint venture of the Society of Professional Journalists and the Reporters Committee for Freedom of the Press. The FOI Service Center offers a handy guide on how to use the federal Public Records Act. The provisions are adaptable to most state acts.

State public meeting acts

All of the fifty states have some legal standards for open public meetings of government bodies, although most of them have exceptions to the rule so that absolute openness is rarely mandatory. Penalties are seldom more than a misdemeanor and are not often invoked, but in some states the courts can throw out decisions made by local government bodies in illegally closed sessions.

No matter how mild, the laws—generally called "Sunshine Acts"—do have a salutary effect if only in their central purpose—that the public should have access to meetings of public bodies. Legal advisors to some elected councils or boards keep a close watch for potential violations of such laws, but ultimately, enforcement depends largely upon complaints lodged by citizens or the media.

As in the area of public records, laws on open meetings inevitably specify exemptions, the most common being sessions to discuss personnel, litigation, or the security of public buildings.

PERSONNEL. Personnel matters are not always easy to define, but the most prevalent uses of this exemption are meetings involving hirings and firings, examination of charges brought against employees, and contract bargaining sessions. The strongest open meeting laws require that the government unit holding the meeting provide general reasons for the closed session and some report of the results.

LITIGATION. The exemption for litigation has its basis in the legal attorney-client privilege under which communication between the two is secret unless the client wishes to disclose it. Discussion of lawsuits in which the government unit is involved, or may be involved in the near future, is the most common reason for closed meetings in the litigation category.

SECURITY OF PUBLIC BUILDINGS. Discussions of the security systems of public buildings if made public would compromise safety.

Policing the government units is complicated by the ease with which a group of officials can discuss official business on an informal basis over the telephone or in unofficial settings such as a coffee shop or a private residence. When this type of episode becomes so organized and so frequent that the evasion of the law is highly noticeable, a formal legal complaint is likely to be successful. At times, it will take only a news story about the practice to bring it to an end.

You should obtain copies of the open meetings law for your state, learn its provisions, and analyze them. Among things to look for are:

• Does the law require advance notice to the media of regular and special meetings?

• Can tape recordings be made of the proceedings?

• Are reports of actions taken at closed sessions required, either immediately after the meeting or at the next regular meeting?

• Are written minutes available after the matter has been considered? If you are aware of the requirements of the law, it is easier to detect violations and to protest formally.

The surest tip that a group is conducting public business in secret is when its members dispose of, with serene regularity, matter after matter without discussion. This can only mean that the topics have been thrashed out beforehand, leaving only the formality of ratification for the open meeting.

Close contact with members of the group and with private citizens who have a particular interest in its activities can lead to discovery of unannounced private meetings. While some elected officials can lie about secret meetings without any apparent twinges of conscience, others will either answer pointed questions honestly or will avoid lying by reticent or evasive answers. Simply questioning the group, individual by individual, ordinarily will reveal whether a secret session was held and what it concerned.

Certain steps should be taken to protect your coverage if a government body decides to hold a closed session. Ask the reason for the closed meeting so that you can challenge it if the reason does not meet the requirements of the law. Know whether the law requires that minutes or a transcript be made of the proceedings. If so, make arrangements to see the record as soon as possible. If no transcript or minutes are required, interview the group's members after the closed session to get an account of what happened.

Patience, knowledge of the law, and your credibility as a reporter usually will make it easier to win the cooperation of members of a government body, and to make sure that public business will not go unreported.

Public disclosure acts

Some states have followed federal guidelines in adopting measures that require candidates and public officeholders to divulge campaign expenditures and personal financial interests. Whether such acts have discouraged persons in certain professions from holding public office is problematic, as is the issue of whether an official's business interests should be published or merely monitored for possible conflicts of interest.

Access to records of the sources and amounts of political funding is a valuable tool in determining whether pressure-group influences are being used to "buy" candidates. Records usually are available through the Federal Election Commission or through state election commissions.

A HELPING HAND

The variety of legal problems that has confronted reporters in recent years has prompted a number of media organizations to produce compact booklets that cover the laws in brief and suggest how you can react to different situations.

The booklets come in different sizes and vary in breadth of coverage and sale price. Pennsylvania's First Amendment Coalition distributes its Media Survival Kit, *a forty-seven-page, pocket-sized brochure, free to Pennsylvania reporters. Some organizations sell booklets, usually at a modest price to cover printing costs. Not all states have such booklets, but the law division of the Association for Education in Journalism and Mass Communication offers a twenty-page guide telling how to prepare a survival kit for your state. The division says a good kit contains a summary of state and federal media law, an outline of procedures to follow when faced with problems, and a card containing a standardized statement that can be read by a reporter should a judge propose restrictions on news coverage.*

If your state press or broadcast organizations do not have survival kits, the law division packet offers suggestions that will help you cope with legal problems. Headquarters for the Association for Education in Journalism and Mass Communication is at the University of South Carolina.

Journalism ethics

In 1887, John Emerich Edward Dahlberg-Acton asserted in England that "in judging men and things, Ethics go before Dogma, Politics or Nationality" (Dahlberg-Acton 1949). Lord Acton, a noted historian and moralist, was addressing historians, but he could just as well have been writing to twentieth-century journalists. As day-to-day historians, journalists could apply Lord Acton's words to their unending efforts to make ethics a keystone of their daily behavior.

Those efforts are vital in enhancing media credibility and in averting the problems that arise when unethical actions extend into illegal actions. A few years ago, the police reporter for an Idaho newspaper found in his typewriter a note saying: "You will find a familiar name on the police blotter today. Please handle it as you would any other." The familiar name was that of the publisher, who had been arrested on a charge of drunken driving. Dutifully the reporter included that familiar name in a story about arrests for drunken driving. It was a legal matter, but the publisher had made an ethical decision in line with another of Lord Acton's beliefs: "If we may debase the currency for the sake of genius, or success, or rank, or reputation, we may debase it for the sake of a man's influence, or his religion, or his party, of the good cause which prospers by his credit and suffers by his disgrace" (Dahlberg-Acton 1949).

The importance of a concern for ethics in journalism is stressed by author John Merrill (Merrill and Barney 1975), who writes that,

> the journalist who has this concern obviously cares about good or right actions; such a concern indicates an attitude which embraces both freedom and personal responsibility. It indicates also that the journalist desires to

SIX WAYS TO HELP AVOID LEGAL PROBLEMS

While there is no sure method of anticipating every potential legal hazard, here are some suggestions to reduce the risk:

- Keep up to date with legal developments in your state. Ignorance of the laws is an invitation to trouble.
- Do not flirt unnecessarily with the outer limits of the laws. Play it safe unless there is a compelling reason to risk a legal entanglement.
- Avoid single-minded concentration on one legal danger. For example, you may avoid a libel suit but overlook something that will involve an invasion of privacy.
- Try to anticipate problems before they arise. Preventive action is better than a battery of lawyers.
- Carry copies of your state's open meetings act or public records act with you if you expect trouble. They will help establish your credibility should you have to question the legality of a government body's action.
- Do not be careless with the facts. Shoddy reporting makes a poor legal defense.

discover norms for action that will serve him as guiding principles or specific directives in achieving the kind of life which he thinks most meaningful and satisfying. Ethical concern is important also for it forces the journalist to commitment, to thoughtful decision among alternatives. It leads him to seek the summum bonum, the highest good in journalism, thereby heightening his authenticity as a person and journalist.

Ethics in journalism rest upon a foundation of individual responsibility, but they also exist within a framework of organizational standards, because the consequences of unethical behavior may affect the institution, not just one person. When a reporter is discovered to have falsified part of a news story, the particular medium may suffer some temporary loss of credibility. The long-term effects can be overcome by a record of reliable, accurate reporting and editing. But when a pattern of unethical behavior develops through the revelation of bad examples scattered across the country, the cumulative result can be a tarnished image for all journalists, and damaged credibility for all news media.

A written and unwritten group ethic exists in journalism. It stresses the importance of operating in the public interest and the responsibility that is placed upon journalists by the protection granted them by the First Amendment. The complicating element reflected in the search for answers throughout the ages is that clear-cut sets of circumstances do not always exist. The decision-making process often entails conflicting values in which the choice is not necessarily one of right or wrong, but one of which decision is the most right or the least wrong. Vast gray areas between all choices make it difficult to establish binding rules that will usually provide the correct answer.

Aggravating the matter is the necessity in many instances for quick decisions that allow little time for reflection and are often made with little knowledge of the philosophy of ethics. The authors of a book on media ethics noted that "the rush of events forces us to make ethical decisions by reflex more than by reflection, like a driver wheeling around potholes, mindful that a blowout sends him into a courtroom at one ditch and into public scorn at the other" (Christians, Rotzell, and Fackler 1983).

While there may be general endorsement of ethical principles, research indicates that journalists occupy varying niches along the spectrum of ethics. A study by Jay Black, Ralph Barney, and Norman Van Turbargen (1979) found that different journalists represent different stages in a sequence of moral development from the morality of arbitrary fixed rules to the morality of universal ethical principles.

A survey of 153 journalists by journalism professor Rilla Dean Mills (1982) revealed a wide range of opinion on ethical decisions. "For the vast majority of respondents in the survey, ethics were viewed as questions of adherence to a rather narrowly defined code of professional behavior. For most, it is not an exaggeration to say that ethics equated with 'objective' news coverage."

The journalists who held objectivity or fairness as a primary ethical goal suggested that they attempt to compensate for their own biases on certain types of stories. For example, a feminist said that certain stories she wrote on the Equal Rights Amendment (ERA) "have been 'overly fair,' if that is possible. In other words, I end up promoting the anti-ERA arguments more than they deserve in an effort to negate my own bias on the issue" (Porter 1981).

Although there may be differences of opinion among journalists about ethical standards, it is clear that there is renewed concern about them. In a recent issue of their journal, Investigative Reporters & Editors, Inc., listed nineteen books on media ethics published since 1980 (IRE Journal 1988).

Codes of ethics

Numerous efforts have been made, with mixed results, to establish written ethical guidelines for journalists. Codes of ethics have been adopted by such groups as the Society of Professional Journalists, the Radio-Television News Directors Association, the American Society of Newspaper Editors, the Associated Press Managing Editors Association, the National Association of Broadcasters, the Newspaper Guild, and a number of individual newspapers and broadcast stations.

The organizational codes are, for the most part, general statements of high principles, stressing devotion to truth, fairness, freedom of the press, and the public trust. Codes of individual newspapers or stations tend to be more detailed and cover such specific issues as the ethical questions involved in sharing transportation to the scene of a news event, soliciting free books and record albums, participating in outside individual commercial activities, and accepting gifts. The promulgation of detailed codes by some newspapers has led to complaints that the codes are enacted more to convince the public that journalists operate under ethical guidelines than to shape reporters' individual judgments.

The *Des Moines* (Iowa) *Register* labels its code as something that "at least will give us all the same minimum guidelines," but recognizes the individual's role in its statement of general principle: "an individual's own good judgment and integrity are the keystones of this code because it would be impossible to spell out every single question that might arise as the result of adopting such a code" (Swain 1978).

THE ETHIC OF OBJECTIVITY

Objectivity in reporting is a keystone of many codes of ethics in both print and electronic media. The following section on Accuracy and Objectivity is excerpted from the Code of Ethics of the Society of Professional Journalists, Sigma Delta Chi (Ethics Report 1986).

Good faith with the public is the foundation of all worthy journalism.

1. Truth is our ultimate goal.
2. Objectivity in reporting the news is another goal, which serves as the mark of an experienced professional. It is a standard of performance toward which we strive. We honor those who achieve it.
3. There is no excuse for inaccuracies or lack of thoroughness.
4. Newspaper headlines should be fully warranted by the contents of the articles they accompany. Photographs and telecasts should give an accurate picture of an event and not highlight a minor incident out of context.
5. Sound practice makes clear distinction between news reports and expressions of opinion. News reports should be free of opinion or bias and represent all sides of an issue.
6. Partisanship in editorial comment which knowingly departs from the truth violates the spirit of American journalism.
7. Journalists recognize their responsibility for offering informed analysis, comment and editorial opinion on public events and issues. They accept the obligation to present such material by individuals whose competence, experience and judgment qualify them for it.
8. Special articles or presentations devoted to advocacy or the writer's own conclusions and interpretations should be labeled as such.

Harlan Draeger of the *Chicago Sun-Times* seconds the idea of individual responsibility and stresses the importance of a strong ethical foundation. "You've either got an ongoing philosophy that's ethical, or you don't," he says (Swain 1978).

Common to the codes of national journalistic organizations is the call for accuracy and fairness, including a willingness to admit and correct errors. Author Martin Mayer believes that all of the ethical and moral issues of journalism involve the "obligation to question one's perceptions, and to fight against the degradation of their transmittal" (Thayer 1980). Mayer points out that it is very tempting to take your own opinion seriously and to feel that you are paid to develop that opinion. . . . The job of the journalist is not to write in such a way that people who read his stuff can find out what *he* thinks. It's much more important to help people find out what *they* think (Thayer 1980).

Conflicts of interest

Most codes of ethics also caution against conflicts of interest, but agreement on what constitutes a conflict is not easy to achieve in the gray shades of real situations. It is easy to agree that a reporter should not accept money from a news source, or should not seek special favors from news-makers or special interests. It is more difficult to decide whether a reporter is guilty of impropriety in accepting a cup of coffee or a lunch from a news source. Common sense may dictate different answers on different occasions.

The appearance of a conflict of interest may be as damaging to journalistic credibility as an actual conflict of interest. A political reporter who put a "Bush for President" bumper sticker on his car could be faulted for lack of professional judgment even if his or her copy showed no trace of bias.

The myriad of possibilities for disagreement about ethical specifics led journalism professor Clifford G. Christians to conclude that "Buckminster Fuller's tetrahedron suggests there are 30 sides or planes or aspects, minimum, to all physical reality. He could legitimately add some zeros to that 30 when thinking of ethics" (Hodges 1981).

Journalism school ethics and the "real world"

In college, journalism students usually subscribe to high standards of professionalism. But what happens to their ethical standards after they spend some time in the "real world," after some time on the job in journalism? Researcher Lee B. Becker and his colleagues (1987) surveyed graduating journalism students at three midwestern universities over a three-year period. In regard to the students' ethical values in college, the researchers found that:

> The large majority of students feel strongly that the news media should pursue (even those) stories that might make the community served appear negative, and that reporters should be willing to protect the identities of their news sources, even

if that means protecting a criminal. Smaller majorities say reporters should refuse all gifts from news sources, and that reporters should not hide their identities. And, while many of the students believe the media should pursue negative stories, a slight majority also believe the media should be willing to run booster pieces about the community. Approximately one-third of students say it is all right for reporters to take promotional trips financed by a business organization, if there are no strings attached. A similar percentage say the media should not run a story suggested by an advertiser, if the advertiser is connected to the story. Relatively few students believe reporters should be willing to break the law to obtain documents, even if they are essential to a story, or that reporters should be willing to publish information if the reporter has promised a source not to use the information. Students also do not think reporters should be willing to give special consideration to loyal advertisers. . . .

There is evidence that the students in the various sequences differ in terms of professional ethics. The public relations students, for example, are more concerned with community image than the news editorial students and believe the mass media should be used to boost that image. The public relations students are also more willing to allow advertisers to have impact on editorial content than are the news editorial students. In general, there is evidence from these data that the public relations and news editorial students assign differing roles to communications in general, and the mass media specifically, in the community.

The researchers then followed up on the graduates by surveying them again after they had been working in their careers for a year. Had job routines and supervisor expectations altered the ethical values of these new recruits? Generally there was little evidence of massive change in the students' values, but there were some shifts. There was some erosion, the researchers say, of an idealistic view of what the media should do, although the change was different for news editorial students as compared to public relations students. Overall the students increased their tolerance for reporters accepting gifts and became less favorable toward reporter protection of sources. Public relations students strengthened their beliefs that media should support the community, while news editorial students showed some increase in their acceptance of news media running stories about advertisers and giving them special treatment. "It seems," say Becker *et al.,* "that the news editorial students became more relaxed in their views of what the media should do, assigning them a somewhat less critical role and giving them less license in gathering the news."

In conclusion, the researchers note that the educational preparation of journalists "is important (or at least as important as work) in determining how students alter their professional values and ethical judgments."

A foundation for ethics

The plentitude of ethical quandaries ensures that reporters will be forced to make difficult choices. In preparing for your professional career, you can lay some preliminary groundwork. A good start would be to take a course in philosophy to become acquainted with the classical philosophers and their views on ethics, or you can read their works on your own. Familiarize yourself with one of the national organization's codes to give yourself at least an inkling of what approaches they take. Refresh your understanding of the First Amendment and the special role it bestows upon the media in serving the public.

Maintain a standard of personal integrity as a protection against unethical actions, whether they involve a temptation to misrepresent one's qualifications on a job application or to slant a news story to please friends or sources. Keep in mind the injunction in the *Washington Post*'s standards and ethics code: "To listen to the voiceless. To avoid any and all acts of arrogance. To face the public with politeness and candor" (Swain 1978).

Ethics or the lack of ethics is a determining factor in the level of media credibility. Journalism ethics are the responsibility of both groups and individuals, making every journalist a partner in the effort to live up to the First Amendment trust.

In Summary

The American philosophy of freedom of the press is built upon the concept that a free flow of ideas and opinions is essential if people are to be able to participate effectively in government. The media are generally considered essential to this free flow. While the media may not be able to tell the public what to think, their focus on a public issue can persuade the public what to think about. Public concern about at least some issues has been found to be media driven (MacKuen and Coombs 1981). The First Amendment to the Constitution, which provides for a free press, is seen by many as primarily a protection against efforts by governments or groups or individuals to hinder the media's role in public issues.

The freedom the media enjoy is not absolute, however. Laws and court decisions that interpret the First Amendment or state constitutions at times do impose restraints upon the news media.

Legal problems that concern the news media most are libel, invasion of privacy, access to public records, court proceedings and public meetings, and various forms of prior restraint. Generally, knowledge of the laws and care in reporting and editing will minimize the likelihood of libel and privacy suits. Such knowledge is essential if the public issues reporter is to avoid problems and ward off attempts at intimidation. Familiarity with public records laws and open meetings laws also will enhance your ability to obtain information from governmental bodies or access to public meetings.

Sometimes ethics and laws overlap, testing the ethical standards you have worked out for yourself or those of an employer or professional organization. An illegal action such as trespassing to gain information for a story involves both ethical and legal questions. Journalistic codes of ethics exist at many media outlets and professional organizations. But there is no single national written code of ethics for journalists as there is for the medical and legal professions. Journalists differ as to the value of the media codes, but even those who disdain them still support the need for ethics in reporting and editing. So ethics becomes in part a mixture of individual and organizational guidelines.

At the heart of journalistic ethics, written or unwritten, is a belief in the importance of reporting the news fairly and accurately. The term *fairly* offers a solution to innumerable questions of ethics because unfair actions by reporters either are unethical or flirt with an ethical danger line. They clearly disturb the American public (*The People & The Press* 1986). Adherence to a fairness standard is not solely an aid to the individual's peace of mind. It helps build media credibility among a public that is often critical of media performance.

References

American Bar Association. 1981. *The Rights of Fair Trial and Free Press.* Washington, D.C.

Associated Press Managing Editors Association. 1980. *APME Red Book.* New York, NY.

Associated Press Stylebook and Libel Manual. 1986. Reading, MA: Addison-Wesley.

Becker, Lee B., Fruit, Jeffrey W., and Caudill, Susan L., with Dunwoody, Sharon L. and Tipton, Leonard P. 1987. *The Training and Hiring of Journalists.* Norwood, N.J.: Ablex.

Black, Jay, Barney, Ralph D., and Van Tubergen, G. Norman. 1979. Moral Development and Belief Systems of Journalists. *Mass Comm Review* 6(3):4–20.

Branzburg v. Hayes, 1972. 408 U.S. 368.

California District Courts of Appeal. 1974. *In re* Farr. 111 Cal. Rptr. 649.

Christians, Clifford G., Rotzoll, Kim B., and Fackler, Mark. 1983. *Media Ethics.* New York, NY: Longman Inc.

Dahlberg-Acton, John Emerich Edward. 1949. *Essays on Freedom and Power,* selected by Gertrude Himmelfarb. Glencoe, IL: Free Press.

Dietemann v. Time, Inc, 1971. 449 F. 2d. 245.

Ethics Report. 1986. Chicago: The Society of Professional Journalists, Sigma Delta Chi.

Gannett v. DePasquale, 1979. 443 U.S. 368.

Hodges, Louis W. 1981. *Thoughts on Ethics.* Journalism Ethics Report. National Ethics Committee. Chicago: The Society of Professional Journalists, Sigma Delta Chi.

Hvistendahl, J. K., and Blinn, E. B. 1982. How Peace Officers and Reporters Interpret Confidentiality of Law Enforcement Records. *Newspaper Research Journal* 3(3):30–36.

IRE Journal. 1988. Books About Media Ethics. 11(3):10.

Langley, Monica, and Levine, Lee. 1988. Broken Promises. *Columbia Journalism Review* 27(2): 21–24.

Libel Defense Resource Center. 1984. *Bulletin No. 12.* New York, NY.

MacKuen, Michael B. and Coombs, Steven L. 1981. *More Than News: Media Power in Public Affairs.* Beverly Hills: Sage.

Merrill, John C., and Barney, Ralph D. 1975. *Ethics and the Press.* New York, NY: Hastings House.

Mills, Rilla Dean. 1982. Newspaper Journalists' Perceptions of Ethical Decisions. Paper presented to the Association for Education in Journalism. Athens, Ohio.

Nebraska Press Association v. Stuart, 1976. 427 U.S. 539.

New York State Newspapers Foundation. 1980. *Legal Handbook.* Syracuse, NY.

Ollman v. Evans and Novak, 1984. 750 F. 2d. 970.

Porter, Sue. 1981. A Declaration of Independence. *Scripps Howard News* 37 (September):2.

Reporters Committee for Freedom of the Press. 1981. High Court Says Media Pledge No Prior Restraint. *News Media & the Law* 5 (October-November):50.

_____. 1982a. $1.4 Million Settlement Reached in Libel Suit Against Alton Telegraph. *News Media & the Law* 6 (June-July):20.

_____. 1982b. Gertz Wins $400,000 in Damages Following 14-Year Court Battle. *News Media & the Law* 6(September-October):21.

Richmond Newspapers v. Virginia, 1980. 448 U.S. 550.

Schenck v. United States, 1919. 249 U.S. 47.

Sheppard v. Maxwell, 1966. 384 U.S. 333.

Swain, Bruce M. 1978. *Reporters' Ethics.* Ames: Iowa State Univ. Press, 117.

Thayer, Lee. 1980. *Ethics, Morality, and the Media.* New York, NY: Hastings House, 256.

The Cost of Libel. 1986. New York, NY: Gannett Center for Media Studies.

The People & The Press. 1986. Los Angeles: Times-Mirror Corporation, 10.

U.S. Congress. House Committee on Government Operations and Senate Committee on the Judiciary. 1975. *Freedom of Information Act and Amendments of 1974.* Washington, D.C.: U.S. Government Printing Office.

This chapter was initiated by Molen. Collaborators were Garrison and Rystrom.

Covering American institutions

In Part 2, we look at three vital components of contemporary American life: economy, business, and labor; education; and entertainment and recreation. Whatever your reporting beat, you will at times find yourself, in effect, covering the economy, because few subjects are untouched by economic aspects. If you are assigned to the business or labor beat, you will certainly confront economic issues. In Chapter 4 "Economy, Business, and Labor," we try to give you enough background, reporting tips, and examples to put you on the way to becoming a competent reporter and interpreter of American commerce, skilled at explaining how decisions in Washington, D.C., or on Wall Street affect audiences in Worchester and Walla Walla.

Few, if any, topics covered by the mass media today affect more people more directly than education. The media are challenged to provide information about education so that the public can make intelligent judgments about its massive investment of people and money in education. "Go and cover that school board meeting" is often a beginning reporter's first assignment. Chapter 5, "Education," orients you to the education bureaucracy, outlines how best to get on top of the beat, and suggests some of the broad public issues waiting to be analyzed.

In Chapter 6, "Entertainment and Recreation," we are not concerned with how to review a play or how to cover a ball game. We are concerned with reporting and interpreting the public policy issues that arise on what are sometimes called "the leisure beats." Leisure is the new American status symbol, and many people are pursuing it with a puritanic, gemhard determination. Questions inevitably arise. In the area of outdoor recreation, for example, how much of our natural resources are we prepared to allocate? In the arts, what is the proper extent of the role of government subsidy? Public issues on the leisure beats are often among the most forgotten issues in the mass media.

CHAPTER **4**

Economy, business, and labor

RARELY do the nation's newscasts and front pages not include at least one story about the economy, business, and labor. In factories, financial centers, and marketplaces, the potential news events take shape. In isolation, each transaction is a microcosm of one of the most delicate and fateful happenings in the world, the functioning of the economic system as it attempts to match supply and demand. This system constitutes a rich source of news for the public issues reporter.

The vast system bridges language and cultural differences, space and time, man-made political boundaries, geographical barriers, and international squabbling and belligerence. On a day when the United States and the Soviet Union may be exchanging diplomatic criticisms and challenges, trade missions from the two nations may be hammering out a commercial transaction. Although the economic system converses in a babel of tongues, it can also convert into universal measurement the dollar, yen, ruble, lira, franc, pound, shekel, mark, peso, guilder, riyal, rupee, drachma, and many other currencies.

The system touches virtually everyone, and every community generates economic, business, and labor news. Thousands of events in local communities, such as the expansion of airline service in Petersburg, Alaska, the rush to file insurance claims after a tornado in Paris, Texas, and the marketing outlook for the garlic crop in Gilroy, California, all affect, and are affected by, national economic trends. Business miscalculations may merely cause inconvenience. When First National Bank of Chicago bought ninety-seven thousand retail accounts from rival Continental National Bank, hundreds of transferred customers waited in long lines while their new bank tried to handle all its new business (Winter 1988). Business errors can also mean disaster. More than five hundred savings and loan institutions were caught with bad loans when oil prices dropped in Texas and the

Southwest in 1987. As of 1990, some estimates of the cost to the country of the savings and loan "bail-out" ran into the low hundreds of billions of dollars.

How well all these developments are covered is questionable. Author Alvin Toffler (American Society 1982) suggests that more issue-oriented reporting is needed:

> When you tell me the following event has occurred — whether that event is an election or an economic downturn or even a story on crime in the community — I think it is the responsibility of a forward-looking newspaper to tell me how that affects other fields. How will that affect education, business, technology, science, religion, family life? I call that horizontal extension. I think it also has a responsibility for saying to me, what are the long-range effects of this change, and that's what I call the vertical extension.

Toffler, a former magazine editor, emphasizes that "high-powered journalists and intelligent people" are needed to carry out this type of reporting. This is particularly true of economic news because the elements of economic subjects are often complex. To foster better public understanding of the economy and the roles of business, labor, and government, you need some knowledge of how the system works and why, sometimes, it does not.

Understanding the capitalist system

Capitalism is a democratic device based upon humanity's desire to improve its lot through free, individual enterprise. At least in theory, the opportunity to establish a business is available to anyone who is willing to risk his or her money or who can persuade others to risk their money. In theory, this also offers any worker the freedom to market his or her individual skills for the best return in wages and job satisfaction.

Although the system does not always live up to its theoretical promises, it is still somewhat astounding that capitalism has worked with such general success. The immensity and complexity of the system seem to suggest that it would be impossible to keep all the components operating reasonably well over a long period of time. Capitalism may have worked so far because, in economist Robert Heilbroner's words, "an enormous fraction of the total life energies and intelligence of society is devoted to making it work" (Heilbroner 1978).

The flow of capital

At the core of the American capitalist system is the flow of capital. Capital finances new products, new plants, new technology, and more jobs. Businesses borrow money, gambling on the chance that the investment will increase productivity and bring in enough additional revenues to repay the loans and improve the profits. Businesses may borrow from banks, insur-

THE FLOW OF MONEY

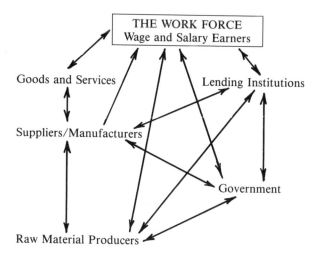

This chart illustrates in simplified form the multiplicity of directions that spending takes. In theory, a single dollar bill could pass through all six points and end up back at its starting point, ready for a new cycle.

The two-way flow illustrates the idea that the income of the work force is generated at the other five points on the chart, and that the income then becomes outgo in the form of purchase of goods and services, investments, taxes, loans, and other expenditures. An individual's $1000 savings account at a bank may be transformed into a loan that enables any of the other economic institutions to function more effectively, multiplied, of course, by the resources of many other individuals or companies.

ance companies, individual entrepreneurs, or other financial institutions. They can also borrow money by selling bonds to investors, the bonds representing debt that must be repaid to the bondholders at a fixed rate of interest at specified times, or they may issue stock, selling shares of company ownership to investors who are willing to risk their capital to make a profit.

Money flows into financial institutions from individual savings accounts, insurance premiums, stock sales, loan repayments, and investments in business. Money flows out of the institutions to people who need capital for various purposes and are willing to pay for its use.

While the process may seem simple, the execution is complex, because in day-to-day operations, a company's decisions are based upon someone's predictions of the future market. The predictions may be logical when the decision is made, but they can go awry if unanticipated changes occur.

Government and the economic system

A pure form of free enterprise capitalism, in which government is not involved, is impossible today, but a persistent, arguable, and important issue is the extent to which the government should influence the marketplace.

In the United States, from city hall to the national capital, government is involved as borrower, lender, buyer, supplier, employer, and regulator. The federal government has the largest role in the economy because of its size and its jurisdiction over interstate commerce. As a reporter, you should know the purpose and function of major government agencies. Too little attention has been paid at times to far-reaching decisions of many agencies, such as those of the nation's chief financial regulator, the Federal Reserve Board.

THE FEDERAL RESERVE BOARD. For about fifty years, the Federal Reserve Board has been overseeing the economy, but until recently, news reports about its activities were confined mostly to periodic announcements on technical financial matters.

The board, often simply called "the Fed," is an independent government agency that controls the money supply. It can reduce the amount of money in circulation by increasing the amount of reserve funds that banks must maintain to back up their deposits. Conversely, by relaxing reserve requirements, the Fed can increase the amount of money available for lending. A goal of the Fed is to maintain a reasonable rate of economic growth and still avoid extreme inflation or recession.

ABC's economics editor Dan Cordtz (Canape 1982) produced this succinct explanation of the Fed's responsibilities:

In a healthy economy, business has to grow to provide more goods and services so that living standards can improve. . . . If there's not enough money, the economy stagnates, and workers are laid off. But if the money supply rises faster than business' ability to produce, we have the classic definition of inflation. Too many dollars chasing too few goods. That's why the Federal Reserve Board is legally assigned the responsibility of regulating money growth.

The Fed thus walks a monetary tightrope.

The administrative structure of the Federal Reserve System is a mixture of government and private enterprise. At the top is a seven-member board of governors. Appointment of the seven, including the chairman, is by the president with the concurrence of the United States Senate. Scattered across the country are twelve regional Federal Reserve Banks that are owned by member commercial banks within each region. Each regional bank is governed by a nine-member board, three of whom are appointed by the Fed's Board of Governors and six elected by the member commercial banks.

The power of the Fed to influence economic developments is concentrated in the Board of Governors and particularly the chairman. The board constitutes a majority on the Federal Open Market Committee, which meets regularly to review the state of the economy and decide what policies to follow in regulating the money supply. The open market committee is made up of the board and five presidents of Federal Reserve regional banks. The twelve regional presidents rotate as voting members of the committee, ensuring that no region will be shut out permanently from the policy-making process. The system also guarantees that the board with its public appointees will always have a numerical majority over representatives from the private sector. Minutes of the closed open market committee meetings are not disclosed for several weeks, but the decisions should be watched closely by reporters because a change in monetary policy will have a nationwide impact.

While coverage of the Fed falls mostly to specialized financial publications and a few large general news operations, other reporters can have access to periodic Federal Reserve Board Reports.

The Fed uses three tactical measures to influence the nation's money supply so the economy maintains a reasonable growth level.

• The Fed sets reserve requirements that determine how much money member banks must hold in reserve, and how much money they can lend.
• The Fed reviews the discount rate set by the twelve regional Federal Reserve Banks. The rate establishes what commercial banks will have to pay to borrow money from the Federal Reserve system.

• The Fed buys and sells government securities on the open market, operating through the trading desk of the New York Federal Reserve Bank.

While those are the primary functions, the Fed has a number of other responsibilities. Of special importance in world commerce is the agency's role in foreign exchange. Through the New York Federal Reserve Bank, the Fed daily buys and sells dollars and foreign currencies to maintain the stability of the United States dollar in foreign exchange.

Its other functions include clearing of bank money transfers throughout the nation, replacement of worn-out money, handling of federal government checks for a variety of Treasury Department programs, supervision of bank-holding companies and state-chartered banks that are members of the Federal Reserve system, and enforcing equal credit and truth-in-lending laws at banks.

The Fed puts out a number of pamphlets explaining its operations. The monthly Federal Reserve Bulletin, which is available for a small subscription price, is helpful. Monthly reviews published by the various regional Federal Reserve banks also offer comment on an analysis of economic developments and are available without charge.

OTHER AGENCIES AND INDICATORS. Covering the economy means more than watching the Federal Reserve Board, because many federal agencies have specialized economic responsibilities. For example, the Department of Commerce gathers commercial statistics, studies general business trends, and conducts the nation's population count every ten years. Census tracts are fertile sources of information about a community or a region, and they are usually available in local government-planning offices. Each month, the Department of Commerce issues an index of twelve leading economic indicators that measure the performance of the economy and forecast the direction it will take. You can use the index for stories about the impact of national trends on the local economy.

A sampling of other agencies involved in economic affairs includes the Securities and Exchange Commission, which oversees issuance and trading of stocks and bonds; the Department of Agriculture, which administers price support systems for various crops; the Bureau of Labor Statistics, which keeps track of unemployment trends; the Federal Housing Administration, which provides credit for home buyers and thus bolsters the construction and real estate industries; the Federal Home Loan Bank Board, which regulates savings and loan associations; and the Commodity Futures Trading Commission, which supervises commodities trading.

STATE AGENCIES. State agencies can often provide information that is relevant to local economic stories. While agencies in different states vary in name and jurisdiction, each state has some government units regulating public utilities, incorporations, insurance companies, banking, business licensing, real estate, and an assortment of other business fields.

ECONOMIC DATA. Statistical measurements abound in the economic world. They come from the Commerce Department, the Federal Reserve Board, the Department of Labor, the Treasury Department, and other agencies. They provide leads to the state of the national economy. The GNP (Gross National Product) represents the value of all goods and services produced in the nation during a specific period. The CPI (Consumer Price Index) charts the fluctuations in the cost of living. The unemployment rate tracked by the Department of Labor offers another base upon which to build local stories.

The M-series figures of the Federal Reserve Board indicate the level of the nation's money supply. M–1 represents the total currency in circulation and in commercial bank checking accounts. M–2 consists of M–1 plus savings accounts at commercial banks. M–3 through M–7 represents money totals in more narrow categories. The money supply figures are watched very closely by the Federal Reserve Board. The board's actions to reduce or expand the money supply are significant. Statistics such as these pour out of government offices and financial institutions by the thousands—daily, monthly, quarterly, and annually—to indicate how the economy is doing.

The data available from various sources are so vast that few individuals can stay current on all of them. Large financial institutions and the government rely upon specialists to evaluate the information in particular fields, but reporters must selectively use the material to avoid foundering in the flood of information. How can you prepare yourself, first, to understand the workings of the economic system so that you can explain developments in clear, nontechnical language, and, second, know which material is most significant?

If you are near a college, consider taking courses in economics or business. An accounting course can be especially valuable. Some universities offer postgraduate enrichment programs for professional journalists, although several years of journalism experience usually is required of applicants. Whatever means of education you pursue, a professional attitude and intellectual curiosity should impel you to expand your knowledge. You should be able to evaluate the effects of economic decisions in Washington, D.C., or in your state capital, and you should know where to seek the information that can make the difference between mediocre and excellent copy.

Reporting on the economy

Only the largest news operations are likely to have reporters assigned full time to the economic beat, assuming that the beat is defined as coverage of the economic system as a whole, involving such subjects as the national and international monetary system, the inner workings of the machinery for setting interest rates, and national controls on multinational corporations. More often, the economic beat is the province of the business reporter, whose title suggests broader responsibilities and less specialization. Small news operations, however, rarely have a full-time business reporter, and sometimes not even a part-time one. Economic assignments may fall to almost any reporter.

ECONOMY IS A LOCAL STORY

Arguably, when it comes to interpreting public issues, local news media do their poorest job in covering economic news.

For example, over the first weekend in January 1990, the wire services carried a story out of New York that several big-city banks were lowering their prime lending rate a half percentage point to 10 percent, the first reduction in nearly half a year, possibly signalling cheaper loans for a broad range of consumers and businesses.

Now wouldn't you think that local news media would try to answer for their constituents the question, "What exactly does this all mean for me here?" Not necessarily so.

One of the authors of this text reviewed a dozen mid-sized daily newspapers for the morning of Monday, January 8. Every one gave the wire story front-page space, but not one took the time to interview local bankers, brokers, real estate firms, and car dealers to get a feel for how soon, if at all, the break in the prime rate would impact the local economy, and in what way.

That's sub-par performance. You can't interpret local economic issues with copy out of New York.

The economic base of your community will determine which indicators you should watch most closely. If the base is agricultural, the United States Department of Agriculture and the county extension agent are prime sources. If the base is industrial, the United States Department of Commerce, a state industrial development commission, or the United States or state departments of labor may be important sources.

Ask the state and federal agencies most relevant to your community's economic base to put you on the mailing list for their reports. But do not overlook local sources, who often are in a better position to know the local effects of an action than the decision makers in the capital.

Watch for the ripple effect. A malfunction in one part of the market place can have repercussions throughout the country. When hard times hit the Detroit auto industry, the negative effects are felt by affiliated suppliers and dealers as well as by many businesses unrelated directly to the auto industry. If you can see the ripple effect touching your community, you can focus the economic picture for your audiences.

You do not always have to approach economics from a highly technical angle. Dave Stewart, a former area editor at the *Finger Lake Times* in New York, recalls a readable treatment of inflation by a reporter armed with a bagful of nickels. The reporter asked shopkeepers what she could buy for a nickel. At best, her nickel would buy some meaningless trinkets, but for the most part it would buy nothing. "She wrote a light, humorous piece, peppered with quotes, about her shopping spree," said Stewart, "Of course, everybody talks about inflation and retail specialization, but this story brought a different perspective to those issues, and in a rather positive way. It wasn't a profound analysis to be sure, but it illustrates the point that economic writing doesn't have to be boring and dry" (Stewart 1983). Anyone doing the story today would have to use quarters, Stewart added.

Reporting business news

News of business and the economy is so intertwined that it is often difficult to separate one from the other. Yet there are differences, most notably in small communities where the business beat ordinarily involves minimal contact with economists and economic agencies and maximum contact with shopkeepers, plant managers, and consumers.

Traditionally, business has had a limited appeal to journalists, possibly because it is frequently associated with relatively unexciting stories about a new business or a new building, or with promotional stories about a firm that also may be a major advertiser. Other beats may seem more exciting.

Adding to a reportorial lack of enthusiasm for business news has been a suspicion that the separation between news and advertising can be threatened if a big advertiser is involved in a business story. In-house friction between advertising departments and newsrooms is commonplace in journalism. Oversimplified, the issue is whether purchase of an advertisement entitles the advertiser to free coverage in a newscast or news column. Editorial employees resist such exchanges, but the fact that they are even proposed increases the skepticism with which reporters view business.

Complaints from business

The resentment is often reciprocated, with business complaining that it is frequently treated inadequately and inaccurately in news stories (Nickel 1980). On the other hand, some research shows that business gets treated very favorably by the news media (Bennett 1981). Some critics say newspaper business sections sometimes serve as a "cheering section" for business (*Arkansas Gazette* 1979).

In bemoaning the economic ignorance of some reporters, steel industry executive Richard F. Schubert (1979) once asked a group of Pennsylvania editors why an editor would run "an article that would get a failing grade in freshman economics? I can't imagine reading a sports commentary by a writer who obviously doesn't understand the sport. Shouldn't the same journalistic standards apply to a subject as important as the national economy?" Schubert, president of the Bethlehem Steel Corporation, suggested that journalists should do a lot of homework on business and economic subjects "that are sure to be prominent in the news for a long time to come."

Even if many complaints by business simply mirror a common criticism that news coverage emphasizes the bad and ignores the good, some attention is needed in newsrooms to make sure that business news — negative, neutral, or positive — is covered fairly. It is true that many business and economy stories require more background knowledge than the writers often possess. You cannot spend thirty to forty minutes reading clippings in the news morgue and expect to be prepared for an upcoming interview dealing with, for example, the local effects of a change in Federal Reserve Board monetary policies. If the clippings contain inaccuracies, you may only compound the errors by repetition, either in your questions or in your stories.

If your source is patient and has the time to interpret the subject in layperson's terms, you may obtain a reasonably good account of the subject. But if you start with some general knowledge of the economy, you will do a far better job, if only because your questions will indicate some intelligence about the subject.

In the public service

When Mark J. Thompson's (1984) five-part series on "mast bumping" appeared in the Fort Worth, Texas, *Star-Telegram,* it dealt with a technical aeronautical problem that had existed for about seventeen years and had claimed the lives of more than two hundred people in helicopter crashes. The series touched off an organized, anguished protest from Bell Helicopter Textron, the second largest employer in Fort Worth, Texas.

Thoroughly researched and documented, the series provided a straightforward report of a business story that encompassed Bell's helicopter designs, bureaucratic procedures involving national defense contracts, and corporate and U.S. army responsibility. Thompson's lead in the opening article of the series summarized its essential theme:

> WASHINGTON, D.C. — Nearly 250 U.S. servicemen have been killed since 1967 aboard Bell helicopters that crashed because of a design flaw that remains largely uncorrected even though the Army discovered it in 1973, according to military documents and former Pentagon safety experts.

The design flaw led to mast bumping, a term applied to a problem in which the spinning, flapping rotor blades of the helicopters teetered too far, chopped into the mast upon which the rotor is fixed, and eventually caused the mast to snap. The loose blades were catapulted into the fuselage. The helicopter occupants were killed either by the blades or by the impact of the crash when the craft hit the ground.

Thompson (1985) said he had first heard of the problem from colleagues in the aeronautics trade press in 1983. His initial investigation brought explanations that mast bumping occurred only after something else had gone wrong with the helicopter, or after the pilots had exceeded the capabilities of the aircraft.

But in early 1983 Thompson saw a trade publication article about a helicopter crash in which the pilot survived. It was the first time a person had survived a severe instance of mast bumping. The pilot told Thompson that he had been flying the helicopter within the prescribed performance limits when the rotor blades broke loose. This was the confirmation Thompson needed to question pilot error as a cause.

He began checking government documents, and talking with families of victims and with Bell employees and former employees. He dug into court records of damage suits that had resulted from crashes caused by mast bumping. He found that prior studies by the U.S. Army and by Bell had pinpointed a mechanical problem that led to mast bumping, but that only minor changes in the mast design had been made as a result of the studies.

Bell officials and other employees reacted angrily to the series, charging that it was sensationalistic. The company promoted a "cancel-my-subscription" drive, and ordered *Star-Telegram* vending racks removed from Bell property. Unions representing Bell employees gathered three hundred cancellations.

Thompson's articles brought different results from the military. The army impaneled a group of experts to conduct a new study of the design. In faulting both the army and Bell for doing too little too late, the panel charged that "the bureaucracy was lethargic." It confirmed Thompson's findings and ordered remedial action—installation of thicker masts. The army also awarded Bell almost $10 million in contracts to design and flight test the use of hub springs to provide more rotor stability (Evans 1985).

Recognition of Thompson's efforts came in three major 1985 awards for public service reporting: the Pulitzer Prize, the Distinguished Service Award of the Society of Professional Journalists (Sigma Delta Chi), and the National Headliners Award of the Atlantic City Press Club.

Significantly, Thompson had received help from Bell employees who had not joined the company protest. As Thompson noted: "What a lot of people don't realize is that the real heroes of this story are the silent ones, people who gave us information when they didn't have to. A lot of them are Bell employees and they'll never get any recognition" (Evans 1985).

Free publicity or news?

One troublesome aspect of business reporting stems from the relatively routine local stories that span the categories of free publicity and news. If you already have a mistrust of business in general, you may consider a story about the grand opening of a new auto parts store a free plug for an advertiser and be inclined to give it short shrift. It may not be news in a metropolitan area, but in a small community such an event has both free publicity and legitimate news value. If a town has a work force of 1000 and a new store adds fifty new jobs, that fact alone has news value.

Kenneth Byerly, a veteran of small-town newspaper publishing, concedes that in the media-advertiser relationship "there is some 'you scratch my back and I'll scratch yours' attitude in the covering of news on business." But, he added, "It is news when a store or other business expands, changes hands, merges with another one, moves to a new location, opens its doors for the first time, or closes down after years of service" (Byerly 1961).

REPORTING ON "SACRED COWS" IN OHIO

Small-town business interests need not be sacred cows if a reporter does his or her homework. Terry Fuchs of the Fremont, Ohio News-Messenger *(circ. 13,962) documented price gouging by a local motel. He won first place for investigative reporting on a small daily paper in the 1985 Ohio Associated Press Competition. The* News-Messenger *was commended for "taking a significant risk for a small paper" (Booher 1985).*

Even the newspaper industry itself, considered by critics of journalism as the most holy sacred cow, is not off limits to good reporters. The staff of the Akron, Ohio, Beacon Journal *took first place in its division of the 1985 Ohio Associated Press Competition for its investigation of the sale of the* Cleveland Press.

Sources

Many different sources of information on business are available to you. You should contact them regularly.

CHAMBERS OF COMMERCE. This type of organization of business-oriented people is standard in most communities. These are booster associations and cannot be counted upon to volunteer much information about negative economic developments, but they can provide information on new businesses, trade volume, and business views on community problems and issues.

OTHER CIVIC ORGANIZATIONS. Clubs such as Rotary and Kiwanis are helpful for the business and professional contacts they can provide. Frequently, their luncheon speakers are newsworthy, but their long-range benefits lie in the knowledge that can be gained from members about community business happenings.

CITY AND COUNTY PLANNING DEPARTMENTS. Since planning agencies are involved when a company wants to build a new plant or a developer wants to put in a new shopping center, the planners are aware of many newsworthy proposals.

BUSINESS LICENSING AGENCIES. These include both city and state entities where a person must file for a business license or a certificate of incorporation. The agencies offer a scorecard on new businesses.

LEGAL NOTICES. Often these are overlooked as a source, but they can lead to stories about construction projects, land sales, changes in business ownership, and other matters that require public notices. Legal notices usually are found in community newspapers or posted in government buildings.

BANKRUPTCY COURT. Federal district courts have jurisdiction in bankruptcy cases. Personal financial plights that end in bankruptcy court are not uncommon. If enough individual bankruptcies are filed, they become a measure of the condition of the local economy. Three basic types of bankruptcy are provided by law:

• Chapter 7 bankruptcies are for individuals or for individuals operating businesses. Under Chapter 7 bankruptcies, the assets involved are liquidated and the proceeds distributed to creditors by the bankruptcy trustee.

• Chapter 11 filings often are used by large corporations in that there is no limit on the amount of income involved. Chapter 11 allows companies to reorganize and remain in business, if creditors agree, so that they eventually can pay their debts.

• Chapter 13 filings are for small businesses or wage earners who want time to reorganize their affairs so they can pay their debts.

OTHER SOURCES. Information from other sources, including government and industry reports, is plentiful. Among the most productive local sources for background and interpretation of economic developments are bank economists, brokerage officials, real estate brokers, professors of economics, state and local government officials, and consumers. From a practical standpoint, your problem will be in finding time to handle all the potential news items.

The investment world

Stock market listings and daily market stories have been part of the news scene for many years. News services provide daily summaries of market activities. You need not follow the stock listings closely on a daily basis unless you are checking on a local company. You should keep up with the news accounts and statistical overviews, such as the Dow-Jones or

Standard & Poor indices, that indicate market trends by averaging the performances of selected stocks. The computer age adds a complicating element that makes the market changes more difficult to assess. Computer technology has made it possible to execute buy-and-sell orders of thousands of shares of multiple stocks within seconds. A result, especially noticeable in 1986 and 1987, has been a more volatile market, one capable of sharp fluctuations in short periods of time.

The largest trading centers are the New York Stock Exchange (Wall Street) and the American Stock Exchange. Major regional stock exchanges operate in several large cities. Reporters should not overlook the possibilities for local news angles in the Over-the-Counter (OTC) market because it is more likely to include stocks of new firms and those with lower asset totals than most companies listed on Wall Street. The OTC market is the nation's oldest and largest securities exchange, but stocks are traded through brokerage agencies rather than on the floor of the New York Exchange or other centralized stock marts. In contrast, OTC listings are dispatched by the National Association of Security Dealers' Quotation Service to brokerage houses that subscribe to its computer-listing service. You can track local OTC stocks through local or area stockbrokers.

The commodity markets

The Chicago Board of Trade dominates the commodity markets, with buyers and sellers dealing in diverse items such as cotton, beef, potatoes, eggs, gold, silver, lumber, and pork. Daily occurrences in the commodity markets affect consumer prices for all kinds of goods. If the bids for frozen pork bellies go higher, you can expect bacon prices in the supermarkets to increase in a few months. By keeping track on the commodity markets of crops grown in your area, you can sometimes anticipate the economic impact of changes in the commodity markets upon local farmers and consumers. For that reason, commodity market summaries and local quotations on regional farm products should be regular reading if you are reporting in an agricultural area.

Tracking the big story

The wisdom of thorough preparation and persistence paid off for Phillip L. Zweig (1983), a staff writer for *American Banker* magazine, when he began a tour in 1982 of western Oklahoma to research an article on how the oil boom in the Southwest had affected small banks. His fact-finding journey soon sent him in a different direction – toward Penn Square Bank of Oklahoma City.

A preliminary study of Oklahoma bank statistics had first brought Penn Square to Zweig's notice because of the spectacular growth rate of its assets in the previous five years. "Operating expenses, on the other hand, were small in comparison, suggesting the bank was booking and monitoring a lot of loans with very few people," said Zweig. Zweig also learned that Penn Square was aggressive in making oil and gas exploration loans.

In his conversations with regional bankers, the name of Penn Square kept surfacing. Zweig sensed that the bankers had misgivings about Penn Square's lending policies, although no one suggested that Penn Square was in trouble. He also became aware that the oil exploration boom was fading, creating the possibility that some borrowers would have to default on their loans. Zweig decided to concentrate on Penn Square rather than on the original small-bank story angle. Zweig (1983) described the development of his story as follows:

> In an early telephone conversation I had with Penn Square chairman Bill Jennings, a flamboyant, old school entrepreneur, he committed the unpardonable sin in business-press relations. He became belligerent when, at one point, I asked him about his 1981 loan losses. This is public information easily obtainable from the FDIC [Federal Deposit Insurance Corporation], but it was not contained in the bank's annual report. Jennings snapped back, "Get them yourself!" which I did.
>
> His attitude convinced me that the bank really did have something to hide, and I soon learned what it was: 1981 loan losses had risen more than tenfold over the year before. It turned out that these losses were taken on loans made for the purchase of racehorses rather than for the production of oil and gas. But problems in the energy portfolio would surface shortly.

Zweig's first story, based on public records and interviews with more than seventy-five sources, focused on Penn Square's questionable loan practices. The article was the first to reveal the weaknesses of Penn Square. Three months later, FDIC officials declared the bank insolvent and closed it. The collapse of Penn Square was a major, national business story, because several giant banking institutions in other cities lost millions on loans they had acquired from Penn Square. The repercussions still were being felt in banking circles several years after the 1982 collapse.

The annual report

While Phillip Zweig was intrigued by what was not in the Penn Square annual report (the information on embarrassing loan losses), many business stories are based upon what is in annual reports. In fact, a common type of business story comes from companies' quarterly and annual reports, in which profits or losses for the period are compared with the same period of the previous year. These stories often originate in press releases, but the complete reports can provide leads for other stories, provided that you know how to analyze the data.

Reporters ordinarily can obtain annual reports from companies or from the Securities and Exchange Commission. Some suggestions from Jane Bryant Quinn (1981), a business commentator and columnist for television, magazines, and newspapers, will help you to analyze annual reports:

• Start at the back of the annual report with the statement of the certified public accountant. "Watch out for the words 'subject to.' They mean the financial report is clean only if you take the company's word about a particular piece of business, and the accountant isn't sure you should."

• Read the footnotes in the back of the report. "The whole profits story is sometimes in the footnotes."

• Don't overlook the letter from the chairman of the board, telling how the company fared this year. "But more important, he should tell you *why*. Keep an eye out for sentences that start out with 'Except for . . .' and 'Despite the. . . .' They're clues to problems."

• Check the balance sheet that shows what the company owes and what it owns, net sales, and net earnings per share, long-term debt, and income statement.

Securities and Exchange Commission

Public companies with more than 500 shareholders are required by the Securities and Exchange Commission (SEC) to file a variety of financial and operational reports. Included among these documents are those known as the 10-K, and 10-Q, and the 8-K. The 10-K is a detailed annual report that must be filed within forty-five days after the end of a company's fiscal year. The 10-Q is an unaudited financial report that must be filed within forty-five days after the end of each of the first three fiscal quarters. The 8-K is used to report changes in company control, sale or purchase of major assets, and any other unusual events. It must be filed within fifteen days after the event.

Most reports are available for inspection at SEC headquarters in Washington, D.C., or, in some cases, at SEC regional offices. Copies of public documents may be obtained at a nominal cost by writing to the SEC Office of Records and Service in Washington, D.C.

Reporting requirements for companies with fewer than 500 shareholders are not as elaborate, and privately held companies are not covered by SEC regulations. For his Penn Square assignment, writer Phillip Zweig noted that some information was difficult to obtain because the bank had only 120 stockholders and its public reports did not have to be as complete as those for companies with more than 500 shareholders. Zweig interviewed many alternate sources to overcome that problem.

Hints for covering business

Legwork, alertness, background knowledge, and intellectual curiosity are requisites to doing a good job in covering business. Some suggestions that may help:

1. Approach business assignments with an open mind. Incomplete and inaccurate coverage may result if you let preconceptions color your view.
2. Do not overlook the potential for stories about small businesses. Many worthwhile stories go unnoticed because reporters are not sensitive to the idea that small-business happenings are newsworthy.
3. Broaden your contacts beyond the upper echelon of authority. The employee grapevine in any business produces abundant rumors. Although few hold any general interest, you ought to investigate those that may. The lead for a story might come from a conversation with a laborer, who might disclose information long before the company was ready to release the information, if, indeed, it ever intended to.
4. Be alert to nonbusiness stories that have economic side effects. For example, a heavy frost in Florida may mean a smaller citrus crop and higher retail prices. An Environmental Protection Agency revision of pollution standards may halt or slow production at a local plant until more efficient equipment is installed. A dock strike may block delivery of parts needed to keep machines operating at an inland industrial plant.
5. Watch for trends. A single business event may not be particularly newsworthy, but the occurrence of several related developments might make an overview worthwhile.

When a packing company announced plans to close two Iowa plants in early 1985, the Cedar Rapids *Gazette* touched bases with company officials, farm representatives, industrial development leaders, union officers, marketing experts, and a community mayor. Reporter Bob Davis (1985) opened his story on the plant closings in this fashion:

SIOUX CITY—While pork-industry watchers expect hog numbers to increase, it will not be enough to save two Swift plants in western Iowa. Swift Independent Corp. announced Thursday it will close two plants, one in Sioux City employing 470 workers and another in Glenwood affecting 290 workers. The company blamed the lack of available hogs for its decision to close the plants.

Davis then devoted space to information about the pork outlook and competition between packing companies before bringing in a tieback to a previous position statement by union leaders:

The United Food and Commercial Workers Union, which represents the 700 workers affected by Swift's announcement, reiterated its charge Friday that the decision to close the plants is a form of blackmail to further reduce wages and benefits. The plants are scheduled to close Sept. 1, the date the current labor contract expires.

After elaborating on the union-management dispute, Davis went to Sioux City and Glenwood for comment on the expected impact in those communities. The story told what was happening, the various reasons for why it was happening, and how it probably would affect pork producers, plant workers, and consumers.

Reporting labor news

While the Cedar Rapids story mentioned earlier did not overlook organized labor, the labor movement generally may be among the most neglected major elements in news reporting on the economy. Rarely is labor covered on a regular basis. Union officials complain that the only time their organizations are mentioned in the news is in connection with strikes or charges of union corruption.

The gaps in coverage may not be quite that extreme, but enough do exist to constitute a major challenge for journalists. As a reporter covering labor, you will have to overcome union suspicions rooted deeply in the turbulent history of organized labor. In reporting on intermittent union-management clashes, you will have to sort through a welter of conflicting claims, a mixture of fact and hyperbole that often obscures the issues.

In appraising news coverage of a major coal strike, writer Curtis Seltzer noted that "understanding collective bargaining in coal requires a grasp of, among other things, history, law, economics, mining technology, industry, finance, workplace practices, and health and pension insurance. Many journalists have lost their way wandering through this maze" (Seltzer 1981). Seltzer's prescription can be applied to virtually all fields of labor.

The labor-media relationship

Labor is a powerful force in the economy. If credit is given for improvements in Americans' standards of living, labor should receive its share for its campaigns to obtain higher wages, shorter hours, and better working conditions. However, labor is not a monolith. It does not speak with one voice, and its diversity at times makes coverage difficult.

Although labor may agree on general work-related goals, unity does not always exist on tactics or execution of means to achieve goals. Within labor's ranks, there often are diametrically opposed viewpoints from such groups as organized labor and nonunion workers, white-collar and blue-collar workers, and dissidents and established leaders. Even within the union movement such independence of opinion exists that a call for a general strike in the United States would go unheeded by many members.

Union labor's attitude toward the media is tinged with suspicion, partly because in its stormy, formative years, labor often found itself out of favor with publishers, whose editorial-page voices tended to side with business. Unions rarely enjoyed overwhelming public support in strikes; they often found themselves isolated and subjected to what they perceived as unfair criticism. Some of the blame for the criticisms was directed at the media, and unions have not yet totally overcome those bad feelings.

Acquiring background knowledge

A starting point for better understanding is to read historical material on the labor movement. Once you are familiar with labor's history, it will be easier for you to follow the union strategy of using political means to gain legislation that will protect workers' rights. It also helps to understand that the labor movement endured a long period of employer and government resistance to the very existence of any organized association of workers. Private industrial security forces and government law enforcement agencies used violent tactics to discourage workers from demanding higher wages or improved conditions. Robert Heilbroner (1978) has summarized the early history of the American labor movement:

> In America, trade union progress was slow. The strong American belief in
> 'rugged individualism'—a belief shared by many workers as well as their
> bosses—a reliance on docile immigrant labor in the heavy industries, and

the use of every legal and many illegal weapons on the part of the employers kept American unionism largely limited to the skilled crafts long after the union movement had finally gained acceptance and some measure of power in Europe.

This changed in the 1930s when President Franklin D. Roosevelt pushed through legislation that sanctioned the right of workers to organize unions to bargain on wages, hours, and working conditions. The National Labor Relations Act of 1935 (the Wagner Act) encouraged the process of collective bargaining and created a National Labor Relations Board to certify bargaining organizations and to adjudicate complaints of unfair labor practices. Other legislation established a minimum wage (twenty-five cents an hour in 1938–39), a maximum workweek (beginning at forty-four hours per week in 1938), premium pay for overtime hours, and restrictions on the use of child labor.

Congress attempted to bring more balance to labor-management relations with the passage of the Taft-Hartley Act in 1947. This act prohibited closed-shop agreements, in which employees were required to join a union before being hired, and emphasized an employee's right not to join a union. It also provided legal means for employers to challenge unfair labor practices by unions. The law does not cover agricultural or domestic labor.

Innumerable other legislative measures have affected labor, including one that established the Occupational Safety and Health Administration (OSHA). Its function is to ensure safe working conditions, but employers complain vigorously about OSHA regulations that increase the cost of business. Although the activities of OSHA have generated some controversy, reporters have given the organization little attention.

The structure of labor

The vast majority of America's labor force works for wages, being paid weekly or biweekly for a fixed number of hours. A smaller part of the labor force is salaried, being paid a fixed monthly wage and having more flexibility in the number of hours worked.

Unions are strongest among wage laborers. Since 1955 the dominant union force has been the AFL-CIO, formed by a merger of two giant labor organizations, the American Federation of Labor (AFL) and the Congress of Industrial Organizations (CIO). Under the AFL-CIO umbrella are affiliated unions representing different skills and trades and operating with a great degree of autonomy. The AFL-CIO is not directly involved in collective bargaining. Instead, it functions as a coordinating agency that promotes the general objectives of organized labor, provides educational materials, lobbies for favorable legislation, and attempts to settle jurisdictional disputes between affiliated unions.

The AFL-CIO operates through state, district, and city councils. The city council, often known as the Central Labor Council, will be of the most concern to you as a reporter of local labor news. It performs the same function locally that the national council does at the top level.

Covering the bargaining process

Collective bargaining, the process by which a group of employees negotiates an agreement with an employer on wages and job conditions, is a prime subject for news coverage. The results usually are of general interest to both business and labor, whether the contract calls for increased employee benefits or for a trade-off of reduced wages for greater job security.

Most contracts are settled quietly year after year, and the ultimate weapon, the strike, is the exception, not the rule. Consequently, negotiations rarely are covered until they reach a crisis stage, although there may be as much significance in peaceful settlements as in a strike.

A major complication in reporting labor news is that bargaining strategy makes both sides unwilling to be frank about their positions for fear they will alert the other to their plans. At times, the bargaining oratory touches more on invective than on the issues. Reportorial persistence is needed to obtain answers that focus on the key points in dispute.

When members of the Professional Air Traffic Controllers Organization walked off their jobs in 1981, the federal government fired the strikers for violating their no-strike pledge. The event provided major news stories for weeks. After surveying the accounts, writer David Kassel (1981) concluded that confusion and ambiguity characterized the coverage:

Neither the union nor the government appeared overly eager to inform the public about what was really going on. Instead, both sides apparently kept much important information secret and concentrated on flinging charges at each other. And the press seemed as passive as the public in its unquestioning acceptance of the public relations announcements of the officials involved (Kassel 1981).

This problem is not uncommon, although the public impact of the air controller's strike was unusually direct, and the coverage of the effects may have drawn attention away from the bargaining issues.

The bargaining process with its sequence of demands, offers, and counter offers, is complex. For reporters, a headache can be involved in sorting through the items on the negotiating table to determine which are crucial issues and which are trade-off points that can be sacrificed to win a concession from the other side. Even a strike vote initially is more of a tactical threat than an actual vote to strike. But when a settlement deadline is set, a strike becomes a serious possibility. Once one or both parties "go public" — that is, announce their positions — your ability to produce a fair account will be tested. Seltzer's advice to reporters is to develop as many contacts as possible among the rank and file on both sides to "avoid becoming prisoners of the information the negotiators feed" to the press (Seltzer 1981).

Reporter James Allen Flanery (1986) of the Omaha, Nebraska, *World-Telegram* did that in December 1986, when labor negotiations reached a critical point at a packing plant in Dakota City, Nebraska, near Sioux City, Iowa. Flanery talked with rank-and-file union members. But he also contacted union and company officials and numerous other sources to give readers a comprehensive view of the dispute. His lead emphasized the widespread implications of the negotiations impasse and possible strike at a plant that had gone through four strikes in the previous seventeen years:

> DAKOTA CITY, NEBRASKA — Ellis Onnen says a lot is at stake in contract talks with meatpacking giant IBP Inc.
>
> "We're negotiating for more than just this plant," said Onnen, 45, a union worker at IBP for 14 years and veteran of three strikes. We're negotiating [a wage standard] for the whole Sioux City area."
>
> Others see even broader import in the contract talks.
>
> Rival packing firms say what is hammered out in Dakota City, Nebraska — with or without a strike — may be a new pay standard for the nation's estimated 35,000 beef-packing workers.
>
> IBP, which by industry estimates kills 27 percent of the nation's steers and heifers, "sets the tone for what others pay," said F. William Nicholson, a Swift Independent Packing Co. executive in Wichita, Kansas.

After establishing the potential national effect of the contract battle, Flanery brought in details of the issues and background on the packing industry and its working standards. Union members gave him information on the company's wage proposal. When IBP officials declined to confirm or deny the union report, Flanery used information from an IBP advertisement in a Sioux City newspaper to explain the company's general position.

To provide perspective, he brought in background information on contracts and labor relations in other packing companies. Government statistics helped. A Securities and Exchange Commission corporate filing gave him earnings figures on the IBP division of the parent company. A United States Bureau of Labor Statistics report provided information on the national decline in the number of packinghouse workers, and a United States

Department of Labor economist explained possible reasons for the decline. Flanery used a United States Department of Commerce formula to estimate the potential financial loss to the Sioux City metropolitan area in the event of a Dakota City strike. The formula indicated that IBP contributed about fifty-eight million dollars annually in salaries alone to the area.

Flanery also consulted industry analysts and interviewed officials from the United States Department of Agriculture and the United States Department of Labor for information on the national wage picture in the packing industry.

A day after the story ran, IBP closed its Dakota City plant at least temporarily when union members rejected a company offer for a four-year contract. In union terminology, it was a lockout. Flanery's use of a variety of sources enabled him to produce stories that made the situation more understandable to readers.

Nonunionized labor

Union members are a minority of the work force; the majority of others either are philosophically opposed to unionism, are unaware of unionism, or are in groups so small that they lack the bargaining strength to form a union. Some small businesses do have employee associations that provide a means to resolve grievances and which perform some bargaining functions.

Michael Hoyt, writing on the state of labor coverage by the media, contended that work in general is not being covered adequately. "Business journalism is a growth industry these days, and the public's economic sophistication has gained. But too much of this expanded coverage of the struggle for profit leaves out labor's perspective. The balance is off. To correct it will take more reporting on work, more economics with the human touch" (Hoyt 1984).

The advantage in dealing with unions, rather than with nonunionized workers, is that they have designated officers and headquarters, so the question of whom to contact is usually clear. There is no simple way to cover the amorphous army of the nonunionized, but some effort should be made to do so. You can be alert to trends that affect all workers—shifts in the type of employment, the effect of an increase in the minimum wage, the difficulties of the inexperienced in gaining entry to the job market.

Still, this is a difficult area to cover unless you have the luxury of devoting full time to reporting about the work force. Few reporters do, but even on a part-time basis you can discover potential stories by an awareness of the job holders you ordinarily encounter—waitresses, clerks, cooks, janitors, dry cleaners, shop supervisors, service station attendants, and numerous others. If you are interested in how they make a living, the story possibilities will come.

Hints for covering labor

1. Make a practice of checking routinely with labor leaders in the community. Once you have demonstrated an interest, union officials will be more inclined to see you as a credible journalist who deserves cooperation.

2. Advise your sources that your objective is to cover the news fairly so they will not be misled into considering you as an ally and a public relations vehicle for their organizations.

3. Become acquainted with independent experts in the labor-management field. Professors, lawyers, bankers, stock analysts, economists, and employment service officials and workers, among others, can provide information that will give depth to your stories.

4. Look for features about the individual worker in the field or store or plant. Their stories may build a better understanding about labor than stories that are more technical and remote from the audience.

5. Look beyond the issues of wages and hours for stories about worker attitudes toward their jobs. Some of the more significant stories about the modern industrial era have pinpointed the mental boredom of assembly-line work and the industrial experiments designed to alleviate the problem. Another type of story occurred in California, where publicity given to the hardship inflicted upon fieldworkers by the use of short-handled hoes led the state to abolish their use.

6. Every labor organization must file an annual financial report with the United States Department of Labor. In addition, a 1974 federal act requires trustees of employee pension funds to submit information on where the money is invested. Both reports are public and are a good source of financial information about unions.

In summary

Economic events of major magnitude touch the lives of virtually every individual in some way. Widespread dislocation of the economic process produces negative waves; a smooth-running and prosperous economy has general positive effects. Interest in the reporting of those events and their effects has increased markedly in the past decade.

Still, the new emphasis has brought complaints from economists, business, and labor that reporting of economic developments is marred by reportorial lack of knowledge. The interrelationships between economic events and the state of business and labor is an important story in virtually any community. To produce good coverage of what is happening and what it means locally or regionally, you must be prepared to explain complicated developments in terms understandable to your audiences.

In a sense, reporters are asked to become students again, learning the basics of economics, the working of the marketplace, and the roles of government, business, labor, and consumers. The decisions of government agencies such as the Federal Reserve System or a state public utilities commission may have an extensive impact but they cannot be reported adequately if you do not understand the purposes of the agencies and how they function. The journalistic techniques are the same as for any other subject area, but background knowledge is essential to enable you to relate the long-term implication for the public.

References

American Society of Newspaper Editors. 1982. Wanted: A New Dimension to the News Report. *Bulletin of the American Society of Newspaper Editors* (December-January):29.
Arkansas Gazette. 1979. TV Reporting Called Biased. Dec. 9, 1.
Bennett, James R. 1981. Newspaper Reporting of U.S. Business Crime in 1980. *Newspaper Research Journal* 3(1):45–53.
Booher, Jake. 1985. Script for Associated Press of Ohio Annual Awards for Investigative Reporting. Columbus, June 16.
Byerly, Kenneth. 1961. *Community Journalism.* Philadelphia: Chilton.
Canape, Charlene. 1982. Putting Stocks in TV Business News. *Washington Journalism Review* (November): 38–41.
Davis, Bob. 1985. Union Charges Swift Plant Closings Tactic to Control Labor; Company Blames Market. *Cedar Rapids* (Iowa) *Gazette,* Feb. 23, 1.
Evans, Christopher. 1985. S-T's Reporter Spurns 'Glitter' in Washington Media Circles. In a special undated magazine reprint, Bell Helicopter Sweeps National Honors for Texas Paper. *Fort Worth* (Texas) *Star-Telegram,* 3.

Flanery, James Allen. 1986. Pact Affects More Than Dakota City Plant; IBP Sets Wage Pace for Industry. *Omaha* (Neb.) *World-Herald,* Dec. 14, 1.

Heilbroner, Robert. 1978. *Beyond Boom and Crash.* New York: W. W. Norton.

Hoyt, Michael. 1984. Downtime for Labor. *Columbia Journalism Review* 22(6):36.

Kassel, David. 1981. Reading Between the Picket Lines. *Washington Journalism Review* 3(8):13.

Nickel, Herman. 1980. The Corporation Haters. *Fortune* 10(12):126–136.

Quinn, Jane Bryant. 1981. *How to Read an Annual Report.* Elmsford, NY: International Paper Co.

Schubert, Richard F. 1979. Sisyphus Had It Easy. Speech at seminar on Pennsylvania's Economy, Nov. 15. Pennsylvania Society of Newspaper Editors. Gettysburg, PA.

Seltzer, Curtis. 1981. The Pits: Press Coverage of the Coal Strike. *Columbia Journalism Review* 20(2):67.

Stewart, Dave. 1983. Analyzing Public Affairs Reporting. Unpublished paper in files of School of Journalism and Mass Communication. University of Wisconsin-Madison (July):10.

Thompson, Mark. 1984. Design Flaw Mars Bell Military Helicopters. *Fort Worth* (Texas) *Star-Telegram,* Mar. 25, 1.

———. 1985. Eye-Opening Body Count to 'Hell of a Story.' In undated special magazine reprint, Bell Helicopter Series Sweeps National Honors for Texas Paper. *Fort Worth* (Texas) *Star-Telegram,* 3.

Winter, Christine. 1988. Bank Customers Deposit Frustrations. *Chicago Tribune,* Aug. 16, 3:3.

Zuesse, Eric. 1981. Love Canal: The Truth Seeps Out. *Reason* 13(10):16–53.

Zweig, Phillip L. 1983. On the Job: Covering Penn Square. *Columbia Journalism Review* 22(5):23.

This chapter was initiated by Molen. Collaborators were Rystrom and Scotton.

CHAPTER 5

Education

WHEN a National Commission on Excellence in Education recently reported "a rising tide of mediocrity in the nation's schools," and called for tougher academic standards, higher pay for better teachers, and other reforms, Wichita, Kansas, *Eagle-Beacon* executive editor Davis Merritt, Jr., decided to "take a comprehensive look at how Kansans are providing for the future in the education of their children." The series was timed to break when the U.S. secretary of education would be conducting a regional forum on the commission report in a local high school. The resulting five-day series, reprinted in a special tabloid distributed beyond the *Eagle-Beacon's* normal circulation area, won an Inland Daily Press Association Award for staff writers Bob von Sternberg, Anne Valentine, Brian Settle, Robert Fisher, Tom Webb, Steve Tompkins, and Michael Ginsberg—all of whom combined their reporting and interpreting talents to explicate the series logo, "Kansas Education: Failing Our Kids."

Headlines of the twenty-seven story series suggest the manifold angles the reporting team looked at in compiling "the facts on which Kansans can base their ordering of priorities in the critical years to come" (Merritt 1983):

Education forum can address school mediocrity

Halting education's backslide: costly, elusive solutions

Wichitan realized too late he wasn't ready for college

Schools, parents seek answers as test scores slip

Studies diverse on educational excellence

State school system feels effects of education's backslide

Non-elected school administrators wield behind-the-scenes power

Experts want tougher required courses

Top students wish they'd learned more

Public discontent benefits private school ranks

Open admissions policy makes work for colleges

Some students lack skills at graduation

Homework, hours in classroom have dwindled

Teachers reflect decline in quality of education

Teacher not sure he'll stay on

Dismissing incompetent teachers a slow process

Teachers say low salaries are driving them from job

Teacher quality under scrutiny

Shortage of math and science teachers worries educators

Budgets rise but test scores slip

School reforms held back by tough math of taxes

Small-Town schools more expensive but personal

Panel studies cost of special ed

Education looks for politicians

Carter H.S. teachers join parents in solving pupils' problems

Competency tests cheered, jeered

Today's children reflect a fast-changing world

The *Eagle-Beacon* coverage was in the best tradition of effective interpretation of a pervasive public issue.

The background

Unlike many other public issues, education is a topic that most Americans feel they already understand. Its intricacies may escape many, but the fact that in America we have virtually universal education mandates at least cursory attention by most newspapers in the country. A study of twenty-one public issues in Louisville, Kentucky, showed that the *Louisville Times* gave education more coverage than any other issue between 1974 and 1981. Public surveys over the same period showed that education and crime were equally strong community concerns, but education still received more press coverage (Smith 1987).

Your job as an education reporter is to recall for your audience yesterday's patterns, report new trends, and personalize complicated issues so your readers will be interested. Education, unlike technology or the environment, has been a public issue for as long as local taxation. Your challenge is to make the latest developments in education seem as important as they are. This is a big job and the press is assigning more reporters to it. According to the *Working Press of the Nation* (1985), the number of reporters covering education increased from 431 in 1963 to 863 in 1985. Another study found that smaller papers were as likely to have a reporter specializing in education issues as larger papers (Yarrington 1987).

You should keep in mind that school officials and the public may not see the same issues as important. While school board members understandably see finances and curriculum development as most important, the public instead sees use of drugs and lack of discipline as more important (*American School Board Journal* 1988).

Elementary and secondary education: strategies and sources

American elementary and secondary education is a huge enterprise, consisting of almost 20,000 private institutions and some 86,000 public schools organized into 16,000 separate systems. But such totals mask the single greatest distinction of American precollegiate education—its diversity. The comprehensive suburban high school teaches everything from automobile mechanics and business math to French literature and integral calculus; in the enduring one-room schoolhouse a single teacher handles six or eight grades; at the run-down urban junior high, graffiti decorates the walls, a haze of smoke filters out of the boys' room, and security guards walk the corridors; in the evangelical Christian private school with a Bible-based curriculum, students say prayers before every class, and administrators ban long hair and jeans; at the traditional Catholic school, the emphasis is on order, discipline, and basic academic skills; and on the campus of a century-old New England academy, tweedy teachers stroll among splendid field houses, and the catalog bulges with college-level courses. Nothing could have been planned to be so diverse (Finn 1981).

So varied are our elementary and secondary schools, and so decentralized is their governance, that no generalization is true of every classroom, not even of all those within the circulation area of a small-city daily paper or radio or television station. Hence, covering the schools is very much a local beat. Yet some of the issues confronting kindergarten through twelfth grade education today are so widespread and pervasive that they can be reported and interpreted properly only if they are viewed in a national context.

EVERY SCHOOL IS UNIQUE

The reporter interpreting education issues has to be on guard lest his or her stereotypic ideas miss what is going on in a particular school system:

Take one good-sized school building, toss in a principal with good leadership abilities, add a few teachers with high expectations and desks full of test scores, and throw in a pinch of discipline. Stir well, let sit for two or three weeks and voila: an effective school.

So goes the theory.

Unfortunately, theory is not fact, and current thought on the qualities of an effective school is full of flaws, according to researchers at the Wisconsin Center for Education Research, a division of the University of Wisconsin-Madison School of Education.

The "effective schools" theory has been popularized in magazines and on national television talk-shows. It has been published in "how-to" brochures for parents and educators, and on flash-cards distributed at conventions and education conferences.

The theory states that there are five indicators of a good school, and instituting those elements in a school building will result in quality education in any classroom for any student.

But 16 months of study have shown that the popular recipe for a good school may be missing some key ingredients, according to UW-Madison researchers Stewart C. Purkey and Marshall S. Smith.

While an emphasis on basic skills in an atmosphere of order, leadership, high expectations and positive attitudes would be conducive to learning, such elements as staff participation and the unique qualities of an individual school must also be considered, they say. "What we came up with is that improving schools can't be done by recipe," Purkey said. "Any program for improving education is going to be idiosyncratic because every school is unique."

As a result, school improvement programs should be "school specific," Purkey said, and should involve staff every step of the way.

"The best kind of school improvement will take place when teachers and administrators sit down together and evaluate the school as it now exists and make plans to improve it," he said.

"Easy-answer solutions" and program changes made without consulting staff may have a detrimental effect on the school, Purkey said.

"I feel it is a disservice to children, particularly low income and minority students, to go blithely ahead thinking we now know everything we needed to know about schools," he said.

"The notion that schools could be changed from the top down or from the outside-in without consulting teachers or relying on their expertise is not only not likely to work, but also further erodes a teacher's sense of responsibility and control over what goes on in the school."

DIANNE PALEY. December 5, 1982. (Madison) *Wisconsin State Journal.*

Understanding the bureaucracy

The bureaucracy is the main and most difficult element of any reporter's initial exposure to public education. The one-room social center of the 1800s became a victim of growing population and the Industrial Revolution in late nineteenth-century America. For industry, automation and assembly lines represented a way to increase productivity. Establishing a system from what had been small, autonomous units grew popular. The legacy of this efficiency model for schools was centralization and unification.

Some schools chose to remain separate, so that within a single community today there still may be several separate school boards and superintendents, each overseeing a small parcel of schools; or there may be separate school boards and superintendents for the elementary schools and for the high schools. Many communities decided it would be more efficient to combine some jobs, such as record keeping and purchasing, rather than to do these tasks independently, so they formed umbrella administrative districts to coordinate such jobs for all the elementary schools or high schools within a sprawling geographic area. Other schools chose unification, which means that they combined jurisdiction for elementary schools and high schools to call themselves a unified school district. The major effect of this unification was to widen the responsibilities of the superintendent and the school board and to remove the district's administrators further from the classroom, making their role more managerial than educational.

The concept of compulsory attendance also became prevalent at the turn of the century, and children who had once attended school fitfully between harvests were required by law to attend classes regularly. By 1900, thirty-one states had passed compulsory attendance laws. Educator John Philbrick wrote at the time that "public instruction cannot be considered as having fulfilled its mission until it secures the rudiments of education to every child. To accomplish this object coercion is necessary" (Tyack 1974).

This commitment to universal education, enforced through various state and local regulations and supported by taxation, is the basis of the educational bureaucracy, which today spends more than $100 billion of federal, state, and local tax money each year to educate the nation's fifty million elementary and high school age children in the public schools. This investment accounts for approximately 7 percent of the gross national product, or roughly $2000 per child per year. Private schools add another $12 billion per year to that total educational expenditure (Education Writers 1985).

Today at the federal level, the education overseer is appointed, not elected. At the state level, chief state school officers may be either elected or appointed. Federal and state governments are administrative funnels for funding. They disburse and regulate the money they control, but political responsibility is still vested in the local superintendent and school board.

Understanding school finance and declining enrollment

Before World War II, public schools were financed mainly by local property taxes. For example, in 1940, 67 percent of public school revenue came from local sources, 32 percent from state government, and 1 percent from the federal government (Education Writers 1985). After the war, the state and federal shares of education began to grow. Today, more than half of the states depend on federal and state sources for more than 50 percent of their funding.

Declining enrollment affects funding. The education visionaries of the turn of the century could see only increased population, and thus a continuing expansion of the need for education, but school enrollment began to decrease in 1970. Since 1970, total school enrollment has dropped by over four million children, a decrease caused by a significant decline in the birth rate in the United States (Education Writers 1985). State and federal aid for education is based on enrollment, so when enrollment declines, schools lose money. A district loses an average of more than $1500 in state and federal aid for each student it loses (Education Writers 1985). Even if the decline in student enrollment is gradual, the district cannot adjust quickly to the change, because a great many fixed costs are tied up in tenured teachers and buildings. Often, a school district sets a minimum enrollment for each school, which if not met, may mean closure of the school. But if the target for a school is 500 children and the school attracts 495 students, the school will usually stay open. The cost of maintaining the building and paying salaries is the same for 495 students as it would be for 500. Theoretically, if this happened in each of twenty schools in a district and there was no offsetting increase at other schools, the decline in revenue (at $1000 per student) could be $100,000, yet the school district's costs for educating the children would remain the same.

The impact of declining enrollment and the shift away from local funding have created complex financial distribution formulas which are different for each state. Each year, every school district must weave its own intricate system of budget projections and expenditures to underwrite the education of every child in the public schools. Fiscal responsibility for education has grown so fragmented that school boards have lost a large degree of monetary control. Yet the boards often find themselves dealing with complaints about underfunded programs or excessive administrative costs, problems that can be handled only at a state or federal level.

Schools — traditional first beat

Into this melee drops the reporter. The school beat, like the police beat, is often the beginning reporter's first assignment. Education writer Mary Ellen Schoonmaker (1985) calls education "the beat that nobody wants." Yet the education and police reporters get more space than any other reporter, at least on some papers, according to Smith (1987). Schoonmaker agrees that education may get a lot of newspaper space, but she says it does not get the comprehensive coverage it deserves. Too much of the education coverage goes to temporary problems, she says.

The good education writer must move beyond temporary problems and investigate persistent issues. Smith (1987) found strong public concern with the issues of public education. A temporary problem might be a teacher strike or school disorder. Persistent issues involve major public policy questions. For example, how should we divide resources to provide both education and vocational training in our schools? How much of our public resources shall we devote to attracting competent teachers? To what extent shall the schools be used for promoting social change? These questions focus on persistent issues that require well-prepared reporters. Smith (1987) found strong public concern with the issues of public education, second only to better-publicized concerns about crime.

The Education Writers of America (1980) identified twelve major contemporary issues in American education. They are (1) Back to Basic Education Movement, (2) Compensatory Education, (3) Student Competency Testing, (4) Declining Enrollment, (5) Desegregation, (6) School Financing, (7) Education for the Handicapped, (8) Parent Activism, (9) Teacher Negotiation/Bargaining, (10) Violence and Vandalism, (11) School Prayer, and (12) Vocational Education. Yet, in a study of ten newspapers, DeRiemer (1988) found little coverage of these major issues. Instead, education writers concentrated heavily on two topics, school administration and student activities.

Education routinely demands a major portion of every community's financial resources. All of us spend a major portion of our lives in public or private schools. Nearly everyone in the community is involved in the education process or affected by it in some way — as parent, teacher, student, or taxpayer. Education issues clearly deserve more serious coverage.

Sources on the education beat

Like all beats, education has its traditional sources: public relations people, employee associations, parent associations, and "leaks."

PUBLIC RELATIONS PEOPLE. Most urban school districts employ a public relations person; most small districts do not. Even a small district will delegate this responsibility to an administrator, however. This person will be your first source, but should not be your primary source, since his or her tendency is to speak with one voice for the administration (often in an effort to minimize problems). Your primary sources should be individual administrators, board members, teachers and other employees, parents, and students whom you have grown to trust.

EMPLOYEE ASSOCIATIONS. Administrators, teachers, and classified employees (the last are nonacademic employees, such as bus drivers and secretaries) usually join individual associations or unions. Associations are often good sources of comparative data—how your district compares to other districts in the state in salaries and benefits, for example. Be aware, however, that unions are interested in expanding membership and influence, and that you can easily become a tool for this purpose (see the section entitled Covering Collective Bargaining, below).

PARENT ASSOCIATIONS. Most commonly, parents join together in local or school chapters of the Parent-Teacher Association (PTA), although parents with special interests (such as parents with preschool or handicapped children) often form separate organizations. The local chapter of a national organization, such as the PTA, can provide comparative national data on issues the organization is following, such as how violence on television affects children. Parent groups especially have a tendency to call press conferences when a pet program or project is threatened, or if a school is being closed. Parents tend to come together sporadically for each issue, so their press conferences may not be the organized, cohesive presentations you would expect. But listen to them. You may learn from these people, whose children are affected every day by all the administrative decisions.

UNOFFICIAL SOURCES. News tips may come from people who are disaffected from the administration or trying to undermine the public credibility of the board or the administration. Of course, you should follow all leads, but question the motivation of people who contact you surreptitiously or anonymously. Be aware that time is the enemy of careful reporting. But despite time pressures, do not overlook the two-source rule: with sensitive stories, always check an independent second source, even a third, to verify the first source's information. With particularly complicated issues, hold the story until you can satisfy any misgivings you have about the information.

Covering the school board

Local school boards dominate the attention of most education reporters, so it is important to understand who the typical school board members are. They are overwhelmingly Anglo-American, middle-aged, with a family income double that of the average family. Most of them have finished four years or more of college; just a little over 25 percent of them are women.

The typical board member is a professional or business/industrial executive. Many large, urban school districts pay their board members salaries, but most board members receive only nominal amounts, less than $5000 a year. Over 90 percent of them are elected to office, rather than appointed, and their campaigns usually are small-scale and heavily dependent on volunteers.

The school board usually appoints the superintendent, although sometimes the superintendent is autonomous, with no board oversight. It is important to remember that a superintendent appointed by a board is constantly trying to please a majority of the board members, since his or her job depends on it. Independent superintendents still must keep the majority of a community content, and hence they are highly susceptible to public pressures.

As recently as the 1960s, according to David F. Hendrix, the superintendent had substantial authority over local schools and in the community at large. Hendrix (1988) says this authority has been undercut by growing teachers' unions, increased federal and state involvement in local education, and public realization that schools have major problems. One result is that no school superintendent's job is safe anymore. The American Association of School Administrators expects one-third of the nation's school superintendents will leave their jobs within five years. There will be many reasons, but one that Hendrix sees is "less than visionary leadership on the part of superintendents" (Hendrix 1988).

Stability among school board members is also declining. One reason is that 75 percent of school board members face election opposition. Others resign because of the time demanded for board work and because they quickly find themselves being blamed for a myriad of school problems. As one school board member told the National Association of School Boards in its annual survey of members, "It's no day at the beach being on the school board" (Cameron 1988). Often the result for school boards is less consistency in educational policy from year to year as superintendents and board members change.

The forum for public debate among administrators, teachers, parents, and school board members is the board meeting. Usually held two or more times a month, board meetings are the public hearing on policy. Approving expenditures is one type of policy decision; firing an employee or closing a school are others. A board's effect lies in how it handles these policy decisions.

Personnel matters and private student matters, such as expulsions, are usually handled in executive session. This session may be held at a separate time from the public board meeting, but most commonly it occurs before or after the public meeting. Reporters and the public are barred from executive sessions. As each issue is brought before the board in private, only the people involved in that issue may be in the room, then they must leave when the next item is considered. For example, a student may have been caught with drugs in his or her locker. The board may meet in private with the student, the parents, and the school principal, and then decide whether the student should be expelled.

Executive session agendas may be distributed, but usually with nondescript headings, such as "Consideration of Student Expulsion" or "Teacher Suspension." Reporters' innate curiosity makes them feel left out in these situations, but rarely will a board member divulge what occurred. Rather than become preoccupied with exactly what happened at the board meeting, why not begin to collect independent information that might make a comprehensive story?

It is a good idea, however, to watch executive session agendas for an increase in certain topics. "Student Expulsion" as an item, for example, may indicate a crackdown. As contract negotiations near, watch for "Meeting with Board Attorney to Discuss Legal Matters." This may signal that the board is beginning to consider the contract. This tactic is much more fruitful than being preoccupied with knowing what goes on in each session.

At the public meetings, each item for board approval must be listed separately on the agenda, and most localities distribute the agenda at least two or three days before each meeting. This practice is an advantage to the reporter who can investigate upcoming issues before the board takes action.

Every reporter should understand how control of the agenda can shape the school board meeting. For example, dissident views may be thwarted if an item does not reach the agenda to be discussed. Many localities also place requirements on the school board agenda that allow board members to vote only on the items on the agenda, and not on any other issues that arise during public discussion.

The public, and reporters, are often confused when an important, unscheduled item is brought to the board by a member of the community at a board meeting and then must be deferred to a future meeting for action by the board because it must be placed on the agenda before it can be considered. The protection for the public in such requirements is that no issue may be decided until adequate advance notice has been given, but this tactic is also a way for board members to delay a decision until a calmer meeting, where the board can vote without confrontation.

If a school district is changing textbooks or building a new playground, the school board must approve the expenditure at a public board meeting. But administrators do not like to lose in public, so usually an agenda item for a public meeting has one of four functions: (1) To approve an action the administration already knows has board consent; (2) To approve routine items that must be made a matter of record, such as insurance claims which are referred to the district's insurance company for payment; (3) To give a public hearing to a controversial issue that the administration cannot decide without board direction; (4) To decide issues unpopular within the administration, but for which the administration wants to direct criticism to the board. Items that are certain to be approved often appear on a Consent Calendar, a brief listing of several items that the board will approve with one vote.

When school board members and administrators battle publicly on issues, it is important for the reporter to remember that most boards do not have their own staff, so they are dependent on the administration for information. A salaried board with its own staff is in a better position to question an administrative decision, since its information may be gathered independently.

The only staff person for a volunteer board may be a school administration secretary shared by all board members. This means that any questions by a board member are filtered through the secretary to the school administration for answers. This early warning system helps the administration defuse controversial issues before they arise before the entire board. This process could insulate the public from information and the education writer should be alert to it.

Hints for covering school boards

Journalism professor Shirley Biagi of California State University-Sacramento has been on both sides of the education beat — as a newsmagazine editor on the one hand, and as a member of a school board, on the other hand. She has been of invaluable counsel in structuring this chapter, and her tips to aspiring interpreters of educational issues at the local level are quoted throughout (Biagi 1986). (Biagi, not so incidentally, is the author of recent books on writing with a word processor, on writing and selling feature articles, and on the art of interviewing.)

For covering the school board, Biagi suggests the following:

1. School issues are usually cyclical and predictable. Do study background beforehand, and write about the issue before the board considers it.
2. Do not believe that big decisions are made at board meetings. Most decisions have been made before the meetings, and a good reporter will be able to speculate successfully based on comprehensive background information.
3. Do cover the schoolchildren. The tendency is to forget that children are at the basis of all the administrative and political decisions being made.
4. Do not spend too much time with administrators. Attend subcommittee and parent meetings for a comprehensive view.
5. Do maintain a rapport with everyone. Credibility is your best insurance.
6. Do not cozy up to one board member at the expense of the others, even if that board member is your ideological clone.
7. Do go where the action is; do not concentrate on administrative or board haggling. If a school is being closed, interview the principal, parents, teachers, and students.

Covering the budget process

While funding for schools may come from diverse sources, the board must give at least tacit approval to each expenditure, whether through a routine vote on a yearly budget or through selected approval of unexpected costs throughout the year. The advantage a reporter has in covering the annual school budget is that the process is cyclical. Budget approval is usually mandated by a certain date each year, so the budget-adoption process is relatively fixed, and can last as long as six months from the first proposed budget to the final draft. Regardless of when the school budget comes up, it is a major influence on the entire school program and still the top problem, according to the National Association of School Boards (1988).

Schools can have either line-item or program budgets. A line-item budget will tell at a glance how much is being spent for teachers' salaries, for instance, but will not tell how much is being spent for industrial arts classes. A program budget will show how much is being spent for industrial arts classes, but will not easily reveal how much of the industrial arts budget is in salaries and how much in materials purchases.

The budget document will usually include an estimate of projected income, show how much was spent in the current year compared to the previous year, and estimate expenditures for the coming year. A comparison will show items the administration wants to increase, but more importantly, it will reveal items to be decreased or eliminated. According to the National School Boards Association, "the most distinguishing characteristic of school system budgets usually is that they reflect the values of administrators—not board members. Through the budget, administrators show who *they* think should get what, when, and how" (Shannon 1980).

Board members must then react throughout each scheduled debate on the budget, inevitably forced to justify publicly any changes they want to make in the administration-drafted document. Members must also endure the lobbying by any teachers or parents with children in programs scheduled to be eliminated or schools targeted to be closed.

One aspect of school budgets that beginning reporters often fail to understand is that most of the costs of a school district are fixed. A school district is not a manufacturing plant, where automation can suddenly save millions of dollars by replacing people. As a service business, schools are people-intensive. Of a school district's total budget, 75 to 90 percent pays for people—teachers, principals, janitors, and secretaries—so when school board members argue over budget decisions, they are disputing only the 10 to 25 percent of the budget available for reapportioning, and items that can be reapportioned may not be truly discretionary—textbooks, for example, or building repair. So while school boards are very visible as receivers of wrath, the measure of their authority is in how much of the budget is fiscally fixed and how much is discretionary.

Hints for covering the budget

Professor Biagi (1986) gives the following hints for covering the budget process:

1. Learn the timetable from proposed to final budget. Since the budget process is cyclical, try to research anticipated budget actions and write about them before they become public.
2. Investigate the sources of funding for your school district. Try to unravel the complex funding formulas so you can, if necessary, explain them to your readers or viewers.

3. Determine the portions of your school district's budget that are fixed and those that are discretionary. Learn which categorical programs your district administers (programs mandated by either state or federal laws that carry their own funding to be used only for those programs).
4. Examine the budget carefully for what is *not* planned for next year compared to what was funded for this year. These are the programs or issues that will most likely be debated at board budget meetings.
5. If a particular program is scheduled for a significant increase or decrease, learn about it. Is the future of the program affected because federal or state funding has changed? What successes make the district want to expand a program? What is being cut to support the increase? Or, why eliminate a program? Has it been a failure?
6. Pay attention to budget deliberations. Other than the selective audience of people affected by program cuts, the public usually stays away from budget meetings. A reporter might conclude that the public is therefore not interested; this is a mistake. Voting on the budget is a school board's most important action each year. Always remember that each piece of money eventually affects children. Whenever you are confused, ask administrators what this budget action will mean for a single child. Then ask the teachers, parents, and children who will be affected.

Covering collective bargaining

As student enrollment grows static, and even declines, the demand for teachers slips, and so do salaries. Since 1970, public school teachers' salaries have lagged behind inflation. The result of this situation has been that the concept of collegiality—where teachers, board members, and administrators would work together toward common educational goals with districts setting pay levels and educational priorities and teachers sublimely accepting—has changed greatly. Not all teachers now belong to unions, but even nonunionized teachers pay close attention to salary levels and working conditions.

Teachers and other school employees now bargain not only for salaries but even debate such issues as who does yard duty and how often. School authorities generally agree that teachers who formed unions were much better prepared for collective bargaining than were school boards and school administrators. The American Federation of Teachers (AFT) began bargaining for better salaries and working conditions for its members soon after it was formed in 1916. The other major teachers' organization, the National Education Association (NEA), did not take on this role until the 1960s, after federal government employees won the legal right to bargain collectively (Berger 1988).

School board members, in contrast, are often ill-equipped to become contract negotiators. Elected from various professional backgrounds, usually as volunteers with a commitment to community service, board members suddenly find themselves required to spend half, even two-thirds, of their time as board members in negotiating sessions with teachers' unions, as well as with unions for administrators and for clerical and maintenance workers.

Some school boards now delegate this responsibility to professional negotiators who are on salary or contract to the board to settle bargaining issues. While the board must approve what is negotiated, the effect of this development on board-union relations is to move the two sides further apart and to create an adversary relationship.

A reporter is easily confused in a stormy collective-bargaining situation. Although in most union negotiations a strike threat exists, most school boards will publicly resist initial union demands. This one-act play is very predictable, and can be compared to a duel by pistols about to take place between two people defending their honor publicly, while behind a bush their seconds are trying to negotiate a settlement so that no one will be harmed.

A strike is an unwelcome choice—employees lose money (although as part of the settlement afterward they may receive pay for the days they were striking), and boards lose face. Neither situation is desirable. It is easy for a reporter to become a pawn in the game that takes place as the two sides posture for the community.

The education writer is responsible for informing the public, a major factor in any collective-bargaining situation. Public opinion is perhaps the key variable that both school boards and employees try to win over to influence bargaining. It is almost as if the bargainers meet in absentia with a third party—the public—through the public pronouncements, rhetoric, and other means of communicating with citizens about issues. When conflict arises, the schools are at center stage, and the education writer is suddenly thrust into the position of being an expert required to answer key questions such as the following:

- Does the board have the money for a pay raise?
- Would it be necessary to cut programs to pay for the salary increase?
- How do the local district teachers' salaries compare with those in the area, in similar districts, in the region, in the state?

• How do the salaries compare with increases in the consumer price index?

• Are teachers' demands related to students' needs or quality education, or do they enhance working conditions?

Hints for covering collective bargaining

Professor Biagi (1986) recommends the following for reporters covering collective-bargaining situations.

1. Like many school issues, contracts are cyclical and predictable. Their terms (usually two or three years) are defined each time they are written. So, for example, if a contract in your school district is scheduled to expire in June, begin to investigate the issue in January before the board faces the issue.

2. Most reporters cover the circus but forget that the public arguments are based on a printed document called a contract. Ask for a copy of the current contract and understand the provisions under dispute.

3. If picketers show up at a board meeting, learn to judge whether the crowd is manufactured or real. Interview people in the audience during recesses to learn how the demonstration was organized.

4. Cover only a minimum of the rhetoric. Do not allow your newspaper or television station to become a platform for each side to throw charges at the other. Instead, go to the teachers and the board members *individually* and ask their positions. Do not believe that the organizational leaders of the union necessarily speak for all the members or that one board member speaks for the board.

5. Investigate both sides of the issues. If the union has called for smaller class size, for instance, ask the administration and the union for cost estimates. Sometimes lowering class size by even one student is a big expense, and then you must ask both sides whether the money could be better spent elsewhere.

6. Realize that bargaining situations are just that—both sides usually begin at extremes and eventually compromise. Neither side expects to get all it asks.

7. A strike is usually the most emotional issue a school reporter faces, but be prepared to overlook the picket signs
at the schools and the "we will not be moved" stance of the
board to learn instead whether any of the contract issues
will really change what happens to the children in the classroom.

Private elementary and secondary schools

Ten percent of the fifty million elementary and secondary students in
the United States attend private schools. Under the private school umbrella
is a disparate array of church-related and independent schools. Most
private schools (85 percent) are church-related. Two-thirds of the private
schools in the United States are Catholic.

"Advocates of public education consider the swing to nonpublic
schools a threat to the democratic underpinning of the nation—a trend that
they say will fragment and divide the population," reports the *New York
Times*. "But supporters of private and parochial schools reject this notion,
arguing that their institutions are a constitutionally permissible alternative
for parents who should be free to decide what sort of education best suits
their children" (Maeroff 1981).

For this freedom of choice, parents may pay as little as $175 a year per
child at a neighborhood parochial school or $6000 a year or more for
private boarding school. (A continuing legislative debate is whether parents
should receive tax credits for the tuition they pay.) To attract parents,
private schools often boast a college preparatory curriculum, and many
brochures for private schools compare test scores of public school students
with those of private school students.

Reporters are received in a variety of ways at private schools. Unlike
public schools, board meetings are private and curriculum decisions are
entirely between parents and the administration. Parents choose a school
because of its curriculum, and enrolling their children gives tacit support to
the school's approach.

Do not assume antipathy between public and private schools; many are
mutually supportive. Questions that an alert reporter should track include:
How widespread are private schools in the community? Is enrollment growing or slipping? What alternatives do the private schools offer? Are those
choices missing in the public schools in the area? To answer these questions,
private school administrators will offer you data to compare with the public
system. Also speak with parents and their children about what attracts
them to the school. But the real answers are in the same place they are in
the public schools—in the classroom.

Higher education: issues and entrees

We are sometimes inclined to speak of America's "system" of higher education, but in fact, it is a nonsystem, so diverse are colleges and universities in their traditions, circumstances, and aspirations. Private institutions vary from the large research university supported in considerable part with federal contract funds to the small college devoted to undergraduate teaching and underwritten by gifts from alumni and friends. Public institutions run the gamut from the junior or community college through the teachers college to the municipal university with a major commitment to evening instruction and on to the sprawling state multiversity with its emphasis on graduate education and extension or outreach. In between are all sorts of permutations. Their numbers and locations are such that it is rare for a daily newspaper or radio or television station not to have a postsecondary institution within its coverage are. Yet many issues facing higher education are so perennial and pervasive that they can be investigated and interpreted accurately only from a national perspective.

Continuing issues

The "continuing problems facing high education," first alliteratively distilled by Scott Cutlip and Allen Center (1952) in the early 1950s, have changed only by degree in the 1990s: function, faith, funds, freshmen, freedom, federalism, and football. All are interrelated.

In varying intensities and ways, American colleges and universities have come to engage in teaching, in research, and in extending campus resources to the public at large. But collectively and individually, they are

GREAT CAMPUS PROBLEMS

I once said in the 1950s as Chancellor at Berkeley that the great administrative problems of the day were sex for the students, athletics for the alumni, and parking for the faculty; but it could better be said now that the problems are, instead, athletics for the students who have gone "straight," sex for the professors with some of whom the counter-culture still finds support, and parking for the alumni as they return for their refresher courses.

CLARK KERR. 1983. *The Uses of the University.* Cambridge, Mass.: Harvard University.

by no means as self-assured as they may seem with respect to the nature of each function. Should they instruct primarily in the classic liberal arts that cultivate the life of the mind, or should they concentrate on courses that teach skills and equip graduates to make a living? Should they investigate basic phenomena or attempt to solve practical problems? Should the campus reach off-campus to the current adult market? And if a college attempts

AN IMPORTANT TIP ABOUT COVERING HIGHER EDUCATION

Most campus decisions are really made outside the formal system of governance, are made in more informal, less bureaucratic ways. The more visible superstructure of governance is less important that the less visible infrastructure. Most decisions about teaching, about curriculum, about research topics and methods, about amount and form of public service are made by individual faculty members. Most decisions made about majors selected, courses taken, time spent on study are made by individual students. And intense competition among institutions of higher education, public versus private and public versus public, means that all are seeking optimum solutions; none can afford to lag too far behind. Decisions made in these three ways—by individual faculty members, by individual students, and in response to external competition through market pressures—are the most accepted, the least contested, and considered to be the most legitimate.

Looking only at what is happening to the formal superstructure of governance is like looking only at a part of the whole—important, but not all that decisive. What are faculty members deciding individually? How are students voting with their feet? What does interinstitutional competition compel? These are more essential questions than what form a coordinating council should take or whether or not there should be a federal department of education.

CLARK KERR. 1983. *The Uses of the University.* Cambridge, Mass.: Harvard University.

to be all things to all people, how can it ration time and effort and reward faculty equitably?

Historically, no country has lavished such faith in higher education as the United States, but at times that faith falters. Free-spirited faculty may seem to threaten traditional values. Equally iconoclastic students may disturb the peace. Administrators may act more like bond salespeople than like scholars. Graduates with Ph.D.s who are driving taxis may suggest that a university degree is not an automatic open door to the good life. So institutions of postsecondary education are constantly taking the pulse of public faith.

The most practical measure of public faith is the funds allocated to higher education. Chancellors and deans never seem to have enough, although back in 1907 one administrator admitted that "palaces rear on the sites of barns, dollars roll in and up merrily" (Mulkeen 1981). Unquestionably, current years are leaner ones for colleges and universities that expanded so steadily in the years after World War II.

In the 1990s, higher education is expected to undergo changes that may affect its fundamental character. Sue Berryman, director of the National Center on Education and Employment at Teachers College, Columbia University, says we will have to rethink all of our assumptions about education. She points out, for example, that higher education in this country is based on lower school models developed earlier. We may simply be using the wrong models (Berryman 1988). Meanwhile, industry and much of the public see education as increasingly irrelevant. Critics say the schools emphasize learning that involves manipulating abstract symbols while the work world is mostly connected to concrete situations (Shanker 1988).

At the same time, state officials with greater budget control are coming forth with their own "solutions" for the problems in education. Teachers find themselves caught between these government planners and newly militant parents groups that want more influence on the way their children are educated. Chris Pipho of the Education Commission of the States suggests this may bring about a different sort of paradox: the states using their new power to force decentralization on public school systems (Fiske 1988).

The past twenty-five years has seen the greatest period of growth and expansion for education in the United States. The next decade may see the greatest period of educational change.

Freedom of inquiry is another running story in higher education. Teachers must have freedom to teach, not merely for the sake of their students but for the future of humankind. Yet the freedom of the professor to teach and of the student to learn comes under frequent attack and on occasion is abridged, frontally or indirectly. Protecting and defending intellectual freedom is a continuing issue.

Among current abridgments of campus freedom is creeping federal-

SPORTS AND EDUCATION

In the 1990s a reporter covering the higher education beat will have to interpret the public issues attendant to the perennial conflict between the maintenance of academic standards on college campuses and the drive to achieve athletic prowess, particularly in the collegiate "money" sports, football and basketball.

"College sport," noted U.S. News and World Report *in 1990, "has grown into an expensive circus, driven by an insatiable appetite for winning, and amateur athletes are getting neither the moral guidance nor the education they bargained for."*

This story is not likely to be covered by media sports departments; an invidious exposé could threaten their world. City and state desk investigative reporters will have to do it. They can take a hint on how to proceed from the U.S. News and World Report *team.*

USN&WR *reporters found that although there are some exemplary colleges that graduate nearly all their athletes, too many fall far short of that goal. Nationally, "fewer than 30 percent of football and basketball players graduate, a rate far lower than for all students, and only a tiny fraction make it to the pros," said* USN&WR. *The reporters traced the problem to the "peculiar economics of college sport. Despite the enormous sums of money involved, athletics are not a profitable enterprise for most colleges." Along with citing some statistics, the reporters quote a college president, who explains:*

> Winning is the thing that ensures the income. Football and basketball have to make money, and they have to win to make money, and that's how the cycle becomes so vicious.

With the national picture as background, USN&WR *gave flesh and blood to the statistics by zeroing in on the University of Georgia football team that won a national championship in 1981. Reporters disccovered that out of the twelve starters on the offensive team, only three had been graduated and only two had made it to the pros, principally Herschel*

SPORTS AND EDUCATION (continued)

Walker. Each of the dozen was interviewed. "Each player's story is distinctly his own," USN&WR *stated, "but each resembles tales that could be told by former college athletes in every corner of America."*

"The Price of Victory" became a U.S. News and World Report *cover story.*

ALVIN P. SARNOFF with JOANNIE M. SCHROFF. 1990. "The Price of Victory." *U.S. News and World Report*, Jan. 8, 44–53.

ism. With federal aid for colleges has come a stream of rules and regulations that challenge an institution's autonomy and are expensive to administer. More than a few faculties have become so inundated with paperwork that they feel as if they have little time to do what they are supposed to do—teach, inquire, and inform the community.

Intercollegiate athletics, personified particularly by big-time football and basketball, are an ever-present center of campus debate. Not only are sports expensive to maintain, they can erode campus academic standards. Yet they have been such a part of the American scene that an institution ceases to play the game, literally, at grave risk to its community, alumni, and student support.

Whether they are or not, faculty members will usually think of themselves as the true managers of the system. The faculty will usually be represented by a deliberative body, frequently called a council or senate, although the real work will normally be done by a wide array of committees. Any higher education reporter should first take a cram course in the administrative and faculty organization of the campus. To assist, the school will normally have a public information person, although he or she may masquerade under another title.

Students may be the most overlooked sources by reporters trying to interpret the travails of higher education today. Not so with Guy L. Pace of the *Pullman* (Washington) *Herald.* Taking a look at "the mass confusion" during registration at Washington State University, Pace not only interviewed the registrar and key faculty, he also stood in the lines and got revealing quotes from representative WSU students (Pace 1987).

Constituent groups are important news sources: for the commuter campus, the community itself; for the private institutions, alumni; for the public institutions, legislators and public officials; for the research university, the federal government and foundations; for all universities, nonacademic staff, and, of course, the students.

Adult education: the hidden agenda

To investigate and interpret American education anywhere today you should also pay attention to the vast network of continuing and adult education devices. In terms of individuals participating, the pursuit of skills and knowledge outside of formal academic classrooms is a bigger story than what is conventionally thought of as the education beat.

Adult education ranges from the technical institute or vocational school, training high school dropouts directly for the local job market, to a seminar in conflict resolution for personnel managers or a discussion group exploring the Great Books. It is the rare American institution today that does not consider itself to be involved in some way in the business of adult education. Industries, museums, libraries, historical societies, bridge clubs, churches, lodges, farm bureaus, colleges and universities, social welfare organizations, professional societies, and sports and volunteer associations all are among the diverse group of institutions that have taken on roles as educators.

Covering this maze of activities is much more difficult than covering local schools or the nearby college. If you are lucky, your city will have a continuing or adult education council, but the information available from these informal consortia will vary in scope and depth. The chief guidance counselor of the local high school may be a good source of information; so may the county agricultural agent, the head librarian, or the employee relations director of the city's largest industry. Weaving the tapestry of continuing education in your circulation area is a challenging assignment, and may in fact render more public service to your readers or listeners than routine coverage of youth education.

Case studies in interpreting school issues

You may have happy memories of your school days, but do not always expect school officials to welcome you warmly when you show up to do a story on a public issue. Public issues by their very nature involve controversy. School officials, like most bureaucrats, want to avoid controversy.

Sigrid Bathen of the *Sacramento Bee* found school officials resistant

ISSUES IN AMERICAN HIGHER EDUCATION

New problems are always developing in education, but certain major issues are prominent today and are likely to remain prominent:

1. What relationship should exist between the contributions higher education makes to the economic well-being of the country and to its noneconomic aims?
2. How can the commitments of higher education to fairness and equality best be reconciled with requirements for efficiency, quality, and the making of judgments of relative value?
3. Who is to decide such issues? What voice should students, faculty, and governments have?
4. To what degree and in what ways are the economic and the noneconomic purposes of higher education mutually supportive?
5. Where do the economic and noneconomic purposes of higher education conflict?
6. Does higher education contribute adequately to economic well-being? Should its efforts be geared more heavily toward increasing economic growth?
7. How effectively is higher education serving the cause of social equality?
8. How should the need to develop fully the talents of the most able students be weighted against the claims of less able and disadvantaged students for assistance?
9. Can we maintain a desirable diversity among colleges and universities without perpetuating undesirable inequality and hierarchy?
10. What is the public interest in private higher education?
11. By what mechanisms should decisions about cutbacks be made?
12. What is the optimum distribution of student financial aid?
13. Is it morally permitted or required for colleges and universities to go beyond race-blind and sex-blind standards in encouraging the prospects of minorities and women? If so, what quotas are permissible and which are not?
14. How can higher education best discharge its obligation to provide expanded opportunities for the handicapped?
15. How should appropriate standards of equity in the distribution of research funds be defined?

MICHAEL S. MCPHERSON. 1983. Value Conflicts in American Higher Education. *Journal of Higher Education.* 54(3):243–78.

and even incredulous when she asked to talk with students who were being suspended in record numbers.

Bathen had been on the education beat for only two months when something on the school board's meeting agenda caught her attention. There was a list of student suspensions attached. The suspension list was routinely passed out along with the agenda but it was new to Bathen so she got the list for a year earlier and compared the figures.

"Often a reporter tends to look at these statistics too routinely," admitted Bathen (1982). But the comparison suggested the suspension figures were anything but routine. Bathen found a huge increase in the number of suspensions even though student enrollment was lower. At one high school the suspension rate had doubled.

Bathen spent the next week interviewing school board members and administrators. "I tried to give some substance to the numbers," said Bathen. "I looked at the reasons for the suspensions. The answer was partly that administrators were coming down on disciplinary infractions, but it also was that children are acting up at an earlier age."

Bathen's story, "Board Grapples with Suspensions," ran on the front page of the "Metropolitan News" section the morning before the board's Monday night meeting (Bathen 1980a).

"I thought the story might bore people with all those numbers," Bathen said. "I was astonished at the interest we got from parents. I realized from the reaction of school administrators that they were terribly concerned that I had perceived the story's significance. They were very defensive, trying to give me reasons that were only a partial explanation or no explanation at all."

Bathen decided the statistical story was not enough. She wanted to talk with some students who had been suspended. She spent the day of the school board meeting trying to find some. Many administrators were unwilling to cooperate. One administrator blanched and said, "Kids? You want to interview kids?" To Bathen the administrator seemed to be asking, "What do students have to do with the process of education?"

Bathen was cautious. She accepted that administrators cannot identify suspended students because of privacy laws. Bathen just went out to the high school with the highest suspension rate at lunch time and started asking questions of students she found. Still, she was worried about verifying the information from the students. "How could I be sure that the students who talked to me had actually at one time been suspended?"

Bathen finally convinced one high school principal that her approach was legitimate. She went to his office and found six students sitting there. She asked if any of them had ever been suspended from school. They all had. She asked the students if they would allow their names and pictures to

SCHOOLS GET REPORT CARD

"Longitudinal" surveys — that is, comparable surveys of the same population conducted at different points in time — can be a very interesting way to cover changes in public opinion on a variety of issues, including the quality of education in the community.

By asking separate samples of city residents the same questions three years apart, in 1987 and again in 1990, the The Milwaukee Journal *discovered that the public seemed to perceive a decline in the quality of education in the city's public schools. Follow-up questions found that those interviewed tended to blame the school board for the decline, rather than the superintendent of schools, whose contract was coming up for renewal. Reporter Priscilla Ahlgren included with the story a sidebar that told readers the details of the polls taken in 1987 and 1990, including the different margins of error in each year.*

In gathering information for the story, Ahlgren also sought comments from the school superintendent and used quotations from various survey respondents who voluntarily agreed to forego anonymity. The quotations added warmth and depth to Ahlgren's article. The copyrighted story led off the top of the front page one Sunday.

PRISCILLA AHLGREN. 1990. Journal Poll: A Report Card on Perceptions of City Schools. *Milwaukee Journal,* July 29, A1, A21.

be part of a story in the *Sacramento Bee.* All but one agreed. But Bathen decided to change their names and not to run their pictures.

After writing the story about the students, Bathen went to that night's board meeting. School board meetings usually had small audiences. "It was a packed house and all of the TV stations were there," Bathen said. "I realized it was because of my story. Then I started to wonder, 'Gee, did I do this?' "

The board finally addressed the suspension issue at 10 P.M. right on Bathen's deadline. "I wrote the meeting story hurriedly, with a few quotes from administrators who came to the podium to try to explain," she said. "But I don't find board meetings particularly productive. The real action takes place behind the scenes."

The next day a short story on the board meeting ran on the front page of the "Metro" section (Bathen 1980b). Alongside it was the longer feature story that included the interviews with the students who had been suspended. In it, Bathen detailed the difficulties she had faced:

> Principal Jones allowed a reporter to interview students in his office. A similar request was denied at Kennedy (High), although reporters were allowed to interview masses of students during their lunch break — an experience which yielded confusing, and largely unreportable results. Some students said they had been fighting, but said other students involved in fighting were not suspended (Bathen 1980c).

Bathen's story made it clear that there was a serious public issue involved. School administrators were facing serious problems of school discipline and were not dealing with them effectively. As a result of the stories, the school board created a task force of principals and administrators to study the entire problem of school discipline.

Bathen's experience shows once more that a resourceful and persistent reporter can deal with a public issue despite the unwillingness of public officials to cooperate. She points out that reporters should not always expect cooperation. "Technically, administrators and principals don't have to talk to reporters, but I have always believed that the schools are public institutions. The press has the right to be there and the public officials have a responsibility, within reason, to cooperate with the media" (Bathen 1982). Bathen's stories represented effective reporting and interpreting of a serious public issue.

Pat Tearney of the *News Graphic Pilot* of Cedarburg, Wisconsin, also found some administrators uneasy when he looked into the growth of girls' sports at area high schools and found some subtle sexual biases remaining. Tearney got a good deal of cooperation from school administrators in the suburban Milwaukee towns his twice-weekly newspaper covers.

Tearney had been covering sports and other assignments for the *News Graphic Pilot* for several years, so he was a familiar figure to many of those he interviewed. But he found some uneasiness as he developed his series on girls' sports over several months. He researched school and sports conference records, interviewed students, coaches and school administrators, and surveyed students on their attitudes toward girls' sports.

"School principals have a very visible and sensitive public position," Tearney commented. "Any time you are touching on potential sex discrimination in school sports or any other school area, you are bound to cause some uneasiness" (Tearney 1988a).

In his first story, Tearney (1988b) traced the growth of girls' athletics in local high schools since the 1972 federal law prohibiting discrimination effectively mandated that girls be given equal opportunity to play school sports. From a starting point close to zero, in fifteen years Wisconsin high schools had developed 2,230 girls' athletic teams in ten sports. In the 1985–1986 school year, 58,689 Wisconsin girls participated in a high school sport.

In Tearney's second and third articles, he focused on some major problems in the high school sports programs for women. One is the small number of college scholarships available for women athletes. Even though their sports and studies schedule is equally demanding, girls who are outstanding high school athletes are much less likely to be rewarded with a college scholarship offer (Tearney 1988c). Another problem is the shortage of women coaches who can serve as role models. Because of home responsibilities, many women teachers just do not have the time for such demanding extracurricular activities like coaching (Tearney 1988d).

The final article in the series pointed out that girls' sports was still a second-class citizen in many high schools. When budgets are reduced, it is often the girls' teams that get cut back or even eliminated. For a time, girls' basketball teams were scheduled in high school gyms on Tuesdays and Thursdays while Fridays were reserved for the boys' teams. It took a lawsuit to get the girls' teams equal time on Fridays. Concluding his series, Tearney found that high school sports programs for girls were always at risk. He wrote: "But budget time is near, tax relief is the watchword of the day, and girls' gymnastics is costly, hard to find coaches for—and attracts almost no fans" (Tearney 1988e).

In summary

Four problems in the reporting of education by the press have been identified repeatedly by researchers and journalists: (1) severely limited coverage of education (Ross 1983; Schoonmaker 1985); (2) imbalance in areas of education coverage (Johns 1984; Schoonmaker 1985); (3) a lack of "education expertise" in reporting of education (Gorton 1984; Ross 1983); and (4) an overemphasis on events rather than issues (Johns 1984; Ross 1983; Schoonmaker 1985). Over the years even the major news organizations seemed to be putting few resources into covering education and then reporting only the surface events without examining the background issues. Ross (1983), for example, examined education coverage in the *Los Angeles Times* over the fifteen-year period from 1960 through 1975. DeRiemer

(1988) analyzed education coverage by ten newspapers in nine states from 1969 to 1984. Both studies confirmed others critical of the scope and depth of education coverage in the mass media.

Education coverage does, however, seem to be improving. Looking at education articles in six daily newspapers in the mid-1980s, Criscuoio (1985) concluded that the facts no longer support popular opinion that newspapers give "scant, primarily negative coverage to education." This supports the earlier study by Hynds (1981) that found education coverage expanding and improving. Most newspapers, according to the study, are now devoting at least 5 percent of their news hole to education. Most are covering a variety of educational activities, including programs for the disadvantaged and for the gifted, as well as problems related to integration of the schools or the misuse of alcohol and drugs by young people. Most now depend on their own staff to provide the majority of their educational coverage, and many newspapers have increased the staff time devoted to education in recent years. However, most education writers still do not have any special training for their position. In the future, the study predicted that more emphasis is likely to be placed on interpretation and analysis in education reporting, and the economics of education is likely to get close attention (Hynds 1981).

Today's journalism students will set tomorrow's standards for investigating and interpreting education.

References

American School Board Journal. 1988. Current Priorities: Board vs. Public. 175(1):21.

Bathen, Sigrid. 1980a. Suspensions: Schools Report Figures Up Despite Decline in Enrollment. *Sacramento* (CA) *Bee,* Nov. 10, B1.

_____. 1980b. Board Grapples with Suspensions. *Sacramento* (CA) *Bee,* Nov. 11, B1.

_____. 1980c. Suspensions Provoke Problems. *Sacramento* (CA) *Bee,* Nov. 11, B1.

_____. 1982. Interview with author, July 12.

Berger, Joseph. 1988. 2 Rival Unions Endorse Plans to Help Teachers. *New York Times,* July 6, 25.

Berryman, Susan E. 1988. Breaking Out of the Circle. *New York Times,* June 26, E7.

Biagi, Shirley. 1986. Interviews with Clay Schoenfeld, September-November.

Cameron, Beatrice H., Underwood, Kenneth E., and Fortune, Jim C. 1988. Politics and Power. *American School Board Journal* 175(1):17–20.

Criscuoio, N. P. 1985. The Public's Attitude Toward Education. *Editor and Publisher* 118(1):16–18.

Cutlip, Scott, and Center, Allen. 1952. *Effective Public Relations.* Englewood Cliffs, NJ:Prentice-Hall, 231.

DeRiemer, Cynthia. 1988. Education Coverage in Award-Winning Newspapers. *Journalism Quarterly* 65(1):171–77.

Education Writers of America. 1985. *Covering the Education Beat.* Woodstown, NJ: Education Writers Association.

Finn, Chester E. 1981. A Call for Quality Education. *American Renewal.* New York: Time-Life, 66–77.

Fiske, Edward B. 1988. Lessons. *New York Times,* July 6, Y25.

Gorton, Richard, and Newsome, M. 1984. School-Press Relations. *Journalism Quarterly* 63(1):184–87.

Hendrix, David F. 1988. Spotlight on Superintendents in School Reform. *School Administrator* 45(4):17–19.

Hynds, Ernest C. 1981. Newspaper Education Coverage Has Been Expanded, Improved. *Newspaper Research Journal* 11(3):70–76.

Johns, J. L., Brownlie, C. F., and Ramirez, R. L. 1984. How Newspapers Cover Education. *Journalism Quarterly* 53(1):177–80.

Maeroff, Gene I. 1981. Private Schools Look to Bright Future. *New York Times,* (Jan. 4,) Sec. 12:1.

Merritt, Davis. 1983. Kansas Education—Failing Our Kids. *Wichita* (Kansas) *Eagle-Beacon,* July 13–17, 1.

Money Still Is Your Top Problem. 1988. *American School Board Journal* 175(1):21.

Mulkeen, Thomas A. 1981. Higher Education in the Coming Age of Limits. *Journal of Higher Education* 52(3):310–16.

Pace, Guy L. 1987. The Last Mass Confusion. *Pullman* (Wash.) *Herald,* Jan. 10, 1.

Ross, Bonnie Lou. 1983. Education Reporting in the Los Angeles Times. *Journalism Quarterly* 60(2):346–52.

Schoonmaker, Mary Ellen. 1985. The Beat Nobody Wants. *Columbia Journalism Review* 23(5):37–40.

Shanker, Albert. 1988. Rethinking Failure and Success. *New York Times,* June 26, E7.

Shannon, Thomas A. 1980. Why Schools Aren't Businesses. *American School Board Journal* 167(6):29–30.

Smith, Kim A. 1987. Newspaper Coverage and Public Concern About Community Issues: A Time-Series Analysis. *Journalism Monographs* No. 101:11–12.

Tearney, Pat. 1988a. Interview with James Scotton, Mar. 12. Milwaukee, WI.

_____. 1988b. State Tournaments—A Long Way From Play Days. *News Graphic Pilot* (Cedarburg, WI), Aug. 15, 6.

_____. 1988c. Athletic Competition Offers Benefits, Enjoyment. *News Graphic Pilot* (Cedarburg, WI), Aug. 17, 10.

_____. 1988d. Where Have All the Women Coaches Gone? *News Graphic Pilot* (Cedarburg, WI), Aug. 22, 6.

_____. 1988e. Girls Play, But Usually in Front of Empty Seats. *News Graphic Pilot* (Cedarburg, WI), Aug. 24, 11.

Tyack, David B. 1974. *The One Best System.* Cambridge, MA. Harvard Univ. Press.

Working Press of the Nation. 1985. Burlington, Iowa. NSRB, Inc.

Yarrington, Roger. 1987. J-Schools Should Encourage Higher Education Writers. *Journalism Educator* 39(1):11–12.

This chapter was initiated by Schoenfeld. Collaborator was Molen.

CHAPTER 6

Entertainment and recreation

PUBLIC ISSUES in the arena of entertainment and recreation—the leisure beats—are receiving increased news media attention and resources. We have more leisure time than ever before, and audience interest in leisure pursuits has multiplied, so public issues underlying what we see in the theater or in our parks, or what we do with our free time, are important items on news agenda today (Peterson 1982).

For example, arts and architecture critic Beth Dunlop of the *Miami Herald* teamed with five other *Herald* reporters in looking at the vitality of the cultural life of south Florida in an era of severe economic constraints on arts funding. Noting the region's attractiveness as a vacation center and its strength as a banking and commerce center, as well as its reputation as a major drug and crime center, Dunlop said the region "hasn't developed a cultural life that in any way compares to the sophistication and diversity of its people." But, the team of reporters said, the potential was there. Their lengthy report in a Sunday "Lively Arts" section assessed that potential and the obstacles preventing its realization.

The reporters analyzed and evaluated the status of the Florida Philharmonic, the Metropolitan Museum and Art Center, the Players State Theater, the plans for and development of new performing arts centers in Dade, Broward, and Palm Beach Counties (the major south Florida population centers), the Cultural Center (home of the Center for Fine Arts, the South Florida Historical Museum, and the Metro Dade Public Library), and other activities in the region. Development and maintenance of these institutions, they wrote, would depend on money, and they noted "a great deal of uncertainty over the financing of the arts."

The reporters conducted dozens of interviews with arts program administrators, artists, financiers, attorneys, and other civic leaders. Almost two full pages of analysis reached a conclusion pointing to leadership as the significant "glue" that would hold south Florida cultural life together in the years ahead. "The prospects for the development of a flourishing cultural life are exciting, not gloomy," the article stated. "The leadership is committed; the puzzle pieces are just waiting to be put in place."

For the reader unfamiliar with the arts in south Florida, the story was informative. For those knowledgeable of the arts, it was a gold mine of analysis. As a result of efforts such as that by the team at the *Herald,* those concerned about the continued growth of the arts knew what had to be done.

The background: work versus leisure

American society seems to be moving in two distinct directions. First, there is a rising percentage of individuals who are working more and more hours per week (Blinkhorn 1990). But second, and more important, the percentage of underemployed and unemployed individuals has increased. "The point," researcher Thomas Kando has said, "is that those persons who have increasing free time on their hands are involuntarily retired, poor, unskilled, chronically unemployed, as well as a volunteer leisure class. Thus, there is a growing category of people committed to leisure, as well as a growing minority of persons who, of their own volition, work increasingly hard" (Kando 1980).

In an article on work and leisure, *Milwaukee Journal* reporter Lois Blinkhorn noted that the definition of leisure has changed from being free time to do what you *want* to do, to time to do what you *should* do, such as exercise or attending to parents or children (Blinkhorn 1990). Researchers have found that the motivations for leisure activities include the desire to improve physical well-being, self-image, and self-esteem, and to maintain emotional balance; and the need for identity, sense of community, learning, social integration, and a means of compensation for voids in other aspects of life. To attain these goals, people do certain things with their leisure time that raise issues for a journalist. At least six areas of questions relate to your leisure issues reporting (Neulinger 1974):

IDEAS. What is your town's idea of leisure? How do residents of your community use their own time? What are their work patterns? What is the government's concept of leisure as exemplified by its policy?

TYPES. What are the prevailing community types, or approaches, to leisure? What are the different philosophies about leisure time usage and activities in your community?

PRACTICES. How do your community's residents spend their personal funds on public leisure activities? How do they spend their time? What do people think, feel, and do about leisure?

PRIORITIES. How are priorities developed? What are the conditions leading to decisions? What role does government policy toward recreation play in community decisions? What role do private sector business policies play?

PROBLEMS. What are the different leisure needs of different sectors of the community? What is government doing to serve the whole community?

PROMOTIONS. What are the best ways of promoting good use of leisure time? What is the role of government in promoting it? How can more leisure time be made available? You probably see the potential here for improving the social welfare of the community. How does a journalist interpret this social issue, particularly in areas in which leisure activity is such a major part of the economy?

Interpreting entertainment and the arts: issues and strategies

As public issues reporters who investigate and interpret issues related to the arts and entertainment, we must first learn what those issues are. How does a community view the arts and its expenditures on the arts, on facilities, and on the general cultural life of the community?

INTERPRETING AMERICAN CULTURE

Once upon a time the arts-and-entertainment beat was exclusively the province of the "reviewer" who wrote critical essays for the divertissement of aficionados. Today, however, issues of public policy permeate the field of the arts and entertainment, calling for sophisticated interpretation on the part of reporters with a grasp of ethics and economics quite as much as esthetics.

EARL BRALY. 1984. *American Culture Revisited.* Palo Alto, Calif.: Palo Alto Press.

Financial support of public programs

In an era when the prevailing government attitude is for private support of the arts as well as of other public forms of entertainment, uncertainty is growing about public arts and entertainment programs and their sources of financial support in this decade. Controversy has arisen over public funding for artistic expression that some segments of the public might find offensive, such as art that depicts homosexuality or desecration of patriotic symbols. Efforts to reduce federal support of the national endowments for the arts and humanities have already had a far-reaching impact. Local programs are scurrying for alternative sources of income to replace grants that no longer will come from the federal government. As you might suspect, there is a domino effect. Once funding is cut and sources become limited, programs accordingly cut back on their offerings to the public. Plans for new facilities are delayed or dropped. Expansion is halted. Yet, as many communities have begun to realize, funding in the future may come from combinations of public and private funding through coalitions and combinations of groups interested in paying the price for art and entertainment.

Marketing the arts for that all-important financial support raises issues itself. A paradoxical attitude toward finance seems to exist among arts administrators. While they call for more funding to meet rising costs, they are unwilling to charge appropriate fees. While they acknowledge more promotion is needed, they generally refuse to allocate funds for such promotion. They often seek more government funding, but want more independence. They want independence, but they also want more public involvement and support. Management of the arts poses many problems, and most administrators face at least four challenges in marketing the arts: (1) the need to stimulate greater attendance; (2) the need to develop a loyal audience; (3) the need to develop long-term support; and (4) the need to raise funds (Mokwa, Dawson, and Prieve 1980).

Public and private facilities

Since the cultural boom of the early 1960s, many communities have spent millions of dollars for splendid new cultural centers for their citizens. Cities of all sizes, such as Atlanta, Dallas, Miami, and Madison, Wisconsin, have recognized the need to provide homes for their operas, symphonies, theater groups, dance groups, film festivals, and other art forms. We have watched many cities renovate old sites, mansions, and other large structures into centers for the arts. Existing cultural centers have been modernized, enlarged, and generally improved for the public interest.

Financing for these facilities comes from a combination of sources. None seems to be able to manage alone these days. Public financing comes from budgets in federal, state, and local governments. Many times several levels of government combine funds for a major project. But with tighter public budgets in the 1980s, managers developing new cultural centers are looking more toward the private sector for additional funds. The private sector includes corporate donors such as Exxon and such as Mellon, Rockefeller or Ford, and the contributions of smaller companies on the local level.

Combined funding of the many programs involving the arts and public entertainment has led to these massive new complexes for our leisure time. And, of course, we have combined resources, with the public programs working with private facilities to generate new offerings for our citizens to enjoy. Operation and maintenance of these facilities—whether they be a complex of buildings or one renovated old theater in a small town—represent a major effort as well.

Here is a checklist of tough issues on which you will report in the years ahead:

- Who manages facilities and at what cost?
- Should these facilities be available to private entrepreneurs?
- Should facilities be financially self-sustaining?
- Should new facilities be built when existing facilities may be modified or renovated?
- Should the city administer the facility or employ an outside specialist?
- What proportions of the community's resources should be devoted to such public facilities?
- Who should set management policies for such facilities?
- How should profits from such facilities be used?
- How should deficits from such facilities be subsidized?

What price art and entertainment?

We have emphasized the importance of funding issues in the arts in the years ahead. More and more news media are beginning to look into the financial state of local and regional arts and ask the question, "What price art?"

This is precisely what Diane Goldsmith, *Atlanta Journal* reporter, did for the "Arts and Entertainment" section of a combined Sunday edition of the *Atlanta Constitution* and the *Atlanta Journal*.

Goldsmith told her readers that art would not remain in the metropolitan Atlanta area unless residents of the area were willing to pay a high price for it. In her lead story, she wrote: "If you're not convinced, just check the figures below, which represent an average performance by the Atlanta Symphony, Ballet, and Civic Opera. What about revenue from ticket sales? It barely makes a dent in the total" (Goldsmith 1981).

Her reporting included figures provided by the symphony, the civic opera, and the ballet. She explicated the high cost of maintaining these programs for the community. Her report demonstrated that only 13 percent of the cost of a production was covered by ticket sales.

Methods for cutting costs were analyzed in her story as well. She quoted the executives of the symphony, ballet, and opera companies. She reviewed budgets and reproduced them on the front page of the section as itemized tables for the reader to study, complete with amounts for each item and percentages of the total budget.

And she looked at alternative means of funding for the arts. She told her audience that the Atlanta Arts Alliance was helping to pay the debts. For example, she explained that a public fund-raising campaign by the alliance provided one-fifth of the needed funding for the symphony. She also pointed out that other fund-raising campaigns, corporate support, and other private sources all support the arts in Atlanta.

She concluded:

> Most important, though, productions of such high quality merit playing to full houses. Atlantans must vote with their feet. With subscriptions for the symphony master season up 10 percent over last year, the balance sheet portends well for the hometown band. Similarly, the gods seem to be smiling over the Atlanta Ballet, which opened to a sold-out house just four days before American Ballet Theater splashed into town. But the opera's production of "Black Widow" played only to a half-full house for the second performance.
>
> If you love the Met when it comes to town each May, isn't our own opera company doubly precious?

Because so much of the future of the arts is dependent upon its financial successes and failures, and because much of this funding is still public in nature, here is a checklist of emerging issues:
- Appropriation of tax dollars to support production of the arts
- Appropriations for new public arts facilities
- Use of public funds for arts educational programs
- Welfare economics and public subsidies to the arts
- Management of the arts: public or private?
- Funding priorities within the arts: which is the "best" art to fund?
- Taking risks in the arts: gambling with public money
- The arts in small communities and rural areas

- Obstacles to appreciation of the arts by the public
- Sharp budget cutting at the expense of the arts
- Coordination of resource solicitation, marketing
- Marketing the arts
- Mismanagement and fraud in the arts
- National administrative structure and management of the arts
- Resource allocation within the arts
- The arts and international affairs: a propaganda tool?
- Organizing on the local level
- Reassessments of need in the arts
- What the government knows about itself and the arts
- Increasing education of pupils in the arts, developing new artists

Some news media actively participate in voluntary campaigns in support of the arts, sometimes by incorporating "mobilizing" information in their news columns. For example, in covering a drive to raise money for the Montana Institute of the Arts Foundation, Christine Meyers (1983) of the *Billings Gazette* concluded a story with the note that "contributions may be sent to Box 1456, Billings, 59103." Her lead was also of the booster variety:

A successful statewide fund-raising campaign has secured a permanent home and gallery for the Montana Institute of the Arts Foundation.

The non-profit arts advocacy organization and its 55-piece art collection will be housed in the old Billings News building at 2405 Montana, in the heart of the city's historic district.

Selection of a Billings home is a coup for the area, according to MIAF members who explain that the choice was based on Billings' position as corporate and transportation center for the Big Sky Country.

The MIAF worked within a budget of $125,000 to secure the building. Of that amount, $85,000 has been raised.

Grass roots culture

Although the arts events that attract mass attention usually occur in major urban settings, covering the arts means keeping an eye on the rural settings as well.

For example, the rise of art colonies in the hinterlands is a current phenomenon rating investigation and interpretation. Reporter Tim Behrens (1983) and photographer Chris Pietsch did investigate the phenomenon by going to Sandpoint, Idaho, where "artists have found sanctuary for creative minds. For both transplanted and native artists, the valleys and mountains provide a stimulating background." Why Sandpoint?

"The Bitterroot and Selkirk ranges," the author explains, "awe with an overbearing presence. Hunting, fishing, and boating provide the antithesis of a mechanized society . . . yet the long winters and short growing season have kept land values low, speculators sparse. The healing and creative atmosphere is fast becoming legend." The artists' love affair with northern Idaho rated a full page in the Spokane, Washington's, *Spokesman-Review.*

Small towns sometimes devote major efforts to promoting the arts. Reporter Gary Peterson (1983) of the Madison, Wisconsin, *Capital Times,* went to a nearby small community to report on grass-roots theater in action:

> In August, the dancers gather on the village green.
> It is the time to Tell in New Glarus.
> Each year since 1938, the people of New Glarus have performed Johan Christoph Friedrich von Schiller's drama, "Wilhelm Tell."
> The play is staged three times on Labor Day weekend in an open clearing on the Tell Grounds east of the village, just off County W. The English version is given on Saturday and Monday; the original German, on Sunday.
> Not only are numerous actors involved in the production—there are duo English and German casts—but also many dancers.
> The Swiss Miss Dancers (second through fourth grade girls), the Wedding Dancers (seventh and eighth graders) and the Usherettes (high school age) all perform before or during the play. Most school age New Glarus children are given the chance to appear in the play either as peasant children in crowd scenes or as choirboys. Seemingly, few in this small southwestern Wisconsin village are left untouched by Schiller's pageant honoring Swiss independence, one of the roots of Western democracy.

A basic issue related to grass-roots culture involves the continuing role that local governments will play in funding cultural programs in the remaining years of the century. How many valuable tax dollars can be devoted to public leisure when, many argue, there is not enough budgeted for basic services? There are many other public issues to consider. Here is a checklist of just some grass-roots entertainment issues:
- Government support of leisure programs for the public
- Government funding of community film programs
- Public television and local programming priorities
- Community theater programs subsidized by local government
- Community cable television content and capacities
- Community development and maintenance of television and radio facilities
- Levels of demand for such public services versus expenditures
- Planning priorities in popular cultural areas of public activity
- Public use of private facilities versus development of public facilities

Interpreting outdoor recreation: issues and strategies

By any measure, today's rush to the great outdoors is staggering. If you add up all the reported visits to parks, forests, wildlife refuges, and other recreation areas in 1985, the total number of visitors exceeds the population of the United States. Even charging entrance fees at more national parks has failed to slow the growth in the number of visitors (Latane 1988). This phenomenon is the result of shorter workweeks, higher wages, an increasingly younger population, a decline of the work ethic, and relatively cheap transportation. Only the end of inexpensive transportation will keep outdoor recreation demand curves from going off the charts.

How to cover outdoor recreation

The media cover outdoor recreation from a variety of perspectives. One way is to devote "how to do it" or "how to get there" columns to each type of recreation. Another way to cover outdoor recreation is to view it as a form of industry. Where tourism contributes significantly to a region's economy, the news media pay a good deal of attention to the ups and downs of various businesses catering to outdoor recreationists. A third way is to view outdoor recreation as a form of impact on the environment — ecological or esthetic — and cover the topic from that perspective, recognizing that the various forms of outdoor recreation popular today are producing intractable environmental impacts. Outdoor recreation can also be covered from the viewpoint of types of recreation areas and the agencies that manage them. Different types of areas include high-density areas,

A MAJOR LEISURE BEAT

Outdoor recreation permeates every segment of our society, and it is a vital part of the lifestyle of most Americans. Over three-fourths of the U.S. people regularly participate in some form of outdoor recreation, and they spend about $250 million per year in its pursuit. . . . There is a critical need to better define and coordinate desirable roles by the private sector and by local, state, and federal agencies.

H. KEN CORDELL and JOHN C. HENDEE. 1982. *Renewable Resources Recreation in the United States.* Washington, D.C. American Forestry Association.

which are intensively developed, general areas, which are substantially developed, natural environment areas, unique natural areas, primitive areas, and historic and cultural sites. In general, private enterprise and municipal governments manage the first two types, state governments the intermediate types, and the federal government manages the latter types, which include national parks, forests, and refuges.

Public policy issues in outdoor recreation

We often take our natural resources for granted. In terms of public outdoor recreational and leisure facilities and their management for the future, there are at least seven categories of public issues and policies that involve outdoor recreation. Consider current public policy issues directly concerned with outdoor recreation as outlined by Marion Clawson and Jack Knetsch (1985):

DEMAND FOR OUTDOOR RECREATION. Should we seek to supply any amount of outdoor recreation that is suggested as likely to be in demand? How in fact do we measure demand? How far must demands for other services and goods be reconciled with the demands for outdoor recreation when they compete for use of natural resources, capital, labor, or management? How far should government at any level stimulate use by provision of free or nearly free outdoor recreation areas? If public agencies persist in pricing park and recreation areas at comparatively low levels, and at the same time, legislative bodies refuse to provide sufficient public revenues, how can the available supply of outdoor recreation best be rationed among the demands for it? How far should the nation go to meet the demand for outdoor recreation of its lower income and otherwise disadvantaged social groups? Will parks and recreation areas be made equally available to minority groups as part of the national effort to eliminate discrimination? To what extent should the whole burden be shifted to private enterprise? These are all major policy issues, with deep emotional, economic, and social roots, as well as with serious practical implications for recreation programs everywhere.

FACT COLLECTION AND RESEARCH. How can we build a factual foundation for recreation planning and management? What level of government should be primarily responsible for this foundation? Should it be the responsibility of recreation operating agencies, of specialized recreation research agencies, of universities, or of others? Are we prepared to pay the costs of gathering pertinent data and making necessary analyses?

RECREATION PLANNING. If reasonable economies are to be achieved in future park and outdoor recreation programs, there must be careful planning, but how do you get a comprehensive, coordinated approach on the part of all the government units and private organizations involved without winding up with centralized control?

RESOURCE ALLOCATION. How much of our natural resources are we prepared to allocate to outdoor recreation? For example, how much will increased camping interfere with timber growth and harvest in a forest? Or to what extent must timber growth and harvest be modified to reduce interference with outdoor recreation? And what will it cost in terms of lumber for housing?

PROPER ROLE OF GOVERNMENT. Government at some levels may play one or more roles in the general field of outdoor recreation; it may act as researcher, planner, financier, resource manager, activity manager, or director, among other roles. In practice, these roles are frequently intermingled and even confused, particularly among levels of government.

PUBLIC USE OF PRIVATELY OWNED LAND. There is a vastly larger area of privately owned land than of publicly owned land in this country, and much of it could be used for recreation, but how can the public use of private land for recreation best be encouraged, and what problems will be encountered in doing so? For example, should hunters have a right to expect hunting on private land to be free of charge? Public aid to private landowners may be an inexpensive way to provide additional recreation opportunity as well as to help solve the income problems of some individuals.

PROTECTING ENVIRONMENTAL QUALITY. For an environmental impact to be judged acceptable or unacceptable, we have to have a base from which to evaluate environmental changes. What if we pick the year 1852 and its environment as a base? Obviously, human intrusions for recreational purposes have had a deleterious effect on the American landscape since then. But what about 1952? Have we gone backward or forward in recent decades? To answer that question, we have to decide whether we are evaluating the overall national environment or local or regional situations. For example, the buildup of second-home cottages may have degraded the pristine beauty of a Minnesota lake, but the total impact of shoreland development on the environment of that state as a whole may have been relatively minor. But, you ask, what do you mean by "relatively?" Well, compared to the ditching, dredging, and draining for agricultural and municipal purposes that have decimated some 90 percent of Minnesota's wetlands since 1852, the impact of shoreland developments on the landscape is minor.

In assessing the impact of outdoor recreation on the environment, it is also important to ask whether we are evaluating the direct, or the indirect, impact. For example, it is hard to imagine that swimming in an area could have any direct impact, but if you consider how many natural fish-spawning beds are buried under the sand blankets of artificially created swimming beaches, then you would have to question whether swimming really is benign.

The impact of recreational development on one area—Northern Wisconsin—was shown in two major stories in one edition of the *St. Paul Pioneer Press Dispatch*. One article (Olson 1988) reported that the wakes from powerboats and water skiers were threatening the nesting area of lake loons. The public issue is whether powerboaters and water birds can share small lakes or should legislation ban such boats from smaller lakes.

The other story (Kerr 1988) reported on the impact of the Lake Superior sailing explosion on the town of Bayfield, Wisconsin. Fifteen thousand sailors enjoy the area's waters each summer and more than four hundred boats berth there. Only 2 percent of the boats are locally owned. While reporter Scott Kerr found local merchants welcoming the business, local residents saw the area being turned into a "yachtie playground."

But there is another side to the story of the impact of recreation on the environment: some of it is positively constructive. For example, political pressure on the part of picnickers, campers, hikers, and sightseers has created a demand for more and better public parks. Without that pressure, priceless natural resources would not have been preserved.

PAYING FOR PUBLIC OUTDOOR RECREATION. The most actively debated policy issues about recreation relate to the best way to pay for it. Public recreation cannot be truly free; some very real costs are incurred, and they must be met in some way. When the total volume of outdoor recreation was much smaller, much of the use was supplied at relatively low cost as a byproduct of public land management, and the issue of how recreation was to be financed was less acute. Now, however, the issue cannot be avoided. In the final analysis, the major policy issue is the degree to which users of outdoor recreation shall pay for it individually and directly as they use it. The alternative is to raise the necessary revenues collectively by general or special taxes. Perhaps as important as whether to levy a user charge is the question of how to do it.

It is difficult to see any of these issues in isolation. Sociologist Max Kaplan, who has examined the basis of leisure activities in our society, says they are all interrelated. "It is impossible to split the economic from the social, political, and technical; we deal with whole systems to see these relationships," he writes (Kaplan 1975). Dealing with leisure activities will require a journalist to understand these relationships.

Travel and tourism

You have no doubt read the travel and vacation section of your local newspaper. Most major newspapers have substantial travel sections. Researchers Neil Cheek and William Burch provide evidence that travel to visit friends and relatives is the leading adult leisure activity over a yearly period, noting that 93 percent of adults engage in this activity at least once in a given year. Driving for pleasure was rated second (76 percent) along with boating, swimming, and picnicking. Also highly rated were out-of-town visits to parks (52 percent) plus fishing, camping, hiking, and hunting (34 percent). Many areas depend on travel and tourism for their primary economic base. Without it, they might not have the revenue to provide the quality of life residents seek (Cheek and Burch 1984).

Weekend and vacation travel is a major leisure activity. The increase in the number of holidays, both official and unofficial, has contributed to its popularity, as has the growth in amount and frequency of vacation time allotted by employers. Foreign travel is increasing, not only among Americans traveling abroad, but among foreign tourists visiting the United States as well. Midwest American cities like Milwaukee and Kansas City that rarely saw a foreign tourist a few years ago are now welcoming them in record numbers (Bluhm 1988). Most of the tourist industry is privately funded, even large leisure complexes such as Disneyworld in central Florida or the Astrodome-Astroworld complex in Houston. Still, states, cities, and even small communities are vitally concerned with promoting tourism and travel and eagerly seek the revenue they can bring. Just some of the 1988 summer efforts to draw tourists to smaller communities include:

Amherst, Massachusetts held a "Teddy Bear Rally" and attracted fifty thousand teddy bears and their owners.
Springfield, Ohio's annual Baseball Card Show brought thousands of dealers and fans from across the country.
The West Virginia hamlet of Jane Lewis got five thousand chili-lovers to its Eleventh Annual West Virginia Hillbilly Chili Cookout.
Indianola, Iowa, hosted two hundred hot air balloonists—and thousands of spectators—at the United States National Hot Air Balloon Championships.

Each of these events and thousands of others can form the basis for a public issues story. Government involvement is almost always present, often in promoting the event, always in handling the traffic and other problems that crowds of people always generate. This is shown by some of the public issues that accompanied the 1988 summer tourist season.

WRITING THE RAILS

One type of tourist attraction that is growing in popularity is a ride on a restored old-time passenger train pulled through the countryside by a snorting, whistling steam locomotive. Usually found in rural areas, these new old-fangled railroads can help the local economy by attracting people who are curious, nostalgic, or just out for fun.

After a rejuvenated steam train began operating over the 65 miles from Williams, Ariz., to the South Rim of the Grand Canyon, reporter Jayne Clark found that the "Grand Canyon Railway" has an even more basic function—providing transportation. Park officials, she found out, are amenable to the train service since it promises to relieve traffic congestion in Grand Canyon National Park, by as much as 300 cars a day.

The automobile, her story notes, was responsible for dooming rail passenger service to the park, which operated from 1902 to 1968. People preferred to travel by car. What does the steam train have to offer in the 1990s? Clark states:

> The train is not for those in a hurry. It hits a top speed of about 35 mph and spends two hours and 45 minutes chugging to the canyon. A car can cover the same ground in slightly more than an hour. Judging from early response, however, many travelers regard the ride as part of the canyon experience.

Demand for tickets has been high, she reports, and the railroad company has plans to expand its service to the Grand Canyon airport, building a train depot there.

—JAYNE CLARKE. 1990. Grand Canyon Train Back on Tracks.
Los Angeles Daily News, June 10, T1.

Maine rock concerts brought in lots of revenue to boost faltering small-town economies, but crowds disturbed the quiet life-style that the local people enjoyed (Donnelly 1988).

Cape Cod's scenic beauties attracted huge weekend crowds that overwhelmed roads and other facilities (Longcope 1988).

New York's lake and ocean visitors ran into the growing environmental problems of the nation when pollution closed beaches at the height of the tourist season (Brown 1988a, 1988b).

Northern Virginia visitors and residents alike found getting in a game of golf can mean a long wait and a hefty greens fee because of urban encroachment on available open space (Malone 1988).

Oshkosh, Wisconsin, had traffic problems on the ground and overhead when its Experimental Aircraft Association convention brought 775,000 visitors, many flying their own planes (Martin 1988).

Any reporter can see a story, even a public issue story, in these events. The public issue journalist must look underneath the physical attractions, the events and even the immediate problems and find the long-term public issues related to travel and tourism. These long-term issues can be placed in five categories:

NATURAL RESOURCES. These include water, climate, and other natural and man-made features. Reporters should look at how these are used, their potential for use, and their limitations. This is a category that merits continuing surveillance by reporters.

SERVICE STRUCTURE. This category consists of the necessary parts of a tourism enterprise, such as the water supplies, sanitation systems, utilities, and transportation (including everything from highways to parking lots).

TRANSPORTATION AND TRANSPORTATION EQUIPMENT. Automobiles, trains, and buses, as well as related facilities, are all a part of this category.

SUPERSTRUCTURE. This includes all aboveground facilities, such as hotels, terminals, restaurants, shops, and museums.

HOSPITALITY RESOURCES. Special events and activities which arise from the social and cultural backgrounds and traditions of an area and its residents may appeal to visitors.

As reporter you will see these public issues in terms of the following specific concerns related to affairs of government and the people. What are these specific concerns?

- Growth of tourism in developed areas

- Limitations of development in ecologically fragile areas
- Public support, development, and promotion of tourism
- Basic objectives of the travel and tourism industry in a community
- Consumption of energy and other resources for travel
- Planning of undeveloped areas
- Public sector and private sector cooperation in development
- The need for major entertainment complexes versus smaller, decentralized centers for travel and tourism
- Development of regional travel and tourism

Spectator and participant sports: some public issues

Until recently, most of our leisure time devoted to sports seems to have been devoted to spectator sports—at least that is the impression we would get from media coverage of sports. But such is far from the case. While the sports sections of our newspapers have only recently increased their attention to the participant sports, Americans have always been active in participant sports as a major, leisure activity. As noted earlier, outdoor activities are among the most popular adult leisure activities. While watching a sporting event is also rated highly by adults (49 percent do so at least once a year), more adults would rather participate in a sport than watch it (Cheek and Burch 1984). And many find the time to do both. With two major league baseball teams nearby, Wisconsin residents are avid fans of the Milwaukee Brewers and the Minnesota Twins. But the state also has the Home Talent League, the nation's oldest and biggest amateur baseball league. The thirty-nine teams involve hundreds of players and attract thousands of fans each week of the season (Hopkins 1988).

A public affairs reporter should be aware of numerous public and private issues in the area of sports and athletics. These include matters of equality of the sexes and the races, of the handicapped and nonhandicapped, of the married and the unmarried, of the organized groups and the unorganized groups, and so on. There are also issues related to public support and regulation of professional and amateur athletes. There are financial issues related to sports, such as ticket taxes, public funding of sports facilities, and even liability for injuries in sports activities.

Journalism professor John Stevens and Sports Illustrated senior writer Craig Neff both see sportswriters devoting little attention to serious public issues. Stevens (1987) says the "middle-class bias of newspapers" is most apparent in the sports pages. He points out that rodeos, bowling, professional wrestling and stock car racing are rarely covered despite their huge blue-collar followings. Neff (1987) cites steroid use, grade fixing for college athletes, and the shortage of minority and women sportswriters as issues that are usually ignored by sportswriters.

There are signs that things are changing. For example, financial relations between professional sports and government is a major public issue because huge sums of money are involved. That is apparent in Milwaukee, where the Milwaukee Brewers and Green Bay Packers play home games in thirty-five-year-old Milwaukee County Stadium. Both teams want a more modern stadium. Under a proposal that looked simple enough, the Brewers would build and own the stadium and the county would provide the land and build the freeway access. But other financial questions are involved. As one sportswriter pointed out, they involved rental fees, concessions, parking, and even the number of private boxes at the new facility. Obviously, Milwaukee believes it benefits greatly from having major league sports teams and wants to keep them. But the financial arrangement is clearly a public issue and deserves continued scrutiny from journalists (Lea 1988).

As the sports scene involves more and more public issues, the sportswriter has to be able to interpret them. The advertisement on page 171, by the *News-Gazette* of Champaign, Illinois, indicates the type of sports reporters that editors want.

Journalists should keep in mind that although thousands are sports spectators, thousands are also participants in community sports. Many more issues could be included in a checklist of both spectator and participant sports. Here are a few:

- A citizen's right to participate in public programs
- Expenditure of public monies for organized sports programs, equipment, and facilities
- Federal and state funding of athletic programs
- Equal spending of public monies for programs for women and other minority sports groups
- Eligibility and availability of athletics programs in public schools
- Conduct and organization of public regulatory agencies in sports
- Government's relationships with private sports enterprise
- Construction of sports complexes for professional sports teams in urban areas
- Public liability for sports injuries
- Creation and maintenance of facilities for participant sports in communities
- Gambling and sports
- Legalized gambling
- Sports as big business: professionalization and commercialization
- Violence in sports, participant and spectator injury, property damage
- Reduction and retrenchment of public schools' sports programs

---

POSITION AVAILABLE: SPORTSWRITER

(March 1985)

Position involves coverage of area high school and college sports and other athletic events, and requires the ability to produce tight, bright copy on deadline and interpretive, in-depth coverage of issues and trends. *Position requires initiative, energy and the ability* to conceptualize in-depth stories.

At least two years of daily newspaper sportswriting preferred.

SALARY: $273.20 to $522 per week, depending on experience

SEND RESUME, WORK SAMPLES, REFERENCES TO:

Paul Walsh

Night Sports Editor

The News-Gazette

15 Main St.

Champaign, Ill. 61820

EDITOR & PUBLISHER. 1985. vol. 118, no. 16: (April): 50.

- Uses of public sports revenues
- Increasing participation of public in recreational sports programs
- Provision of parks and other participant sports facilities
- Adult participant sports programs development and maintenance
- Increasing costs of all sports programs for public budgets
- Public spending on sports versus other spending priorities
- Monetary exploitation in sports of athletes and facilities

Bill Gjebre (1983), a reporter for the afternoon *Miami News,* took a look at the condition of the public recreation program in the city of Miami. He produced a story that told readers the recreation program was in bad shape and that it needed to be completely reorganized. He interviewed the city's chief administrator, the city manager, to find out what measures were planned to strengthen the recreation program. His most useful source, however, was a report released by the city's Operations Analysis Division. Here is Gjebre's lead as it appeared in the *Miami News:*

> Miami's Recreation Department is in bad shape—from top management to drooping tennis nets—and will undergo a "comprehensive reorganization," City Manager Howard Gary says.
>
> "We need to make improvements," said Gary yesterday, in the wake of a blistering report on the department by the city's Operations Analysis Division (OAD).
>
> The report, undertaken at Gary's request, found the following deficiencies in the operation of the department, which runs the city's parks, tennis courts, swimming pools, golf course, boxing gyms and various other recreation centers:
>
> Lack of management direction and control.
>
> Ineffective communication among employees.
>
> Improper assignment of responsibilities to several staff members.
>
> "Unsatisfactory" condition of some recreation facilities and equipment.
>
> Lack of an inventory control system.
>
> Lack of coordination with Parks Department personnel.

The story shows how public issues reporters are getting more and more involved in stories about the issues underlying participation sports.

Key sources for entertainment and recreation reporters

The general news media will tell you what is happening in entertainment and recreation. To anticipate important developments that may become public issues, the reporter must use more specialized sources.

Specialized media

This is an age of specialized publication for all ages and interests. The entertainment industry has dozens of publications which generate numerous, excellent story ideas for reporters who wish to modify their approaches to their own situations. Music-industry publications such as *Billboard* and *Cash Box* are good examples. Recommended technical publications in the arts include: *Communication Arts, Design, Daedalus, American Artist, High Fidelity, Stereo Review, Music Educators Journal,* and *Opera News.* General circulation publications in arts and entertainment include: *Arts Magazine, Art in America, Rolling Stone, Performing Arts,* and *Film Comment.*

In the area of recreation, there are literally hundreds of publications for individuals interested in specific recreational activities such as travel, sports, hobbies, and continuing adult education. We recommend only a few in each area here. Examples in travel and tourism include regional publications such as *Southern Living, Sunset, Arizona Highways, Holiday,* and *Travel and Leisure.* Countless other publications, such as airline publications, automobile association publications, and various tourist guides, also specialize in travel. Sports publications are flourishing. More than one publication is available for each sport. For example, in golf, there is *Golf Magazine, Golf Digest,* and a dozen more. In tennis, *Tennis Illustrated, World Tennis,* and *Tennis.* Persons interested in the major issues and story ideas concerning outdoor recreational activity should check *Camping Journal, Boating,* or *Sail.* Hobbyists are also in good company with hundreds of publications to suit their interests. Reporters seeking information on specific activities need only to consult the general circulation section of a recent edition of the *Gale Directory* for listings.

The general circulation news media — daily newspapers, weekly newspapers, and magazines — are also good sources of ideas. Coverage of arts and entertainment is growing, and in some publications it rivals the emphasis placed on sports and other recreational activities. Other publications, such as those from newspapers across the state or from other states, always generate sound story ideas.

Government agencies

A reporter seeking a leisure beat story may find sources in any branch of the government at just about any level. Just as you have seen in other areas, various administrative agencies within the executive branch are good starting points. Certainly, the legislative branches are worth considering, since legislation affecting the arts and recreation originates and becomes law there.

At the federal level, the National Endowment for the Arts is the major agency controlling funding for the arts and is an excellent source of information about financing, grants, and development. Similarly, the National Endowment for the Humanities operates to provide federal funding for the arts on local levels. Another source is the Federal Council on the Arts and Humanities, which acts as the advisory board of the two endowments. Parallel groups and agencies operate in various states, but clearly with less financial clout than the federal agencies. With funding shifts from the public to the private sector, however, government sources may be less useful in the years ahead.

For sports and other recreational activities, federal sources generally lie in the Department of the Interior, which controls parks and land use. There is little help to be found in the federal government on sports in general, although there are hearings before Congress on topics related to sports. Much sports and recreation information from the government will be available at local government levels, primarily through parks departments, school systems, and local legislative bodies.

It is difficult to generalize about sources for the reporter covering recreation as a public policy issue. There is little uniformity among the echelons of government with respect to who is concerned with the matter at what level. At the municipal level, there will probably be a city park commission and superintendent, but it is unlikely that either will have a broad perspective on outdoor recreation other than of those activities taking place in urban parks. At the county level, there is likely to be a parks director and a county board and parks committee, but neither will have comprehensive data. In some states, most outdoor recreation programs and activities will be centralized in a department of natural resources or some similar department, but in other states, the responsibilities will be divided among several bureaus. Where federal recreation lands are concerned, only the individual park, forest, or refuge administrators can serve as sources of some data.

The best source of comprehensive recreation data in a particular state is likely to be an office in the cooperative extension service of the state land grant university, or the academic department of parks and outdoor recreation management at the university. Some state park programs and various recreation societies have official publications. It may also be profitable to talk to staff members of key state legislators, or to legislators, county board members, and city councilpersons themselves.

The private sector

With support for the leisure activities moving from government to private sources, the importance of these sources is underlined. Today, you must be more sensitive to the issues and financial needs of the arts and their relationships with sources of private funding. Larger and larger amounts of dollars are needed from private contributions to make budgets balance, either on a public funds matching basis or as outright donations. Private sector sources of information include corporations (such as the Corporate Fund for the Performing Arts at the Kennedy Center, or corporations such as Exxon and IBM), foundations (such as the Ford, Rockefeller, and Mellon Foundations), and, of course, personal contributions solicited on the local level.

Much information on recreation is also available from private sources.

Countless sports organizations exist at all levels and provide important information to reporters. Professional sports maintain league and team offices, and there are major amateur sports organizations as well. The National Collegiate Athletic Association (NCAA), the Amateur Athletic Union (AAU), the United States Olympic Committee (USOC), the National Association of Intercollegiate Athletics (NAIA), and other groups serve as umbrella organizations for athletes competing in an organized fashion in dozens of sports, all at the amateur level. General participant sports maintain professional and amateur groups as well. In golf, for instance, the Professional Golfers Association (PGA) and the United States Golf Association (USGA) are two examples. Of course, there are national organizations for specific sports, such as the Little League, and local subdivisions which are good sources for information. In general, these groups are available in your community and at the regional and national levels. A local contact can provide information on regional and national sources as well.

Case study: interpreting convoluted entertainment-recreation issues

Increasingly, entertainment-recreation issues involve taxpayer monies. The *Loveland* (Colorado) *Daily Reporter-Herald* ran into a controversy involving funding the city's lake. Reporter Dave Downey (1983a) led off a long series with this anticipatory story:

> Area residents may see their recreational privileges on Lake Loveland go down the drain unless the city is able to reach a new rental agreement with the lake's owner. The agreement expired at the end of 1982 and the Greeley-Loveland Irrigation Co., which owns the lake, has given Loveland city officials until March 1 to reach a new agreement.
>
> The company has offered the city two alternatives: purchase the surface use rights outright for $400,000; or enter into a 10-year lease at $25,000 a year for the first five years, and $35,000 for the next five years—a total of $300,000 for the 10 years.
>
> The Loveland City Council will discuss the proposals at its special work session Monday at 5:30 p.m. in the council chambers.
>
> The city had a 10-year agreement in effect through 1981 which cost the city $2,500 annually in rental fees. Then, in 1982, the city paid a one-year $7,500 fee as the agreement was extended for one year to allow for continued discussions on another long-term contract.
>
> Gary Havener, parks and recreation director, said acceptance of either of the Greeley-based company's offers would greatly increase the cost to city taxpayers of having recreational privileges at the lake. "I think it's

going to boil down to an economic question: Can we afford the money? If we can't, we might lose the right to swim there," he said.

Downey and the *Reporter-Herald* then covered practically nonstop meetings of the city council, culminating in "a counter offer by the city to purchase the surface recreational rights on Lake Loveland outright for $50,000 or enter into a 10-year–lease-purchase agreement at $7,500 a year"—an offer the Greeley-Loveland Irrigation Company turned down flat.

As negotiations continued to drag on Downey (1983b) asked the question that was on everybody's minds—how could a lake in the middle of a city be controlled by private parties? He explained the answer in a background story: a hundred years ago there was no controversy over the price for recreational privileges on Lake Loveland.

Lake Loveland didn't even exist then, except in the minds of the directors of the Greeley-Loveland Irrigation Company who dreamed of turning a swampy, natural depression into a 12,000 acre-foot agricultural irrigation reservoir. Their vision became a reality in 1894.

When the snowmelt runoff came gushing into the newly built facility in the spring of 1895 via the rebuilt Barnes ditch, the water level of little Hays Lake in the bottom of the depression was increased by 40 feet to form Lake Loveland—then a half-mile north of the town.

Today, the city completely surrounds the lake which has become a popular recreational area. The city of Loveland is presently in the process of negotiating a long-term contract with Greeley-Loveland for continued access to the recreational privileges the reservoir provides.

In the first years of Lake Loveland's existence, cattle grazed along its banks. The beautiful homes on the lakefront today weren't there. Neither were the summer crowds of recreation enthusiasts.

In fact, it wasn't until 1954—after the first houses were built on the lake when the Foote Addition went in on the lake's southeast side in the late 1940s—that there was any agreement at all between the irrigation company and city for recreational privileges.

"Before then there just wasn't anybody around the lake," noted Ron Brinkman, secretary-treasurer for the Greeley-based irrigation firm. "I don't think there was much recreation out there (before the Foote Addition was constructed)."

The first lease agreement gave the city the rights for boating, swimming, fishing, hunting, ice skating, camping, picnicking, ice boating and other recreational privileges for five years, Brinkman said. There was no dollar amount attached, he said, but only the requirement that the city provide safety patrol and carry adequate accident liability insurance.

The first agreement expired in June of 1959. "The other leases were all patterned after it," Brinkman said.

When the Irrigation Company announced "there will be no recreational privilege on Lake Loveland this summer—not for the general public nor for the 109 homeowners around the lake," reporters Downey and Greg Pornula went looking for public reactions. Here's what they found: The decision by Greeley-Loveland Irrigation Co. to ban boating, water skiing and swimming on Lake Loveland this summer has brought a mixed reaction from those around the Loveland community.

Some are extremely upset and say the irrigation company has been very unfair in negotiations with the city for a new lease, or purchase, for access to the lake's surface. Yet others think the Loveland City Council could have given a bit more in the negotiations.

State and county recreation officials predict only little, if even noticeable, impact on the volume of boating and swimming at other area lakes. Realtors predict little, if any, impact on the property values of homes fronting the lake.

In an interview with a retired judge and lakeshore resident, the *Reporter-Herald* uncovered an interesting angle—without a recreational agreement, the city could not be sued if an accident, such as a drowning, occurred.

In the continuing saga, lakefront homeowners eventually worked out a deal with the irrigation company to purchase lake recreational rights for $400,000 and permanent easements to the waterline. In turn, the city worked out a deal with a newly formed Loveland Lake Recreation Club (the homeowners) to trade two boat ramps on Lake Loveland for public swimming privileges at a designated beach.

In the best traditions of public affairs reporting, the *Reporter-Herald* had gone out of its way not only to provide blow-by-blow coverage of key meetings but also to provide historical perspective, reaction from residents, and details on continuing informal negotiations. The series won an Inland Daily Press Association Award.

In summary

Working on the entertainment and recreation beats does not mean just reviewing the latest album or film; nor does it mean just knowing where parks are located or just checking out the local fairs, festivals, and tourist attractions. Important public issues affecting entertainment and recreation are developing daily. Frequently financial and environmental issues clash at the community level.

For example, the 1988 Experimental Aircraft Association convention crowded the Oshkosh, Wisconsin, area with 775,000 visitors, but they contributed an estimated $65 million to the local economy (Martin 1988). Some of Maine's small towns were disturbed by the rock concerts, but the summer fans spent thousands in each of them (Donnelly 1988). Meanwhile, Cape Cod's summer roads may be crowded at times, but the Cape's were narrower and less well maintained before the tourist dollars came (Longcope 1988).

We must also report the underlying relationship of government to entertainment and to public outdoor and indoor recreation. Government officials are very aware that good recreation opportunities can bring new industries as well as visitors to their area. Even a hint that a major league team may move to another city can bring major government reaction. The trade of a single sports star, Canadian hockey player Wayne Gretzky, to a Los Angeles team was considered a major economic event (Allen 1988). Government involvement can be buried in such mundane concerns as concessions fees and parking facilities (Rinard 1988). It is the job of the public issues journalist to find and report on all the public issues involved.

Journalists cannot simply provide readers with an entertainment calendar or schedule of games and be satisfied that they are adequately covering the beats of entertainment and recreation. There is much, much more.

References

Allen, Kevin. 1988. Gretzky's Trade Fills Other Pockets. *USA Today,* Aug. 12, 2C.

Behrens, Tim. 1983. A Haven in North Idaho: Sanctury Provides Balm to Soothe Artists' Soul. *Spokane* (Washington) *Spokesman-Review,* Aug. 7, E-10.

Blinkhorn, Lois, 1990. What Leisure? *Milwaukee Journal,* July 15, G1.

Bluhm, Donald A. 1988. High Tide of Foreign Visitors to US Sweeps Into View. *Milwaukee Journal.* Aug. 7, H1.

Brown, Phil. 1988a. Lake George Beach Closed-Bacteria in Water. *Times Union* (Albany, NY), July 23, B1.

————. 1988b. Long Island-Harbor is Suspect in Shore Debris. *Times Union* (Albany, NY), July 23, B1.

Cheek, Neil H., Jr., and Burch, William R., Jr. 1984. *The Social Organization of Leisure in Human Society.* 2d ed. New York: Harper and Row.

Clawson, Marion and Knetsch, Jack. 1985. *Outdoor Recreation.* 2d ed. Baltimore: Johns Hopkins Univ.

Donnelly, John. 1988. Maine Villagers Beset by Rock Concertgoers. *Boston Globe,* July 17, 59.

Downey, Dave. 1983a. Owner Could Pull Plug on Lake Loveland Pact. *Loveland* (Colorado) *Daily Reporter-Herald,* Feb. 19, 1.

Downey, Dave. 1983b. New Long-Term Contract Sought: Nobody Made Waves Over Lake Rights Until 1954. *Loveland* (Colorado) *Daily Reporter-Herald,* April 2, 3.

Dunlop, Beth. 1981. Turning Point for the Arts. *Miami Herald,* Oct. 11, 1L, 12L.

Gjebre, Bill. 1983. Report Scores City Recreation Department. *Miami News,* July 7, A2.

Goldsmith, Diane. 1981. What Price Art? *Atlanta Constitution and Journal,* Nov. 21, E1.

Hopkins, Steve. 1988. For 60 Years League Has Been a Big Hit. (Madison) *Wisconsin State Journal,* Aug. 21, A1.

Kando, Thomas M. 1980. Leisure and Popular Culture in Transition. 2d ed. St. Louis: C.V. Mosby.

Kaplan, Max. 1975. *Leisure: Theory and Policy.* New York: John Wiley.

Kerr, Scott. 1988. Bayfield Changing as Sailboating Booms. *St. Paul* (Minnesota) *Pioneer Press Dispatch,* July 17, B1.

Latane, Lawrence. 1988. National Park Fees Haven't Hurt Growth. *Richmond Times-Dispatch,* July 31, C1.

Lea, Bud. 1988. Packers Are Committed to Playing in Milwaukee. *Milwaukee Sentinel,* Aug. 18, Part 2, p. 1.

Longcope, Kay. 1988. Partying Poses Problems — Cape Town Eyes Options After a Raucous Fourth. *Boston Globe,* July 17, 59.

Malone, Roger. 1988. Country Clubs Cash In. *Arlington* (VA) *Journal,* July 28, 1.

Martin, Chuck. 1988. Event's Participants Pump Millions Into State. *Milwaukee Journal,* July 31, D1.

Mokwa, Michael P., Dawson, William M. and Prieve, E. Arthur (eds.). 1980. *Marketing the Arts.* New York: Praeger.

Myers, Christine. 1983. Art Foundation Needs More Help. *Billings* (Montana) *Gazette,* June 23, A3.

Neff, Craig. 1987. Portrait of the Sportswriter as a Young Man. *Gannett Center Journal* 1(2):47–55.

Neulinger, John. 1974. *The Psychology of Leisure: Research Approaches to the Study of Leisure.* Springfield, IL: Charles C. Thomas.

Olson, Kathy. 1988. Vigilance of 'Loon Lady' Helps Save Placid's Birds. *St. Paul* (Minnesota) *Pioneer Press Dispatch,* July 17, 1988, B1.

Peterson, Gary. 1983. New Glarus Folks Become Actors For 45th Return of Wilhelm Tell. *Capital Times* (Madison, WI.), Aug. 18, 6–7.

Peterson, Richard A. 1982. Measuring Culture, Leisure, and Time Use. In Vol. 3 of *Mass Communication Yearbook,* edited by D. Charles Whitney and Ellen Wartella. Beverly Hills, CA: Sage.

Rinard, Amy. 1988. Talks Begin on Sale of Parking Structure to Bradley Center. *Milwaukee Sentinel,* Aug. 13, 1.

Stevens, John. 1987. The Rise of the Sports Page. *Gannett Center Journal* 1(2):1–11.

This chapter was initiated by Garrison. Collaborator was Schoenfeld.

3

Covering social conditions

In a sense, all the issue areas covered in this book represent social conditions, but in Part 3 we are reserving the term for important societal affairs that do not fall neatly into the other chapters of the book.

It is tragic that a constant social condition is crime, but it is a crucial public issue to cover. The emphasis in Chapter 7, "Crime and Justice," is on reporting and newswriting with the whole picture in mind, not as fragmentary, isolated accounts of discrete events.

Problems of social welfare are everywhere. Some are unique to particular communities or regions; others are universal. Some are so blatant that they thrust themselves on public attention; others exist just below the level of community perception until enterprising reporters make them public issues. Some give rise to vigorous, sustained social movements; others attract only ephemeral interest. Some social problems provoke government programs and legal sanctions; others are the concern largely of private organizations. In

Chapter 8, "Social Issues," we take a look at various representative social problems. Investigating and interpreting such problems in a comprehensive, sensitive manner is one of the most difficult tasks facing you as a public affairs reporter.

A growing but still somewhat neglected form of covering social conditions is the subject of Chapter 9, "Consumer Affairs." Everybody is a consumer, and the issues and problems facing today's consumers can make up a specialized beat, although it has overtones, of course, of covering governmental affairs and of covering business and the economy. As a consumer affairs reporter you may operate under some real or imagined constraints—the indifferent track records of regulatory agencies and consumer activist groups, pressures from your advertising manager, consumers who don't seem to want to be protected, your editor's allergy to libel. How to accommodate these constraints and do a constructive job of aiding consumer protection is a rewarding challenge for public affairs reporters.

CHAPTER 7

Crime and justice

LAW ENFORCEMENT WORK and reporting have some common elements. Both deal with society's problems and both rely upon observation and interviews to obtain information. The similarities end with the way the information is used. For the law enforcement officer, the objective is the protection of society through apprehension of criminals and prevention of criminal acts. For the reporter, the task is to inform the public of what is happening, what is being done about it, and how well it is being done. Neither law enforcement officers nor reporters are uniformly successful in achieving their goals.

In fact, criminologist Alan J. Butler believes that the burden upon the law officer is exacerbated by unrealistic public expectations. The officer is "supposed to solve the problems of society that have developed over hundreds of years, formed by forces of national consequence over which he has no control, and insoluble by politicians, professors and pundits" (Butler 1976). If Butler is right, the media must bear some responsibility for contributing to those unrealistic public expectations.

Butler's conclusion suggests some questions about mass media coverage of crime: Does media concentration upon major sensational crimes distort the public view of the extent of crime? Is media coverage fragmented, incomplete, and, as a sociologist contends, ignorant of "the sociohistorical circumstances surrounding the event?" The answers will vary from city to city, from medium to medium, and from case to case, but the assertion that most crime reporting is one-dimensional is indisputable.

Issue-oriented reporting pops up sporadically, most often on subjects such as child or spouse abuse and drug trafficking. In-depth treatment of crime issues is still, however, the exception. Coverage generally is typified by single-event reporting similar to this news lead:

A Kenosha woman's finger was slashed by a knife-wielding man who

DRUGS HIT SMALL TOWNS TOO

Drugs and drug-related crime are not only the province of inner-city police and federal drug enforcement agents, as one crime reporter found out:

Just as worship services were about to begin at a Methodist church one recent summer, the church music director was summoned to the pastor's office. There she learned that her 28-year old daughter had been arrested that August morning in a drug bust in which 27 other people were charged.

"This skirmish in the nation's war on drugs was fought not on an inner-city street or steel-barred crackhouse, but in a small town amid the romantic scenery of the rolling Wisconsin countryside," James Rowen wrote in leading off a four-part 1990 *Milwaukee Journal* series on "Drugs in Dairyland."

Rowen interviewed dozens of police officers, counselors, and local residents in 19 villages and towns in nine counties in south-central and western Wisconsin to find that "drugs in most forms are easily available in rural Wisconsin," and that "part of the problem is too few officiers with too large an area to cover."

JAMES ROWEN. Drugs in Dairyland. *Milwaukee Journal,* January 7, 1990.

took her purse in an incident at 10:45 P.M. Wednesday (*Kenosha News* 1988).

This kind of factual approach to hard news events is essential, but it does not obviate the need for more thorough exploration of the larger issues.

Complicating the media responsibility to provide information about crime are people's attitudes. The public displays an ambivalence toward crime news that gives rise to a perennial issue: do the media carry too much crime news? The accusation that they do surfaces frequently, usually after some particularly shocking crime. The criticisms often suggest a cause and effect relationship between crime news and crime: a potential criminal reads or hears or views a news story and is motivated to commit a similar crime.

Research has yet to establish evidence of a direct link, but the charge is difficult to either prove or disprove (Einsiedel et al. 1984).

Whatever the contradiction that makes crime news both repelling and fascinating to the audience, the media cannot ignore it. Despite assertions that the media sensationalize crime news to cater to the basest public appetite, the need for information is real, if only to alert people psychologically and physically for self-protection.

Background

The pervasiveness of crime and the many forms it takes make almost every reporter a crime writer at times. Just as crime spills into every layer of society, so it transcends the lines that delineate traditional reporting beats. This makes it imperative that you understand the operation of all agencies involved in law enforcement. It is also important that you learn about the nature of hard-to-detect "white-collar" crime, which can have such an impact on a community.

Who covers crime?

At some time in their careers, most reporters write about some sort of crime. They may cover illegal campaign financing, rape, grocery coupon frauds, terrorism, tax evasion, child abuse, and any other of a number of offenses. In general, these forays into crime writing constitute a thin slice of a reporter's duties.

Consider the lead paragraphs of a McClatchy News Service story (Avery 1983) from June 22, 1983:

SACRAMENTO—State Controller Kenneth Cory and Gilbert W. Chilton, former chairman of the State Teachers Retirement System, engineered a $50 million loan from the teachers pension fund last September to finance a shaky Texas oil drilling scheme operated by a convicted oil securities swindler. Chilton has since abandoned his family in Fresno and disappeared, the oil investment seems to have gone sour, and investigations have been launched by the state attorney general and the Federal Bureau of Investigation.

The unprecedented loan that went to TXPACCO, Inc., of Denver could mean the loss of up to $11 million that was invested in behalf of 354,000 active and retired public school teachers in California, state officials told The Bee. While such a loss poses no danger to the remainder of STRS' $10 billion investments portfolio, it has proved to be extremely embarrassing.

Cory, in an interview Tuesday, defended the loan and said he still believes it is a wise investment that will not lose any money for the pension fund.

The main story and several sidebars were the work of three reporters, none of whom was assigned to a police beat. Jim Lewis was a legislative reporter for the state capitol bureau of the *Sacramento Bee;* Jim Boren was a political reporter for the *Fresno Bee;* and Paul Avery was a metro staff reporter for the *Sacramento Bee.*

The subject of the story was sensitive, because no charges had been filed, but the public interest warranted thorough coverage by the *Bee* newspapers. Each article was loaded with documentation from public records and statements from interviews that raised questions about the loan procedures and possible wrongdoing by Chilton. Subsequently, a federal grand jury indicted Chilton on charges of criminal fraud.

This type of story does not pop up in routine police coverage; rather, such stories can be encountered in almost any area of reporting. For a police reporter, the news is more likely to fit into more traditional categories of crime. Only the police reporter finds crime the dominant part of an assignment sheet, and follows intimately and regularly the events in the often seamy world of the lawbreaker.

Law enforcement agencies

Most local crime stories come from the police department, the sheriff's office, and the state highway patrol. These agencies are closest to the public, the most visible enforcers of the laws, and the most regular sources of news.

In a few metropolitan areas where city and county governments have been merged, the police department is the principal law enforcement unit. For most of the nation, day-to-day policing is shared by police and sheriff's officers, the police handling crimes within the city limits, and the sheriff's office responsible for crimes in rural areas and unincorporated settlements. The role of the state highway patrol varies in different states, although highway traffic usually is its major field of enforcement.

More specialized law enforcement jurisdiction is held by some state and federal agencies, the best known being the Federal Bureau of Investigation (FBI). The FBI is the closest in function to a federal police force of any organization in the United States. FBI jurisdiction includes bank robbery, kidnapping, civil rights violations, subversion, fraud against the United States, and other offenses prohibited by federal law unless they have been assigned specifically to other agencies.

Justice Department guidelines limit the information the FBI is authorized to release, but this is not an onerous handicap since you can obtain the data essential to most crime stories. A greater problem is an FBI policy that puts at least a partial gag upon local FBI agents. Detailed information often must be obtained from regional offices or from the national headquarters in Washington, D.C.

An FBI Uniform Crime Report is issued annually. It offers statistics on seven crimes: murder, rape, robbery, and aggravated assault (crimes against persons) and burglary, theft, and auto theft (crimes against property). The report is helpful both in indicating trends and in providing a peg for a story comparing local with national rates. Some caution is advised in their use, because the statistics cover only reported crimes, and many offenses go unreported. You can supplement the statistics with interviews with local law enforcement officers and crime victims, and turn what could be a dreary recitation of figures into a story with human interest and readable significance.

Some local crime stories will involve other federal agencies, such as the Treasury Department in counterfeiting cases or the Immigration and Naturalization Service (INS) in illegal immigration arrests. The INS is a particularly important news source in seaport cities or in states bordering Canada and Mexico. United States marshals, who are officers of the federal court, can be helpful in providing leads about cases that will be brought before a United States magistrate. Occasionally, the marshals will make news in more direct fashion, as in a 1984 operation in which they teamed with local agencies to locate and arrest more than 2000 fugitives being sought for violent crimes.

More than one hundred federal agencies have some statutory role in crime prevention, but most of them are infrequent news sources because their criminal jurisdictions are narrow.

Each nonlocal agency has its own organizational structure and information policy. When reporters are seeking information, it may be common for field representatives of the agency to pass the buck to someone higher in the chain of command. The same may be true in a local agency, but there, it is easier to reach the highest authority (the police chief in a community, for example) than it is to reach the national or regional director of an agency whose headquarters is hundreds of miles away. An offsetting factor is the possibility that some lower-echelon employee will talk if the reporter promises confidentiality.

Understanding criminal behavior

Accumulating knowledge of criminal motivation and behavior can be fascinating and frustrating because no policy manuals outline precisely why people deviate from society's rules (Wellford 1983). In this century two major studies of crime have been made by presidential commissions — the Wickersham Commission in 1931 (National Commission 1931) and the President's Commission on Law Enforcement and Administration of Justice in 1967. Neither was able to isolate definitively the causes of crime. "No single formula, no single theory, no single generalization can explain the vast range of behavior called crime," the 1967 commission reported (President's Commission 1967).

Theories abound. Some appear to be valid for certain types of crime, but even with a valid theory solutions or remedies are elusive. Nevertheless, reading periodicals and books, talking with authorities, and observing the happenings on the police beat can give you an inkling of probable causes. The literature of criminology, psychology, and sociology teems with articles about deviant behavior. Of special value to journalists are *Police Magazine* and *Corrections,* two magazines that provide solid examples of issue-oriented reporting on the processes of police and correctional work.

In recent years the use of drugs has been used to "explain" criminal behavior. Policies and programs have been proposed to deal with what is seen as a menacing national and international problem, but the scope of the problem and its proposed solutions tend to overwhelm the public.

Jay Merwin of New Hampshire's *Concord Monitor* focused on local people involved with illegal drugs in his community. Merwin found more victims than criminals among small-time drug dealers. He showed Concord's drug problem was part of the social fabric of individuals' lives.

Merwin's "Dealers and the Damage" (1988) report provided the figures on the extent of the drug problem in Concord and in New Hampshire. But Merwin focused on the drug dealers themselves. He found that the small-time dealers, eventually hooked on their own product, usually wound up in jail. He showed his readers the broken promises, lost careers, shattered families, and physical deterioration they shared. One dealer and user even wrote a poem of thanks about being in jail, away from his addiction. The three-story report put an enormous social problem in human terms that Concord readers could understand.

White-collar crime

In one type of crime, virtually every law agency may at times get into the act. This is variously labeled white-collar crime, occupational crime, or corporate crime, depending on how narrowly or how broadly it is perceived. It can encompass such diverse offenses as international bribery, computer-data theft, Medicare fraud, stock scams, on-the-job theft of supplies, and embezzlement.

The computer era has provided new challenges and opportunities for thieves. Corporate security no longer is exemplified by night watchmen. Computer specialists who can devise safeguards to balk thievery by computer are now vital to security.

Because corporate crime is often hidden by a facade of respectability, it is seldom obvious to an outsider. Reporters have difficulty locating incriminating information because much company information is not public. Compounding the problem is the fact that some thefts involve complex bookkeeping schemes or tortuous efforts to launder stolen money, so the trail is difficult to follow.

A crime may continue for years before it is detected. A Merced, California, deputy tax collector systematically stole an estimated $1.7 million in county funds over a twelve-year period before she was arrested. Former Vice-President Spiro Agnew resigned in the face of accusations that he received payoffs from Maryland contractors for at least a decade for favors rendered when Agnew was a Maryland public official. In another case that involved almost a decade, a doctored record of financial success made the Equity Funding Corporation a darling of stock investors until its falsified records were exposed. Twenty-two company officials eventually were convicted of participating in the scheme.

While most business and government officials are honest, the tentacles of white-collar crime have enmeshed enough of them to create a major law enforcement problem. Unless someone privy to the wrongdoing blows the whistle, regular coverage of an office or of an official is not likely to uncover the crime. Most news stories on white-collar crime have developed after inside sources have talked to the press or after a government entity has initiated legal action.

Informants often face a problem in finding someone who will believe their story. Charges of wrongdoing are easily brushed aside as the work of a malcontent or an incompetent. Even if the accuser's credibility is suspect, you should consider the complaints worthy of investigation. It also is wise to treat denials by an accused person or firm with some skepticism. Even claims of innocence by individuals one may admire and respect should be weighed carefully, especially if they are not accompanied by some substantiation of innocence.

Although the amounts of money involved in white-collar crime often are astronomically higher than the amounts involved in more common crimes, sociologists Marshall B. Clinard and Peter C. Yeager contend that " 'crime in the streets' generally receives more attention than 'crime in the suites' " (Clinard and Yeager 1980). One reason may be that white-collar crime rarely is a cause for fear, unless one values property above life and physical safety. It is also probably true that a $20 million securities fraud would have less impact on the average person than would a $450 burglary at a neighbor's house. Clinard and Yeager's comment does suggest, however, that the media need to be more alert to trends and effects of white-collar crime.

Investigative reporter Jerry Urhammer (1980) advises reporters to learn to follow the paper trail:

> Every individual in this world, every corporate entity, leaves a paper trail. It starts with a birth certificate; it ends with a death certificate. In between, you have mortgages, real estate deeds, driver licenses, car registrations. Anytime you get into court, you leave a helluva paper trail around. There's a great mass of information out there if you know where to tap into it.

In Florida, a city public works director was indicted by a grand jury for misuse of city equipment and personnel, in part because the *Fort Lauderdale News* and *Sun-Sentinel* followed a paper trail. The newspaper discovered that:

• The public works director maintained a secret business partnership with a lawn service operator who held a $298,000 city contract.

• The director had public works employees do repair work at his home while they were being paid by the city.

• The director had city employees do major engine work on his private camper at a city garage during normal working hours.

The *News* and *Sun-Sentinel* broke the case by investigating rumors of malfeasance in the office of the director. Dan Lovely, an experienced records researcher, dug through department files, page by page, to build up documentary evidence. Beat reporter Rocky Moretti staked out the public works director's home to determine whether city workers were indeed doing repairs on city time. The resulting series won an Inland Daily Press Association Award.

Race and crime coverage

An issue that spreads across urban, suburban, and rural boundaries is the complaint from minorities of inadequate police protection, police bias, and distorted media reporting. Criticisms of the media generally follow two lines: (1) that most stories about ethnic groups still deal with crime, particularly when a minority member is a suspect; and (2) that the media often ignore the fact that minorities are more often victims of crime than perpetrators.

Associate Editor Ernie Sotomayor of the Dallas *Times-Herald* points out serious public issues that should be addressed by the crime reporter. On the one hand, minority crime victims get little attention from the news media. At the same time minority members accused of crime get major coverage if the victim is white. Reflecting this, a 1985 *Times-Herald* study found the killers of white people are twice as likely to get the death penalty than the killers of blacks (Sotomayor 1986).

In addition, a bias of neglect has left untouched many important stories about the effects of crime upon minority communities. Coverage frequently has suffered because reporters have not been familiar with and sensitive to minority problems. If you are a member of an ethnic minority, you probably already are aware of stories that have not been covered — but should be. If you are not a member of an ethnic minority, you can still begin working to establish contacts that will help you to acquire a better understanding of a particular group. It may take time and effort to establish your credibility, but the goal is worthwhile.

Officer-reporter relationships

Effective crime reporting is not easy. The subject is an often odious aspect of life. The effects of stories upon the people involved can be long-lived and deleterious, if not ruinous. The relationship between law officers and news reporters is sensitive; an antagonistic situation may constrict the flow of information. You may find that needed reports are not available, or that the officer in charge of an investigation suddenly becomes difficult to find. Failure to realize the problems police officers face in doing their job can make your job tougher.

Conversely, if you are too cozy with the law enforcement agency you risk becoming half police officer, half reporter, and subordinating your news principles to your police loyalties. It is possible to maintain cooperation without sacrificing your professional standards. Cooperation in some circumstances may be justified. But veteran journalist Clark Mollenhoff warns that a reporter should make it clear to law enforcement agents that cooperation "does not insulate them from possible criticism" (Mollenhoff and Raskin 1981).

Situations occasionally warrant coverage that may put a law enforcement agency in an unfavorable light. Overnight, that friendly warmth you have enjoyed with the agency turns into a chill. If you have won an agency's respect for your accurate, fair reporting, the cold-shoulder treatment may pass quickly. The chill may be prolonged if officers previously have developed distrust of your abilities. It will be difficult to get information on the most routine matters.

Police reporter Edna Buchanan of the *Miami Herald,* a 1986 Pulitzer Prize winner for general news reporting, says clashes between police and reporters are inevitable. "When it happens, I do not take complaints to their bosses or mine. . . . It is better, whenever possible, to handle it yourself, person to person. . . . We should be able to work things out without ratting on each other" (Buchanan 1986).

Should you find yourself in a strained situation, put on a tough skin to withstand the barbs and follow your normal reporting procedures until the furor subsides. Remember that the more contacts you have within an agency, the less likely that a curtain of silence will block off all information.

Another danger is getting caught up in the routine and missing a significant public issue. There were lots of newsworthy arrests by sheriff's deputies in Polk County, Florida. But reporters Terrence Tomalin and Tom Arthur noticed that more of them were being made by auxiliary sheriffs. They discovered that many auxiliary sheriffs had little training. Some judges questioned their authority and saw their arrests as illegal. Instead of reporting on crime, Tomalin and Arthur (1986) explored the issue of who should have the authority to enforce the law in their community.

A perennial public issue, of course, is the cost of law enforcement to the taxpayers. Stories critical of these costs regularly come out of community budget hearings. But Matt Bartel and Bill Wilson of the *Newton Kansan* looked behind the political rhetoric and compared costs in various communities. The reporters showed that the city was seriously underfunding its police department. Their prize-winning article also suggested that the result was increased crime (Bartel and Wilson 1987).

Understanding one another

Lack of mutual understanding magnifies the problems reporters and law officers encounter in dealing with one another. A survey of 170 Pennsylvania police chiefs pinpointed this as a source of difficulty. About 42 percent of the survey participants, who represented departments of various sizes, said media knowledge of police procedures was poor or unsatisfactory. But 30 percent also said their own understanding of media practices and policies was also poor or unsatisfactory. "Seventy-one percent said there should be more contact between police and news media," researchers Michael Singletary and Gene Stull reported (1980).

You can understand police practices better by learning the structure of community law enforcement agencies, and by knowing the procedures, the limits of the law, and the constrictions under which officers work. Better understanding of officers' motivations, their problems, and their frustrations will help. Officers' patience is tested regularly in dealing with people, some of whom can be quite nasty. Officers are cursed, spat upon, and sometimes assaulted. In a burst of hyperbole one day, August Vollmer, a colorful police chief in Berkeley, California, put it this way:

> The citizen expects police officers to have the wisdom of Solomon, the courage of David, the strength of Samson, the patience of Job, the leadership of Moses, the kindness of the Good Samaritan, the strategical training of Alexander, the faith of Daniel, the diplomacy of Lincoln, the tolerance of the Carpenter of Nazareth, and finally, an intimate knowledge of every branch of the natural, biological, and social sciences. If he had all these, he might be a good policemen (Tappan 1960).

Access to information

Since laws allow law enforcement agencies to withhold some facts about ongoing investigations, gaining access to information can become particularly troublesome. If an agency already is inclined toward withholding information, the laws will make it easier to justify the practice.

The ease of access varies in different communities, although the chief administrators of local law enforcement agencies ordinarily try to keep some control over what is released. Ideally, an agency always will have someone available who has the authority to release information, but the ideal is not always achieved. More than one official has found it expedient to sidestep freedom of information requirements.

The size of the law enforcement unit has some bearing upon its information policies. Large departments may have a full-time public relations officer. Medium-sized units may simply give public relations liaison duties to someone on a part-time basis. In a small town, the police chief may keep control of information in his or her own hands; in some hamlets, the constable may be the sole agent of law enforcement and the sole source of news.

Access to daily reports is crucial to effective reporting. In local agencies, these reports usually include a blotter or complaint sheet that sketchily notes all calls received during a twenty-four-hour period, an arrest sheet, and investigative reports that provide more detail on cases.

The federal Public Records Act and most state Freedom of Information acts allow agencies to withhold investigatory records on current or pending criminal investigations. Investigatory records legally can be withheld if their release is likely to interfere with an investigation, deprive a person of the right to a fair trial, create an unwarranted invasion of privacy, reveal the identity of a police informant, disclose investigative techniques, or endanger law enforcement personnel. Whether the blotter or complaint sheet falls within that exemption is not always clear. You should check your state laws and state legal opinions related to access.

Even when withholding documents is legal, many agencies will make the information available to you if they respect your integrity. It is helpful to know what investigations are being carried out and what progress is being made, although the price for the knowledge may be an agreement to sit temporarily on the information. A request to hold a story may be justified if publication would jeopardize the arrest of suspects. If the requests occur too frequently, or too indiscriminately, however, you will have to weigh the question of whether the compromises are being made only on your side.

In Sheridan, Wyoming, several years ago, the *Press* turned a conflict over restrictive police information practices into an educational forum for the police and the public. *Press* reporters dug up examples of the impact of restricted information on community life. A thorough roundup of police information procedures around the state showed the situation in Sheridan to be aberrant. Despite its obvious professional concern over the principles at stake, the *Press* gave Sheridan police and court officials attention and space to comment. Throughout the coverage, the emphasis was on showing how the public was affected by government restrictions on information. The series won the *Press* a first place award from the Inland Daily Press Association.

The issue of brutality

One long-standing issue that can generate friction between police and the press is a charge of police brutality. The point at which justifiable force in subduing a prisoner becomes unjustified brutality is often blurred, and the police version may be authoritative, but incomplete or distorted.

Complaints of civil rights violations involving brutality are investigated by the United States Department of Justice, but it may take months before an investigation is concluded. You need not wait that long. Many agencies conduct their own investigations through internal affairs procedures, and you can follow the progress. You can also check previous records to determine whether there have been earlier cases of injuries during arrest. You can track down people who may have knowledge of the immediate complaint. If enough accusations of unnecessary force are found and some substantiation turns up, you have a news story.

Charges of brutality are not always well founded, and sometimes they are politically motivated, but you should always check them thoroughly. You also ought to keep an eye on law enforcement programs in community relations to determine their effectiveness in reducing citizen alienation from officers. This can be done without necessarily arousing hostility (Mollenhoff 1981).

Tracking down injustice

The tip that newsman Mike Masterson received in the mail from an Arkansas state prison was intriguing. It was also twenty-four years old. A white prison inmate wrote of having seen two officers in civilian clothes beating a young black man in the Conway, Arkansas, jail in 1960. The convict had written similar letters to the presiding judge in the county, the prosecuting attorney, the FBI, other officials, and at least one other newspaper. Only the letter to Masterson brought results; the others apparently did not take it seriously.

"It was one of those things that struck me as odd," Masterson (1985) recalled later. This was not the usual letter from a prison inmate proclaiming his innocence. This was from a man who apparently wanted to seek justice on behalf of a person he probably had never known. Masterson's instinct was that this claim should be investigated.

In 1960, Marvin Williams, a twenty-one-year-old, black ex-paratrooper, then a painter for a bus manufacturing company, was arrested by Conway police as he sat in his car outside a restaurant. The next morning he was found dead in his cell.

A hastily impaneled, all-white coroner's jury was convened the following day. The two arresting officers told them that Williams, whom they described as being stuporously drunk, fell and hit his forehead on the steps while being taken to jail. The jurors, without waiting for the formal results of an autopsy performed on the previous day, ruled that Williams's death had not resulted from foul play by police.

In June 1984—twenty-four years after the incident—Masterson began searching for records and witnesses. The yellowed news reports in the Conway newspaper were sketchy, the minutes of the inquest and the autopsy report were missing, and the death certificate was incomplete and studded with errors. (The autopsy report was later found at a Conway funeral home. The minutes of the inquest turned up when Masterson was nearly two months into the investigation.)

In late July 1984, Masterson's first article (1984) on the incident ran in the *Arkansas Democrat* of Little Rock. The lead paragraph went as follows:

> CONWAY—An *Arkansas Democrat* investigation into a case closed last month by the FBI has turned up evidence that a young black man died of a bludgeoning rather than from a fall while in the Faulkner County Jail 24 years ago.

The story then detailed Masterson's findings. The autopsy report was especially revealing. It showed that Williams had suffered a major skull fracture behind the left ear, although the officers had testified that he had fallen forward, striking the front of his head and causing a minor bruise and laceration. The autopsy also showed that Williams's blood had tested negative for alcohol content, refuting the claims that Williams had been drunk.

Masterson also talked with people who had known Williams or who had been with him the night of his arrest. His companions attested that Williams had not been drinking and was anxious to get home because he had to be at work at 7:00 A.M. Masterson also found that Williams had been the valedictorian of his high school graduating class, had a good reputation, and was a member of a reputable family.

A Freedom of Information Act request for the FBI files on the case brought results. The files revealed that an informant had tipped the agency the day after Williams's death that the young man had been beaten and that authorities were trying to cover up the circumstances. The FBI conducted a limited investigation and forwarded the results to Washington. Apparently, nothing further was done until June 1984 when the FBI regional office in Little Rock received the letter from the inmate, then routinely declared the case closed once again.

The investigation by the *Democrat,* however, raised enough questions to warrant an official reexamination of the case. Masterson wrote more than twenty-five stories, leading to the governor's order for a special grand jury investigation. In early 1985 the grand jury returned indictments charging the two arresting officers with first-degree murder.

Masterson's fight against injustice brought him the Heywood Broun Award of the Newspaper Guild for outstanding reporting on social issues. Masterson also received the $250 Paul Tobenking Award from the Graduate School of Journalism at Columbia University. He used the $250 award to establish a scholarship in Menifee in Williams's name.

While the Williams case was one of unusual flaws and even injustice in our legal system, it is not unique. Within one month recently, two men were freed from American prisons after rulings that they had been convicted by mistake. A Milwaukee, Wisconsin, man had served eight years of a sixty-year sentence for rape when a new technique for analyzing sperm and blood stains on clothing proved he had been convicted by mistake. In Oakland, California, a man who had served nine years of a sentence for two murders was released after new evidence led the attorney who had prosecuted him originally to believe the man had not committed the murders.

These cases show that the legal system makes errors that on rare occasions a reporter can remedy. Much more important, however, is for the reporter to realize that bad journalism can contribute to these errors. Special care is mandatory in writing crime stories, because people's reputations, safety, freedom, and even their lives can be affected by careless and inaccurate reporting. Journalists also must be cautious of the rights of crime victims and be aware of the mounting criticism of their exploitation by the news media (Seymour 1986).

While it is generally true that an arrest suggests that some evidence has made a person suspect, the arrest process is not perfect. As the Associated Press (1986) repeatedly warns its reporters, you should be cautious about premature conclusions of guilt when an individual is accused, arrested, or even indicted in a criminal case.

The psychology of fear

One effect of crime, the kindling of fear, is to some degree a byproduct of selective media coverage. When the front page of a newspaper contains two or three stories of violent crimes or the evening newscast opens with a succession of four or five crime stories, the audience may decide there is a crime wave. They will be even more convinced if the news report itself labels the series of offenses a crime wave.

If police perceive that the media are interested in a certain type of crime, they are likely to bring more such instances to the attention of reporters. Thus, several stories of crimes against the elderly can stimulate police reports on others. Public officials are then likely to perceive crime against the elderly as a developing public issue. Their comments to the news media further add to the elderly's fear of crime (Scheingold 1984).

A team of Arizona State University sociologists, after a year-long survey of crime coverage and its effects in Phoenix, concluded that people become more fearful when the newspapers tell them that crime is getting worse (Baker et al. 1983). A New Orleans study of newspaper and television coverage of crime produced a similar result. The research team found that "the public gains a sense of increasing crime, not by summing the cases about which it hears or reads, but by noting the stories of increases presented by the media" (Sheley and Ashkins 1981).

Yet national data suggest that the average person in the United States is unlikely to be a victim of a serious crime in any given year. Political scientists George E. Antunes and Patricia A. Hurley (1977) contend that public concern about crime is heightened by media emphasis upon murders, rapes, and spectacular armed robberies, "while the more routine, mundane and frequent crimes of larceny, burglary, assault and auto theft" receive scant, if any, coverage.

DISTORTION ON THE CRIME FRONT

In 1981, Los Angeles was in the grip of a crime wave — or was it?

David Johnson, who covers the politics of the Los Angeles Police Department for the *Los Angeles Times,* contends that people received a skewed view of the crime scene because of media overemphasis on violent crimes, especially by area television stations. An analysis of crime statistics was needed to put the situation in perspective. Johnson explained it this way:

The relentless recitation of stories on mayhem and murder was great for ratings. But not for improving viewers' understanding of the world around them. . . .

There was no crime wave, even though the phrase was routinely used by both electronic and print reporters in the Southland [Southern California]. I even used it once in a lead.

The only "crime wave" was because of the theft of automobile stereo sound systems, especially the theft of Blaupunkt radios from BMWs. They were up 16.8 percent. But when *reported* car burglaries and thefts from vehicles — called "car clout" crimes by cops — were excluded from the police statistics on *reported* major crimes in Los Angeles, major crime was actually down almost 1 percent. . . .

Car clouting and murder are not the same in nature, their threat to society, or their indication of the nature of street crime. But when police chiefs issue their crime figures, they often emphasize the total number of *reported* crimes. When dealing with major crime totals, a stolen Blaupunkt counts exactly the same as a cold-blooded murder — one.

Excerpted from feed/back. 1983. California Journalism Review. Winter.

What to know about the law

The First Amendment to the Constitution is the keystone to American press rights, and every reporter should know it, in addition to knowing how the United States Supreme Court interprets it. In law enforcement reporting, you should also be familiar with the Constitutional amendments that pertain to the administration of justice. These are the Fourth Amendment, which prohibits unreasonable searches; Fifth Amendment, which prohibits self-incrimination; Sixth Amendment, which gives the right to trial by an impartial jury; Eighth Amendment, which prohibits cruel and unusual punishment; Tenth Amendment, which delineates federal and state jurisdiction; and the Fourteenth Amendment, which grants equal rights to all citizens of the United States.

Reporters should also be familiar with legal principles such as the due process to which everyone is entitled and the systems of statutory, regulatory, and common law. Introductory textbooks on law, including those on media law, are a good starting point. They usually are available in community libraries or the law libraries that are maintained by county governments in many states. Some state judges' associations or bar associations provide explanatory booklets to help people understand the workings of the court systems. These are particularly good in explaining the system of the state. Once you have acquired a basic knowledge, you can go on to more specialized legal materials such as those most relevant to your reporting interests or responsibilities. You need not know all the statutes that govern crimes, but some crimes are encountered so frequently that you ought to understand the difference between certain terms. A few of the most commonly encountered terms are defined below.

FELONY AND MISDEMEANOR. A felony is a major crime with penalties as severe as death or imprisonment in a penitentiary. A misdemeanor is a minor offense, such as a traffic violation or a petty theft, ordinarily with a maximum punishment of a fine or up to one year in a local jail.

BURGLARY AND ROBBERY. Burglary is breaking into a building to commit a theft or some other felony. Robbery is taking personal property from an individual in his or her presence and against his or her will by force or fear.

SIMPLE ASSAULT AND AGGRAVATED ASSAULT. Simple assault usually is a threat to injure someone without actually doing so. Battery is the actual use of force, so assault and battery commonly refers to a physical beating. Aggravated assault is committed with the intention of carrying out an additional crime or with particularly outrageous violence.

HOMICIDE, MANSLAUGHTER, AND MURDER. Homicide is the killing of one person by another. Manslaughter is an unlawful killing, but without malice. Murder is the killing of another with malice aforethought or premeditation. First-degree murder is a premeditated killing or one committed during a felony. Second-degree murder is one in which a deliberate intent to take a life is lacking.

These are general definitions; the exact legal meanings may vary in different states. Accusing someone of a specific degree of offense before formal charges are filed can be unwise because, for example, a charge that may initially appear to be first-degree murder may end up being manslaughter or even justifiable homicide when all the evidence is in.

Care in word choice

A gray area exists between the time an arrest is made and the time formal charges are filed. Accusations against an individual are damaging enough without being compounded by careless language. An arrested person may never be charged or may be charged with a lesser offense than that presumed to be warranted. In a story about an elderly woman who contended she had lost a large sum in what appeared to be a swindle, a television reporter named a suspect and said indictments were expected momentarily. No indictments were returned and the television station had to broadcast an apology to avoid libel action.

Even the use of a wrong preposition or verb can connote guilt and unfairly besmirch a person's reputation. For example:

John Doe was arrested last night for murder. (It translates as John Doe murdered someone.)
John Doe was seized by police last night in connection with the death of Jane Doe. (This does not directly accuse John Doe of a crime, but suggests he knows something about a crime, an impression heightened by an overly strong verb.)
John Doe is being held for questioning in the slaying of Jane Doe. (This does not accuse John Doe of a crime and does not prematurely call the death a murder.)

The differences are slight but important should you have to defend the wording in court.

The word "alleged" is often used to indicate that an accusation has not been proved. Disagreement exists about its use, however, and some critics argue that it is not a legal defense against libel. Nevertheless, it is a handy term.

You should avoid using the word "confession" to describe a statement given to authorities. It is a powerful word that connotes guilt. The "confession" may turn out to be false or only an admission of a pertinent fact, not of a crime. Many confessions are retracted; others are ruled inadmissible as evidence.

Hints for reporting on crime

1. Double check names and addresses obtained from law enforcement reports. Mistakes are not unknown in police reports. The city directory or the telephone book are common sources for correct spellings.
2. Routine crime stories seldom justify a creative approach. It is better to be direct and simple in style than to be clever, reserving the more personal flair for features, analytical pieces, and the occasional big story.
3. Keep in contact with rank-and-file officers. Friendly relations with them can bring tips that may not be forthcoming from department executives.
4. Do not overlook the story possibilities in noncrime matters. It has been estimated that a police officer spends no more than 25 percent of the workweek on crime-related assignments. The remaining time is spent in such activities as traffic and crowd control, general assistance, and information services.
5. Do not depend upon officers to be totally open with you. Law enforcement work involves extensive secrecy, at least on a temporary basis, and there will be times when the most cooperative officer will withhold information.
6. Be careful not to inflame public fear through overly broad generalizations. Suppose that a reporter interviews two people who have been robbed and beaten in their homes by armed assailants, and that the resultant story tells of fear sweeping the city. Such a conclusion should be based upon more thorough research than was made in this instance.

Enterprise reporting

The millennium in which the world will be free of crime is not in sight, so reporting of antisocial behavior will continue to be a demanding and important job.

A good job of crime reporting requires that you delve beyond the bare facts of law violations and arrests, statistics, policy statements, promotions, and retirements. It requires articles that explore the nature of crime and its far-reaching effects upon a community. These stories need not involve official corruption or wrongdoing. Sheer curiosity and sharp observation should bring to mind innumerable angles that have interest and significance.

The significant issue usually lies behind the crimes that are making the headlines. In 1982 and 1983 an elusive serial killer claimed the lives of forty-six women, most of them teenagers, in an area of high prostitution near Seattle. The murders stopped in January 1984. Instead of leaving the story, reporters Carlton Smith and Tomas Guillen of the *Seattle Times* analyzed all the facts they could gather about the murders. First they found that poor law enforcement policies contributed substantially to the ability of the police to stop the killer. For nearly two years police kept arresting teenage prostitutes in an effort to keep them off the streets and out of danger. The women were quickly released by the courts and simply moved to another area. So did the killer.

The murders finally did stop and prostitution dropped, Smith and Guillen found, when police shifted their focus from the teenage prostitutes and arrested their customers. This, the series suggested, should have been the policy from the start. But the killings could resume, the reporters warned. Five years after the killings began, Smith and Guillen concluded, the Seattle area had no effective program for dealing with teenage prostitutes. In a six-part series, the reporters dealt with the public issues behind the front-page headlines (Smith and Guillen 1987).

Reporters covering crime should always look beyond the crime scene, the police station and even the courtroom. Crime reporter Ted Cilwick of the *Kansas City Times* looked into Missouri's parole system after he found many familiar names on police arrest sheets. It was not easy. Unlike most states, Missouri continued to keep its parole hearings, votes, and key records secret. In addition, Cilwick found records so confused that Missouri's Department of Corrections was not sure how many prisoners were being paroled from state institutions.

Cilwick checked courthouse files around the state and interviewed more than forty judges, prosecutors, legislators, police officers, and crime victims. He found that Missouri prisoners were serving less time before parole and were returning to prison because of new crimes at twice earlier rates. Prisoners with more than a dozen arrests, half a dozen convictions, plus escapes and parole violations on their records were getting paroled. Cilwick's four-part series, "Back On The Street," exposed a parole system that critics called "out of control" (Cilwick 1985).

Overcrowded prisons are a nationwide problem. As judges "get tough" on crime in response to public pressure, the nation's prison systems have to cope with record numbers of inmates (Inman 1988). The public issues involved reach all levels of government. Reporters and editors at the *Eagle-Tribune* of Lawrence, Massachusetts, discovered this in 1987 when a sexual assault story turned into a year-long investigation into state prison furlough policies. The results became an issue in the 1988 presidential campaign.

The story began when an alert *Eagle-Tribune* editor saw something unexpected. Reported arrested in a sexual assault in Maryland was William R. Horton, Jr. In 1975 Horton had been convicted of murdering a Lawrence gas station attendant. The *Eagle-Tribune* editor thought Horton was still serving his life sentence because there had been no report of an escape or a parole.

A year later, after nearly two hundred stories, two young reporters had exposed a furlough system that let convicted murderers out of overcrowded prisons. Susan Forrest and Barbara Walsh did it by doggedly pursuing both public officials and public records. Along the way, they learned how to get a major story when government officials refuse to cooperate. State officials

BUREAUCRACY AT BAY

Reporter Susan Forrest kept calling Massachusetts Correction Commissioner Michael Fair to get his views on the furlough of convicted murderer William Horton. One call was transferred to department spokesperson Mary McGowen. Forrest asked to speak with Commissioner Fair:

McGowen	Forrest
"He is not available."	"Do you know when he will be available?"
"No, I don't."	"Will he be available tomorrow?"
"Nope."	"The day after tomorrow?"
"No."	"Next week?"
"No."	"Will he ever be available for me?"
"No."	

SUSAN FORREST. Massachusetts Prison Chief "Will Never Be Available." *Eagle-Tribune,* April 17, 1987.

"just wanted us to go away," said Walsh (1988). The reporters also had to get lots of background information. "I had no idea of how the prison furlough program worked. I had to learn a lot," said Forrest (1988).

Eagle-Tribune executive editor Dan Warner sensed a major story and committed the resources of the small (circulation 60,000) daily. The refusal of government officials to talk about the furlough system just made the *Eagle-Tribune* staff push harder. "The arrogance of the Department of Corrections was a big part of it," said Walsh (1988).

When Forrest did get to question Massachusetts prison officials about the Horton furlough, she found they "cannot recall specific details about the case" (Forrest 1987a). Forrest fought for Horton's prison records to see if official claims that he was a model prisoner were true. Officials said privacy laws made the records unavailable (Forrest 1988). She asked to talk with Horton's fellow prisoners, but state officials refused. She posed as a murderer's girlfriend and got her interviews on visitor's day. Horton's fellow prisoners told her that he used cocaine and heroin while in prison and even they opposed his furlough (Forrest 1987b). When she could not get through to Governor Dukakis, Forrest staked out his car for five hours.

In four months Forrest wrote more than one hundred articles in the case. She wanted to talk with the Maryland rape victim but police refused to disclose her name. Then one day Forrest received a call from Maryland. The rape victim had heard about the paper's crusade. "I thought nobody cared about us," the woman told Forrest (1988). Forrest went to Maryland. Her story about the brutal treatment of the rape victim and her boyfriend, who had been beaten and slashed repeatedly by Horton, stunned readers (Forrest 1987c). The story earned Forrest the Investigative Journalist of the Year Award from the New England Press Association.

Meanwhile Walsh, who continued working on the story when Forrest left the paper temporarily, tried to get information on Massachusetts's prison furlough policy. State officials insisted it was similar to those in other states. Walsh called twenty-five experts in an attempt to verify this, but got no clear answer. "We decided that we were in this and we would just keep going," said Walsh (1988). She spent a week calling fifty states and found the Massachusetts prison furlough system was very different (Walsh 1987). "It was a rubber stamp policy to help prison officials with their own problems of control and overcrowding," said Walsh (1988).

Editorials, petitions, and legislative hearings were erupting across the state over the prison furlough issue. It was rapidly becoming an issue in the Dukakis presidential campaign (Bidinotto 1988). After months of public pressure, the Massachusetts legislature passed a law prohibiting furloughs for first-degree murderers. Governor Dukakis, still facing what he termed "one of the most crowded prison systems in America" (*Berkshire Eagle*

1988), signed the bill on April 28, 1988. *Eagle-Tribune* reporters and editors had looked behind a tragic crime and found an important public issue before the public. Their year-long series brought the *Eagle-Tribune* the 1987 Pulitzer Prize for General Reporting.

High-crime neighborhoods

An example of enterprise reporting would be a story on high-crime sectors and what makes them that way. Law enforcement agencies in cities generally have data on the incidence of crime in various sections. Sometimes a story about a high-crime area provides the impetus needed to mobilize community action to alleviate the problem.

In a small town, officers may not have statistics to pinpoint centers of trouble, but you should be able to learn where they are by studying crime reports and talking with town officials. Any such story should include reasons why an area is high in crime. Reasons might include quality of housing, income levels, and type of environment. In shabby, deteriorating neighborhoods, crimes against persons may be excessively high; in more affluent areas, crimes against property may be more prevalent. No magic is needed to produce this type of community service reporting, but you have to dig deeper than the police blotter listings to find the more significant stories. The possibilities are endless, and the stories' value to society is incalculable. That value may be more within reach if you write with the whole of the picture in mind, and not just fragmentary, isolated events.

In summary

Crime is one source of a constant flow of news. The newsgathering assignments on almost any newspaper or broadcast station call for regular contacts with law enforcement agencies. But readers have mixed feelings about it. Although they sometimes complain that the media contain too much crime news, they still follow the accounts closely.

For the media, crime constitutes a compelling subject. For a police reporting specialist such as Edna Buchanan, the police beat is never dull. "It is all there: greed, sex, violence, comedy and tragedy," she says. "You will never learn as much about people on any other newspaper beat" (Buchanan 1986).

But crime coverage is more than covering criminal incidents. Criminal activity affects the entire community. That is good reason why reporters should seek the underlying issues. The most effective reporting is done by people who know law enforcement procedures, who understand the patterns of crime, and who keep in mind the impact of crime upon general society.

References

Antunes, George E., and Hurley, Patricia A. 1977. The Representation of Criminal Events in Houston's Two Daily Newspapers. *Journalism Quarterly* 54(4):756–60.

Associated Press. 1986. *Associated Press Stylebook and Libel Manual,* 5, 17, 102.

Avery, Paul, Boren, Jim, and Lewis, Jim. 1983. State Pension Oil Loan Investigated. *Fresno* (CA) *Bee,* June 22, 1A.

Baker, Mary, McCleary, Richard, Nienstedt, Barbara, and O'Neil, Michael J. 1983. The Impact of a Crime Wave: Perceptions, Fear, and Confidence in the Police. *Law and Society Review* 17(2):319–35.

Bartel, Matt, and Wilson, Bill. 1987. *Inlander,* Oct. 25, 9.

Berkshire (MA) *Eagle.* 1988. Crowded State Prisons Pose Tough Problem for Dukakis. July 21, B11.

Bidinotto, Robert James. 1988. Getting Away With Murder. *Reader's Digest* Vol. 133, no. 795 (July):57–63.

Buchanan, Edna. 1986. Advice from One of the Best Police Reporters Around. *The Bulletin of the American Society of Newspaper Editors* 686(April):10–12.

Butler, Alan J. 1976. *The Law Enforcement Process.* Port Washington, NY: Alfred Publishing.

Cilwick, Ted. 1985. Back on the Street. *Kansas City Times,* June 5–8, 1A.

Clinard, Marshall B., and Yeager, Peter C. 1980. *Corporate Crime.* New York: Free Press.

Einsiedel, Edna F., Salamone, Kandice L., and Schneider, Fredrick P. 1984. Crime: Effects of Media Exposure and Personal Experience on Issue Salience. *Journalism Quarterly* 61(1):131–36.

Forrest, Susan. 1987a. No One Recalls Freeing Killer. *Eagle-Tribune* (Lawrence, MA), May 27, 1A.

_____. 1987b. Convicted Killers Say Horton is Giving Them Bad Name. *Eagle-Tribune* (Lawrence, MA), May 13, 1A.

_____. 1987c. How 12 Hours Shattered Two Lives. *Eagle-Tribune,* Aug. 16, 1A.

_____. 1988. Interview, July 20.

Humphries, Drew. 1981. Serious Crime, News Coverage, and Ideology. *Crime & Delinquency* 27(2):191–207.

Inland Daily Press Association. 1982. Sustained Coverage of Public Issues. Annual Contest Program.

Inman, William H. 1988. Leader of Free World Also Leads in Inmates. *Richmond Times-Dispatch,* July 31, 1A.

Johnston, David. 1983. Bureaucrats with Guns. Feed/back, *California Journalism Review* 9(2):22–23.

Kenosha (WI) *News.* 1988. Woman Hurt in Robbery. Aug. 18, 4.

Masterson, Mike. 1984. Inquiry Finds New Facts in Death at Conway Jail. *Arkansas Democrat* (Little Rock), July 25, 1A.

_____. 1985. Personal Correspondence in Author's Files, June 17.

Merwin, Jay. 1988. Dealers and the Damage. *Concord Monitor,* June 28, 1A, 3A.

Mollenhoff, Clark, and Raskin, A. H. 1981. Where Should the Boundary Line Be Drawn? *The Bulletin of the American Society of Newspaper Editors* 641(April):40–41.

National Commission. 1931. *National Commission on Law Observance and Enforcement.* Washington, D.C.: Government Printing Office.

New York Times. 1967. Text of Summary of 18-Month Study Made by a Special Presidential Commission. Feb. 19, 68.

President's Commission. 1967. *The Challenge of Crime in a Free Society.* President's Commission on Law Enforcement and Administration of Justice. Washington, D.C.: Government Printing Office, 12.

Scheingold, Stuart A. 1984. *The Politics of Law and Order.* New York: Longman, 80–82.

Seymour, Ann. 1986. Victim Advocate Suggests Code for Journalists. In *Crime Victims & the News Media,* edited by Tommy Thomason and Anantha Babbili, 31–33. Fort Worth, TX: Fort Worth Star-Telegram.

Sheley, Joseph, and Ashkins, Cindy D. 1981. Crime, Crime News, and Crime Views. *Public Opinion Quarterly* 45(4):492–99.

Singletary, Michael W., and Stull, Gene. 1980. Evaluation of Media By Pennsylvania Police Chiefs. *Journalism Quarterly* 57(4):665–58.

Smith, Carlton, and Guillen, Tomas. 1987. Green River: What Went Wrong? *Seattle Times Special Report,* Sept. 13–18.

Sotomayor, Ernie. 1986. A Victim's Race: Does It Make a Difference? In *Crime Victims & the News Media,* edited by Tommy Thomason and Anantha Babbili, 11–14. Fort Worth, TX: Fort Worth Star-Telegram.

Tappan, Paul W. 1960. *Crime, Justice and Correction.* New York: McGraw-Hill.

Tomalin, Terrence, and Arthur, Tom. 1986. Sheriff's Auxiliary: Too Big, Too Powerful. *Ledger* (Lakeland, FL), May 11, 1.

Urhammer, Jerry. 1980. The Investigative Reporter. Speech at San Joaquin Valley Professional Journalists' Conference. California State Univ., Fresno, Oct. 30.

Walsh, Barbara. 1987. Most States Would Not Have Furloughed Horton; 'Out of the Question,' They Say. *Eagle-Tribune,* Apr. 17, 1A.

———. 1988. Interview, July 20.

Wellford, Charles F. 1983. *Research in Criminal Justice.* Vol. 4 of *Encyclopedia of Crime and Justice.* New York: Free Press, 1375–78.

This chapter was initiated by Molen. Collaborators were Meier and Scotton.

CHAPTER 8

Social issues

THE most challenging, and perhaps the most important, type of public issues reporting is investigating and reporting problems that exist largely below the level of public perception. You cannot assume that these social problems will reveal themselves if you confine your coverage to the usual beats of covering events and the agencies that enforce or create the rules of society.

Poverty, for example, is not illegal, yet it is a social problem of significant scope in virtually all sections of the country. Child abuse is in fact a crime, but only its most serious manifestations reach the formal legal process; much of it is subtle and well hidden, and it is a topic that people are reluctant to admit and discuss openly. Laws have been passed prohibiting racial discrimination in hiring, housing, and so on, but racial discrimination often takes more subtle forms than refusing a person a job because of the color of his or her skin. Even if laws are not broken, discrimination may still exist. Human rights questions, sex discrimination, and all forms of abuse are further examples of social problems that exist, to some extent, outside the formal regulation of the government (Bassis, Gelles, and Levine 1982).

Pervasive problems

While each community is beset with many unique social issues, some general problems will be of concern to all communities. These include civil rights, discrimination, various minority groups, poverty, aging, the "teen syndrome," and others. Each poses certain challenges for reporters.

Civil rights, human rights, and discrimination
The 1960s was a turbulent era in which black Americans asserted their right to equality in the United States. The term civil rights was attached to their efforts, and the movement spread nationwide in that decade. Since

INTERPRETING TRENDS: THE GROWING UNDERCLASS

Faced with the inevitable analysis of trends in social issues in the decade ahead, Wisconsin Associated Press Bureau reporter Joya L. Wesley did a superb job for the state's dailies on Jan. 2, 1990. The text:

Social observers warn Wisconsin's population is aging rapidly, and poverty, crime, and drug abuse will increase in urban centers and spread into suburban and rural areas unless public officials address forthrightly the problems of a growing, ethnically diverse underclass.

But Wesley didn't just write off the top of the head. The perceptive report was based on interviews with such diverse sources as:

A professor of educational policy and community studies at an urban university;

A demographer with the state department of administration;

A professor of rural sociology at a landgrant university;

A professor of communications at a private college;

A volunteer director of a county council on alcoholism and other drug abuse.

The result was an in-depth interpretation of "the time bomb we're sitting on if we don't address the complex needs of this growing underclass."

JOYA L. WESLEY. 1990. Growing Underclass: A Wisconsin Time Bomb. *Oshkosh* (Wisconsin) *Northwestern,* Jan. 2, B1, B4.

then, civil rights have remained a concern of black leaders, but the concept has expanded. Other racial and ethnic minorities, women, homosexuals, the elderly, the handicapped, Vietnam veterans, and other groups with special needs and problems began to assert their claims to equal rights. These movements have caused conflict and tremendous amounts of legislative and social change throughout the country.

The civil rights movement asserted the right of all people to equal treatment in terms of education, employment, housing, and the freedom to enjoy all aspects of American life. Changes that came about were often the result of violent public protest and action; many of the changes came about only after the government passed new regulations outlawing previous practices. The courts, likewise, handed down decisions declaring certain practices, such as separate but equal facilities, unconstitutional. In fact, in the 1960s, the government took an activist role by making such changes as passing the affirmative action laws, which were intended to overcome racial, and, later, age, sex, and religious discrimination in hiring.

The civil rights conflict reached its culmination in the mid-1960s, when riots flared in cities across the country from Los Angeles to Detroit to Newark (Commission on Civil Disorders 1968). The burning, looting, and killing that took place were a sudden reminder that discrimination and racism were indeed very serious problems. After that series of violent outbreaks, many new laws and changes were enacted. But the civil rights battle eventually drifted away from the media spotlight, to be replaced by other concerns — particularly the war in Vietnam. Racism, however, was not completely gone. In 1980, riots broke out in Miami after the police were acquitted of criminal charges in the killing of a black doctor during an arrest attempt. More than thirty people died and millions of dollars worth of damage was done. Suddenly, people were reminded that racial problems were not dead.

Other forms of discrimination had similarly lain unattended by journalists because nothing was happening to bring them to public attention. The plight of women came to the fore in 1978 with the International Women's Year. With attention formally turned to the subject, people became aware of the discrepancy in pay suffered by many women, of inequitable laws that afforded women and men unequal treatment and of many more problems that had existed for years but had never been challenged (Chafe 1977). Even such a sensitive issue as the sexual harassment that many women find on the job is now getting media attention (Jones 1988).

Handicapped people have also suffered from discrimination for many years (Clinard and Meier 1979). Buildings have been physically inaccessible to them, employers have discriminated against them because of their handicaps, and programs to help them overcome their handicaps and become productive citizens have been either limited or nonexistent. Their problems received more media attention in 1982, the International Year of the Handicapped.

What do all of these examples of discrimination have in common? They all existed for many years and were taken for granted by people who were not affected by them (Commission on Civil Disorders 1968). It was not until activists — people who aggressively pushed to make the problems part of the public dialogue — appeared that the public was forced to recognize the existence of these problems. Civil rights activists of the 1950s and 1960s, led by Martin Luther King, Jesse Jackson, and the more controversial Eldredge Cleaver and Malcolm X, made the problems public issues through protests, parades, and demonstrations. Likewise, the problems of women were forced to the forefront in the 1970s by a group of activists headed by such leaders as Germaine Greer and Gloria Steinem, and by the members of the National Organization for Women. Vietnam War veterans faced problems such as readjustment and posttraumatic stress disorder. Many Vietnam veterans also claim adverse health effects from exposure to the defoliant, Agent Orange. These issues were made salient by groups of Vietnam War veterans, who often felt alienated from society as well as from traditional veterans' organizations. Not until well into the 1980s was at least some recognition afforded to these veterans, and the government still has a poor record of providing programs for them, and business a poor record of hiring them (MacPherson 1984). Even the popular Vietnam Veterans' Memorial in Washington, D.C., "came about through the hard work of veterans," notes political writer Myra MacPherson (1984), "who were left to raise the money to pay tribute to themselves; it was not a gift from a grateful nation."

Sometimes, even the more popular media are sensitive to social causes. In the later 1980s, television programs such as "China Beach" and "Tour of Duty" and popular films such as "Platoon" and "Born on the Fourth of July" gave a more sympathetic view of Vietnam veterans. Auster and Quart (1988) say that the change in film portrayals of wounded Vietnam vets — from the 1970s depiction of the vet as dangerous to the 1980s version of the vet as morally strong, courageous, and deserving of compassion — took place because audiences had finally become "ready to confront the painful reality of the Vietnam War directly on the screen." Among some members of the public, viewing of films such as "Platoon," which depict vets as being personally changed by their Vietnam War experiences, is associated with the viewers having greater empathy for Vietnam veterans — that is, perceiving that the problems many of the vets face are attributable to the war (Griffin and Sen 1989).

Other groups became actively involved in promoting the causes of homosexuals, retarded citizens, and others with special problems and concerns. People soon became aware that the only way they could get their problems solved was to bring them to the attention of the nation, and that meant getting the attention of the media. In fact, many of the protests staged by activists were produced solely for the media.

The media have been manipulated by the proponents of many causes, sometimes with very positive results and sometimes with negative results. The most difficult thing for most media to do in covering areas such as civil rights is to avoid media productions, demonstrations, protests, and so on, and produce independent stories that look objectively at the problem.

One excellent example of doing so came in 1985. On Maryland's Eastern Shore, where racial rioting had broken out in 1963, the editors of the *Star-Democrat* (1985) in Easton decided to take a look at racial relations in a much calmer period two decades later. The small daily put seven reporters to work examining schools, employment, government, churches — even social clubs and volunteer fire departments. They interviewed both black and white residents over several months. The result, a twenty-eight-page supplement published on New Year's Eve, asked, "How Far Have We Come?" The editors concluded that only slow progress had been made toward closing the economic, educational, and other social gaps between black and white citizens in the area.

Nearly half way across the continent in Illinois, Joan Norsworthy and Bill Oakes (1985) looked at the Hispanics in the Chicago suburbs. In two weekly issues the *Palatine Countryside* reported on how Hispanics were struggling to live the American dream. Norsworthy and Oakes contrasted the lives of the low-income newcomers with those who had settled earlier and more comfortably in the affluent suburbs of a metropolitan area. Their articles on "Hispanics: Finding the American Dream" won first prize for public affairs reporting in the Suburban Newspapers of America contest. Not all civil rights issues can or need to be covered this extensively, but there is a need for a more detached and balanced look. Too often, the charges of a vocal activist group and, perhaps, the countercharges or denials of another group appear in the media, but little is done to provide more objective information that puts the conflict into context and helps people determine which of the charges are accurate and which are not.

When you deal with civil rights issues, you are dealing with three basic groups of people: those who feel they are being denied certain rights; those claimed to be denying the rights of others; and the majority of the people who may not have a strong interest in the confrontation. The concept of equal rights is a cornerstone of American society, but frequently those who have rights are not willing to extend them to others, especially if some cost is attached. As a reporter dealing with issues of civil rights and discrimination, the key point to remember is that these issues are emotional, and that the people most actively involved are likely to have strong feelings about them. These people should not be used as sole sources, and every effort should be made to obtain as much objective material on the subject as possible.

Aging

As their opportunities and problems have grown, so too have the activism and political power of elderly people. They have gained concessions in terms of mandatory retirement, increasing the retirement age from 65 to 70 or in some cases, eliminating it entirely. They have used their economic power to gain special discounts and programs from businesses. An eight-page *Milwaukee Sentinel* "50 & Fun" section aimed at older readers was full of special advertising offers from businesses that recognize their new economic power (*Trend* 1988). As their numbers grow, older citizens will become an even more important economic and political force (Harris and Cole 1980).

Already, their political might can be felt at the state and local level. For example, despite the fact that older drivers are far more likely to be involved in traffic accidents, only six states have any special requirements for older drivers. Legislators see any law requiring additional tests for older drivers as "political dynamite" (Sussman 1988). Another example was the school bond election in a suburb of Phoenix, Arizona. Voters in Sun City, a retirement community, repeatedly defeated bond proposals to build more schools. Their rationale was that because they had no children in the schools they should not have to pay to support the system. It was only after the community was taken out of the district that Peoria voters were able to pass the necessary bond issues.

News coverage of aging in the future will continue to deal with the problems that plague the elderly—poor health, lack of adequate housing, fixed incomes and inflation, and the increased incidence of violent crime against the elderly. You will need to become more aware and cognizant of these problems. With the elderly becoming an increasingly large portion of the population, their political importance becomes a greater concern for all people. The increasing need for facilities and various forms of aid, such as Social Security, continues to place a larger burden on younger, taxpaying workers. And, since most of us hope to become one of the elderly someday, we are concerned with the future that awaits us. Since we will all face the problems, we are all concerned, to some extent, about them now. Effectively covering aging often becomes a matter of reminding people that parents and grandparents face the problems today that the younger generation will face tomorrow.

Effective coverage of the aging can also mean getting substantial background in the new and complex area. One such area is the guardianship system, what Fred Bayles and Scott McCartney (1987) called "a crucial last line of protection for the ailing elderly." Associated Press reporters, in a year-long project, found abuses in a system that is supposed to protect the elderly. They found victimized elderly citizens in retirement communities in

INTERPRETATION OF RESEARCH ILLUMINATES MINORITY'S STRUGGLE

Morton Lucoff and Karen Payne are veteran reporters for the Miami News, *a medium-sized afternoon daily serving metropolitan Dade County. Their city has gone through considerable changes since the beginning of the decade—influx of Mariel refugees from Cuba, racial tensions in the Liberty City and Overtown neighborhoods, and a massive movement of Haitians from their native island of Hispaniola to the Bahamas and then to south Florida. Thousands of new residents poured into south Florida, particularly Dade County, in a brief period, creating many housing, employment, and other similar social problems.*

Lucoff and Payne believed that the story of one such group, the Haitians of Miami, needed to be told. That story was illuminated in a mid-1983 story based on a research study by the Behavior Science Research Institute of Coral Gables:

An unreleased study of Little Haiti provides the most vivid picture to date of the plight of Haitians in Miami and their impact on this community.

It shows a people who have had a hard time finding work, who face an imposing language barrier and pay a lot for substandard housing—but depend on welfare no more than the rest of Dade and are trying hard to get an education to improve their lot.

"This should settle a lot of fears and anxieties about Haitians," said Robert Ladner, executive director of the Behavior Science Research Institute of Coral Gables. "People think they are in the backyard killing chickens and goats. . . . No doubt that exists, but more of them are a bunch of incredibly industrious, hard-working people."

The institute's study for the City of Miami and Dade County found:

• Unemployment rates in Little Haiti are eight times higher than Dade County averages.

• Two-thirds of the households in Little Haiti exist on an income of less than $150 a week.

• Half of the Haitian population can't speak English.

• Most live in crowded, deteriorating housing, but pay high monthly rents.

But the study, commissioned by the two local governments to get an idea of what services and programs the Haitians might need, pointed to many positive factors:

• Haitians show no greater dependence on welfare, Social Security and other forms of poverty aid than Dade averages.

• School attendance rates are high. Among 16- to 19-year-olds, the rate is 25 percent higher than Dade's average, and one of every three adults attends school.

INTERPRETATION OF RESEARCH ILLUMINATES MINORITY'S STRUGGLE (continued)

• Even with health problems and high pregnancy rates, fewer than 30 percent of Haitian residents go to Jackson Memorial Hospital for public care and half go to private clinics.

Ladner said the survey was based on interviews with 624 adult Haitian householders living in the two-square-mile Edison-Little River area of Miami, bounded on the south by 36th Street, the north of 85th Street, the east by Biscayne Boulevard and the west by NW 7th Avenue.

The area is home to an estimated 22,855 Haitians, about half the total in Dade—making it the "largest single known concentration of Haitians in the United States . . . as well as the oldest and most well-established known urban Haitian community," the survey said.

Miami and Metro commissioned the study to help determine what services and programs the Haitian community needs. Miami paid $22,000 and the county $20,000.

Ladner said the research shows the Haitians, as a group, are following the traditional pattern of other immigrants settling into life in America.

MORTON LUCOFF and KAREN PAYNE. Interpretation of Research Illuminates Minority's Struggle. *Miami News.* June 19, 1983. D1.

Florida (Sewell 1987) and the Southwest (Macy 1987). But abuses were found as well in New York (Landsburg 1987), Indiana (Wyman 1987), Nebraska (Day 1987), Washington (Ryckman 1987), and many other states.

An estimated 350 thousand elderly citizens were living under the guardianship of others because they were ruled incompetent to handle their own affairs. Probate court records revealed that many lost their life savings as well as their freedom to unscrupulous and unsupervised legal guardians. With the nation's elderly population projected at nearly 35 million by the year 2000 (Bayles and McCartney 1987), your own community is certain to become involved in the guardianship system. As a journalist interested in public issues, so should you.

Youth

At the other end of the aging scale are the youth of America, who have become involved in some of the country's most serious problems. Social problems that have plagued adult Americans for many years have worked their way into the teen and preteen groups, and one of the most pressing concerns in the country is helping youth to deal with these problems.

Among the most severe problems are alcoholism, drug abuse, crime, and pregnancy. In an effort to grow up faster than their chronological age will allow, teenagers have picked up many of the negative aspects of their elders. And, in turn, many preteens have picked up the same problems by emulating their teenage models.

Covering the problems of youth can be a delicate situation. In addition to convincing the victims, the youth, that what they are doing is wrong, people attempting to deal with the problems must cope with protective or disbelieving parents who swear their child could not be involved in certain activities.

The youth of a community are among its most jealously guarded resources, and people are reluctant to admit their youth are having problems. Most states still have some sort of prohibition that prevents the media from releasing the names of juvenile criminal offenders. Juvenile courts and assistance agencies operate in strict secrecy, making information difficult for a reporter to obtain at times. Additionally, there is a tremendous amount of disagreement over the causes of the problems and what should be done about them. Many families resist outside involvement in their problems. They do not want other people to teach their children about sex, alcoholism, drugs, or other moral issues. They jealously guard such rights as their own, but may be reluctant to take responsibility for their child's problems. At the same time, there may be little that parents, teachers, or other adults can do in solving the problems. Teenagers and preteens are very susceptible to peer pressure, and they may continue to do what their friends do no matter what adults tell them to do.

Faced by attempts made by adults to protect youths, by denials that problems exist, and by arguments over cause and responsibility, you as a reporter face a delicate task in dealing with youth problems. Generally, stories about problems in other communities have little impact. The standard reaction is, "Yes, but that doesn't happen here." To gain attention, you must localize problems: drinking and drug use in the local high school; the number of teenage pregnancies among young girls in the community; the crimes committed by juveniles. Privacy acts and juvenile court secrecy can also pose a problem. About the only way to evade those problems is to find youths, parents, and other "victims" who are willing to give up their privacy and tell their story.

This is not always easy. Courts and other social agencies usually will not provide the names of children whether they are charged with a crime or innocent victims. Lawrence Lebowitz of the *Times Record* of Middletown, New York, had to fight New York state, county, and court officials to get the truth about the beating to death of an infant. After weeks of patient interviewing and reviewing available public documents, Lebowitz identified the victim. He also found that the state's child protective system was simply overwhelmed by the demands placed on it. Lebowitz's stories helped persuade the Family Court judge involved to abandon the tradition of closed hearings so that "the public learns about the plight of children who enter the child protective system" (Winerip 1988).

A social issue such as protecting young children does not deserve attention only after a community is shocked by a tragic event. Bill Eichenberger of the *Columbus* (Ohio) *Dispatch* found working women in the area especially concerned about child abuse as they looked for safe day care. Eichenberger (1988) discovered the problem was a big one for the community and the nation. More than twenty-four thousand children in the county lived in families headed by single mothers. Nationally, 52 percent of mothers with children one year old or younger were in the labor force. Good day care was in such short supply that some working women started looking for reliable day care even before they got pregnant, Eichenberger found. He discovered that some of their anxieties were well founded.

Ohio does have an office that sets standards for day-care centers and does require that they be licensed. But Eichenberger found that only four day-care centers in the entire state held such licenses. Eichenberger interviewed mothers before presenting the issue to *Dispatch* readers. He laid out the costs of good day care and suggested how parents could pick out the good ones. He concluded with a list of questions parents should ask when looking for a reliable and safe day-care center.

Poverty

Poverty is a problem that haunts every part of the country (Harrington 1962, 1987). It exists in virtually every community. It may be minimal and hidden in some, but it is still present. Many see a direct relationship between poverty and America's increasing crime rates. One result of this, William H. Inman (1988) of United Press International pointed out in the *Richmond Times-Dispatch,* is that building and running state prisons takes more money than schools, highways, or police. Poverty is clearly a basic social issue for the media.

Dealing with poverty in the media poses a number of problems. Many times, the people who are poor would rather not be identified as so. The phrase "poor but proud" evokes dignity, and for many poor people, dignity is a prime possession. On the opposite side, people who are not poor may resent the attention given to those who are. First of all, they may feel it reflects poorly on the community in general to point out that some of its residents live in poverty. Secondly, many people view poverty not as a condition that society is responsible for, but rather as a condition that is the fault of the people who are poor. Such people resist the idea that the poor should be singled out for special assistance (especially if the nonpoor have to pay for it). Additionally, poverty is difficult to personalize. Because most people cannot envision themselves being poor, they have a difficult time empathizing with those who are.

On a more practical basis, it is often difficult to define poverty. Just where is the cutoff between poverty and low or middle income? The federal and state governments set income guidelines that are used to define poverty, but these guidelines are open to a number of interpretations, and the cost of living can vary widely from one part of the country to another. Such relative standards make poverty difficult to define and cover. Poverty is also difficult to report on because it is often too subtle to be noticed. Poor people may dress in neat clothes, keep their houses clean and trim, and not manifest outward signs of poverty. The poverty of many older people especially is well hidden. They live a modest life and receive little attention until a crisis occurs. For example, during heat waves and cold spells old people sometimes die when they refuse to turn on the air conditioning or the heat, because they are afraid they cannot pay the utility bills.

As a reporter attempting to cover local poverty you will face problems in terms of defining it. You will also face problems in terms of personalizing it, because the people involved frequently do not want to be singled out. When you do focus on a specific person or family, others' attitudes may lead them to think the person is an exception or that people are poor because of their own shortcomings. In addition, reporters who attempt to single out certain people and report on poverty are often accused of sensationalism. As much as any other social problem, reporting on poverty on the local level requires persistence, because it can take a long time to convince the nonpoor that the problem really exists and that something must be done about it (Lewis 1978).

Editorial problems

Just how effectively does the metropolitan press cover social issues? Not very, in the view of Professors Michael Ryan and Dorothea Owen. In analyzing the content of eight representative dailies, they found less than 10 percent of the news content devoted to social issues, and the stories were marred by a higher than average number of errors—perhaps because covering these various kinds of social problems presents problems for reporters themselves (Ryan and Owen 1976).

INTERPRETING THE SOCIAL WELFARE SCENE

Often people most in need of help do not know where to get it. William Wineke tells readers where they can find help:

If You Need Help, Don't Despair, Someone Cares

If you're more than 55 years of age and need a job, the Over 55 Employment Service, 1045 E. Dayton St., may be able to help.

The Madison Urban League, 151 E. Gorham St., has an employability development training and job placement program for young people between the ages of 16 and 21; the first session begins Nov. 29.

The Madison Community Health Center, 1133 Williamson St., offers a variety of low-cost health services to people without money.

A peer support group for the unemployed meets every Thursday noon at Pres House, 731 State St.

Vets House, 147 S. Butler St., offers free employment counseling and job placement services to Dane county veterans and women who meet CETA low-income guidelines.

Those activities are representative of the hundreds of community-service programs offered by an almost bewildering variety of agencies in Madison and Dane County for the unemployed and for others who need help.

A week ago, the Wisconsin State Journal asked its readers to tell us about agencies trying to help people hurt by the current economic conditions.

The very least one can say about the services offered in this area — some of which are well-known and some of which have operated almost anonymously — is that the people of this city care about each other.

For persons who need help in some aspect of his or her life, perhaps the most important is the "First Call for Help" service operated by the United Way of Dane County. According to Wendy Barton, who directs the service, First Call for Help keeps track of more than 1,000 agencies. The number includes subsections of government departments.

The First Call for Help number is 241–5100.

"We average between 35 and 40 phone calls a day," Ms. Barton said. "Most of the callers need food or housing or help with the justice system."

What Ms. Barton and her staff do is match those callers with agencies which can help.

WILLIAM R. WINEKE. November 14, 1982. (Madison) *Wisconsin State Journal.*

Determining significance

The significance of a problem is one of the first things you as a reporter must establish before becoming fully involved in discussing it. What is a significant problem? Is it defined by the number of people involved or, perhaps, by the number of people who potentially may become involved? Problems that seriously affect a majority of the population will not remain hidden for long. Yet if you wait until a majority of the people are directly affected before reporting a problem, your report may be too late to warn people of impending effects on their lives. Even major health problems seldom affect a majority of the people within an area. For example, there are few, if any, communities in the country where 50 percent of the population is plagued by alcoholism. And who is to say that a problem that seriously affects only a handful of people is not a problem with which society should be concerned?

One commonly used method of determining community interests and singling out significant community problems is public opinion polls. These help to isolate the concerns of the public — their attitudes on various issues, their knowledge of social problems, their perceptions of causes and effects, and even the reasons for their concern. They provide an excellent starting point from which to uncover relevant social problems (See "Surveys" in Chapter 2). But it is not enough to say that a large portion of the public is against something without going deeper into the subject and finding out why, and whether the situation can be corrected. Extensive public disinterest in a topic should, likewise, not be sufficient reason for deciding not to deal with a subject. Apathy does not lessen the severity of a problem. Also, relying totally on public opinion polls may not uncover key problems that people are aware of or concerned about, but reluctant to discuss.

How do you as a reporter decide which social problems to cover? Many decisions are made for you. Events happen that suddenly thrust subjects into the spotlight. Reporter Brad White and news editor Ernie Ford of KSL-TV in Salt Lake City started their award-winning expose of the conditions of local nursing homes after they received word of an elderly woman who had drowned at a nursing home while she was left unattended in a bathtub. In looking into the situation they began to uncover other instances of neglect — patients left unattended, unsanitary conditions, and poor health care. Their five-part series, "Out of Sight, Out of Mind" (Television Award 1981), resulted in the indictment of the owner of eight of the homes plus an investigation of state inspection procedures — and follow-up coverage of both those events by the local daily newspapers.

Yet if you always wait to cover an issue until something draws attention to the problem and gives it instant significance, many problems may never be uncovered. For example, the *Milwaukee Journal* in 1985 ran a series of articles investigating legal, procedural, and ethical questions regarding the incarceration of individuals for failure to pay municipal fines, a practice that discriminated against the poor. No salient "events" brought this problem to the forefront of attention — just alert and sensitive reporters. Within weeks, Bernstein (1985) could close out her series by reporting that the courts and police had changed the system to help alleviate the problem. Many official investigations, changes in laws, and criminal proceedings have come about after newspapers and television stations have run stories exposing problems. As Shepard Stone of the Ford Foundation has observed, "A race riot is news. But there was news, significant news, in the city before the riot, news of the conditions and forces that led to it (Stone 1967).

Many stories on social problems begin as complaints from readers and listeners who contact reporters to complain about something. Others come from observations made by reporters either as they cover their beats or as they simply move about the community. Andy Young, a reporter and runner, was pursuing his hobby when he literally ran into a story that developed into a prize-winning series in the *Elyria* (Ohio) *Chronicle-Telegram*. While running through the Eastern Heights area of town, he noticed that black families had moved in. His research into a "changing neighborhood" introduced him to the mysteries of mortgages and banks' lending practices. Using the federal Home Mortgage Disclosure Act, Young was able to gather information on hundreds of home loans to show how banks' lending policies can either hinder or promote housing integration. How did he get on the trail of these lenders? He just went to the yellow pages of the Elyria telephone book and looked up the banks and savings and loan institutions doing business in the community.

One thing you as a reporter must guard against is the temptation to make all passing comments, complaints, or other such leads into major stories. Many of the complaints and comments you receive will be nothing more than self-serving mutterings by people who feel they have been unfairly treated. Many will be exaggerated, distorted, or even blatantly false. Attempting to find important stories in such leads can result in creating a bigger story than what really exists. That warning should not prevent you from checking out as many of the leads as possible, however, for there is no way of telling which will yield important, fruitful information unless you make those checks.

Civic pride

Many communities have social problems that have existed for years but have been overlooked, accepted, or hidden and denied. Poverty is one example of such a problem. It exists to some extent in most communities but many citizens would rather not see it publicized. Drug use and drinking among students at local schools are also stories that many people may feel should be handled quietly and not spread across the columns of the local press. Critics often claim that the media exaggerate these situations, and that problems such as students' abuse of drugs and alcohol are personal, to be handled within the family and through the proper authorities. The community and its leaders, especially in smaller communities, are usually interested in putting forth the best possible public image to the outside world, and they may not look favorably at shortcomings being discussed in the local media.

When community leaders do mount a program to deal with a social problem, the media still cannot take the role of cheerleader. Reporter Patricia Ahlgren looked into a summer jobs program that found work for 5,092 teens in the Milwaukee area. She reported that many of the teenagers found their jobs kept them busy, made them feel independent, and let them save some money for school expenses (Ahlgren 1988). But Ahlgren also reported that the majority of the jobs involved child care, graffiti removal and neighborhood cleanup. She quoted critics who saw such jobs teaching little about the real world of work. She also reported that the program used public money to put youth to work in private businesses (Ahlgren 1988a). Carefully balancing the critics and supporters of the jobs program, Ahlgren provided a look at a continuing social problem.

Public apathy

It is not unusual for a reporter and editor to ferret out what they believe is a significant problem only to have the audience refuse to recognize it as such. For example, poverty among certain members of a community may not be looked at as a community problem, but rather as the problem of a small group of people (Coleman and Rainwater 1978). Members of the community may see no reason to take interest in, or responsibility for, something they feel they had no hand in creating. Similarly, problems such as alcoholism and drug abuse are frequently not viewed as community problems but rather as the problems of the individuals who are troubled by them. Community members usually become interested in the problems only to the extent that the problems affect them directly: when, for example, a drunk driver causes an accident in which they are personally involved; or when their taxes are increased to pay for social assistance and welfare programs; or when the unemployment rate of the community skyrockets and they see their own businesses decline. Public apathy may be the greatest obstacle a reporter must overcome in reporting a social problem within a community.

REPORTING THE PROBLEM NO ONE ADMITS

Logan (Utah) *Herald-Journal* reporters Nancy Williams, Jim Thalman, and Veda Travis faced a number of problems in doing their award-winning series on child abuse in the community in the summer of 1980. Statistics released by state agencies showed that Utah had one of the highest incidents of child abuse in the country, and the reporters were curious about how those statistics were manifested locally. What made the story even more important was a tip from their managing editor.

Local funeral directors had been stopping in regularly to complain about the number of children who were dying under what they thought were suspicious circumstances. The death of twin brothers on the same night (the deaths were attributed to Sudden Infant Death Syndrome) caused one director to complain to the managing editor that the children appeared to have been abused but that nothing was being done about it. Local doctors were reluctant to accuse anyone of child abuse and were, in fact, covering up suspected cases.

The Logan area is dominated by the Mormon church. The heavy religious emphasis on the family and a similar emphasis on the rights of the parents to raise their children without interference made investigating the parent-child relationship difficult. "The parents seemed to look at their children as property and they exercised the same rights over them as they did any other property," said Thalman. This sanctity of the family has resulted in the development of strict family court regulations in Utah, and these regulations reach into the Department of Social Services (DSS). "All we could get from the DSS or the courts was numbers, statistics," says Williams. "They wouldn't add any details" (Cassady 1982).

Even the agency statistics were questionable. Because of the influence of the church, many family problems are handled by the clergy. An untold number of abuse cases never reached the courts or agencies (or the statistics). And the church leaders were as closed-mouthed as the governmental agencies in providing information. If anything, the reporters suspected, the church leaders were downplaying the seriousness of the problem. In addition, stories based strictly on numbers, statistics, and government reports would tend to lack the human element the topic required.

Where, then, could the reporters go for information? "Most of us knew people who had been exposed to or involved in abuse situations," says Thalman. "We had to rely on them" (Cassady 1982).

The resulting five-part series depended heavily on personal sources. In addition to the introductory, background story and a story about the problems police encountered in handling abuse cases, there were three stories that centered on people who had been involved intimately in child abuse matters.

▶

REPORTING THE PROBLEM NO ONE ADMITS (continued)

One story provided an emotional account of a man who had waited too long to become involved in what he suspected to be child abuse by his neighbor. It included his remembrance of the child dying in his arms as he waited for the ambulance. The story was a strong statement on public apathy and reluctance to become involved. Another segment was the first-person account of a young woman who had overcome an incestuous relationship with her father. The final installment of that story was not even planned at the beginning of the series. After the first segment ran, a woman who had chosen to give up her young child because she could not control her abuse of the child called and volunteered to tell her story.

All of the people were local, all of the stories were true, and although the reporters did not imply that these situations were common, they did point out many of the more serious aspects of the problem.

The reporters won state and regional awards for the series. No laws were changed, no arrests were made, and no new programs were started as a result of the series. Yet, as Thalman says, "if we made people aware, if we convinced people who needed help to get it, or if we persuaded hesitant bystanders to become involved, we accomplished something" (Cassady 1982).

NANCY WILLIAMS, JIM THALMAN, and VEDA TRAVIS. The Problem No One Admits. *Logan* (Utah) *Herald Journal*. June 23–27, 1980.

Needed: initiative and continuity

Another major difficulty many reporters have in dealing with social issues is that the problems are continuous while most newspaper, radio, and television journalism is not. The media rely on incidents to bring problems to their attention and, unfortunately, to justify coverage of an issue.

Such an event-oriented approach to the coverage of social issues produces several problems. For one, it suddenly presents to the public a problem in a distorted manner without adequate background or prior understanding. It takes the problem out of context. Additionally, the coverage is frequently shortlived; once the incident disappears, so, frequently, does the coverage. This forces people who are seeking to bring about change to invent incidents continually in order to obtain media coverage.

This invention of incidents biases media coverage of the problem unless opposing groups also invent incidents. Even when opposing groups exist, their information is likely to be as biased as that of the original group, and coverage frequently deteriorates into a repetition of distorted charges and countercharges. The reliance on incidents to bring social concerns to the fore and to justify their coverage in the media also means that reporters frequently must cover rather small and petty concerns. A vocal minority may get coverage for its cause simply because it is vocal and because it is skilled in manipulating the media (Cohen and Young 1973).

While coverage of such incidents will continue, reporters are finding it increasingly necessary to define and investigate social problems on their own, before the incidents erupt. What Stephen Hess calls "social science journalism" is concerned less with events than with the currents that cause events. It is an attempt to identify and write regularly about problems before they become crises, and to explore important but hidden areas of news that exist in the gaps between traditional beats (Hess 1981).

Your role as a social issues reporter thus becomes twofold: (1) to uncover and report on social conditions that are unknown to the community, but that are nevertheless of interest and importance; and (2) to report on social conditions that are known but, for whatever reason, are not admitted or discussed by the local citizenry.

Sources

Four basic kinds of sources are available to you as a reporter doing stories on social problems: government agencies specializing in the problems; private agencies, such as charities and special interest groups; the victims, who are directly affected by the problems; and the bystanders, who are not directly affected. Each type of source can provide certain kinds of information, but each has certain interests and perspectives which must also be taken into account.

Government agencies

Originally, communities dealt informally with their own social problems. But as society became larger and more complex, much of the responsibility for dealing with problems was taken over by government agencies. Local, state, and federal agencies were formed to deal with a myriad of social issues.

You can obtain many kinds of information from government agencies. As the administrators of the programs dealing with social issues, they are most likely to have information about them. Statistical data, the results of surveys and reports, and budget information are all available. People working for government agencies, particularly those in offices most directly associated with the people they serve, are among the most knowledgeable sources available. They are familiar with the statistics, reports, and regulations, as well as with the more personal problems that the regulations do not cover. Local officials of government agencies are also among the most knowledgeable sources on the local situations with which you may be most concerned. They are able to localize the severity and extent of a problem and to point out the aspects that make the local situation unique.

Various levels of government are involved in social problems. Depending on its size, your community may have local branches of various federal agencies. Most states have their own agencies for dealing with such social problems as poverty, alcohol, and drug abuse, although the responsibility for various problems varies from state to state. In rural areas, regional agencies may cover one or more counties, depending on how severe the problem is and how many people need to be served. Virtually every community in the country has some form of access to government expertise and programs covering a range of social problems.

There are, of course, some caveats for dealing with government agencies. For one, the top officials are frequently appointed or elected and may well lack the necessary background or expertise to provide solid information. Additionally, as political officeholders, they are subject, as are other government workers, to pressures that may make them cautious in the kinds of information they provide. Government workers, like many others involved with public activities, are also conscious of their own image and are frequently reluctant to provide information that would reflect badly on themselves or their offices. Primarily, though, government agencies can be major sources for information and expert opinion on most social issues.

Overall, the government's legal and financial involvement in the solutions to social problems necessitates a tremendous amount of information gathering and research, most of which is open to you as a matter of public record. Many times, obtaining information from government agencies is a matter of finding a sympathetic official who is willing to give you more than the official information and statistics.

Private organizations and charities

Private citizens have developed organizations to deal with many social problems. Battles against diseases, programs to aid handicapped citizens, facilities to take care of orphaned children, and programs to provide aid for people in times of disasters have all come into being because of the concern of private citizens. Similarly, organizations have come into existence in efforts to gain recognition of or redress for certain causes. Activist groups have dealt with human and civil rights causes, trying to convince government leaders that a formal action or regulation was needed. Other groups have been formed, even in cases when government action has been taken, to provide additional, alternative ways of dealing with problems.

The nature of these organizations ranges from lobbying groups seeking increased aid and more equitable treatment for certain people to charitable groups concerned primarily with raising money and supporting facilities to treat a problem. While neither type of group has any formal regulatory power, they can exert tremendous influence on how a problem is dealt with. And the less government control there is of an issue, the more control the private agencies may enjoy.

These organizations provide excellent sources of information for you for a number of reasons. As is true with government agencies, they can be major sources of factual information about problems. These organizations acquaint themselves with statistics, trends, pitfalls, and possible solutions. For example, Alcoholics Anonymous would probably be able to provide as much factual information as you could desire about the problem of alcoholism. Additionally, these organizations are informed on the controversies surrounding problems, the controversies over possible solutions, the causes of the problems, and so on. In fact, they may provide a useful source of alternative opinion to the assertions of government employees.

The people working for private organizations, often as volunteers, are usually motivated by a genuine interest in the subject matter. They may be willing to make extra efforts to get material that you request. Their intense interest can cause problems, however, for it can produce a single-sighted attitude toward their cause. This is especially true among activist groups, whose members are not likely to spend much time involved with ideas that do not support their causes. Even charities may overstate their cases to stir up more public sympathy and contributions.

In addition to providing information about social problems, private organizations themselves can often be the subject of excellent stories. For activist groups, questions of motives, membership, leadership, hidden agendas, finances, and more can surface. For example, is a group becoming active because of a sense of need in solving a problem, or for purely political reasons? Is a politician leading a protest because of a deep concern for the inequity at issue, or as a means to generate votes in the next election?

Charities also can be the subject of stories about things other than their outward activities. How much money does a certain charity raise? On what is that money spent? How much of it goes directly toward dealing with the problem, and how much goes into other things such as administrative and overhead costs? Who are the top people in the organization, what is their background, and how much do they get paid? Charitable and other nonprofit organizations are required by the Internal Revenue Service (IRS) to file certain tax information regarding how much money they raise or spend. Many states and communities require any organization soliciting money within their boundaries to register with local authorities. Investigation of charitable organizations, particularly those whose names are not easily recognized, can produce instances of fraud. On the positive side, such digging can also inform potential contributors more fully about relatively unknown, yet worthy, charities.

Victims

Victims are an obvious source of information about social welfare issues. They can help to localize the problem and provide flesh-and-blood examples. They are also intimately acquainted with the problem, although usually only with their particular manifestation of the problem. This is probably the biggest difficulty in dealing with victims. Are these people typical of a more common problem, or are they unique in their situation and their perspective? There is a danger of overgeneralization on your part, especially if the situation is particularly graphic or intense, which can lead the public to believe the problem is more severe (or less severe in some cases) than it really is.

Victims are seldom sources of factual, objective material. If they have taken the time to gather such material, they generally have gathered only what supports their own causes, and they may have colored the material with their own perspectives.

The definition of "victims" does not simply apply to individuals; it can also apply to groups. However, you must be careful not to define the existence of a social problem just because more than one person becomes vocal about the subject at the same time. Many people have learned that they can manipulate media coverage of their concerns by providing a seeming display of "community" concern at the appropriate time. Few people generally attend local city council meetings, so if a dozen or so vocal citizens appear at one time to protest the same matter it can make quite a demonstration of concern. This sudden show of interest may convince many reporters that a "significant" problem exists, when really only the dozen people who are present care about the problem.

Bystanders

Despite their seemingly limited scope as sources, bystanders—people who are not directly affected by a problem—can be extremely useful sources of information for one major reason: solving the problem generally will require their participation and approval to some extent. Their participation may involve raising money, either through donation or government sources. It may take the form of passing new laws and regulations that may require at least a tacit approval from a majority of the people to their elected representatives. It may mean a display of concern on the part of the majority to show the people who are setting priorities which problems are considered most crucial.

Bystanders are sources of information in terms of their opinions about the problem. Thus, it is usually necessary for a journalist to obtain information from a variety of bystanders, particularly those who are in some position to help solve the problem—politicians, community leaders, business people, and financial leaders. Reporters should remember that bystanders are like victims of a crime or disaster. They may not accurately report what really happened and they probably do not accurately reflect the main opinions in the community. Thus, surveys of community knowledge, perceptions, attitudes, and behavior regarding the problem are also very useful.

Hints for covering social issues

1. Humanize your stories as much as possible. Social problems involve people and the best way to demonstrate a social problem is to offer a human example. This will also help make ordinary, dull, statistical material more interesting.
2. Social problems involve a great deal of emotion. Be aware of this when interviewing people involved in the problem.
3. Many social problems do not have a right or wrong side, per se. Do not look for a wrong side or a right side but, instead, approach the issue as a problem that needs solving.
4. Do not be afraid to identify something as a problem, but in reporting it be sure to look at it from more than one perspective, that of the nonvictims as well as the victims.
5. Government agencies, charitable organizations, and special interest groups are the best sources of background information. Dealing with problems is their main purpose, and

part of that purpose means gathering relevant information. You may have to dig for those facts that do not reflect favorably on their efforts, however.

6. Do not expect everyone to agree that what you define as a problem is, in fact, a problem. Your job is to convince them. If there is not enough proof, perhaps there really is not a problem.

7. It is easier to sell a social problem as a problem if you can demonstrate its potential effects on a large number of people.

HUMANIZING THE PROBLEM

Eric Newhouse, chief of the Associated Press bureau in Charleston, West Virginia, has read plenty of statistics about unemployed coal miners. His state has led the nation in unemployment. So how was he to bring out the pain of unemployment? Newhouse talked with social workers, clergymen, unemployment counselors, and—above all—with out-of-work miners themselves. Avoiding statistics for the moment, Newhouse's lead was:

Is there life after unemployment security benefits for an out-of-work miner?

Earl Barker wonders. He made $14,800 in the first half of last year before being laid off. Then the government paid him $148 a week to tide him over until he got a new job. Those checks quit last month.

Now he's about to apply for welfare, which would give him $140 a month in food stamps.

"Anyone who says you can live on that is crazy," says the burly miner, hands clamped anxiously on a cup of coffee. "It will keep you from starving but not much more."

Newhouse's sensitive treatment of the stresses faced by unemployed miners ran in West Virginia and national news media in June 1985.

In summary

All societies have social problems. Some are dealt with formally through the enactment and enforcement of laws and regulations. Others are more subtle. They harm no one but the victim. They are not criminal acts. They do not affect a majority of the people. These problems frequently go uncovered by the media until the victims themselves become vocal enough to make the media notice.

Covering these problems is difficult, because it is difficult to convince those people not plagued by them that they are significant problems and that something should be done about them. Many times, the victims themselves are reluctant to publicize their problems. Many of the problems rest in highly sensitive areas dealing with children, morality, and beliefs. Identifying such problems and dealing with them in a sensitive yet nonemotional manner is one of the most difficult tasks facing you as a public issues reporter.

References

Ahlgren, Priscilla. 1988. Jobs Help Teens Feel Busy, Independent. *Milwaukee Journal,* Aug. 7, 17A.

_____. 1988a. Are Summer Jobs Worth It? Value of Programs Disputed. *Milwaukee Journal,* Aug. 7, 1A.

Auster, Albert, and Quart, Leonard. 1988. *How the War Was Remembered: Hollywood and Vietnam.* New York: Praeger.

Bassis, Michael S., Gelles, Richard J., and Levine, Ann. 1982. *Social Problems.* New York: Harcourt Brace Jovanovich.

Bayles, Fred, and McCartney, Scott. 1987. Declared "Legally Dead" by a Troubled System. *Guardians of the Elderly.* Associated Press Special Report, Sept. 1.

Bernstein, Nina. 1985. Municipal Courts Alter Rules. *Milwaukee Journal,* May 16, 1.

Cassady, David. 1982. Interviews, Mar. 17–18.

Chafe, William Henry. 1977. *Women and Equality.* New York: Oxford Univ. Press.

Clinard, Marshall D., and Meier, Robert F. 1979. *Sociology of Deviant Behavior.* 5th ed. New York: Holt, Rinehart and Winston.

Cohen, Stanley, and Young, Jock (eds.) 1973. *The Manufacture of News.* Beverly Hills, CA: Sage.

Coleman, Robert P., Rainwater, Lee. 1978. *Social Standing in America.* New York: Basic Books.

Commission on Civil Disorders. 1968. *Report of the National Commission on Civil Disorders.* New York: Bantam Books.

Day, Dan. 1987. Elderly Con Victim: "I Didn't Know an Older Person Needed Protection." *Guardians of the Elderly.* Associated Press Special Report, Sept. 17–18.

Easton (Maryland) *Star-Democrat.* 1985. How Far Have We Come? Dec. 31, supplement.

Eichenberger, Bill. 1988. In Search of Good Day Care. *Columbus* (Ohio) *Dispatch,* Aug. 1, 1B.

Griffin, Robert J., and Sen, Shaikat. 1989. "Causal" Communication: Media Portrayals and Public Attributions for Vietnam Veterans' Problems. Paper presented to the Communication Theory and Methodology Division, Association for Education in Journalism and Mass Communication, Washington, D.C., August.

Harrington, Michael. 1962. *The Other America.* New York: Macmillan.

Harrington, Michael. 1987. *The Next Left: The History of A Future.* New York: Henry Holt.

Harris, Diane K., and Cole, William E. 1980. *The Sociology of Aging.* Boston: Houghton Mifflin.

Hess, Stephen. 1981. *The Washington Reporters.* Washington, D.C.: Brookings Institute.

How Far Have We Come? 1985. *Star-Democrat* (Easton, MD), Dec. 31.

Inman, William H. 1988. Leader of Free World Also Leads in Inmates. *Richmond Times-Dispatch,* July 31, A1.

Jones, James T. 1988. Harassment Is Too Often Part of the Job. *USA Today,* Aug. 8, 5D.

Kluger, Richard. 1975. *Simple Justice.* New York: Knopf.

Landsberg, Mitchell. 1987. New York's System Haphazardly Administered. *Guardians of the Elderly.* Associated Press Special Report, Sept. 6.

Lewis, Michael. 1978. *The Culture of Inequality.* New York: New American Library/Meridian.

MacPherson, Myra. 1984. *Long Time Passing: Vietnam and the Haunted Generation.* New York: Doubleday.

Macy, Robert. 1987. Growing Senior Citizen Population Poses Problems. *Guardians of the Elderly.* Associated Press Special Report, Sept. 26.

Norsworthy, Joan, and Oakes, Bill. 1985. Hispanics: Finding the American Dream. *Palatine* (Ill.) *Countryside,* Aug. 6, 7, 8, 10, 11, 13.

Report of the National Commission on Civil Disorders. 1968. New York: Bantam.

Ryan, Michael, and Owen, Dorothea. 1976. A Content Analysis of Metropolitan Newspaper Coverage of Social Issues. *Journalism Quarterly* 54(4):634–40.

Ryckman, Lisa Levitt. 1987. Foundation Works to Patch System's Cracks. *Guardians of the Elderly.* Associated Press Special Report, Sept. 20.

Sewell, Dan. 1987. *Woman Fights Back From Coma, Then Against Guardianship System.* Associated Press Special Report, Sept. 10.

Stone, Shepard. 1967. The U.S. Press: A Critical View. In *City Hall and the Press,* edited by Raymond L. Bancroft. Washington, D.C.: National League of Cities, 34–59.

Sussman, Lawrence. 1988. Aging Drivers Create Touchy Issue in State. *Milwaukee Journal,* Aug. 7, A1.

Television Award. 1981. Television Award for Public Service Reporting. *The Quill* 69(6):24–25.

Winerip, Michael. 1988. A Judge Moves to Shed Light on Family Court. *New York Times,* July 29, B1.

Wyman, Thomas P. 1987. *Noble County Farmer Challenges and Beats Guardianship.* Associated Press Special Report. Sept. 25.

This chapter was initiated by Cassady. Collaborator was Meier.

CHAPTER 9

Consumer affairs

BECAUSE everybody is a consumer—even reporters and editors—covering the issues facing consumers today is high on the new media agenda. The *New York Times* regularly includes a "Consumer's World" (1988) section. The "Weekly Mortgage Rates" (1988) now share space with stock market tables in the *Cape Cod Times* and many other papers. Reporting on consumer affairs at the most basic level can involve a shoppers' guide of comparative supermarket prices, warnings from the community's Better Business Bureau about a confidence game in the area, or a newspaper or television station "action line" feature in which reader or viewer "gripes" are selected, researched, and discussed. But the consumer affairs beat can also call for interpretive and in-depth reporting that places these events into a meaningful context of ongoing consumer concerns.

Enduring consumer issues

As is the case with so many other public issues, consumer issues involve questions of responsibility and trade-offs. Underlying most consumer affairs news events are the following ongoing concerns:

- What is the quality and safety of consumer products?
- Who is responsible for protecting the consumer?
- How much protection is necessary or desirable?
- What level of risk is acceptable?
- What are the relative costs and benefits of safety standards?
- How important is the consumer's freedom of choice?
- How can the consumer be protected from deception and unfairness?
- What special protection is necessary for vulnerable or disadvantaged consumers (for example, children, the poor, the elderly, people in Third World countries)?
- How just and effective are procedures for consumer redress after sale?

• What overt and covert pressures are applied by manufacturers and merchants?

Along with manufacturers, merchants, and individual consumers, the primary participants in the consumer affairs arena include regulatory agencies and consumer groups.

The rise and (sometimes) fall of regulatory agencies

In a 1981 address to the American Academy of Advertising, Stanley E. Cohen (1981), Washington editor of *Advertising Age,* contended that through the years, the pendulum has swung back and forth in the consumerism movement, as reflected in the history of the Federal Trade Commission (FTC). When the FTC was established in 1914, it was involved primarily in preventing unfair advantage by one company over a competing company, rather than in working directly to protect consumers (Holsinger 1987). In *FTC* v. *Raladam* in 1939, the Supreme Court examined the role of the FTC in dealing with false and deceptive advertising, and ruled that the FTC could not stop advertising that was harmful to the consumer unless the advertising hurt a competing business in some way (*FTC* v. *Raladam*). Remedial statues passed in the 1930s gave the FTC specific power to deal with false advertising promoting the purchase of food, drugs, devices, or cosmetics; and during the same period a consumer research laboratory was created to test products. Results were published in a *Consumer Bulletin,* listing products by brand names.

But as Cohen (1981) pointed out in his talk to the advertising academy,

in the decades that followed, there were many swings of the pendulum. . . . In the Truman and Eisenhower years, upward mobility created suburbia and a generation of optimists. Shopping centers and the shift to self-service retailing brought revolutionary changes to marketing strategy, all the way from product design to hard sell ad copy.

Consumers were beginning to sense that something had changed, in terms of product quality, service, and their ability to rely on advertising. In those placid Eisenhower years, the Federal Communications Commission and other regulatory agencies were in the hands of policymakers who were reluctant to add to the burdens which businessmen endure. . . .

The Eisenhower euphoria began to lift. During the 1960 campaign John F. Kennedy promised a New Frontier . . . consumerism would have White House status.

In 1963, President Kennedy developed a Consumer Bill of Rights. In 1966, the year after Ralph Nader's book, *Unsafe at Any Speed,* launched the author to national prominence, Congress passed the National Traffic

TV STATION LOCALIZES CONSUMER REPORTING

Possibly because the subject lends itself to visuals, local television stations often do a very fine job of covering consumer affairs. For example:

In 1990, TV station WREX in Rockford, Illinois, ran an indigenous series examining a range of products: bacon (it's the cost per pound after frying that counts), hair-growth stimulants (they don't work), diuretics (they're dangerous to your health), mouthwashes (they're no substitute for flossing), shotgun shells (if they're loaded with lead pellets, you're in trouble with federal game wardens), and so on.

In each case, the station consumer-affairs commentator quoted local authorities to buttress his national sources.

and Motor Vehicle Safety Act, as well as the Fair Packaging and Labeling Act. During the Nixon administration, newly created agencies included the Consumer Product Safety Commission in 1972, and the controversial Occupational Safety and Health Administration (OSHA) in 1973.

The rise and (sometimes) fall of consumer groups

Concurrent with the creation of government regulatory agencies was the rise of citizen-initiated consumer groups, such as Consumers Union, the publisher of *Consumer Reports.* No group created a greater stir or received more national attention than Ralph Nader and the consumer activists who rallied around him and came to be known as "Nader's Raiders." The rise of this consumerism phenomenon began in 1966, when United States Senator Abraham Ribicoff was conducting open hearings on the potential role of the federal government in highway safety. Nader was expected to testify; then Ribicoff learned that General Motors, anticipating that the auto industry critic would be a witness, hired private detectives to follow Nader. Consequently, Ribicoff began the hearings by questioning General Motors executives as to their motives in spying on a private citizen. Nader, an apparently unassuming young attorney, subsequently became a folk hero who had taken on a powerful national corporation and won. During the next ten years, Nader and his growing band of supporters were responsible for founding at least twenty consumer-oriented organizations concerned with such topics as aviation, law, engineering, public health, auto safety, pollution, tax reform, and public interest research groups. But Hays Gorey (1975), who covered Nader for *Time* magazine for almost ten years, notes that

> Ralph Nader has experienced both spectacular success and frustrating failure, responding to each in much the same shrugging manner. He has not lacked for critics nor for devotees. His role, too, has evolved, moving beyond a surfeit of rapierlike thrusts against government agencies, corporations, labor leaders, presidents, the Congress, to a more sophisticated, durable, and perhaps more effective strategy of sustained oversight. . . . After nearly a decade of pressing, probing, pushing and — yes — pillorying, is Nader wearing out his welcome? Has he become, quite suddenly, obsolete?

The Reagan administration in the 1980s produced an atmosphere of deregulation, a laissez-faire attitude of the federal government toward the activities of private business. By 1990, however, there appeared to be growing concern in the country regarding the effects of such a "hands off" atmosphere on consumer safety.

In looking to the future of the consumer movement, Mayer (1989) said that:

> The consumer movement will have to develop its own moral vision for the 1990s and beyond. . . . The new consumerist vision must seek to link consumer issues — but without subordinating them — to the long list of progressive issues involving civil rights, demilitarization, gay rights, feminism, and employment security. Finally, a compelling consumerist view for the future must address consumer problems that are increasingly global in nature. . . . The movement has already shown that it can deliver the goods. It has prevented unsafe products from being marketed; ensured that consumers have access to timely and accurate information; guarded against anticompetitive practices that raise prices and lower quality; and guaranteed that consumers have somewhere to turn when a new car is a lemon, a household appliance starts a fire, creditors make harassing phone calls in the middle of the night, or fraudulent investment schemes rob senior citizens of their life savings. Its next challenge is to preserve the ability to solve everyday consumer problems while building a new moral basis for the future movement.

Consumers who do not want to be protected

A common and paradoxical problem is that consumers often do not seem to want to be protected or even informed. Investigators in law enforcement agencies and reporters have been stymied by this phenomenon, especially in dealing with victims of various con games. Human nature being what it is, no one wants to admit that he or she has been "fleeced"; and the more outlandish the scheme, the more reluctant the victim is even to complain, much less to cooperate with those trying to expose the scam to the public.

Even more puzzling, perhaps, are the consumers who do not actively seek information, even on major purchases, that would help them with their decisions. In an article for the *Journal of Consumer Research,* four researchers examined two basic methods by which consumers acquire product information: internal search (retrieving previously acquired information from their memories) and external search (actively seeking new information). They concluded that the average external search for all but the most expensive durables is quite limited. Consumers normally visit only a few stores, rarely seek out unbiased third-party sources, such as *Consumer Reports,* and, in general, do not actively seek information. When the consumer does conduct an external search, the research usually comes from one of three categories: seller-related sources such as advertising or retail salespeople; direct inspection of the merchandise; or disinterested third parties who have no special interest in the purchaser's decision. Research indicates that third-party sources offer substantial benefits to consumers. However, the availability of this type of source in many markets is currently limited. One of these limitations may be a paucity of quality consumer affairs reporting (Beales et al. 1981).

Another curious phenomenon is the apparently lackadaisical consumer response to many product recalls. The Consumer Product Safety Commission (CPSC) usually relies on press releases and media coverage to publicize recalls. The commission's task force on recall effectiveness has concluded, however, that the media have often not responded with the type of attention the severity of the hazard would warrant (*Consumer Reports* 1981). Even when consumers are aware of the recall, many do not respond. Reasons for consumer inaction cited by *Consumer Reports* (1981) include the trouble or inconvenience involved, a lack of incentive, doubts about the quality of repairs, and the decision to solve the problem in some other way (for example, by throwing the product out or by consumers fixing the product themselves). "I believe there is a recall resistance among adults," a CPSC commissioner is quoted as saying. "With so many recalls, many adults seem to have become numbed to the hazards" (*Consumer Reports* 1981).

INTERPRETIVE CONSUMER ISSUES REPORTING

A local and timely angle can make enduring consumer issues alive and relevant for people in your community. In the following story, reprinted from the June 7, 1983, Dallas Times-Herald, *reporter Marcia Smith uses the human interest appeal of health and safety as a springboard for giving readers some background on the role of regulatory agencies, and the trade-offs that must be considered, in consumer product safety:*

New mowers less dangerous because of regulation

Doris Nelson, R.N., has seen a lot of mangled feet limp into the emergency room at Parkland Hospital.

This spring, the hospital's emergency room director has greeted a man with three lacerated toes, a man with a piece of metal embedded in his thigh, and a two-year-old with a severed toe. A walk-behind lawn mower was responsible for each injury.

What happens, says Ms. Nelson, is that hands and feet make contact with the mower's blade or the mower runs over some debris and sends it flying. Often, people lose toes when they set their foot on the mower while trying to start it. The foot slips beneath the mower and hits the blade.

"I've seen cases where the blade cut through a boot," Ms. Nelson said.

And, of course, it's not always the person mowing the lawn who gets hurt. Someone sitting in the yard while the mower is in operation can catch a flying rock, piece of glass or metal.

Last year, Ms. Nelson saw a woman who had to have a piece of metal surgically removed from her abdomen: She had been standing in the path of a lawn mower's discharge chute.

In 1979, there were 79,000 blade contact injuries in the United States, says Terrence Scanlon, a commissioner with the federal Consumer Product Safety Commission. Most accidents happen when the mower operator reaches into the chute to remove chunks of grass or when the mower is being started, the CPSC found.

Because of demands by consumer groups to decrease the number of injuries caused by the common household machine, the CPSC issued lawn mower safety standards in January 1979. The standards specifically require that all walk-behind rotary lawn mowers manufactured after June 30, 1982, must have a blade that stops within three seconds after the operator lets go of the handle. (The blade also must not turn unless the user continuously activates a control.)

INTERPRETIVE CONSUMER ISSUES REPORTING (*continued*)

The standards also call for shielding and labeling: A mower must pass a foot probe test to ensure that the user cannot stick his or her foot into the whirling blades and a "Danger Keep Hands and Feet Away" label must appear on the machine.

With the new standards, the CPSC expects 60,000 injuries can be avoided annually, Scanlon said. The effects of the standards can be more accurately measured after the new mowers have been on the market longer. While the standards went into effect last summer, mowers meeting the standards didn't reach outlets until this spring.

According to a report in the June issue of *Consumer Reports,* lawn mower manufacturers resisted the CPSC's standards. The CPSC wanted power mowers to have a "deadman" control that would stop the blade three seconds after the user released the handle. Under one system, the deadman control would stop the engine, thereby halting the blades. But CPSC and the mower makers disagreed over the mechanism that would restart the engine after it was stopped.

The controversy led the two groups into court and Congress. In an effort to keep costs down, the mower makers wanted a mower that could be restarted by hand; the CPSC preferred a mower that could be restarted electrically. The fighting delayed the new standard and kept the new mowers off the market for a while. Finally, the issue was resolved: Both manual and powered restarts now are available.

Also available is a blade-brake/clutch model. When the user releases the handle, the blade but not the engine stops. When the user grasps the handle, moving the deadman control back into position, the clutch engages the blade again and brings it back up to speed.

The new, safer mowers will be more expensive than older walk-behind models. According to Dennis Dix, executive director of the Outdoor Power Equipment Association Inc., in Washington, DC, the new standards will raise the average price of a lawn mower from $160 to $180–$225.

Some 4.5 million lawn mowers are sold each year, Dix said. The new costs mean consumers will spend about $200 million for new lawn mowers this year.

Spokesman for Briggs & Stratton Corp., the largest maker of the small engines used in lawn equipment, said the company invested millions of dollars to modify its engines, increasing its prices 20 to 40 percent.

The CPSC's Scanlon said he thinks the extra cost is worth it because "children walking behind Dad could be hurt. Or kids who mow lawns for extra money in the summer. Just being careful with your old mower may not be enough."

▶

INTERPRETIVE CONSUMER ISSUES REPORTING (*continued*)

The CPSC three-point standards apply only to rotary, walk-behind lawn mowers. A rotary mower is a power lawn mower in which one or more cutting blades rotate horizontally on a vertical axis. (The other kind of lawn mower, the reel-type, cuts grass by rotating one or more blades horizontally to provide a shearing action. Only the labeling standard applies to reel-type mowers manufactured after Dec. 31, 1979.)

A walk-behind mower, according to the CPSC, is "a grass cutting machine either pushed or self-propelled, with a minimum cutting width of 12 inches, that employs an engine or a motor as a power source and is normally controlled by an operator walking behind the mower." That definition excludes the riding lawn mower and commercial lawn mowers not customarily produced for or sold to customers.

Lawn mower dealers still are selling pre-regulation 1982 models. Bobbie Hickey, a lawn mower saleswoman at a local Sears store, said she has very few of the old lawn mowers left because "my customer's don't want the new features. They say it's an inconvenience—that when they go to pick up a rock, the lawn mower shuts off.

"We have to point out the safety of the new mowers as a selling point. I tell them they may save a child's life. We tend to be careless when we're mowing the yard. The new mowers are going to make us a lot less careless."

MARCIA SMITH. New Mowers Less Dangerous Because of Regulation. *Dallas Times-Herald.* June 7, 1983.

You can find a series of articles on communication and the consumer in the March 1985 issue of the *Journal of Consumer Research* (Consumer Research 1985).

The future of Consumerism

In an overview of a conference on consumerism at the University of Maryland, Paul N. Bloom (1982) saw consumerism continuing as an important public issue. He said the most hotly debated consumer issues will concern how far regulatory reform should go and how to help less-privileged consumers in this country and the Third World. Bloom also expressed concern about the "information priests" who, he said, control the nature and content of consumer information.

In expanding on the notion of information priests, an idea developed by Dorothy Leonard-Barton (1982), Bloom (1982) describes them as the controllers of the information that consumers have, or have access to, in making purchase decisions. "How to get 'good' consumer information from 'information priests' like big business, big government, the traditional media, the new telecommunication industries, and others may prove to be a major overriding issue," Bloom states. Debates, he says, will arise over questions of who should collect and pay for consumer information. Because of the cost of consumer information, Bloom asks, will only the rich be able to utilize it? Changes in the regulatory environment, and consumer needs for unbiased information to be used in making purchase decisions, may bring about changes in the roles of journalists in the years to come.

The role of the consumer affairs reporter

What is the role of the reporter of consumer affairs, and how might it change in the decade of the 1990s and beyond? If the regulators quit regulating, there will be no government efforts in consumerism to be covered. Should the media then assume a quasi-regulatory role in consumer protection by increased concentration on areas of consumer interest and intensified investigative reporting? Or should they have been doing this all along, despite the swings of the pendulum in the consumer movement? These are questions that must be answered not only by individual reporters, but also by editors and news directors of individual newspapers and broadcasting companies in the years to come. And the answers may be influenced in many cases by the attitudes and pressures of those who support all the media—the advertisers.

Advertising: the velvet cloud

Within the organizational structure of the average newspaper, radio, or television station exists a somewhat adversary situation between the departments in charge of gathering news and the departments in charge of gathering the money to pay for the enterprise. Advertisement salespeople see reporters as the nonrevenue-producing segment of the organization, and business managers may view the reporting staff as a considerable drain on the budget, resenting any expenditures that seem unnecessary. Reporters, on the other hand, may view with disdain the business and advertising people, who make no contribution to the true purpose of their media—informing the public on pertinent issues.

In fact, part of the reason for the breakdown in what should be an adversarial relationship between vendors in the marketplace and reporters of consumer affairs may lie in the paradoxical role of the advertiser in the mass media. Reporters, along with the rest of the reading or listening public, utilize advertising as a source of information in making most of their purchase decisions. But many reporters perceive the advertiser as a silent villain, lurking in the background, waiting to try and squelch publication of any consumer-oriented story. With tens of billions of dollars being spent on advertising, the consumer or business reporter may feel that he or she has just cause to worry about the pressure that might arise from advertisers as a result of investigations of consumer issues.

Advertising scholars and other observers seem to have varied opinions about the actual existence of pressures by advertisers and about the extent of the problem. To some, a very real, if not always observable, threat exists. Others see little evidence of such pressure. According to S. Watson Dunn, professor of marketing at the University of Missouri, and Arnold M. Barban, professor of advertising at the University of Illinois, the pressures and threats may take a variety of forms:

> Advertisers may from time to time be interested in omission, or "burying" an embarrassing news story; coloring a news story involving them; extra publicity favorable to them; or shading editorial opinion to agree with their opinions. . . .
>
> There is some evidence that the small, financially insecure newspaper is more likely to be influenced than the large, financially stable one. There is little evidence that large prestigious papers cater particularly to advertisers . . . [or] that magazines, except those that cater to a particular trade group, are unduly sensitive to pressure (Barban and Dunn 1978).

In fact, competition among the media may provide a built-in check on potential influence by advertisers. News directors must report news that is of interest to their readers or viewers, for fear of being "scooped" by the competition, even if the news adversely affects one of their own advertisers. Another factor might be that, in many cases, the advertiser needs the media even more than the media need an individual advertiser's money.

The *Record* of Hackensack, New Jersey, took on a major advertiser in its 1987 series on an auto dealer it accused of deceptive practices. Three writers, a researcher, and other staff members worked on the four-part series for a year. They interviewed customers, former salesmen, other auto dealers, and state officials and found that "deceptive practices are commonplace" (Stark and Locklin 1987a).

Court records showed that customers of two Paramus auto dealerships owned by William J. "Wild Bill" Peretti had brought 140 law suits in six years, almost twice as many as those against any other dealer. *Record* reporters also checked on two Dallas dealerships formerly owned by Peretti. Texas officials told them that those dealerships generated so many customer complaints that Texas passed its first law regulating automobile advertising (Innes and Locklin 1987).

Although the wheeling-dealing of "Wild Bill" Peretti made interesting reading, the *Record* focused on the public issue involved. The issue was this: Why was New Jersey's Office of Consumer Protection not doing something? The Consumer Protection agency had been getting complaints about the Wild Bill auto dealerships for years. Reporters Karl Stark and Bruce Locklin (1987b) found the agency understaffed, demoralized, and ineffective. As one agency investigator told them, "We're not a law-enforcement agency—just a paper tiger."

The investigation found that civil service employees in the Consumer Protection Office had been replaced by political appointees. Most worked only part-time. Meanwhile, neighboring New York, working with a small staff, was doing much better in policing consumer fraud. The *Record* found that even most New Jersey auto dealers wanted the consumer-fraud office to crack down on deceptive practices.

News that the *Record* was looking into the Consumer Protection Agency stirred New Jersey's attorney general to act even before the "Car Buyer Beware" series was published. He promised more staff and more action on behalf of consumers. In a windup editorial (Wild in the Showrooms 1987), the *Record* said that if New Jersey could not produce tougher enforcement against consumer fraud it should abolish this sham operation altogether.

Sources—reliable and otherwise

Although not perfectly protected, consumers have a variety of organizations concerned about their complaints and problems. Some of these organizations are easier for the reporter to work with than are others. Some are certainly more reliable than others. The reporter must, however, cover them all.

Government agencies

One of the most uncomfortable alliances for the beginning reporter, who usually expects an adversarial relationship between government officials and journalists, is the consumer affairs reporter's utilization of agency administrators, who share the reporter's goal of consumer protection. What is supposed to be a traditional battle of reporter versus bureaucrat can effectively be transformed into a "holy alliance," especially when the combination includes a conscientious public servant and an equally conscientious reporter. Both, however, must have the flexibility to accept with equanimity some help from a preconceived adversary. One of the best examples of this situation is the cooperation that can exist between the reporter and the regional office of any state attorney general. The assistant attorney general in charge of consumer protection can be a valuable source for the concerned reporter in the communities served by such an office. An additional source would be in the state capital of any state that has a consumer protection division.

Citizens groups and the BBB

Other sources that should not be overlooked include citizens organizations that devote their time to consumer issues. These include Common Cause, the League of Women Voters, Consumers Union, farmers' associations, citizens groups, and special interest groups such as those that deal with the aging or minorities. Other sources are utilities commissions, ethics committees of various professional associations, universities with consumer complaint services, legal-aid services, environmentalist groups, and even some churches.

The Better Business Bureau (BBB) is another potential source for reporters in most cities. The BBB may be viewed with skepticism by some reporters, since it is composed of dues-paying members of the business community. But the BBB has begun to assume many of the local functions of the FTC. Although the bureau does not carry the clout of the FTC in terms of possible legal action, it operates in three areas to deal with deceptive advertising practices reported by the public.

The least effective of the BBB approaches is what members term "moral suasion," but the two other methods, threatened expulsion if the firm is a member of the organization, and adverse publicity, have proved increasingly effective (Bligh 1981). Even the busiest news staff will usually take the time to edit and run a news release from the BBB on con games going on in the community, and some will follow up on the story by assigning a staff reporter to pursue a particular situation for an in-depth article. By maintaining a good working relationship with the local BBB director, an investigative reporter can frequently gain more insight into a potentially worthwhile consumerism story than he or she will gain from a simple press release.

In the early 1980s, the National Council of Better Business Bureaus joined forces with the American Advertising Federation to form local advertising review boards for each of the 161 offices of the BBB. These local committees, composed of an equal number of members from each group, were designed to meet monthly and review advertising in the local media in order to discover any deceptive practices. Details of their investigations, of course, would not be open to the public until a case was resolved, but as an enterprising reporter you could serve as your own review board by familiarizing yourself with deceptive practice regulations, examining advertising daily, and conducting your own investigations. When you get involved in situations that concern an advertiser, remember that many publishers will be reluctant to get involved. But the potential for eventual disclosure by other local media might enable you to "morally suade" your own chief to go with the story.

Tips

Another source not to be overlooked is the most basic of all sources — tips from readers or viewers of the media. As an established reporter you can come to expect a certain amount of prank calls concerning real or imaginary grievances; but you also will gain with experience the instinct that tells you when to follow up on such tips. The beginner might be well advised to follow up on all tips he or she has time for, since one or more might be a legitimate source of information. The potential stories to be derived from such sources must be approached with caution, because many tips come from persons with particular axes to grind — former employees disgruntled over particular policies or procedures by a company, former customers disgruntled over a perceived injustice, and so on. But you must remember that even information from the disgruntled can lead to a story that could be of importance to the general public.

Polls, surveys, and field experiments

Among the many research tools available to you as a consumer affairs reporter are polls and surveys. Some media traditionally conduct a "marketbasket" survey every week or every month by comparing the prices of selected items at local supermarkets. You can also do an investigative survey of consumer misperceptions of goods and services in your community by asking a sample of consumers for their beliefs about the attributes of a particular brand or product (for example, warranty protections, interest rates on savings accounts, differences between sale and list prices), and then

CONSUMER FIELD STUDIES BOOST RATINGS

A television station in Texas, competing in a medium-sized metropolitan area with two other stations, consistently was finishing last in the ratings for the evening news. The station manager, while not willing to put on an additional full-time staffer to do consumer reporting, approached a journalism professor at the local university with the idea of doing a series of consumer-related specials, on a contract basis, to run for a few minutes each night as part of the regular newscast. Three such specials were produced: a three-part series on prescription drug prices; a ten-part series on automobile repair shops; and a ten-part series on television repair (Rooker 1981).

The drug series was relatively inexpensive, both in staff time and financial outlay, involving a spot check of several commonly prescribed medications in a variety of drug stores, selected randomly throughout the city with a population of approximately 150,000. The largest expense for the television station came in the automobile repair shop investigation, followed by the television repair investigation. In the latter two cases, the station paid the bills for alleged repairs as they were incurred. The plans were simple, but effective.

In the case of the auto repair comparisons, a used car was repaired and inspected for any existing problems by two experts—auto mechanics teachers from local vocational schools with no commercial interests in the project. A young female was enlisted to pose as the car owner, and a connection on the car's alternator was deliberately broken off by the mechanical experts. The automobile was then taken to ten different repair shops, selected on the basis of geographical location in the city and including the shops of some leading automobile dealers, some independent garages, and some service station shops, selected at random.

The results were presented in three-minute segments on the nightly news, with a tag line each night announcing which garage would be explored on the next night's newscast. Of the ten garages patronized, the least any mechanic did was to replace the entire alternator with a new one, and the least amount charged was $80. The highest recommendation was for a complete overhaul of the engine, a suggestion the "consumer" rejected. All other repairs were paid for when the car was picked up. At the end of the investigation the car was taken to an auto mechanics class at a local high school. The students found the problem in less than an hour, and the repair bill was a total of $18 for the part and labor.

CONSUMER FIELD STUDIES BOOST RATINGS (*continued*)

The television repair scheme, also aired in ten segments, was conducted in a similar manner, with a minor tube being burned out, and with similar results.

For the price comparison of prescription drugs, the investigator obtained from a physician the brand names of six commonly prescribed drugs including types of antibiotics, a heart medicine, an arthritis medicine, and a hormone, then telephoned the selected pharmacies to ask their prices. During the conversation an objective third party listened on another phone and also noted the figures quoted by the respective pharmacists, to serve as a double check.

From the standpoint of the station owner—as well as of the consumers—the series was a complete success. What had been anticipated as a loss of revenue of $100,000 to $120,000 from canceled commercials turned out to be less than half that amount—and the straying advertisers soon returned to the fold. In addition, the newscast went from last in the ratings to number one, with ratings higher than both the other stations combined by the final week of the series. As icing on the cake, the investigative piece won a state award from the Texas Association of Broadcasters (Robert Rooker. Personal conversation with author, July 1981).

You should be aware that such undercover tactics, sometimes called infiltration, are a highly effective technique but usually require some falsification of background and identification. Because of this, they may border on invasion of privacy in cases involving private businesses, groups, or individuals. Some news media organizations consider undercover tactics unethical or at least improper. They should never be used without legal counsel and the approval of your news executives.

comparing those perceptions to some verifiable or objective standard. This approach is similar to that commonly used to measure deception in advertising (Liefield and Heslop 1985).

Another common type of research in investigative consumer reporting is the field experiment. In using this approach, the reporter sets up the situation to be investigated—for example, bogus automobile repairs—then selects a random sample of repair shops to investigate. Such field experiments are limited only by your imagination, the budget of your news director, the time you have available to devote to the project, and the ethical considerations involved.

Other sources

Other sources you might want to have on hand include:

• *Consumer's Resource Handbook,* published by the United States Office of Consumer Affairs—lists local, state, and federal consumer protection agencies.

• *Help: The Indispensable Almanac of Consumer Information,* edited by Arthur E. Rowse, published by Everest House Publishers, New York—contains practical information on a wide range of consumer topics plus addresses for Better Business Bureaus and federal and state consumer agencies.

• *Evaluations of Firms and Professionals Who Provide Consumer Services,* by Gregg B. Jackson and Francine H. Meyer, published by Washington Center for the Study of Services (funded by the United States Office of Consumer Education)—an annotated bibliography of consumer studies on topics ranging from opening a checking account to choosing a summer camp.

• Consumer affairs periodicals (for example, *Consumer Reports* and the *Journal of Consumer Research*).

Special problems in consumer reporting

Time is a critical factor in investigating consumer affairs. The budget, work schedules, and a myriad of other factors, most importantly the reporter's time, all must be considered in conducting an investigation. For the broadcast media, this problem is compounded by the time the finished product will take up on a subsequent newscast or special report. In an article in the *Investigative Reporters and Editors Journal,* Bill Kucera (1981) of KUTV News in Salt Lake City described some of the problems his station had with its documentary series "Paper Land," concerning a Utah/Idaho land scheme:

> After three months of digging, not one frame of video had been shot. . . . What we had to show for our effort was a three-foot-high stack of documents, hundreds of pages of notes and a growing sense of frustration about television investigative reporting. . . . It would take 45 days to complete the needed shooting and more than 15 hours of videotape would be used. . . .
>
> After hearing the complaints (about the land company), we felt the

sales pitch was something we wanted to witness. Despite having reservations about the "hidden camera" approach to journalism, we felt it was necessary to attempt to record a sales pitch on tape. It was decided that the result would never be allowed to stand on its own, but only used to buttress complaints from buyers.

Kucera described the difficulty in setting up the camera, microphone, and newspersons in a remote section of the 10,000 acres of land, most of which offered little protective covering. Successfully completed, this and other interviews were combined with pictures of the land and voluminous documents, including a fifty-page computer printout showing the company's sales:

> We summoned the help of a journalism class from the University of Utah for the arduous task of calling many of the 1800 people on the list in order to ask what they thought they had purchased. After making more than 500 phone calls, we found that a startling 40 percent of the people we spoke to thought they owned a conventional lot. The printout code clearly showed they owned an undivided interest in the land. . . .

Discussing the problems of presenting all this information in a manner that would lend itself to video, Kucera said much imagination had to be used to help break the visual monotony. A variety of photographic methods, stills, and video graphics were used. "In the end," writes Kucera, "a 30-minute documentary, possibly preconceived as too visually slow for television, played quickly. Most importantly, documents considered by some as not stimulating enough for television actually allowed viewers to become part of the investigative paper trail that reporters find so interesting" (Kucera 1981).

The cost factor

Another critical factor in consumer affairs reporting is funding, especially for investigative projects on small- to medium-sized media. You should consider the bottom line when evaluating projects. Think in terms of costs and benefits. That may sound nonjournalistic, but you should think about what your project will cost and try to develop an estimate of the cost involved with the story, because funds for it must be set aside and not used elsewhere. Small- and medium-sized newspapers simply do not have unlimited resources on which to draw. Human and economic resources are precious.

Working for a paper with a staff of about forty people, your news budget may be somewhere around $700,000 a year, and it is eaten up by little things. You cannot expect an editor to fund a project that requires large outlays of money up front. If you are going to ask an editor to fund a project, it is advisable to reduce the required money into segments and then deliver your project in a sequence of smaller pieces.

The commitment factor

Your own commitment is a big factor, more critical than money for a small paper. You might persuade your editor to let you have the time to work on an investigation. See if those in charge will give you an extra week of vacation in the summer—normally that does not cost them anything. Tell your editor you are not going to work on the story on their time, but on your week of vacation. Editors like that. Block out one or two hours a day to work on that story and use your time effectively. If you are not willing to invest your own time in your career, you may be static for a long time.

The trust factor

A key factor in consumer reporting or in any other investigative reporting assignment is gaining the trust of your editors.

At some point in your career you will probably find a good story—a controversial story that will require your editor to be confident you will do it right. It is probably too late to try to win that trust only when you get that story. Most editors will tell you that the most important thing you can do is to build the trust of your editor day by day. You do not build it on the big, wonderful stories. You build it on the little things—getting names right, turning in clean copy, meeting deadlines, and displaying the attitude that you are working on this medium to learn.

Team reporting

An approach that can make efficient use of both time and money is the team method of doing an investigation. Any paper or television station not large enough to have a full-time consumer reporter could utilize this method by sparing a little time each day for several reporters to work on a special consumer story. Most experienced reporters and editors recommend a strict definition of the goals of the story and the responsibilities of each team member. Some recommend using no more than a two-person team, but other newspapers use more. The important thing is to get hard-working, dedicated people, including at least one good interviewer.

In summary

Although consumer reporting is a relatively new field, there is a rising interest by the general public in this area of specialization. Major expense areas, such as the confusing car rental rates (Hinds 1988), and less costly items such as restaurant tips (Taylor 1988), interest consumers and should attract consumer reporters. As Americans become increasingly health conscious, health spas are a focus of consumer interest (Teitell 1988).

Cost factors are not the only possible approach. *Consumer Reports* (1987a, 1987b) examined both cable television service and paper towels in one issue. The articles advised consumers to check most carefully on the service a cable company offers. A Sunday *Cape Cod Times* article pointed out that leaving home for a vacation without checking on your insurance can be risky (Owens 1988).

Factors influencing the scope and breadth of the media's attention to this subject include the sometimes unpredictable role of the myriad of regulatory agencies, the activity of various consumer groups, and the influence of advertisers on the individual news organizations. Other factors that must receive media attention are cost, time, and the consumer who does not seem to want to be protected. Editors or newsroom directors must weigh these factors against reader or listener demands in order to determine what the reporter's role should be.

References

Barban, Arnold M., and Dunn, S. Watson. 1978. *Advertising: Its Role in Modern Marketing*. Hinsdale, IL.: Dryden Press. 97–98.
Beales, Howard, Mazis, Michael B., Salop, Steven C., and Staelin, Richard. 1981. Consumer Research and Public Policy. *Journal of Consumer Research* 8(1):12.
Bligh, Allan. 1981. Personal interview. Lubbock, Texas, Dec. 11.
Bloom, Paul N. 1982. Consumerism and Beyond: A Overview. In *Consumerism and Beyond: Research Perspectives on the Future Social Environment,* edited by Paul N. Bloom. 1–3. Cambridge, MA.: Marketing Science Institute.
Cohen, Stanley E. 1981. The Ronald Reagan Era: Another New Beginning. *Journal of Advertising* 10(2):3.
Consumer Reports. 1981. The Failure of Product Recalls. 46(1):45–48.
_____. 1987a. Cable TV. 52(9):547–55.
_____. 1987b. Paper Towels. 52(9):581–83.
Consumer Research 1985. The Effects of Communication on Consumers. *Journal of Consumer Research* (Special Issue) 11(4):849–961.
Consumers World. 1988. *New York Times,* July 16, 54.
FTC v. *Raladam,* 1931. 283 U.S. 643.
Gorey, Hays. 1975. *Nader and the Power of Everyman.* New York: Grosset and Dunlap.

Hinds, Michael deCourcy. 1988. The High and Secret Cost of Car Rental. *New York Times,* July 16, 54.

Holsinger, Ralph L. 1987. *Media Law.* New York: Random House.

Innes, Charlotte and Locklin, Bruce. 1987. Wild Bill's Rough Ride to the Top. *The Record* (Hackensack, NJ), Feb. 8, A1.

Kucera, Bill. 1981. Paper Land. *IRE* (Investigative Reporters and Editors) *Journal* 4(4):4.

Leonard-Barton, Dorothy. 1982. Professionals as "Information Priests" in the Diffusion of Innovations: The Case of Dentists. In *Consumerism and Beyond: Research Perspectives on the Future Social Environment,* edited by Paul N. Bloom. 123–29. Cambridge, MA: Marketing Science Institute.

Liefield, John, and Heslop, Louise A. 1985. Reference Prices and Deception in Newspaper Advertising. *Journal of Consumer Research* 11(4):868–76.

Mayer, Robert N. 1989. *The Consumer Movement: Guardians of the Marketplace.* Boston: Twayne Publishers.

Owens, Robert O. 1988. Steps to Take to Insure for a Carefree Vacation. *Sunday Cape Cod Times,* July 17, 56.

Rooker, Robert. 1981. Personal Interview. Lubbock, Texas, July 20.

Stark, Karl and Locklin, Bruce. 1987a. Wild Bill's Deceptive Deals. *The Record* (Hackensack, NJ), Feb. 8, A1.

_____. 1987b. Little Action on Complaints. *The Record* (Hackensack, NJ), Feb. 9, A8.

Taylor, Kimberly. 1988. Restaurants Consider Putting Tip in the Bill. *Eagle-Tribune* (Lawrence, MA), July 18, 14.

Teitell, Beth. 1988. Buyer Beware. *The Cambridge TAB* (Cambridge, MA), July 12, 1.

Weekly Mortgage Rates. 1988. *Sunday Cape Cod Times,* July 17, 57.

Wild in the Showrooms. 1987. *The Record* (Hackensack, NJ), Feb. 11, A26.

This chapter was initiated by McVay. Collaborator was Cassady.

4

Covering
social
frontiers

The components of the category we call social frontiers are subject to change. For example, while specialized science reporters have been around since the 1920s, the environmental reporter did not appear until 1969, and the energy beat was created overnight to cope with the 1973 oil crunch. New beats will emerge in the coming decades.

Stimulated by space-age explorations, the American fascination with science has been dramatized in recent years by the appearance of specialized magazines, television documentaries, public network radio programs, syndicated newspaper columns, and local specialized reporters. Chapter 10, "Science and Health," discusses the task of reporting on advances in research, development, and health issues. It includes discussion of the growing role of news media as reporters and interpreters of the political and social issues that arise in a world increasingly affected by the test tube, the computer, and Medicare.

Chapter 11, "Energy," discusses that

adolescent beat, the dimensions of which vary somewhat from city to city. In general, if you draw the assignment you will be concerned with the supply and costs—economic, social, and physical—of conventional sources of energy in your area, as well as with developments in alternative sources of energy and with collective and individual energy conservation efforts. Controversial issues—the future of nuclear power, subsidies for the installation of solar heating, off-shore oil drilling, the potential for gas rationing, the equity of risks—demand balanced, insightful coverage.

The bottom line in ecology, and in newsrooms today, is that "everything is connected to everything else." On the environment beat, many of the key aspects of public issues come together—urban and rural affairs, government, politics, business and labor, the economy, education, outdoor recreation, social currents, consumer affairs, science, and energy. Chapter 12, "Environment," discusses the specialized task of interpreting the myriad of fragile mechanisms of the natural world, of investigating human impacts on those mechanisms, and of reporting society's attempts to repair or alleviate the adverse impacts.

CHAPTER 10

Science and health

SHORT of Point Barrow, Alaska, you cannot find a much more remote place in the United States than on the Delmarva Peninsula—the Eastern Shore of Delaware, Maryland, and Virginia, the out-of-the-way land James A. Michener immortalized in his novel *Chesapeake.* Yet if you are a reader of the *Onley* (Virginia) *Eastern Shore News,* you would have seen the following story by reporter Curt Badger (1983), representing the ubiquity of science and health as a public issue:

Health officials on alert for rabid animals

A rabid animal has not been caught on the Eastern Shore of Virginia since 1976—and the local health department is glad. During the three-month period from June 1 to Sept. 1 of 1982 environmental health officials in the two counties investigated 29 reported animal bites. That's almost one every three days. Luckily, rabies was not found in any of the animals and none of the victims had to undergo the costly treatment.

Yet state health officials report that an outbreak of rabies has spread this year from eastern West Virginia across northern Virginia and eastward, into Maryland and Pennsylvania, in epidemic proportions. Over 400 cases of rabies have been confirmed in northern Virginia, mostly in raccoons. These cases were primarily in Loudoun, Fairfax, Fauquier, and Prince William counties, but health officials say it now appears to be moving south. Rabies has been found in several raccoons in Orange and Stafford counties. Some people have already had to be treated because they were bitten or scratched by a rabid, or suspected rabid, animal.

Rabies is a fatal illness in humans once it develops. The only way to fight rabies is to prevent it. The newest method of prevention after a person is bitten by a rabid animal is a shot of special human rabies immune globulin (HRIG), followed by a series of human diploid cell vaccine (HDCV), six shots given over a period of 28 days. Fortunately, this vaccine is a lot less painful to the victim than was the previous 14-21 shot series—

except for its cost. Medical supplies may cost as much as $500, not including the cost of visits to the family doctor.

"While the span of the Chesapeake Bay is a natural barrier, the possibility of the outbreak spreading to the Eastern Shore is very real," says Francis C. James, environmental health manager for the Eastern Shore Health District, "especially with the amount of tourism here. For instance, the family pet may have been exposed to rabies at home, and then come along with the family on vacation to the Eastern Shore—not to mention the stream of migrant workers and their pets that pass through every summer."

Because of the danger of rabies spreading to the Shore, the local health department recommends the following:

• Trappers, hunters, and other persons who handle wild animals should get pre-exposure shots, a series of two shots of human diploid cell vaccine. This vaccine would protect them in the event they were scratched or bitten by a rabid animal.

• Get the family pet, cat or dog, vaccinated.

• Keep trash cans tightly covered. Raccoons are known scavengers of trash cans. This is a real concern since the family pet may fight a raccoon that invades the back yard.

If you are bitten or scratched by any animal, pet or stray:

• Wash the wound immediately with soap and water. See a doctor for treatment if the wound is severe.

• Report the animal bite to your local health department. The animal must be examined for rabies. This does not mean the animal will be killed. Often it is only confined for a period of time and then released if no symptoms of rabies appear.

For safety, report the animal bite.

The background

Uncomplicated as that *Eastern Shore News* story is, it illustrates well many key points about reporting and interpreting science and health.

The social programs, technology, and medical care originating in scientific research have an enormous impact on our daily affairs. Each week, new knowledge, discoveries, applications, questions, and problems arise with the potential to affect the nature and quality of life. An increasing number of personal decisions depend upon an understanding of science and the developments associated with it. Yet while the production of new scientific knowledge is continuous, the National Science Foundation (NSF) acknowledges that, other than high school science courses, "society has no organized plan for bringing new scientific knowledge to the general public," so "the science literacy of the American public depends upon a combination of electronic and print media" (Dunwoody 1981).

The discoveries of laboratories and libraries can be promptly and effectively applied in field and factory only if the news media engage in comprehensive reportage. *Washington Post* science writer Victor Cohn believes, for example, that "the role of the media in long-term changes in Americans' health habits is virtually undeniable, though impossible to quantify. Take the changes of the past few decades in the American diet, the changes in smoking habits, and the more recent drop-off in use of the risky pill. None of these would have happened without much plain reporting" (Schoenfeld 1982). Reporter Badger did a good job of pointing out rabies-prevention measures.

Science and health are not so much technical subjects as they are public issues. Because economic and social angles abound, science and health today are "political" in the best sense of the term. As Dave Perlman, science editor of the *San Francisco Chronicle,* points out: "Coverage of the politics of science, of the interaction between science and politics and public affairs and public decision-making in scientific and technological subjects, is one of the most important things science reporters can do" (Schoenfeld 1982). Reporter Badger did not neglect his story's economic angle.

Scientists and doctors are becoming aware that they cannot live in cloistered labs on public monies and remain immune from public scrutiny. Says psychologist Robert A. Baron: "It's become very clear to me that often as scientists we are guilty of not communicating with our friends and neighbors, with the general public, with the people whose tax dollars support our research. If we're going to continue to get public support for our research, we have an obligation to do this as clearly and crisply as possible" (Schoenfeld 1982).

An example of clear writing that helped readers understand modern physics was a five-part series on "The Quantum Leap" in the *Oregonian* of Portland, Oregon. One article began with this dramatic quotation from physicist Neils Bohr: "Anyone who is not shocked by the quantum theory does not understand it" (Kidder 1988). Although its topic was unfamiliar to most readers, the series carefully fulfilled psychologist Baron's basic communication requirement by describing modern physics "in terms that people who are not in science can understand" (Schoenfeld 1982).

To protect the public from quacks, sound science and health care must have their stories told repeatedly and well. Interpreters of science, technology, and medicine should be constantly on guard against "firsts," "seven-day wonders," and "cure-alls." Scientists prize the recognition that comes with being first to present a discovery, and they compete strenuously to attain it, some even to the point of violating the canons of their calling by disseminating inconclusive data. Reporter Badger was blunt about the fact there is no cure for rabies.

The public is interested in news of science and health, and wants more of it. As early as the 1950s, a major study of the public's consumption, understanding, and appreciation of science and health news indicated a lively interest in science, close attention to a considerable proportion of health care news, and a desire for more. Professor Clyde Nunn (1979) offers more recent supporting data; readers in a 1977 survey rated the science-related categories of energy, public health, and environment first, third, and sixth, respectively, among categories whose content they found "very interesting." Ten other national opinion polls, conducted from 1966 to 1990, show a steady increase in persons proclaiming "great confidence" in science.

The media's power to bring issues before the public entails a special responsibility for science and health reporters, because they cover highly technical subjects whose social impact is often a topic of great professional and public controversy. As in any other area of public issues reporting, a primary objective is to present to the public the substance of timely debate as fully and as accurately as possible. The potentially broad impact on the public of scientific, technological, and medical innovation brings science reporting into prominence as a significant link in the policy-making process. Communication scholars Nancy Pfund and Laura Hofstadter (1981) view "greater public involvement as essential," and they feel "more aggressive press is the only way to realize this goal."

In recent decades, the reporting of science and health news has received growing attention from social scientists as well as from news professionals. Several studies have been done on the increasing specialization of the science reporter as a journalistic type, on the special problems involved in interpreting scientific findings and theories for a mass audience, on the competence with which science, technology, and medicine are covered by communication professionals, on scientists themselves as a group, and on the interaction of scientists and reporters (Friedman 1981).

Interpreting science and health: sources and strategies

Good science reporting is marked by the same qualities that underlie good journalism of any type. But there are some special problems for the journalist interpreting science and health to the public because the public is unfamiliar with the way science works. Many scientists have traditionally

STATISTICAL LITERACY

As a reporter, your knowledge of some basic principles of statistics is very important. Even if you are not reporting on science, you will likely be doing your professional newsgathering in our culture, which relies heavily on numbers. You will be reporting and interpreting events and issues to an audience that, for the most part, knows little or nothing about statistical reasoning. The audience will rely on you to help them make the correct sense of things. Sharon Dunwoody comments on the importance of statistical literacy for journalists:

I do know that statistical literacy can make a big difference. A couple [of] years ago, when three San Francisco 49ers players came down with Lou Gehrig's disease, a rare nerve disease with no known cause or cure, speculation focused on the possible role of a processed sewage sludge. Milorganite, manufactured and sold by the Milwaukee Metropolitan Sewerage District, had been used to fertilize the team's practice field. Someone wondered if trace amounts of heavy metals in the sludge might have caused the disease cluster.

One of Milwaukee's two daily newspapers, *The Milwaukee Sentinel,* bought the cause-and-effect link. In copyrighted stories, the newspaper's reporters examined the incidence of Lou Gehrig's disease among sewerage district employees and among county residents, and told of several incidents where individuals exposed to Milorganite in other capacities had come down with the disease.

The Milwaukee Journal, on the other hand, remained silent for several days, finally entering the fray with several front-page stories that argued, among other things, that (1) there was absolutely no evidence of a statistical link between Milorganite and Lou Gehrig's disease, (2) that the three football players represented a disease cluster that could easily have occurred by chance, and (3) that the incidence of Lou Gehrig's disease among county residents did not differ in a statistically significant way from the national incidence of the disease. In other words, there was no proof that Milorganite was even associated with—not to mention caused—Lou Gehrig's disease.

SHARON DUNWOODY. Using Numbers in the News. *Sciphers.* 10(4):1–2. Spring 1990.

wanted it that way, preferring to work isolated from the public. A journalist must therefore work harder at helping audiences to understand scientific issues.

Accuracy

All journalists of course, are concerned with accuracy. But as a science writer you must be doubly attentive. Otic law, "Accuracy Always," is amended for the science writer to read "Precise Accuracy Always."

BUT HOW PRECISE? One veteran science writer says there are two kinds of accuracy, both equally legitimate—that of the technical journal and that of the newspaper or magazine report. Edwin E. Slosson, former editor of Science Service, wrote that "the would-be popularizer is always confronted by the dilemma of comprehensible inaccuracy or incomprehensible accuracy, and the fun of his work lies mainly in the solution of that problem" (Colton 1949).

Need a reporter be as precise as the scientist, and thus run the risk that the information he or she is trying to convey will be incomprehensible to readers, or is it acceptable for a reporter to engage in the colloquial?

For example, suppose you are explaining what a "contour line" is. A geologist would probably say, "a contour line is a brown-tinted line on a geodetic map, representing an unmarked yet surveyed line on the surface of the earth, all points on which are at the same elevation above a mean datum plane." Now that is, of course, an accurate definition, but it would probably confuse the average reader. On the other hand, without really sacrificing accuracy, you could say something like "contour lines are lines on a map that give you a mental picture of the lay of the land itself." In other words, the scientist must establish accuracy to five decimal points, but the science writer can usually deal in round numbers.

"These differences exist primarily because the products serve two very different audiences," Sharon Dunwoody (1986) explains. "While journal articles are 'must' reading for scientists in the field, the mass media audience must be lured into the story. . . . To keep them interested the media use simple versions of words and concepts and eschew detail. This last point is important. While readers of a journal article will pore over their colleagues' research, readers of a newspaper science story will read for only a few main points. . . . Most of these readers will be interested in what the researchers found and why it is important to their daily lives."

In an analysis of the relative accuracy of science reporting, D. L. Pulford (1976) found that while the error rate in science news stories is similar to the mean rate found in accuracy studies of general news stories, most inaccuracy in science writing resulted from errors of omission. Evaluating the accuracy of science news in mass circulation magazines, Susan Borman (1978) also reported that while the general level of accuracy was "good," the most frequent error was the omission of information relevant to a clear understanding of events: failure to name investigators, to explain research methods, or to supply statements distinguishing fact from speculation. More recently, Lea Lundberg (1984) found much the same thing.

UNDERSTANDING AIDS

AIDS is a deadly disease. It is "one of the most serious health problems that has ever faced the American public," according to a brochure sent in May 1988 to all postal customers by United States Surgeon General C. Everett Koop.

Because of taboos on discussing sexual issues in society, there was little discussion of the AIDS-related issues until the death of film star Rock Hudson in 1986. "But now we must discuss them," Surgeon General Koop tells us on the cover of the AIDS brochure. "It is important that we all, regardless of who we are, understand this disease."

The brochure explains that AIDS stands for acquired immunodeficiency syndrome. It is caused by a virus. There are two main ways you can get AIDS. "First, you can become infected by having sex—oral, anal, or vaginal—with someone who is infected with the AIDS virus. Second, you can be infected by sharing drug needles and syringes with an infected person."

It is not just the health community that recognizes AIDS as a threat to every community. Also in May 1988, a Pulitzer Prize was awarded to Jacqui Banaszynski of the *St. Paul* (Minnesota) *Pioneer-Press* for her series on "AIDS in the Heartland." Her series reported on the last year in the life of an AIDS victim from a small town in Minnesota. She told Marquette University's 1988 Journalism graduating class, "You don't have to work for a newspaper like the *New York Times* to do important stories on serious issues."

"Understanding Aids." HHS Publication No. (CDC) HHS–88–8404. Washington, D.C. U.S. Printing Office. 1988.
"Aids in the Heartland." Jacqui Banaszynski. *St. Paul* (MN) *Pioneer-Press.* June 21, July 12, August 9, 1988.

SCIENCE SOURCE HOTLINE

Seeking expert sources for science coverage? You can get free help from the Media Resource Center run by the Scientists' Institute for Public Information (SIPI) in New York City. You merely need to call, toll free, 800-223-1730 and indicate what information you need. The center will search its computer data base and give you names and phone numbers of possible sources by return phone call, often within an hour of your request. The institute also issues a free bulletin on current scientific issues that you can get by writing SIPI at 355 Lexington Avenue, New York, New York 10017.

Clarity

So fraught with public misunderstanding is information about science and health that reporters covering the beat have a special obligation to strive for clarity in their reporting and interpreting. One of the best ways to achieve clarity is to adopt the outline principle explained in Chapter 2, that is, to organize your materials carefully and then make that organization obvious to your audience.

In the following excerpts from a story on the rising costs of health care, note how medical reporter William R. Wineke (1983) leads his readers by the hand through rather complicated data by asking a direct question, supplying a concise answer, injecting another question, and so on. He makes his skeleton outline apparent through the flesh of his story in a (Madison) *Wisconsin State Journal:*

> If you want to know why your health insurance premiums are so high, the Health Care Financing Review has some mind-boggling statistics to explain the problem.
>
> According to review authors Mark Freeland and Carol Schendler, in 1950 the per capita expenditure for health care services in the United States was $82.
>
> That means that an average of $82 was spent by each American during the course of the entire year.
>
> In 1983, per capita spending on health services is expected to reach $1,521. By 1990, that figure will almost double to $2,982.

If those figures seem modest, take a look at the national aggregate figures:

In 1950, the total American health care bill was $12.7 billion. In 1983, it will jump to $362.3 billion; in 1990, it will increase to $755.6 billion.

Where is all that money going to come from? . . .

Where is the money going to go? . . .

Why are health care costs escalating? . . .

Why is new health care construction rising? . . .

All of this means that no matter how mind-boggling health care cost increases have seemed in the past, we haven't seen anything yet.

The worst is yet to come and no one has so far devised any good means of paying for it.

Completeness

Concentration on the "hard" sciences may lead to gross lack of completeness in science coverage. Because social sciences can be an important source of information for lay audiences, S. Holly Stocking (1981) of Indiana University warns science reporters not to overlook the "social" in science. One very important role for the science reporter is to help the public separate valid scientific findings about human behavior from the often speculative pronouncements found in popular books and other mass media.

The social impact of science, technology, and medicine is also a critical part of news coverage. Medical costs, for example, can present a hardship to patients, their families, and the community as a whole. The entire problem of medical costs was examined by Diane Hollenshead (1984) for the *Shreveport Journal*. With help from other *Journal* editors and reporters, Hollenshead covered every aspect of the issue from emergency-room costs to paying the hospital bill. The *Journal* also co-sponsored a symposium on "A Medical Challenge/The Shreveport Plan." The *Journal's* special section was published on the day of the symposium. Hollenshead, 23, had joined the *Journal* just seven months earlier as an education reporter. A four-day seminar and plenty of reading and interviewing helped prepare her for the issues she tackled in the *Journal's* thirty-two-page supplement.

Veteran medical writer William R. Wineke (1987) of the (Madison) *Wisconsin State Journal* also looked beyond the test tubes of medical research to related human issues. He examined the pros and cons of a "med flight" helicopter in the service of a local hospital. Was the helicopter cost effective? Was the hospital, in fact, using it to "steal" patients from other hospitals? Did its life-saving capabilities, in fact, make up for its noise contamination of surrounding residential areas? Wineke's answers: yes, no, and maybe.

Human interest

Adding human interest to your subject involves timeliness, appeal, geography, significance, and names.

TIMELINESS. News, by its simplest definition, is new. That is why the reporter urgently presses for information instead of waiting patiently for a researcher to mail a copy of his or her paper after presenting it at a meeting. As a science reporter, you cannot become so immersed in the relatively timeless aura of laboratory and library that you forget that science stories should be timely.

APPEAL. Just as the science story must be timely, so must it have psychological appeal. The story must deal with the essential elements of reader appeal: struggle, love, suspense, and personal identification.

An item of scientific news seldom appeals to the nonscientific reader because it happens to relate to botany, astronomy, or medicine; the appeal is in the story's emotional value to the reader as an individual. This interest may be purely personal, to the extent that the revelations of the laboratory are used to better daily life; the result of curiosity, either ordinary or scholarly; the result of an interest in progress and the future; or romantic interest in the scientist on the frontiers of research.

Science writers, in other words, should concern themselves with people doing things that are unusual and/or important and not with projects, conceptual schemes, test tubes, and questionnaires.

As intrinsically appealing as any science story is, you still have the obligation, as Edmund Lambeth puts it, to "engage the reader" (Lambeth 1979). To show how to do it, Lambeth uses Christine Duerr's prize-winning piece in the Providence, Rhode Island, *Journal-Bulletin* on "Bay Life." Here's her lead:

> If all the life in all the oceans of the world were suddenly threatened with complete annihilation, and mankind had the resources to preserve only one small body of water from that fate, which would you choose?
>
> Oceanographers would be very likely to choose Narragansett Bay. They know better than most of us what a rich treasure we have here — that our bay is uniquely suited by geography, climate, geology, and topography to nourish an abundance of life.

The special vocabularies of science can seem arcane and inaccessible to the layperson, but not if you relate scientific terms to more familiar matters. Duerr writes of "phytoplankton," the one-celled marine plants that "when magnified they look something like semi-transparent grapefruit, popbead chains, and millstones." She says that diatoms, one of 150 varieties of phytoplankton in Narragansett Bay, "live in an incredible variety of 'glass houses': tiny geodesic domes, delicately ribbed A-frames, bizarrely shaped igloos. The styles haven't changed for millions of years, nor have the building materials. The sturdy little houses in which diatoms live are made of silica, the crystalline compound from which glass is made." In portraying the life cycle of the Bay, Duerr notes the importance of bacteria as they break down plant and animal life into food for other forms of life and keep dissolved organic material from reaching toxic concentrations: "If anemones are the flowers of the sea and jellyfish the dancers, then bacteria are the janitors and recyclers."

GEOGRAPHY. A bricklayer in New York may find it difficult to relate the latest harvesting techniques in Texas cotton fields to his or her own life and times. A steelhead fisherman in Oregon will need to be told the pertinence of trout management in Michigan. A Vermont farmer will wonder whether California architecture could withstand the test of New England winters. So the science writer who does not make every possible attempt to find a logical, local angle to his or her story is missing a bet. For science writers concerned with filling a column in a daily newspaper, this technique requires that you devote the bulk of your articles to local situations or at least to the local application of national developments.

Local ideas and sources

"The majority of people in the United States read local small-town newspapers rather than large national papers," Friedman (1986) and her colleagues note. "Most of the smaller newspapers do not employ full-time specialty reporters. Yet science-related problems such as toxic wastes, air pollution, and groundwater contamination all hit home in small communities, where they must be covered by general assignment reporters who have little training in the understanding of science."

The problems small-town reporters face in covering science include interpretation as well as knowing where to go for the information (Friedman et al. 1986). "Scientists and small-town reporters aren't used to working with each other, and their relationship can be tenuous at best," comments David W. Crisp (1986), one-time reporter for the *Palestine* (Texas) *Herald-Press,* who won an award for science writing. Scientists might seem intimidating to the reporter, says Crisp. "But dealing with scientists can often be a pleasure because they tend to be intelligent, articulate, and dedicated to their work . . . But experts usually aren't indigenous to the community, so they are hard to find and it takes a lot of long-distance phone calls to talk to them." Cultivating such experts, however, can really pay off, says Crisp, "when a national issue hits a small town."

Crisp notes that, along with the big issues, there are many opportunities to report science, even in small communities, if scientists are available to help. Developing a firm background for yourself and your audience is essential. "You can't write a good story about the city sewers without knowing something about gravity flow and bacteria," Crisp advises. "You can't evaluate a standardized test or a poll without knowing something about probability theory and sampling error. You can't write a good story about the price of gasoline without knowing where the oil is and what it takes to get it out."

Here is how "localizing" science might work in a variety of situations:

• You are aware of the international debate about the Greenhouse Effect, the claim that air pollution is gradually causing a warming of the world. What do local weather records say? The summer of 1988 may have set temperature records, but what about the past one hundred years? Has spring been arriving earlier? Have winters been warmer? The summers? Also there may be years of drought, but is there any discernible trend in the past century?

• You and your car-pool mate are comparing notes on the development of your respective one-year-olds. One weighs twenty-three pounds, is walking and talking. The other weighs eighteen pounds, is still crawling, and has yet to say a word. Is anything wrong with either one? You decide to talk to a local pediatrician. You find you are both victims of "statisticitis," and that "average" babies exist only in textbooks. Like every adult, every baby is an individual; no baby develops according to a set pattern. The pediatrician gives you a good deal of background reading, and you come up with a medical story that could bring comfort to those parents who are forever comparing their babies to a chart. You should, of course, also note that a truly marked abnormality should be brought to the attention of a doctor.

• You read a short story in the metropolitan daily serving your area about two university professors who have come up with a simple process that makes better clay products for less money. You wonder what impact their discovery may have on production in the local brickyard and on local brick prices. You interview the local brickyard manager. The development is so new that he has not heard much about it yet, but he is planning to attend a convention to learn. You make plans to call him back in a month. You follow up. He is now using the B-T process, as it is called, involving the controlled addition of soda ash to clay. He says his production costs have dropped, and his bricks are choicer, tougher, and more durable.

• Your publisher has to go to a hospital in a metropolis 160 miles away for her prescribed cardiac surgery. Why does your local small-city hospital not perform the operation, which is relatively routine? Are the surgeons not available? Are the special facilities not available? What would it cost to add the service? Could quality be assured? There may be medical and social-work specialists in your city who could supply answers to these questions.

If you are near a college or university campus, you have access to a ready supply of local stories stemming from research. "A campus is without exception the best place to write stories about how science and technology are changing our lives. Scientists, engineers, philosophers, sociologists, economists, lawyers, and educators can be found who are thoughtful and articulate," says Lorraine Wechsler, journalism professor at Iowa State University (Schoenfeld 1982).

For example, Andy Alm (1985), science reporter for the Eureka, California, *Times-Standard,* visited the campus of Humboldt State University in nearby Arcata one day and came away with two stories, one on seaweed culture and one on a strange mammal, the ringtail. His leads went as follows:

Humboldt Bay seaweed may mean big money

You can eat it, fertilize fields with it, feed it to cattle, use it to thicken ice creams, or turn it into fuel for your furnace or automobile.

Seaweed culture is a multi-million dollar business in Japan, but has barely gotten its feet wet in this country.

Part of the problem is nobody is quite sure whether it can be done here. Humboldt State University biology professor Robert A. Rasmussen intends to find out.

Ringtails researched

Richard Callas recalls that his grandfather used to tell stories about squirrel-sized animals that looked like a cross between a raccoon and a cat.

Callas thought nothing more about these accounts until, years later, a friend discovered one of the creatures injured on Highway 299. Until then, he thought the animal was just legend.

Curiosity whetted, Callas began studying the ringtail, or *Bassaricus astutu,* as it is known in scientific circles. Today this nocturnal mammal is the subject of his master's thesis in natural resources at Humboldt State University.

Significance

For science writers who are building feature articles for a national syndicate or magazine, the perspective of geography requires that they give their reportage as broad a geographic base as possible. As the editor of a national outdoor magazine once told his correspondents: "Get the national-level interpretation. Our magazine is distributed in all 50 states. What's important in Cow Creek near Lonesome Valley isn't worth a damn in New York City [unless it is] given a clever treatment, either as humor, human interest, or timeless news" (Stein 1949).

As a science writer, you must get to the heart of each issue. You must alert your readers to the big picture—the implications and significance of a single event in the context of a larger scheme—as well as to the momentary account of that single event.

To separate the news of real scientific advancement from insignificant or unsound scientific claims, you should generally ask two questions of each potential science story: (1) Does it show how research and engineering are helping to overcome human failings and physical limitations? and (2) Is it on a subject of interest to all readers who wish to be informed?

Lest a reader become confused, good science writing must provide "orientation"; that is, it must supply a context that gives meaning to the reported facts (Lambeth, 1979). As an example, Lambeth (1979) cites Peter Stoler's prize-winning account of the fossil searches of anthropologist Richard Leakey. Stoler wrote:

> He (Leakey) and his dusty band are looking, almost literally, for footprints in the sands of time, for clues to the mystery of man's origins. Their ambitious goal: to establish the nature of the creatures that veered off from the ancestral line of apes onto the evolutionary path that eventually led to man. In this pursuit, Leakey's team has turned up at the Turkana site alone more than 300 fossilized bone specimens from an estimated 180 of man's ancestors. All told, during a decade-long search, Leakey has found more and better pre-man and early man fossils than any other anthropologist. His work has helped upset many long-held ideas on evolution and has forced science to write a new scenario for man's slow progress from ape to Shakespeare's paragon of animals, Homo sapiens.

Many scientists are involved in what is called pure, or basic, research—a search for knowledge with no thought of immediate application. Indeed, basic research underlies all applied research and technology. Its importance should not be overlooked by reporters; neither should practical applications be implied when none are pertinent. An overly eager reporter once tried to enliven a story about an esoteric discovery in biochemistry by suggesting that the enzyme just isolated might someday lead to a cure for a certain type of cancer. An even more careless editor supplied "New Cancer Cure" as a headline to the article. Hundreds of desperate cancer patients wrote to the laboratory for free samples of the "medicine" — a tragic example of the damage sloppy science and health reporting can exact.

Names

That names make news is, of course, a journalistic truism, and one that you as a science writer must constantly bear in mind. Test tubes, microscopes, documents, and most of the other gear of science are inanimate and essentially dull; but people are interesting. The use of names will personalize any story and will also lend it authority.

Some scientists vigorously protest the use of their names in stories on the grounds that it amounts to personal glorification, which can be a device used by charlatans to promote their own trade. This is an unfortunate line of thinking, for a scientist's name in a story is some protection for the public against careless reporting. A statement without a reference is not a solid statement.

Of course, the use of too many names will clutter up a story. It is unwise to burden a story with a long list of names and affiliations of all those who have contributed in a minor way to the results being reported. Most of the names will mean nothing to readers, and they will take up precious space and impede the story's readability.

From his study of press coverage of marijuana, Gordon Shepherd believes that science reporters tend to err by seeking out sources who are celebrities in the field of science, rather than going to persons at the cutting edge of research in a particular field, whose names may be unknown to the general public, but whose news may be more substantial than that of the well-known scientists. "If reporters write a story on the performance of athletes on the playing field," says Shepherd, "their first informants will be the athletes themselves, not their coaches, managers, or club owners. If mass publics are to be informed of scientific evidence bearing on controversial issues, who better to query than those specialists whose own research has won them the recognition of their scientific peers" even though they may as yet be unknown to the public in general (Shepherd 1980).

One good way to inject names, and hence, living, breathing people, into science and health reporting is by adopting the focus principle explained in Chapter 2.

"How dangerous is acid rain?" was the headline of a story by Margot Hornblower (*National Wildlife* 1983). Her theme was that "across much of North America, the latest scientific research points to the ominous conclusion that acid rain is widely endangering the eco-system. What once seemed to be a problem confined to a few hundred poorly-buffered, high-altitude lakes and streams in Canada and New York's Adirondack Mountains is now recognized as a far more pervasive threat."

Hornblower lends human scale to her story by introducing us at the outset to a representative scientist and his work:

> Hubert W. Vogelmann, a University of Vermont botanist, gazes wistfully at a slide projected on the screen: a verdant forest of fir and spruce, thick, luxuriant, blanketing Camel's Hump Mountain. "I took this picture in 1963," he notes. "See how green, how healthy the vegetation is?"
>
> With a flick of the finger, Vogelmann changes the image. "Here's the same mountain photographed last fall," he adds, gesturing toward an expanse of gray skeletons now covering Camel's Hump. "It looks as if someone has taken a blow torch and swept through the trees."
>
> As far as Vogelmann and his fellow scientists are concerned, the explanation is obvious. "Every time it rains in Vermont, the rain is 30 to 40 times more acid than normal rain should be," he says. "Week after week, month after month, we are being deluged with acid precipitation."
>
> The botanist's research shows that, since the mid-1960s, half the spruces have died over a broad area on four mountaintops, where high elevation, frequent showers and fog expose trees to high acidity. Trunk cores show that growth rates there have slowed dramatically since the late 1950s — a period that coincides with steady increases in the levels of sulfur emissions and other air pollutants in the eastern half of the country. Seedlings have since disappeared entirely from parts of the forest floor. The soils have lost crucial nutrients. The damage, Vogelmann says, "may well be irreversible."

History, past and future

Every story has a past, as well as a present and a future. The science reporter who fails to suggest whence the development being covered came, and what and who lie behind it, has an incomplete story.

The failure of reporters to give credit where it is due is one of the complaints scientists most frequently level at the press. Scientists argue that their own work is built upon the work of their predecessors, and they usually underscore this point in any learned report of their work. Consequently, they expect journalists to illuminate that point also. Some scientists are so insistent on this point that one gets the impression that any mention of, say, the law of inversity, should be traced back to Darwin's discoveries. Too much historical information would make a science story read like a textbook, which is what some scientists probably would prefer. You cannot write a definitive history of science in every half-column account of a research development, but handled briefly and simply, the historical perspective can serve a very useful purpose.

Science, as Edmund Lambeth (1979) points out, is a lengthy pageant, some of whose participants prefer that references be made to the research giants on whose shoulders they themselves sit. Such background need not consume much space. Witness this touch of history in Mike Lenehan's prize-winning piece on "The Essence of Beeing" in the *Chicago Reader:*

> Part of this tendency (on the parts of bees) to work one flower at a time is no doubt attributable to the famous 'dance language' of bees, first noted by M. J. E. Spitzner in the 1780s and later fully described by Viennese-born biologist Karl von Frisch, who shared a 1973 Nobel Prize for his work. Von Frisch described two basic types of dance, the 'round dance', which is used to tell of a food source within about 100 yards of the hive, and the 'wag tail dance', which tells of a more distant source (Lambeth 1979).

Market sense

Another important perspective in science, technology, and medicine reportage is that of the market for whom you are writing. As a science writer, you should develop an ability to "slant" your work away from the scientist and toward the public press, be it magazine, newspaper, or television. To make your writings understandable to a mass audience, fill them with references to the equipment and practices of ordinary folks. In other words, be human. Many writers are concerned more with their message than with their delivery, and consequently, they fail to convey their intended message. To avoid this pitfall, writer David W. Ewing recommends a "situational approach" to writing, in which writing depends on the readers and their relationship to the writer (Schoenfeld 1982).

Research into readability of science writing supports the use of the traditional rhetorical devices taught in English composition classes: simple words, short sentences, active voice, relating the unfamiliar to the familiar, graphs, charts, illustrations, examples, parables, and, in particular, metaphor. The more "passive" the use of the message by the audience, the more important are such readability techniques (Bostian and Byrne 1984, and Bowes et al. 1978).

Qualification and reservation

University of Missouri journalism professor Donald Brenner says that "a major problem with science reporters is their inclination to over-promise, to talk about miracle cures when there are none. They want to describe breakthroughs. Scientists never voluntarily talk about breakthroughs" (Schoenfeld 1982).

Medical writers, for example, frequently fail to make a distinction between a "treatment" and a "cure." With faintly concealed exasperation, scientists wonder why reporters cannot follow a simple procedure to avoid this misrepresentation. Having stated that a technique will work, or may work, under certain conditions, the journalist should quickly state under what conditions it will not work. This will decrease the chance for confusion in the reader's mind.

Always be absolutely certain of all your facts. At all times avoid embarrassing your source with exaggerated claims. Do not write more into an advance in technology than is actually there. If a technique is merely a step toward better methods, present it as a step and not as a seven-league stride.

As a science writer, not only should you present any and all facts with their appropriate and specific qualifications, but you should approach the entire story with a generally reserved attitude. You should avoid an overly positive or overly emotional tone. You should also leave the door open for disagreement by other experts, for failure in a new set of circumstances of the success you are reporting, and for new developments that will outdate the discovery you are reporting. For example, Barbara Beckwith charges in the *Columbia Journalism Review* that the news media have embraced genetic explanations of sexual differences with "trendy zeal," all but ignoring the profoundly controversial aspects of these sociobiological theories (Beckwith 1984). Professor Lambeth emphasizes the point that good science and health writing will always qualify scientific assertion. To illustrate, toward the end of the account of Richard Leakey's fossil searches, writer Solter points out that "doubts about the sequence of man's emergence remain. Scientists concede that even their most cherished theories are based on embarrassingly few fossil fragments, and that huge gaps exist in the fossil record. Anthropologists, ruefully says Alan Mann of the University of Pennsylvania, are like the blind men looking at the elephant, each sampling only a small part of the total reality" (Lambeth 1979).

In trying to find reality, journalists must deal only with its small parts. But they must still keep looking for the significant parts. Unfortunately, says Fred Jerome, director of the Media Resource Service program of the Scientists' Institute for Public Information, "for the most part, science in the mass media has remained a sales contest in which headline makers, cover illustrators, and TV admen scramble to come up with the newest newness, and major policy issues continue to be downplayed or ignored" (Jerome 1986).

COVERING MEDICINE CAN BE HAZARDOUS TO YOUR HEALTH

Like medicine itself, medical news can be a life-or-death business. . . .

The amount of medical information has been snowballing for years, and with it the amount of controversy. Nowadays, even such accepted treatments as coronary-bypass surgery and aspirin for children's ailments are being challenged on TV, and debates continue to rage over herpes and the causes of cancer. In response to the strain, some doctors just sigh and quote Thomas Jefferson: "It is better to know nothing than to know what is wrong."

If medical news burdens doctors, it's even more of a burden on journalists who have to keep up with it, understand it and—hardest of all—present it correctly. Invariably, their reports are carefully worded: "Researchers *believe* alcohol causes birth defects"; "Aspirin *might* prevent strokes"; "Interferon *promises* a cure for cancer." But such qualifiers slide by easily, and many viewers hear what they want to hear.

"We are very protective because we're dealing with vast populations of people who are desperate, and desperate people grasp at straws," says George Strait, an ABC News medical correspondent. And the dangers of self-prescribing are compounded by the common attitude that "If some is good, more is better . . . "

The fact that so many alleged medical advances reach the screen prematurely also fosters false hopes and fears. Normally, a researcher reports his findings in a professional journal following peer review, even though his conclusions may well be tentative. The networks all subscribe to the major medical journals. They regularly pick up the lead stories, squeeze a half-dozen pages of text into a minute and a half, add a dramatic gloss and air them—at the rate of about three stories per network news show per week. But because they prefer to report "news," TV journalists sometimes select items too new or speculative to be interpreted, even by experts.

CAREY GOLDBERG. Who Knows Best—The Doctor or the Reporter? *TV Guide.* 30(48):432–45, Nov. 27-Dec. 3, 1982.

Cooperation

Working together, scientists and writers can accomplish what neither group can accomplish singly.

It is a rule of thumb among scientists that the report of a development should initially be made available to "the trade" through a learned journal. To violate this standard operating procedure is to jeopardize or destroy professional contacts. If the project has been completed, but not yet announced in a professional or technical publication, you can offer to time the release of your story to coincide with the date of publication of the journal. If the project is completed, or if some results have been achieved but will not be released until a paper has been presented before a scientific body, offer to write the story based on the paper, and release it simultaneously with the presentation of the paper. If a project is still in the earliest experimental stages, a story should not be written at all unless the scientist or scientists involved do not object to a bare announcement that the project has been launched.

An article published in a reputable journal does not represent merely the opinions of its author; it bears the imprimatur of scientific authenticity, as given by the editor and the referees consulted. This provides extra protection for the reporter.

What we have just said, of course, applies to relations with scientists in the nonindustrial world. Industrial scientists' publications are usually withheld for periods of as long as one year or more until discoveries can be patented, because patent laws usually deny patents on work already published.

Admittedly, cooperation has its pitfalls. Professor Phillip Tichenor (1970) and his colleagues have found that reporters can be co-opted by the science establishment, losing their objectivity and becoming little more than "flacks" for individual scientists or whole research centers. In so doing, reporters quickly lose standing within the journalism community and, sooner or later, within the scientific community as well. So cooperation must not become a synonym for subservience.

Wariness

Many reporters and scientists are very cautious about dealing with each other. For some scientists, this caution stems from being "burned" due to inaccurate media accounts of their work in the past. For some journalists, wariness is due to their lack of scientific knowledge, a sense that scientists are hard to understand, the reporter's inability to separate good science from bad, and a fear of being used or misled.

"Scientists are no more neutral than anyone else," claims Nicholas A. Ashford (1983), a Massachusetts Institute of Technology professor of technology. "The thing that is dangerous is that they cloak their values in terms of their scientific expertise." In addition, some reporters fear that the few

UNTANGLING THE NUMBERS

The best journalists typically bring to their stories a healthy skepticism that makes it extremely difficult for unscrupulous or ignorant sources to use or to wildly mislead them.

But the normal, healthy skepticism rarely manifests itself when journalists write about complex research reports written by faceless researchers or bureaucrats who are unavailable to explain their work.

Most journalists seem unable to judge whether numbers are really meaningful or accurate. Consequently, they either trust all figures or they trust none; and they tend to focus exclusively on a report writer's conclusions, while ignoring specific numbers and data collection techniques.

But journalists can take a more realistic approach to stories based on someone else's figures if they will consider the following guidelines for evaluating, understanding, and reporting research reports and the numbers they contain:

1. Is a study that uses a non-probability sample being passed off as sound scientific research?
2. Is a report writer trying to generalize beyond the population from which the study's sample was drawn?
3. Does the use of large doses in an experimental study need to be explained?
4. Is correlation likely to be confused with causation?
5. Have possible contaminating variables been controlled for in an experiment?
6. Are intercoder reliability figures reported for content analysis studies?
7. Can estimates of health risks from potentially hazardous materials be reported in a meaningful way?
8. Can a legitimate research report be reported in a way that does not make it seem trivial?
9. Is a research report so trivial or so poorly done it is not worth a story?
10. What is the credibility of the channel through which the report is published?
11. Do scientists involved in the preparation of a study have vested interests or conflicts of interest?
12. Is the research report an example of advocacy research and not worthy of a story?

JAMES W. TANKARD, JR., and MICHAEL RYAN. 1982. Untangling the Numbers: Journalists Can Cope with Complex Research. *Newspaper Research Journal.* 3(4):61–68.

scientists they encounter may try to scoop competitors who are on the same research track by making a public announcement of their findings. Reporters can alleviate some of these problems by using multiple sources, emphasizing trends rather than a single discovery claim, and by finding out whether the scientist's findings have been published in a learned journal or read to a convention or some other scientific body (Minten 1985).

Many scientists do not know much about journalism, Sharon Dunwoody (1986) observes, mainly because they have no reason to learn. Most scientists encounter reporters occasionally, at best, and may harbor stereotypical views of journalists as sensationalizers.

Dealing with journalists can be particularly risky for scientists, Dunwoody says, in that "the scientific community does not reward its members for informing the public, and in some instances it may punish them for doing so." A scientist, she explains, is expected to be preoccupied with doing high-quality research. Unless the scientist is well established within the research community, he or she may get reprisals from other scientists for taking time out for such activities as communicating with the public. "Charismatic teachers," she notes, "don't win Nobel Prizes."

Nonetheless, some scientists do feel rewarded for public communication activities, Dunwoody observes. Among the rewards, she says, are personal satisfaction in helping the public understand science, recognition by the public, their employers, and some of their peers, and the type of visibility that can help them obtain research grants.

Public policy

In interpreting science and health, your goal should be to present an articulated scenario of public policy issues and not just a series of disjointed, newly breaking stories. A dean of science journalists, Hillier Krieghbaum (1979), points out that "science reporting has to move beyond the stage of 'Gee Whiz!' coverage. Social implications of science and health care have become increasingly important, and so have the politics of science and medicine."

After performing in-depth studies of press coverage of biomedical innovation, Nancy Pfund and Laura Hofstadter (1981) offer these criteria for effective science and health journalism today:

• Match an understandable translation of technical material with a clear conveyance of its social context and possible ramifications.

• Increase coverage of issues as opposed to spot news.

• Examine possible conflicts of interest.

• Recognize that scientists are not the only legitimate spokespersons for the consequences of scientific innovation.

• Convey controversy and opinions of diverse experts.
• Faithfully reflect the increasing complexity of progress in science and health.

Reporting on health risks

There has been increasing concern about the ways in which information about health risks (for example, the likelihood of death or disease from chemicals in the environment, from nuclear radiation, from radon in homes) is conveyed to the public. Research shows that members of the public tend to rely on the mass media for information about such risks (Freimuth et al. 1987). News reportage of risk could therefore affect public understanding, public opinion, and public policy (Cohn 1990).

One problem that reporters face is that communicating about risks is essentially communicating about probabilities (Wilkins and Patterson, 1989), such as the annual risk of death from smoking a pack of cigarettes a day. Most people have difficulty understanding probabilities and how these risk statistics would relate to the everyday decisions they make (Dunwoody and Neuwirth, 1988). In addition, most reporters are not themselves well versed in statistics. Generally, the news media have difficulty covering and interpreting such risks for the public (Sandman et al. 1987).

The media tend to overemphasize some risks, and under-report others, says *Washington Post* medical reporter Victor Cohn (1990). He blames both journalists and their scientific sources for coverage shortcomings. For example, scientists may pre-judge reporters as being incompetent and may need to improve their own communication skills; reporters usually seek controversy, tend to be too trusting of officials, and often look for the scare *du jour*. Complicating matters, Cohn says, is that even the experts disagree about risks from health hazards. Some tips for coverage of health risks are offered by Cohn, by *Philadelphia Inquirer* reporter Jim Detjen, and by Vincent Covello, head of Columbia University's Center for Risk Communication (Cohn et al. 1990). They suggest that journalists should be suspicious of:

• A definite estimate of a risk; for example, "327 out of 1 million will develop cancer from exposure to chemical X." Risks should be presented as an estimate or as a range, usually starting with *zero*.
• Anecdotal cases used to back up a theory. Risk should be estimated from a pattern among several studies over a long period of time.
• Use of comparisons. It is often inaccurate to compare the risks of one hazard to the risks of another.
• Bias: "I wouldn't have seen it if I hadn't believed it."

REPORTING PUBLIC RISK PERCEPTIONS

Reporting on health risks can mean covering social science as well as medical science. In her article, "Risk vs. Reality: How the Public Perceives Health Hazards," reporter Cristine Russell told *Washington Post* readers about some of the dynamics of the public's reactions to risks, based on the findings of social science research. Her lead introduced the subject in terms of a public issue:

New Jersey had a problem. A cancer-causing, radioactive substance was widespread in homes throughout the state, threatening the health of thousands of residents. State officials worried that publicity about the hazard could cause a panic.

But just the opposite happened.

Two years after announcing the health problem, officials are confronting a surprisingly different problem — apathy. Many New Jersey residents have ignored a major risk that is literally in their own back yards: radon gas that occurs naturally in uranium-containing rocks and soils and seeps into basements. . . .

Yet public hysteria did erupt when state officials tried to dispose of dirt containing low levels of radon-emitting industrial waste from an old luminescent paint factory. . . .

The writer then introduced the broader perspective:

Why did the public ignore government warnings about the danger of high levels of natural radon while panicking about what state experts saw as the insignificant threat of low-level radioactive waste?

Understanding why experts and the public fail so frequently to agree on the nature of health risks is of growing concern not only to government officials but to academic researchers and environment activitists, as well.

Efforts to bridge the gap — studying how the public perceives risk and how best to explain it — have created a burgeoning new field called "risk communication."

Reporter Russell then interviewed a researcher:

"The core of the problem is that the risks that kill people are often not the same as the risks that frighten and anger people," said Peter Sandman, head of the Rutgers University environmental communication research program. . . . "Risk for the experts means how many people will die, but risk for the public means that plus a great deal more. Is it fair or unfair? Is it voluntary or coerced? Is it familiar or high-tech and exotic?"

When it comes to the *perception* of risk, radon in rocks is not the same as radon in industrial wastes. . . .

REPORTING PUBLIC RISK PERCEPTIONS *(continued)*

Russell's article explains some of the factors—for example, whether risks are voluntary, local, natural, well-known—that affect a person's reactions to risk, and explores some concerns related to communicating information about risks to the public. She raises the issue of whether communities and the public will ignore what could be a flood of information about hazardous chemicals present in their communities, as this information becomes publicly available under the Emergency Planning and Community Right-to-Know Act, passed as Title III of the Superfund Amendments and Reauthorization Act (SARA) of 1986.

Overall, the article is a fine example of interpreting science as a public issue.

CRISTINE RUSSELL. 1988. Risk vs. Reality: How the Public Perceives Health Hazards. *Washington Post.* June 14, Health section, 14–18.

They recommend that reporters ask sources:

- How do you know? How can you be sure?
- What are your numbers? How did you get them?
- How valid (accurate) and reliable (reproducible) are the results?
- What is the normal occurence rate? What is the probability of chance causing the same results?
- Has the study undergone peer review? Who reviewed it? What are their credentials? What are their biases?
- How many people or animals were used in the study?
- Has your work been duplicated in other labs?
- Who are your critics?
- Would you expose yourself or your children to this risk?

Generally, the media should be more sensitive to covering potential hazards before they occur, so that events become follow-up stories, observes Bud Ward, executive director of the National Safety Council's Environmental Health Center. "The best stories," he says, "will come prior to any news peg" (Leistner 1990).

Research projects that investigate risk communication have been sponsored by the Environmental Protection Agency and various research centers. This research promises to provide further guidance to journalists regarding ways to communicate effectively with the public about risks from health hazards.

Case studies

The following case studies are examples of science and health reporting that delve beyond events and bring interpretation to bear on discussion of public policy.

"Broken promises"

Bemused by what *Parade Magazine* science writer Earl Ubell has called "the incredible journey" of advances in science and health care in the 1980s, science, technology, and health reporters can easily fall into a trap of believing that God is in his heaven and all is right with the world. It took CBS's "60 Minutes" until the night of March 24, 1985, to discover that all might not be right with the world of nursing home care, for example, but a pair of reporters for the *Champaign-Urbana* (Illinois) *News-Gazette* had made that discovery a year earlier.

In 1979, the Illinois General Assembly had adopted tough new legislation to clean up the state's widely criticized nursing home industry. Its much publicized "reform" act was hailed as perhaps the strictest law of its kind in the country. Critics of the industry—including a number of newspapers—joined the applause for the improvements they had helped inspire.

Five years later, two *News-Gazette* reporters took the first hard look at whether those reforms had accomplished their purpose locally. In an investigation that culminated with four months of full-time effort, they found many of the same problems that had prompted the new law. They found "reforms" that existed only on paper, and a state agency that would not—perhaps could not—enforce them. Examining hundreds of documents, Mike Howie and Steve Bauer found violation after violation of state law recorded on the state's own inspection reports and few if any attempts to enforce compliance with the reform act. They interviewed dozens of sources—almost all of them identified in the stories by name.

Their six-part series (Howie and Bauer 1984) revealed unsanitary and unsafe conditions, understaffed facilities, and unlicensed administrators at the East Central Illinois nursing homes they examined in detail. The series revealed so-called "surprise" inspections by the state that came as no surprise to the nursing home personnel, and a state bureaucracy that admitted it had never implemented key portions of the reforms. The series concluded with articles on how the public could help nursing home residents, on how a family could find a good nursing home, and on the alternatives to nursing home care.

These headlines impart the flavor of how Howie and Bauer went about their task:

Broken promises remain from nursing home act

Despite state codes, violations continue

Nursing home reform bark worse than bite

Wanted: elixer for nursing homes

Institutional care takes toll on quality of life

Questions, visits may lead to best nursing home

Within weeks of the series, an ad hoc organization of volunteers, senior citizen groups, and local public agencies responded by forming a task force to improve the quality of life in the area's nursing homes. Prompted by the *News-Gazette* series, the group started a movement to increase volunteer involvement in nursing homes and to conduct its own inspections of facilities. The series won an Inland Daily Press Association Award.

"The deadly cure"

Methadone, the drug pushed by Uncle Sam as the way to halt heroin addiction, has contributed to thousands of deaths during the past decade while becoming a significant drug of abuse in its own right.

Its victims include patients who sought a cure for their drug abuse, thrill-seekers who bought it on the streets, and unborn children carried by methadone-using mothers.

And each year, more narcotics abusers treated with methadone become trapped in a closed cycle of addiction, dropping in and out of treatment but never able to break completely free of the clinics that dispense this government-sanctioned, government-subsidized drug.

The federal government accepted responsibility for the safety of patients treated with methadone in late 1972 when officials decided to approve the drug's use and help pay for its distribution, which has cost American taxpayers more than $1 billion.

After 11 years, no one knows the full extent of the injuries and deaths related to methadone; until the *Fort Lauderdale News* and *Sun-Sentinel*

began a year-long review of the national methadone program, nobody even had an idea.
Government records disclose:

So began the first of forty-four stories by medical writer Fred Schulte (1983), who won a first-place Inland Daily Press Association Award given for a series reporting and interpreting public affairs. How Schulte went about generating his data is a dramatic example of the use of computers to decipher obscure public records.

Schulte began investigating the treatment of narcotics addicts after receiving a plaintive phone call from a south Florida methadone patient. As he dug into the story he discovered government officials had little hard information readily available, so he began filing formal requests for data under the federal Freedom of Information Act.

Slowly, information started to come in. Obscure statistical reports from university research libraries and the archives of the National Institute on Drug Abuse showed that few of the hundreds of thousands of addicts treated with methadone were able to shake off their addiction. A printout of data never before extracted from computers of the Food and Drug Administration showed thousands of adverse reactions to methadone. A computer run never before attempted by the Drug Enforcement Administration—titled "The Fred Schulte Report" by a waggish bureaucrat— showed thousands of deaths and injuries attributed at least in part to methadone.

Schulte searched page by page through two years' worth of medical examiners' files in two counties, and examined police reports in seven jurisdictions to piece together portraits of some of the methadone casualties in south Florida. Reports on every inspection of methadone-dispensing clinics in the state over ten years were assembled and punched into the computers of the *News* and *Sun-Sentinel* for a statistical analysis. Schulte traced the genesis of both methadone therapy and the national drug-abuse treatment bureaucracy through forgotten files in the National Archives. Officials there said they did not believe the files had ever been examined before by anyone other than archivists. The upshot: the government's own records showed methadone to be what Schulte called "The Deadly Cure."

Hints on getting started in science and health reporting

Veteran science writers, general assignment reporters interested in science writing, scientists and instructors met several years ago at Lehigh University for a three-day workshop on how to

improve investigating and interpreting science and health issues, particularly for small- or medium-sized local newspapers. At the workshop's close, Professor Sharon M. Friedman, its organizer, summarized the major workshop
suggestions (1981):

1. To write good science-related articles, use a number of sources, both for
   story information and for checking out slant, objectivity, and veracity of
   the material and the prime sources. Put more background research into
   these articles and know your topics fairly well.
2. Understand the numbers involved in such stories, be they sample sizes or
   energy curves. Sometimes studying the numbers reveals obscured information and provides a better story.
3. Be accurate, and this includes checking back with sources to ensure accurate copy. Every science writer—like every journalist—makes mistakes.
   Expect a few, but do not let them discourage you. The more you write
   about science-related topics, the fewer mistakes you will make.
4. Always be learning. David Perlman, science editor of the *San Francisco
   Chronicle,* has said "a science writer is probably the only reporter on a
   newspaper staff who gets paid his salary for attending, albeit haphazardly,
   a never-ending graduate school in all of his favorite subjects."
5. Try to do as much interpretive reporting of science-related issues as you
   can. Do not be afraid of taking an explanatory feature approach to
   science stories—they are the "bread and butter" of science writing. You
   still will have to work within a hard news peg some of the time, but try to
   convince your editor that in-depth articles are more interesting and serve
   readers better. Explain why science-related articles take more time in
   terms of accuracy and research, and try to get two or three days to write
   such articles rather than two or three hours.
6. Avoid the approach of the lazy reporter who overlooks major issues
   because he is too busy covering routine meetings. Also, go back to old
   stories and follow them up. Keep a date file on when to check back.
7. Remember, often science-related stories need that extra step beyond regular reporting to find, understand, translate, and write the article. You
   should try to initiate many of your own story ideas because you will
   probably have a better sense of what science-related topics are important
   or need to be covered than your editor. This is particularly true for complex topics involving in-depth reporting.
8. Editors can be a stumbling block because of their unfamiliarity with
   science and perhaps even their disinterest. But they can be shown that
   these articles have reader appeal; the better the material you turn in, the
   more they will be convinced.
9. Scientists, too, can be stumbling blocks, but keep in mind that they have
   different perspectives and sensitivities when you deal with them. Be aware
   of and sensitive to their problems with the press. Good preparation on
   your part will help ease their discomfort.
10. Local stories that are interesting, even exciting, can be found if you put a
    little effort into the search. Checking with local universities and research-
    oriented industries on a regular basis can provide both good article ideas
    and good contacts. Getting on the mailing lists of national scientific
    groups for press releases and background materials also can alert you to
    story ideas that will interest your readers.

By responding to such suggestions, you can join the growing cadre of journalists bringing sharper skills to the interpretation of issues in the field of science and health.

SCIPHERS

Practitioners, students, and professors of science writing have their own newsletter, Sciphers, *a quarterly review of books, articles, and research reports, news of internships and awards, and helpful how-to analyses. For information, write* The Science Journalism Center, University of Missouri, Columbia, MO 65205.

In summary

"Modern culture differs from classical culture primarily because of the scientific revolution," observes physicist Hugh T. Richards (1988). Unfortunately, Richards adds, few individuals have an educational background adequate to follow and appreciate the evolving world that is as much influenced by scientific developments. These developments are behind such issues as arms control, genetic engineering, space exploration, acid rain, depletion of the ozone layer, and alternative energy sources. "Decisions about the scientific and technological issues faced by society are of increasingly critical importance," Richards asserts, "and must not be left to a few inside scientific advisers . . . For rational decisions we need desperately that the educated class be scientifically literate."

While educational institutions must play a key role in the scientific literacy of the populace, there is no doubt that coverage of science by journalists can contribute to the public's understanding of science. More importantly, journalists must put health and science issues into a full and clear context if wise decisions are to be made on these public issues.

As pressing public issues, science and health deserve the best interpretive reporting journalists can muster. In this chapter we have talked about the perspectives that journalists must have—including accuracy, clarity, completeness, and wariness—if they are to cover these issues. The fascinating and demanding task of making sense for your readers and listeners out of science and health news requires that you have them all.

References

Alm, Andy. 1985. *Eureka* (CA) *Times-Standard,* Nov. 17, 6, 11.
Ashford, Nicholas A. 1983. A Roundtable Discussion About Science at EPA. *Environment* 25(6):6–14.
Badger, Curt. 1983. *Eastern Shore News.* Onley, VA. June 2, 16.
Beckwith, Barbara. 1984. He-Man, She-Woman. *Columbia Journalism Review.* (January/February):46–47.
Borman, Susan Gray. 1978. Communication Accuracy in Magazine Science Reporting. *Journalism Quarterly* 55(2): 345–46.
Bostian, Lloyd R., and Byrne, Thomas E. 1984. Comprehension of Styles of Science Writing. *Journalism Quarterly* 61(3):676–78.
Bowes, John E., Stamm, Keith R., Jackson, Kenneth M., and Moore, Jeff. 1978. *Communication of Technical Information to Lay Audiences.* Seattle, WA: Communication Research Center, School of Communication, University of Washington.
Cohn, Victor. 1990. *Reporting on Risk: Getting It Right in an Age of Risk.* Washington, D.C.: The Media Institute.
Cohn, Victor, Covello, Vincent, and Detjen, Jim. 1990. Questions/Answers. *Sciphers* 10(4):3.
Colton, F. Barrows. 1949. Some of My Best Friends Are Scientists. *Scientific Monthly* 69(September):156–60.
Crisp, David W. 1986. Scientists and the Local Press. In *Scientists and Journalists,* edited by Sharon M. Friedman, Sharon Dunwoody, and Carol L. Rogers, 73–78. New York: Free Press.
Dunwoody, Sharon. 1981. *Selected Bibliography: Research on Science Communication.* Washington, D.C: American Association for the Advancement of Science.
_____. 1986. The Scientist as Source. In *Scientists and Journalists,* edited by Sharon M. Friedman, Sharon Dunwoody, and Carol L. Rogers, 3–16. New York: Free Press.
Dunwoody, Sharon, and Neuwirth, Kurt. 1988. Coming to Terms with the Impact of Communication on Scientific and Technological Risk Judgments. Presented to the Symposium on Science Communication, Annenberg School of Communications, University of Southern California, Los Angeles, December.
Freimuth, Vicki S., Edgar, Timothy, and Hammond, Sharon L. 1987. College Students' Awareness and Interpretation of the AIDS Risk. *Science, Technology, and Human Values* 12:37–40.
Friedman, Sharon. 1981. Communicating Effectively About Science and Technology. Science Writing Workshop. Bethlehem, PA: Lehigh University.
Friedman, Sharon, Dunwoody, Sharon, and Rogers, Carol L. 1986. *Scientists and Journalists.* New York: Free Press.
Hollenshead, Diane. 1984. A Medical Challenge. *Shreveport* (LA) *Journal,* August 29.
Hornblower, Margot. 1983. How Dangerous is Acid Rain? *National Wildlife* 20(3):4–11.

Howie, Mike, and Bauer, Steve. 1984. *Champaign* (IL) *News-Gazette,* Sept. 16–21.
Jerome, Fred. 1986. Gee Whiz! Is That All There Is? In *Scientists and Journalists,* edited by Sharon M. Friedman, Sharon Dunwoody, and Carol L. Rogers, 147–54. New York: Free Press.
Kidder, Rushworth M. 1988. A Weird World Underlies "Reality." *The Oregonian* (Portland, OR), Aug. 18, C1.
Krieghbaum, Hillier. 1979. Perspectives on Science Writing. *Journal of Environmental Education* 10(3):16–20.
Lambeth, Edmund B. 1979. Teaching from the Prize Winners. Paper presented to the Science Writing Educators Group, Association for Education in Journalism, Aug. 5. Houston, TX.
Leistner, Juli. 1990. AAAS Risk Workshop. *Sciphers* 10(4):1–3.
Lundberg, Lea. 1984. Comprehensiveness of Coverage of Tropical Rain Deforestation. *Journalism Quarterly* 61(2):378–82.
Minten, Jay. 1985. Science and the Media: The Boundaries of Truth. *Health Affairs* 4(1):5–23.
Nunn, Clyde Z. 1979. Readership and Coverage of Science and Technology in Newspapers. *Journalism Quarterly* 59(3):406–13.
Pfund, Nancy, and Hofstadter, Laura. 1981. Biomedical Innovation and the Press. *Journal of Communication* 31(2):138–47.
Pulford, D. L. 1976. Follow-up of Study of Science News Accuracy. *Journalism Quarterly* 53(1):119–21.
Richards, Hugh T. 1988. The Tragedy of Scientific Illiteracy. *L&S Magazine.* Madison, Wis.: University of Wisconsin, 5(1):7–8.
Sandman, Peter M., Sachsman, David B., Greenberg, Michael R., and Gochfeld, Michael. 1987. *Environmental Risk and the Press.* New Brunswick: Transaction Books.
Schoenfeld, Clay. 1982. How to Write About Science. In *Effective Feature Writing,* edited by Clay Schoenfeld, 128–29. New York: Holt, Rinehart, and Winston.
Schulte, Fred. 1983. The Deadly Cure. *Fort Lauderdale* (FL) *News and Sun-Sentinel,* June 15-July 29.
Shepherd, R. Gordon. 1980. Selectivity of Sources in Science News. Paper presented to the Science Writing Educators Group, Association for Education in Journalism, Aug. 10. Boston, MA.
Stein, Gilbert (Editor of *Hunting and Fishing*). 1949. Letter to author, Jan. 12.
Stocking, S. Holly. 1981. Don't Overlook the "Social" in Science Writing Courses. *Journalism Educator* 36(2):55–57.
Tichenor, Phillip, Olien, J. N., Harrison, A., and Donohue, G. A. 1970. Mass Communication Systems and Communication Accuracy in Science News Reporting. *Journalism Quarterly* 47(4):673–83.
Wechsler, Lorraine. 1982. Quoted in Clay Schoenfeld. *Effective Feature Writing.* New York: Holt, Rinehart, and Winston, 131.
Wilkins, Lee, and Patterson, Philip. 1989. Risky Business: Covering Slow-Onset Hazards as Rapidly Developing News. Presented to the International Communication Association annual convention, San Francisco, May.
Wineke, William R. 1983. No End In Sight To Rising Health Care Costs. (Madison) *Wisconsin State Journal,* May 23, 1:6.
_____. 1987. Critical Service Med Flight Proves Worth; Questions Still Hover. (Madison) *Wisconsin State Journal,* Jan. 11, 3:1.

This chapter was initiated by Schoenfeld. Collaborator was Griffin.

CHAPTER 11

Energy

$\mathbf{S}$OME ECHO of an energy issue, whether booming or faint, can be heard on just about any news beat, in large communities and small. If you cover a hearing on utility rates or do a story on the rising or falling price of gasoline at local filling stations, you are certainly covering an energy story. But you will also find overtones of energy issues when you interview the elderly about living on Social Security benefits, cover layoffs at the local auto plant, investigate mass transit ridership, write a feature about the resort industry, or do an article about respiratory diseases. The list of such stories can get very long, since energy reverberates throughout the vexing issues of economic growth, population growth, environmental quality, health, inflation, nuclear proliferation, foreign relations, defense, social equity, urban design, transportation, poverty, and even the more nebulous problem of adjusting our personal aspirations and expectations of the future to the exigencies of the present.

It is a sad state of affairs that media and public concern about energy seems to rise and fall with the cost of gasoline at the pump. Energy is a serious, long-term, chronic problem that demands ongoing attention. Yet most media energy coverage is dictated by dramatic events. The lessons of the oil shocks of the 1970s were mostly forgotten through the 1980s, until the news media and the country rediscovered the energy problem in the wake of Iraq's invasion of Kuwait in 1990. "If the latest oil crisis shows anything," stated *Newsweek*'s Sharon Begley and Mary Hager (1990), "it's how quickly Americans forget."

Your job as a reporter is to help people in your community see beyond the surges of singular energy-related events, to understand how problems of energy supply and demand have arisen, and how these problems will affect them. It is just as important to tell them clearly what they can do about the impact of energy on their lives. Some of the most important decisions affecting the future availability of energy are made across kitchen tables as well as in Congressional caucuses.

Getting some energy background

Homework does not end when you are graduated from college. You need to gain background information on any story before you cover it. Thus, the first step in covering energy is to understand something about the history, economics, technology, and terminology of energy. If you do not understand an energy story and its context, neither will your readers. In fact, you need to understand energy well enough to interpret in words your readers can understand the technological and economic jargon used by your sources. How can you do so?

Experts

If the community in which you work has a college or university, the public relations office might help you find one or more professors with an active interest in some aspect of energy. These professors could be in just about any department: engineering, economics, sociology, mass communication, and others. Many of these scholars may be willing to give you a briefing on local dimensions of the energy problem that fall within their expertise. Retired utility executives and ex-officials of regulatory agencies can also give you valuable background.

For example, the small number of science writers who had established links with expert sources had a great advantage in covering the famous and complicated story of the breakdown of a nuclear power plant at Three Mile Island in 1979 (Sandman and Paden 1979). Remember to maintain a healthy journalistic skepticism, however. Does your source moonlight as a consultant to the utility? Head the local antinuclear coalition? Taking a political stance or working professionally in the field does not necessarily render unreliable an otherwise-qualified source, but you should be a bit more cautious when dealing with information from that source.

Many reporters have taken good advantage of the Media Resource Service (MRS) of the Scientists' Institute for Public Information (SIPI), a nonprofit group. Reached by a toll-free number, MRS will refer a reporter to a handful of scientist sources with a wide range of views on specific topics. This handy system gives even the smallest newsroom access to science consultants (Colglazier and Rice 1983).

Readings

When you do your energy homework, there is no substitute for reading the literature of the field and keeping abreast of developments. The past fifteen years has seen a proliferation of publications dealing with all aspects of the energy problem. Some of the most insightful are at times controversial in their approach or conclusions. Therefore, you should not confine your homework briefing to only one or two sources. Among the most useful books are:

Energy Future: Report of the Energy Project of the Harvard Business School (Stobaugh and Yergin 1979);
Energy: The Next Twenty Years (Landsberg et al. 1979);
Uncertain Power: The Struggle for a National Energy Policy (Zinberg 1983);
Energy Use: The Human Dimension (Stern and Aronson 1984);
Energy and Conservation (Long 1989).

Many other publications and periodicals that can give you background, updates, or both are available from the government, citizen groups, industry, and private organizations. From the Superintendent of Documents, United States Government Printing Office, Washington, D.C., 20402, you can get a free *Subject Bibliography Index*. Use the index to order free bibliographies in the subject areas of your choice, including energy. You can get energy-related publications from the Department of Energy and a variety of other federal government agencies, including the Bureau of Mines, the Department of Commerce, the Environmental Protection Agency, the National Bureau of Standards Office of Energy Conservation, the National Referral Center's Science and Technology Division, the Nuclear Regulatory Commission, and the Office of Consumer Affairs, all in Washington, D.C. You can also get relevant publications from the Consumer Information Center in Pueblo, Colorado, 81009, and the National Technical Information Service in Springfield, Virginia, 22161. Many local and state government agencies concerned with energy may also be able to provide you with background reading, as can local citizen groups, such as the League of Women Voters, and local utilities. These latter sources, along with information you can glean from your news organization's library, can give you a sense of the agenda of past energy issues in your community, and their chronology. Be sure to exercise caution, especially when dealing with background information either from citizen action groups or from the energy industry.

Other sources
    Along with those already mentioned, other national sources for energy information are the United States Department of the Interior and the Nuclear Regulatory Commission, the House of Representatives Interior and

Insular Affairs Committee and the Science and Technology Committee, the Senate Energy and Natural Resources Committee and the Environment and Public Works Committee. Other organizations from which you can obtain information include: the National Coal Association; the American Institute of Mining, Metallurgical and Petroleum Engineers; the American Gas Association; Edison Electric Institute; the United States Association for the Club of Rome; the Center for Science in the Public Interest; and Resources for the Future.

In nearly every state you will find some kind of utility regulatory commission. These state agencies set customer rates for electricity and natural gas and also monitor related activities by the utilities. Utilities regularly file requests for rate changes. A number of states also have energy agencies attached to the executive branch and agencies to oversee mining and drilling. Some states have agencies to regulate the use of water, which is used to cool electric plants. State transportation and development agencies may also be useful sources of information.

Along with universities, utilities, and citizen groups, local sources of energy information can be quite varied and include business and industry; petroleum, coal, and bottled gas distributors; a mass transit agency; and of course, local residents who are using innovative ideas to save energy. Many utilities have performed "energy audits" of customers' homes, and have suggested to customers the steps they need to take to save energy. Homeowners who have had such audits to tend to take more actions to save energy in their homes. This pattern is especially true among the elderly, who otherwise would have difficulty saving energy and its costs (Griffin 1989). Such programs can be grist for some interesting and useful local energy stories.

An energy primer

The energy problem can take on somewhat different faces depending upon where your community is. If a nuclear power plant is nearby, there may be a citizen group voicing concern about safety. If you are in a coal-producing region, local energy concerns will include the economic benefits of coal to the community, as well as the problems of black-lung disease and damage to the environment from mining. If you are in or near a city, the cost and availability of energy for homes and transportation will be among the salient energy issues, especially if your community includes a large portion of persons living on low or fixed incomes, such as the elderly and some minorities. If you are in a part of the country that depends on tourism, the cost of energy for taking a vacation could affect the local economy. If your community has a lot of lakes, acid rain will be a possible problem. From community to community, the face of energy-related problems can seem as changeable as the sides of a Rubik's Cube, but they are all pieces of the same energy puzzle. It is important for you and for your readers, viewers, or listeners to understand how that puzzle works, how what is happening locally fits into the overall scheme, and what can be done about the energy problem.

Some terminology and history

A commonly used unit of measurement for energy is the British Thermal Unit (BTU), which technically is the amount of energy required to raise the temperature of a pound of water one degree, from 39.2 to 40.2 degrees Fahrenheit. A barrel of petroleum, for example, contains 5 to 6 million BTUs. A large unit of energy often used in planning is the "quad," a quadrillion BTUs. The United States used 74.3 quads of energy in 1973, reduced consumption to 70.6 quads in 1975, steadily increased energy use to 78.9 quads in 1979, then again reduced consumption to 70.5 quads in 1983 before reaching a new peak of energy consumption, estimated at 81.2 quads in 1989 (U.S. Energy Information Agency 1990). As the graph on page 292 shows, however, most of the reduction in energy use during the mid-1980s had been in industry, which fell on hard economic times in the 1980s. The amount of energy used in the United States for transportation, and for residential and commercial use, had increased in the decade and a half from 1973 through 1989. This occurred despite exhortations to conserve and some reduction in use during the interim. The country used 18.6 quads for transportation in 1973 and 22.2 in 1989; 24.1 quads for residential and commercial use in 1973, 29.6 in 1989. Without conservation efforts, however, there is no doubt that energy use would have been much higher, especially given the increasing national population.

Oil is the source of nearly half of the energy used in the United States, followed by natural gas, coal, and, in relatively small portions, hydropower and nuclear energy. Other energy sources, such as solar and wind power, have yet to make substantial impacts.

The technology and style of life in the United States and many other countries depend a lot on petroleum, especially for transportation. About half the oil America consumes is used to get people or things from place to place. Therefore, the efficient use of cars, trucks, and mass transit systems is an important problem. As is true with other fossil fuels (natural gas and coal), the earth's supply of oil is limited, and known deposits are more plentiful in some parts of the globe than in others. About two-thirds of the world's known oil reserves are in the Mideast, a region that writer Robert

SHORT MEMORIES:
THE ENERGY ROLLER-COASTER

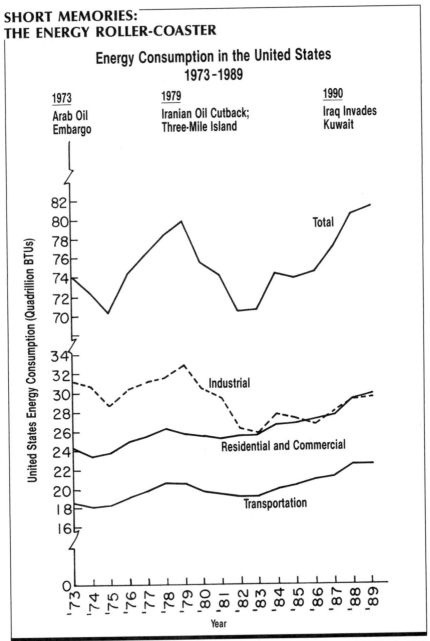

Energy Consumption in the United States
1973-1989

<u>1973</u>
Arab Oil
Embargo

<u>1979</u>
Iranian Oil Cutback;
Three-Mile Island

<u>1990</u>
Iraq Invades
Kuwait

Total

Industrial

Residential and Commercial

Transportation

United States Energy Consumption (Quadrillion BTUs)

Year

Annual data from U.S. Energy Information Administration (1990).

Samuelson (1990) terms "a permanent powder keg." Therefore, where the United States gets its oil has, especially since the 1970s, become a critical problem. Oil production in the United States peaked in 1970, then declined as less expensive imported oil began to pour into the country to meet our growing demands. In 1973, after the United States had become much more dependent on foreign oil, international political tensions prompted the Arab oil producers to place an embargo on oil to the United States, reduce shipments to other countries, and unilaterally quadruple oil prices (Stobaugh and Yergin 1979). Shortages arose throughout the country, and the economic repercussions—reinforced by other events—lasted into the 1990s.

After the 1973 embargo, the United States shifted toward a goal of reducing dependence on foreign oil. The Alaska Pipeline was approved in 1973; a fifty-five mile per hour national speed limit enacted in 1974; the United States Department of Energy was created in 1977; and the gradual deregulation of prices of newly discovered natural gas was approved in 1978. Late that same year, again in the politically volatile Middle East, the overthrow of the Shah of Iran interrupted production of oil in a country that supplied 10 percent of the world's petroleum. Shortages again resulted. The Organization of Petroleum Exporting Countries (OPEC) once again raised oil prices. A new era had arisen in which supplies of oil were relatively expensive and continually insecure. As the decade of the 1970s drew to a close, another major energy event—an emergency at the Three Mile Island (TMI) nuclear power plant in Pennsylvania—made more apparent the fact that any solution to the energy problem would involve some difficult trade-offs.

Through the 1980s, the nation was still without a comprehensive and long-range energy policy. Government support for development and use of non-polluting, "renewable" energy sources (e.g., solar and wind power) was cut dramatically. The Department of Energy, founded to lead the country to energy self-sufficiency through conservation and development of alternative fuels, became preoccupied with the development of nuclear weapons (Behm 1986). Across the country, the notion of an energy "crisis" had largely disappeared. Some spoke of an energy "glut," implying that problems were past. OPEC even lowered its crude oil prices to recapture its share of the market.

By mid-decade, however, many experts noted that lower OPEC prices were again resulting in greater use of, and dependence on, foreign oil. About 28 percent of the oil America used in 1983 was imported. That portion rose to 33 percent in 1986, 41 percent in 1989, and 50 percent during the first part of 1990. The country had reached a new high in dependence on foreign oil. Exploration and production of oil in the United States had dropped significantly during the decade. Oil and gas rigs in the

Southwest were shut down, producing local economic shocks. Meanwhile, America's total use of energy for homes, businesses, and transportation was again on the rise. The nation's energy efficiency had begun to decline (Wald 1989). The speed limit on rural interstate highways was raised to sixty-five miles per hour in 1988. Opponents of the higher limits stressed safety considerations, not energy conservation.

GOOD GRAPHICS HELP TELL THE ENERGY STORY

When Paul Hayes of the Milwaukee Journal *wrote an update on the energy situation for readers of the paper's Sunday magazine on December 11, 1988, he culled many sources of statistical information in order to tell the story. To show how trends in population growth, changes in the work force, automobile efficiency, gasoline*

A SLOWLY GROWING WISCONSIN POPULATION. . .

Millions of people

Wisconsin's population, 1970-1987
(Source: Wisconsin's Blue Book)

IS DRIVING FARTHER IN WISCONSIN THAN EVER. . .

Billions of vehicle miles

Total miles driven in Wisconsin, 1970-1987
(Source: Wisconsin Dept. of Transportation)

LARGELY BECAUSE OF AN ENORMOUS INCREASE OF WORKING WOMEN.

Workers (100,000s)

Men

Women

Wisconsin Labor Force, 1970-1987
(Source: U.S. Census Bureau and U.S. Bureau of Labor Statistics)

1970 '71 '72 '73 '74 '75 '76 '77 '78 '79 '80 '81 '82 '83 '84 '85 '86 '87

Adapted from PAUL G. HAYES. 1988. The Last Oil Binge: Our Crash Course Toward the Next Energy Crisis. *Milwaukee Journal, Wisconsin* magazine, Dec. 11, 11–17.

Noting that the country was returning to patterns like those that led to the 1973–1974 and 1979–1980 energy crises, Allen E. Murray, president of the Mobil Corporation, said in the June 10, 1985, issue of *Newsweek* that "we are headed for another round of shortages. Certainly by century's end. Possibly before" (Murray 1985). On February 18, 1987, United States Interior Secretary Donald P. Hodel said on the "Today" show that another

costs, and miles driven on highways all affect the energy picture, Hayes and Journal *illustrator Kristin Pelisek put together a series of graphs, run in color. These graphs are examples of the way in which diverse statistics can be brought together for readers, and in a lively manner.*

THE CARS ARE MORE EFFICIENT THAN BEFORE. . .

Average
miles per
gallon

Automobile efficiency, U.S., 1970-1987
(Source: U.S. Energy Information Agency)

19
18
17
16
15
14
13

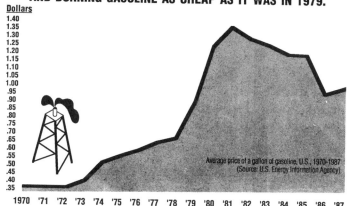

AND BURNING GASOLINE AS CHEAP AS IT WAS IN 1979.

Dollars

1.40
1.35
1.30
1.25
1.20
1.15
1.10
1.05
1.00
.95
.90
.85
.80
.75
.70
.65
.60
.55
.50
.45
.40
.35

Average price of a gallon of gasoline, U.S., 1970-1987
(Source: U.S. Energy Information Agency)

1970 '71 '72 '73 '74 '75 '76 '77 '78 '79 '80 '81 '82 '83 '84 '85 '86 '87

energy crisis was very likely in the near future unless domestic oil production was increased. Economics writer Jane Bryant Quinn observed that "true believers are buying their tickets to the next energy crisis well in advance" (Quinn 1987).

Then, in August 1990, Iraq invaded Kuwait and appeared poised to invade Saudi Arabia. President George Bush said that Iraqi leader Saddam Hussein was not only a threat to the flow of oil but also to "our way of life" (Budianski 1990). Formidable military forces were dispatched to the Mideast, and an economic embargo of Iraq initiated, with the support of many other nations, including other Arab countries and Iraq's former ally, the Soviet Union. Oil prices again rose. Energy again became a salient matter, but more stress was placed on protecting oil supplies than on reducing demand.

Sending American military men and women to the Mideast added a whole new dimension to the energy picture. "We delude ourselves if we think this is merely a passing episode," Samuelson (1990) wrote in *Newsweek*. "We have started down a new path." While there was considerable early support for the United States' action, some voices questioned whether the country would have been quite as concerned about Iraq's aggression if the United States had not continued to become increasingly dependent on foreign oil. Words of caution were expressed by some observers, such as *Milwaukee Journal* reporter Paul Hayes (1990):

> For the third time in 17 years, the United States has failed to face up to its future of using less oil. Instead, it has waited for another crisis, and it has responded with another wasteful national effort.
>
> This time, however, the Bush administration has put American lives on the line. American troops are in Saudi Arabia not to defend any moral principle as much as to insure that the rest of us can drive our big, mostly empty cars into and out of cities during rush hour. In the two earlier crises, the nation responded with safer, albeit misguided strategies. . . .
>
> This reality remains, however: Industrial economies founded years ago on cheap oil should have policies in place to decrease their use of oil, especially now that they understand the resource to be finite and maybe scarce in the next half century.
>
> This message is especially unsettling for citizens of the U.S., where the oil age began and which is the very prototype of an oil-based economy. . . .
>
> We used oil so profusely and so cheaply for so long that an element in the U.S. has come to believe that cheap oil is as much an American birthright as freedom of speech. That is what is meant when President Bush says that "a way of life" is at stake in the Persian Gulf.
>
> That way of life, while it may be the envy of the world, is not sustainable.

Many commentators, including former President Carter, strengthened their call for the development of an effective national energy policy that includes conservation. "No plan will totally free us from a significant dependence on imported oil," Carter (1990) said. "We can, however, with a modicum of forethought and creativity, greatly increase our ability to weather future crises."

Thus, oil gluts and shortages are simply short-term snapshots out of the everchanging and ongoing energy picture. "As citizens and consumers," Hughes et al. (1985) observed, "we face an energy future that will shape our existence."

Energy issues

The notion that the cost of oil or any other form of energy will rise when demand gets ahead of supply is easy enough to understand. But there are hidden factors that influence the availability, cost, and use of energy. Energy is not simply an economic problem. The reporter must know and explain to the public the hidden trade-offs that make the energy problem a social dilemma.

SUPPLY AND DEMAND. At the heart of much of the energy debate is the question of whether increased supply (energy production) or reduced demand (energy conservation) is the better way to ensure that we have enough energy to meet our needs. The former is an expansionist, growth-oriented approach that is traditionally American: expanding production and consumption are seen as good for everyone, and science and technology are depended on to develop and exploit new sources of energy when necessary. The latter approach suggests that expansion has already gone beyond the earth's ability to sustain it, that the growth of energy supply cannot continue, and that disaster can be avoided only through redistribution of wealth and changes in production, lifestyles, values, and institutions. Future generations and the less affluent are seen as penalized by the growth of energy use by the wealthier minority (Schurr et al. 1979).

In reality, of course, solutions that have been proposed for various energy issues are often mixtures of these two views. The federal government has tended to promote conservation as well as the development of new sources of energy, although the Reagan administration decreased direct support for solar energy research and opted instead for more nuclear development.

EXTERNALITIES AND EQUITY. There are enough energy resources in the world to meet reasonable estimates of demand into the foreseeable future (Lands-

LOCALIZING THE ENERGY PROBLEM

Soon after the 1990 Iraqi invasion of Kuwait, Minneapolis
Star-Tribune *reporters Bob van Sternberg and Josephine*
Marcotty put the energy problem into perspective with a page
one Sunday article headlined "Consumers feel crunch despite
trying to conserve." Their story is a fine example of localizing
a problem that has global implications. Some excerpts:

It shouldn't have come as such a shock.

Iraq's invasion of Kuwait is exactly the kind of threat to the world's
supply of Middle East oil that the experts have been predicting since
the last energy crisis.

So, why didn't U.S. consumers do anything to prepare for it?

They did—but it turns out they didn't do enough. And they haven't
done much for the past five years.

During the past five years, U.S. citizens have burned petroleum just
like in the good old pre-OPEC days, because in a lot of ways, they
were just like those days. In real dollars, gasoline costs less than it
did in 1970.

But that couldn't last, and it didn't. The new oil crisis triggered by
Iraqi President Saddam Hussein merely demonstrates how devoted
U.S. citizens are to their internal-combustion way of life. . . . [If]
consumers' behavior during the earlier crises is any indication, only
intolerably high prices will force people out from behind the
wheel—and any decline in consumption will only be temporary. . . .

But some Minnesotans complained last week that they've heeded
their pocketbooks in recent years—buying smaller cars, cutting back
unnecessary driving, accepting the conservation ethic—and they still
feel victimized.

Phyllis Gard had just filled up her big Chevy Blazer in Lakeville late
last week. At $1.279 a gallon, the fill-up cost $5 more than it had a
week before. "It really cuts down on a person's feeling of independence," she said. "I've always tried to be careful, not to make unnecessary trips, that kind of thing. But you still like to believe you can
do your own thing."

Greg Holman, an energy analyst for the Minnesota Department of
Public Service, explained that the gasoline price jolt "is not much of
a shock for people, kind of a here-we-go-again thing. But these days
people don't want to hear about it when you talk conservation."

LOCALIZING THE ENERGY PROBLEM *(continued)*

Even if the current political spasm in the Mideast keeps oil prices high long enough to revive the domestic oil industry, any new oil flowing through the nation's piplelines will remain expensive. And consumers will either pay up or look for other ways to travel.

If the experiences in 1973 and 1980 are any indication, they'll probably do the former. Both times, metro area commuters took the bus and carpooled in larger numbers, but ridership for both alternatives has nose-dived. Despite the scary headlines of the past week, there's no indication that either bus ridership or [car] pooling has increased. . . .

Bill Lazarus commutes 13 miles from his Shoreview home to the St. Paul campus of the University of Minnesota. He called [the local car pooling co-ordinators] last week. "If gas prices keep going up, it might be worth thinking about," he said. "But the problem is, look at the real price of gas—it isn't any higher. There you are. People value their time, the convenience of going where they want to go, when they want to."

BOB VAN STERNBERG and JOSEPHINE MARCOTTY. 1990. Consumers feel crunch despite trying to conserve. Minneapolis *Star-Tribune,* Aug. 12, 1A, 12A.

Local quotations of this type help illustrate the human side of the energy issue, and can provide the basis for conducting a sample survey of local residents to find out how widespread such feelings really are.

berg et al. 1979; Schurr et al. 1979). The energy problem, at this time, consists primarily of the costs—economic, social, political, health, and environmental—of procuring, producing, and using these resources. These costs include, for example, health risks such as those produced by mining and burning coal, environmental risks of disposing of spent nuclear fuel, and national security risks of depending on foreign sources of oil.

While some observers believe that letting prices rise to reflect costs will contain energy prices in the long run (e.g., Ford Foundation 1979), others believe that market factors alone will not, ultimately, determine levels of energy supply and demand. If the energy problem could be solved by economic forces, Sam Schurr and his colleagues observe, energy would have "no practical importance as a public policy issue" (Schurr et al. 1979). They believe, instead, that the way we use energy is likely to be increasingly affected by public policy decisions.

Robert Stobaugh and Daniel Yergin believe that the market system can be relied on as long as corrections are made to allow the various alternative energy sources, including solar energy and energy conservation, to compete equally (Stobaugh and Yergin 1979). These adjustments would have to take into account the "true costs" of energy, including what are referred to as "externalities." Externalities are subtle or hidden costs of various kinds, including health, environmental, and foreign policy costs, paid by some or all segments of the public but not otherwise paid directly by the consumer. Simply put, a given consumer gets the benefit of using the energy re-source—electricity, for example—without having to pay the real cost. In-stead, part of the cost is borne unequally by others. The cost of a kilowatt-hour of electricity may be partially subsidized by a coal miner's health or by the potential risk to the safety of persons living near a nuclear power plant. Traditional government regulations have kept the prices of domestic oil and natural gas artificially low, compared to their economic value, and have indirectly subsidized the use of fuels, such as coal and uranium, to produce electricity, despite what Stobaugh and Yergin term "external costs of suffi-cient importance to cause major political controversies." Some external costs could be made internal by tactics such as including in the price of coal the costs of returning strip-mined land to its original contour. But many externalities would still remain.

Among changes that have been suggested in energy pricing, along with deregulation of oil and newly found natural gas, are changes in electricity rate structures so as to reflect the costs of generating power during times of peak loads, the enactment of pollution taxes, and placing high taxes on gasoline, as is done in many European countries to discourage use. "Higher energy costs," according to Hans Landsberg and his study group, "are a reflection of physical facts: the easy sources are about gone, while the plentiful sources are expensive to use safely" (Ford Foundation 1979).

Large increases in energy prices, however, can cause hardships for the poor. Paying for energy requires a much larger proportion of their house-hold budgets than it does for the rich, and the poor have fewer frills and amenities to sacrifice if necessary. A national study (Kissinger 1988) found that low-income households on the average cut their residential energy con-sumption fourteen percent between 1972 and 1985, but the amount of money they spent for this energy more than tripled, from $284 to $969 annually. The study found that the poor often use dangerous means, such as turning the thermostat down to unhealthy levels, to cut their bills; that these energy costs are making housing unaffordable for the poor; and that the elderly are among the hardest hit by the cost of energy.

The American public's use of energy, Stobaugh and Yergin (1979) observe, is based largely on individual choices by each member of the public. This is a decentralized pattern of choice, they note, quite unlike the decisions to produce energy, which usually are in the hands of relatively few people. Moreover, they say, consumption decisions are made by people who are often poorly informed. Government-sponsored energy education efforts, which flourished in the latter 1970s, nearly disappeared in the 1980s. In the schools, according to a spokesman for the National Assessment for Educational Progress, an affiliate of the Educational Testing Service, "our nation is producing a generation of energy illiterates" (Warren 1989).

Energy source conflicts

With every energy source comes conflicts involving advantages and risks. There is no ideal energy source. One energy source may appear to have great advantage at one time or another, but even the reliance on a single energy source is itself a risk.

FOSSIL FUELS. Oil, coal, and natural gas have been the fuels for home, transportation, and industry for generations. But these fossil fuels are nonrenewable resources that were produced only once in the formation of the earth. Largely because these fuels are exhaustible, their use is embroiled in conflict.

Oil is particularly valuable because it is easy to carry around. This makes it useful in transportation. Alternative souices of energy for transportation, such as synthetic liquid fuels, are still much more expensive than oil, and their future is uncertain. Although automobile engines that run on petroleum produce a variety of air pollutants, there is concern over the extent to which tighter emission-control standards, and the resultant modifications in automobiles, might harm fuel efficiency. At considerable cost, oil can be recovered from reservoirs that have already been milked of their easily attainable oil. Petroleum can also be extracted from shale deposits, which are huge and distributed worldwide, and from tar sands, also at high cost. The impact of unconventional technology on oil recovery is controversial, as are decontrol of oil prices and breaking up the structure of domestic oil companies. In addition, none of these measures is likely to increase United States oil production (Stobaugh and Yergin 1979). Drilling for oil in various offshore regions of the United States risks environmental damage. In addition, these offshore reserves contain only enough oil to delay for a few years the country's need to cut back on the use of oil (Hayes 1990).

Despite the drawbacks, the world is likely to remain dependent on oil for quite a while (Ford Foundation 1979). Disruptions in the Mideast and subsequent fluctuations in the cost of oil have demonstrated the foreign policy and national security risks of reliance on oil imported from an unstable area of the world where the resource is concentrated in a form relatively easy to produce. More shocks are likely.

Coal is plentiful in the United States, which has been called the "Persian Gulf of Coal," but coal also brings with it many problems. Among them are black-lung disease and other hazards to miners, environmental damage from mining, and an array of health and air pollution problems that result from burning coal, including acid-rain damage to distant lakes and streams. Key questions about the use of coal concern the equity of the distribution of these hazards among the population.

From procurement through burning, natural gas is environmentally cleaner than coal. Natural gas also lacks the waste disposal problems of nuclear power, and unlike oil, its production for Americans has been almost entirely domestic. It is also the focus of heated arguments concerning government regulation of its prices, even since the passage of the Natural Gas Policy Act of 1978, which gradually decontrols the price of newly discovered natural gas. Generally speaking, such decontrol is designed to encourage exploration for new sources of gas, but it also results in higher costs for consumers. Gradual decontrol is designed to soften economic impact. Even if natural gas is deregulated and prices reflect market value, production at best will remain about the same (Stobaugh and Yergin 1979). One new source of gas could be the vast United States coal fields. Coal can be turned into gas through a process called coal gasification. However, this is such an expensive process that its product would not currently be marketable.

Burning of fossil fuels generally is suspected of contributing to some long-range warming of the world's climate — the so-called "greenhouse effect" — through a buildup of carbon dioxide in the atmosphere. Small variations in climate have produced major disturbances in the production of food in various parts of the world, a factor that is increasingly being considered in debates over these traditional sources of energy (Ford Foundation 1979). Strip-mining of coal reserves in some portions of the United States, furthermore, can disrupt some of the country's prime grain-producing lands, and growth of ocean transport of oil can threaten marine fisheries through increasingly likely oil spills (The Leonardo Scholars 1975). Even spills that are not as severe as the Alaska spill from the tanker Exxon Valdez in 1989 can seriously threaten the environment and require very costly efforts to clean up.

NUCLEAR ENERGY. The growth of nuclear generation of electricity, which at one time was expected to provide power "too cheap to meter," has come to a virtual halt under the influence of spiraling costs, an economic climate not conducive to building nuclear plants, reduced projections of future demand for electricity, worry about hazards of radiation and waste disposal, and concern prompted by Three Mile Island. The second half of the decade of the 1970s, even before the incident at TMI, saw a virtual moratorium on new nuclear plants as orders dwindled and numerous previous orders were canceled or delayed. Many existing plants may face shutdowns in the future if problems of disposing of spent fuel are not solved (Bupp 1979).

Much uncertainty remains about the social, environmental, and economic costs of nuclear power, especially for future generations. "The fundamental disagreement," I. C. Bupp (1979) observes, "is how to deal with uncertainty." On the overall risk-balance sheet, nuclear power may be safer environmentally than coal (Nuclear Energy 1977). But grave concern exists about the safety of nuclear power plants and especially about the potentially catastrophic effects of a serious nuclear accident.

Multifaceted controversies have also surrounded the fuel for nuclear power. The problems of disposing of spent fuel have become pressing. Nuclear planners had originally expected that nuclear generation would grow to such a large scale that it would be economical to reprocess the fuel; that is, to reclaim unused uranium and plutonium from otherwise spent fuel. Reprocessing, however, has been thwarted not only by the slowdown in the growth of the nuclear power industry, but by security considerations, in that recycling of this fuel risks exposing it to theft. This nuclear material could be used to produce nuclear weapons. Meanwhile, the used fuel is being stored primarily in short-term holding facilities at nuclear power plants.

Methods of long-term disposal of the waste, which remains hazardous for thousands of years, are still debated. Two of the options are to store the waste in underground salt caverns, and to develop the Liquid Fast Metal Breeder Reactor ("Breeder") to "burn" the long-lasting plutonium. The breeder reactor, which can actually produce more nuclear fuel than it uses, would also extend the supply of uranium indefinitely. However, like recycling, the breeder may not be economical and poses security risks. The breeder can result in nuclear proliferation if the technology is exported to other countries. Another side effect of breeder technology would be the necessity to keep the long-lasting radioactive plutonium out of the biosphere and out of the hands of terrorists. The social and political costs could be a loss of individual liberty and constraints on social change due to the requirement for continual surveillance and protection of the fuel (The Leonardo Scholars 1975).

All options for disposing of the spent fuel have uncertainties and side effects. "What makes nuclear power unique among the energy sources,"

CHERNOBYL AND TMI

Two major incidents involving nuclear power plants have become focal points for debate over use of this form of energy.

On April 26, 1986, the Chernobyl Number 4 reactor in the Ukraine area of the Soviet Union, about eighty miles north of Kiev, caught fire and exploded due to errors in human judgment combined with a design problem. At least thirty-one people were killed, more than two hundred suffered acute radiation sickness, nearly three billion dollars of damage was done, and more than one hundred thousand people were forced to leave their contaminated homes. A cloud of radiation from the disaster went around the globe. The press in the United States initially reported various rumors and judgments from experts about the number of people killed near Chernobyl in the immediate wake of the explosion. Afterward, stories continued that dealt with the likely long-term effects of the radiation on people who lived nearby and their offspring. Only time, of course, will indicate the effects of Chernobyl.

The worst accident in the history of commercial nuclear power started in the early morning hours of March 28, 1979, at Unit Two of the nuclear power plant at Three Mile Island (TMI), in the Susquehanna River just downstream from Harrisburg, Pennsylvania. Before dawn, the unit was going about its task of using nuclear fission to heat water to produce steam to turn an electric generator. Starting at about 4 A.M., a chain of mechanical failures and human errors at TMI resulted in the loss of primary cooling water around the radioactive core and the accidental dumping of radioactive water into an auxiliary building not secured for that purpose. The fuel rods in the core, which were left inadequately cooled for sixteen hours, were damaged. (Not long before, Columbia Pictures had released a film, *The China Syndrome,* about a fictitious nuclear plant accident, that had made popular the term "meltdown," referring to the catastrophic melting of the radioactive core of a nuclear power plant.) Metropolitan Edison, which operated the nuclear plant, declared a "general emergency," the first ever at a commercial nuclear power plant in the United States. TMI, later investigation showed, came within twenty minutes of a meltdown. During the incident, there was profound confusion among the public, the press, and the experts in charge; radiation was released into the atmosphere; and a gas bubble containing hydrogen, which some thought could produce a chemical explosion, developed inside the reactor vessel. The crisis subsided when the Nuclear Regulatory Commission (NRC) finally announced that the bubble never had been explosive, and was nearly gone. Protesters still voiced concern in 1985, when plans were made to restart the undamaged Unit One of the plant. TMI's concave, cylindrical cooling towers have become nationally known symbols of a troubled nuclear industry.

While these two events are important, they should not obscure concern about more common problems, such as the disposal of spent nuclear fuel and the aging and decommissioning of nuclear power plants.

Stobaugh and Yergin (1979) state, "are the pervasive external costs it imposes on future generations — generations that will inherit caches of spent fuel that will emit radioactive rays for many centuries."

Some researchers believe that nuclear fusion could some day be used to generate electricity. Fusion may have fewer safety risks than the fission technology now used, but a large number of technical problems have yet to be conquered before the system could work.

ALTERNATIVE ENERGY. A diverse set of energy sources, including solar, water, and wind power, are often referred to as "alternative energy." These sources have in common the fact that they are "renewable" in that their supply is replenished. Most uses of alternative energy are also compatible with the natural ecosystem.

Solar power most commonly refers to energy derived directly from the sun. Such energy is used to warm homes, to heat water, and to provide heat for industrial or agricultural processes. Solar energy can also be converted to electricity by the "photo-voltaic cell," used by the space program. In the summer of 1990, photo-voltaic cells were even used to power some experimental cars in a a race from Florida to Michigan. Solar energy, however, also is the ultimate source of some other alternative energy sources including electricity that is generated by the motion of wind (by windmills or more properly, wind generators) and water (through wave power and hydroelectric dams). From organic matter and wastes ("biomass"), which store solar energy, fuels such as alcohol and methane can be derived. Even firewood is stored solar energy.

Solar-heating technology consists of "active" and "passive" systems. Passive solar heating involves strategy, such as designing a house to take maximum advantage of the sun. Active solar systems concentrate the sun's rays in special collectors and use them to heat (or even to cool) spaces and to heat water. Homes using solar heating most commonly have a hybrid system, with auxiliary energy from electricity or natural gas.

Although solar energy is generally nonpolluting, it still involves numerous technical problems, economic uncertainties, and environmental trade-offs. Wind generators, for example, can be noisy and could disfigure the landscape. Some interesting legal battles are developing over "solar rights," a question of whether, for example, a neighbor's building can block sunlight to a solar collector. Solar energy, even if centralized, may require use of greater expanses of land.

Another energy source that is partially solar and partially lunar is tidal energy, which might be tapped for generation of electricity. Geothermal power — steam or hot water from the earth — may also become useful.

Solar technology generally holds the promise of reducing or eliminating dependence on nonrenewable energy resources, which become more costly as they become more scarce.

CONSERVATION. Perhaps the most important "source" of energy is conservation. "If the United States were to make a serious commitment to conservation," Yergin (1979b) believes, "it might well consume 30 to 40 percent less energy than it now does, and still enjoy the same or even higher standard of living." This strategy involves hundreds or thousands of little actions, none very glamorous, such as insulating homes, closing drapes at night, turning down the thermostat, wearing a sweater, making cars and appliances more efficient, capturing wasted heat, designing buildings to be energy efficient, and "cogenerating," combining the production of heat and power for homes, offices, or industry. (For industry, cogeneration could cut in half the amount of energy required to produce steam and electricity separately). The amount of energy that could be saved through conservation, Yergin notes, is greater than the amount of energy provided by imported oil. Conservation offers the challenge of ingenuity and strategic planning. Like solar power, it is decentralized and relies extensively on individual efforts, which makes what is simple in concept complicated in realization.

The human factor

Why do some motorists in your community drive under the speed limit, even when no police officers are nearby? Why does one family in town keep the home thermostat set low despite the chill of winter, while their neighbor's living room seems to be missing only a grass roof and a few palm trees?

The reasons why some people conserve energy and others waste it have come increasingly under the scrutiny of social scientists. Those who study the behavior of humans and their institutions have investigated the social and psychological factors that can contribute to the solution of the energy problem (the so-called "social fix"), looking beyond marketplace solutions (the "economic fix"), and the biophysical and technical remedies (the "technological fix"). A number of the studies by social scientists have implications for journalists.

The "social fix"

Coping with changes in the cost and availability of energy has probably brought about some changes in the daily lives of people in your community. Many of these changes, such as keeping homes less warm in winter,

GRASS-ROOTS ENERGY EFFORTS

Beginning in 1980, the Milwaukee Journal *periodically ran a series of articles that spotlighted in-the-home energy conservation efforts of various residents of Wisconsin and Upper Michigan, and contained tips for do-it-yourselfers. The series, entitled "Serious Energy Savers," also contained energy conservation success stories that commended those who saved energy and may have enlightened and encouraged others, regardless of whether they lived in large cities, small towns, or in the countryside. Simultaneously, the paper co-sponsored a home energy-saving contest. Included among the success stories were:*

• A family who cut the amount of energy used for space heating in half over a period of eight years. They did it by nibbling away at waste through a variety of methods that were simple and often innovative (Davidson 1980).
• A skeptical rural tinkerer who did not think solar energy would have much effect on home heating until one below-zero Sunday afternoon when he built a small, doghouselike structure with glass on one end, and set it outside. After he added some black paint to absorb heat, the meat thermometer he set inside this structure read 210 degrees. After a couple of years of thinking and tinkering, and with a minimum of high technology parts, he built a solar collector that rests on his garage (Wilhelms 1981).
• A suburban woman who found that a small solar collector easily installed into her window helps heat her kitchen and is useful when she wants to dry her hair. Two local men developed the unit, manufactured it, and made it commercially available. The woman decided to use the unit because it allowed her to try solar heat without a large commitment (Dennis 1981).

These stories usually contained information on how much money and energy had been saved and some practical how-to information. Most of them had some human interest appeal, and were peppered with quotations that illustrated the motivations of the people who took the steps to save energy.

may have involved some discomfort or sacrifice. Individuals' perceptions of how much others are also giving up could influence how readily they accept such changes. Julie Honnold, Lynn Nelson, and other researchers, in fact, suggest that widespread changes in energy lifestyle will probably occur only if they are reinforced by social norms that support them or by definite economic rewards (Honnold and Nelson 1979). A more recent study found that a cable television program that dramatized the social and economic rewards that come to energy conservers resulted in long-term energy conservation among viewers (Winett et al. 1984).

After an extensive review of more than one hundred national and local surveys, Barbara Farhar and her associates observed that most Americans have viewed the energy situation not as a "crisis" but as a moderately serious problem that will be chronic for the foreseeable future. Generally, the public has viewed conservation as an important and effective means of dealing with the energy problem by reducing demand, although they would prefer government intervention and technological innovations to increase supply. Persons may be more likely to believe that the individual citizen can and should do something to alleviate the energy problem if they believe that individual behavior is a large part of the cause (Farhar et al. 1979). In this vein, Russell Belk and his research associates suggest that "the task of generating public support of a specific *response* to energy shortages may be reduced to educating the public about the *causes* of the shortage" (Belk, Painter, and Semenik 1981). Interpretive reporting could play an important and ongoing role in bringing about this type of understanding.

It is, of course, simplistic to assume that journalists, via reportage or editorials, can have an unmitigated impact on public behavior, because so much depends on psychological, economic, and social forces beyond the journalist's reach. Nonetheless, it does seem that what a person knows about practical energy alternatives—for example, how to carry them out, what the advantages and disadvantages of each are, what others are doing, and whether personal attempts to save energy are having an effect—may be an important ingredient of individual decisions about energy conservation, even though knowledge itself may not directly produce actions (Griffin 1985). Although relatively few surveys have investigated what people know about how to conserve energy and what sources they trust for information, the data that do exist indicate that the public is strongly in need of technical facts that would make conservation more effective (Farhar et al. 1979). To help alleviate this information deficit, at least one newspaper has printed an easy-to-clip table listing the average amount of electrical energy used by a wide variety of household appliances per use and per month. The information came from the local electric utility. Specific energy-saving tips were included in the accompanying story. Such practical knowledge can help

DOWN-HOME INTERPRETATION

When the Junior Women's Club of the medium-sized community of Appleton, in Wisconsin's Fox River Valley, planned an "Energy Home Tour" of some local residences, the Post-Crescent *could have covered the event with a brief five-line filler announcement. Instead, staff writer Pat Stenson explored in advance the meaning of the tour in a sixty-three-inch article in the March 6, 1983, edition:*

Energy saving theories, ideas and applications are no longer only to be found in articles, at energy fairs or on a builder's drawing board. In concrete form now, they are to be found in homes throughout the Valley.

Active and passive systems, heating and cooling designs, new and retrofitted homes, will be available for examination as the Appleton Junior Women's Club presents the area's first Energy Home Tour.

"Appleton already has so many home tours," admitted . . . [the] chairwoman of the fundraiser. "But this one's different. For people interested in energy conservation, this is a way to see ideas in practice. We tried to get a variety of homes—newer, older, different types."

After some sentences of transition and detail, Stenson introduced readers to the various homeowners and explored not only what they had done to save energy but also what they could contribute to the public's energy education. One homeowner observed:

People confuse energy efficiency with energy source. If you take a home and add a solar collector you have only changed your energy source, not the home's energy efficiency. You can spend a lot of money or a very small amount on energy sources. But if the home is energy efficient you have a very small heat requirement to begin with and the source isn't as important.

Said another homeowner:

"Many of the design principles are nothing new. . . . The Greeks used them. The Indians used them. It's nothing more than good sense. . . ."

homeowners who have pro-conservation attitudes take concrete actions to save energy in their homes (Griffin 1985).

According to a national survey, the news media are considered second behind consumer groups as reliable sources of information about energy conservation (Farhar et al. 1979). Techniques of investigative reporting might help to uncover some information, especially on a local level, essential to conservation decisions in the home. A reporter for the Syracuse, New York, *Herald-Journal,* for example, conducted an experiment to see whether turning down the thermostat actually saved fuel. On various days with various outside temperatures, Benjamin P. Burtt adjusted his home thermostat to different settings. He then kept a record of how long the oil burner ran each day. The results: by turning the thermostat down from 75 degrees to 65 degrees, he saved 22 percent of his fuel bill. Burtt's investigative effort was reported in his story, headlined "Tests Prove You Can Save Fuel, Electricity" (Burtt 1973).

Furthermore, interpretive techniques might also assist energy conservation endeavors. Social commendation coming from an interpretive reporter or editorial writer might not have the impact of reinforcement from a reader's friends and associates, but it might buoy energy conservation among some groups by rewarding sacrifice. Information about what others in the community are doing to save energy, especially if a concerted effort, may alert people to conservation as a social norm for behavior.

The challenge of energy reporting

How have the media responded to what has been termed the "unprecedented challenge" of covering energy? Generally, not well, according to various voices inside and outside the media. Public confusion over the energy situation, some have suggested, may be partially the result of inadequate coverage (Yergin 1979b).

There was relatively little media discussion of energy issues prior to the energy shortages and the Arab oil embargo of 1973, and the media coverage that did exist was more like a thermometer than a barometer, as events of that year triggered a gusher of energy stories. Generally, the news media did not anticipate the upcoming problems of energy supply and demand, despite major discussions on energy policy in the federal government dating to the 1950s, congressional hearings on oil import policy spurred by a 1970 cabinet task force report (Zentner 1976), and some warnings by the oil industry which, in the early 1970s, embarked on a multimillion-dollar advertising campaign revolving around the theme that "A Country That Runs on Oil Can't Afford to Run Short." Early media coverage, according to economic writer Robert Samuelson, also tended to oversimplify the energy issue. Fingers were pointed directly at the oil companies, who were suspected of engineering shortages for their own benefit. "Most stories," Samuelson says, "simply sidestepped what is now the central issue: the availability of energy and the price we have to pay for it—not simply in dollars, but in terms of damage to the environment, dependence on foreign suppliers, and sacrifice of personal freedom." The news media, he says, had to learn how to deal with the "intricacies of energy choices" (Samuelson 1974).

Roger Morris of the *New Republic* says the media have tended to rely too much on statements from official sources, to trim the background out of stories, to be concerned primarily with today's events, and not to have the expertise or fortitude to check the basis and background of statistics. Morris also observes that shallow reporting in some segments of the press is being rationalized with the notion that readers cannot understand complex ideas, and do not want to (Morris 1976).

An official of the United States Department of Energy has taken the press to task for concentrating energy coverage too much on Washington, D.C., ignoring the issues' complexities, and being preoccupied with "How much is it going to cost at the pump?" He says the press should concentrate instead on what is being done around the country to solve energy problems, what private industry's planners are doing, and what the economic implications of the energy situation are. "This is a long-term, 20 year planning story," he states. "It doesn't happen every minute." The official also notes that conservation of energy needs better coverage, even if it seems "boring," since it will provide most of the energy for the near future (SNPA Bulletin 1980). Conservation may be the least reported of energy options, partly because the media tend to embrace the idea that some technological solution—be it nuclear, solar, or fossil—will solve the energy problem (Yergin 1979a).

Morris suggests the need for change in reporters' perspectives on energy issues, underscoring the idea that energy news needs to be covered in more depth than it is by coverage of today's events in Washington, D.C. Morris states that resource issues are like light reaching the earth from a distant star. The issues that have become visible only today, because of the absence of good journalism, are based on events of the past, and tomorrow's energy problems are being shaped now. "For journalists to wait for those events to have their perhaps irremediable effect on all of us," he says, "is to fail in a basic responsibility to the public" (Morris 1976).

Whether the news media will keep a constant watch on the energy problem through the 1990s remains to be seen. However, as energy expert Daniel Yergin has observed, many reporters who had been covering energy for major papers and television stations have been shifted to other beats (Hayes 1985). Thus, the job of keeping an eye on the energy picture has shifted back to reporters whose main task is to keep watch on other things.

What journalists know about the economic, social, political, and technological dynamics of the energy issue will no doubt play a key role in the quality of tomorrow's coverage. Lambeth (1978) concludes that, if the media expect to exert influence in new areas of coverage such as energy, "they will have to develop means to be at once more knowledgeable and useful to their readers" (Lambeth 1978).

Hints for covering energy issues

Here are some suggestions for improving your coverage of energy issues, based on what we have learned about media performance:

1. Enhance your knowledge of the technical, economic, and social aspects of energy issues. Various publications and even university courses can improve your understanding of energy.

2. Cultivate local, unbiased sources of energy information. Professors and retired officials and executives are possibilities. Do not rely simply on "official" sources.

3. Master the essential terminology so that it does not intimidate you. Scientific sources rely on technical language because of its precision, yet their jargon can often confuse and intimidate you, holding you back from probing and digging.

4. Pursue background and context as well as the fact.

5. Interpret the meaning of statistics and never take them at face value. Always probe to understand how the figures are derived. Have the fortitude to track a statistic through the thicket.

6. Look for the causes and the effects of energy events.

7. Be suspicious of claims of one-shot solutions to the energy dilemma.

8. Remember that economics is a critical component of the energy dilemma, but not the whole story.

9. Do not cop out by believing that energy is too complex an issue for the public to understand.

10. Get beyond the coverage of single events. Crises pass, but the energy problem is ongoing and by no means solved.

In summary

Energy is a public issue in which individual actions do have an impact. Long-run and short-run solutions to energy problems call for a multitude of decisions by a multitude of people, choosing from among a constellation of energy options to find an optimal set of trade-offs. Information, often lacking or erroneous, plays a critical role in these decisions. As a journalist, you are in a unique position to provide the public with the best available facts about energy options. But this information should be presented in a context that allows readers to make comparisons among energy sources with knowledge of their true costs and side effects. Coverage of credible grass-roots efforts to deal with problems of energy supply and demand, along with other practical energy information, could help readers realize the options available to them for coping with the energy problem. The biggest part of the challenge is to help people in your community see beyond gluts and shortages to the real, long-range energy story.

References

Begley, Sharon, and Hager, Mary. 1990. Alternative Energy: Time to Get Serious. *Newsweek* 116(9):40.

Behm, Don. 1986. Energy Giving Way to Weapons; Department's Priorities Change Sharply Under Reagan. *Milwaukee Journal,* Aug. 3, 1A, 4A.

Belk, Russell, Painter, John, and Semenik, Richard. 1981. Preferred Solutions to the Energy Crisis as a Function of Causal Attributions. *Journal of Consumer Research* 8(3):306–12.

Budianski, Stephen. 1990. Poised to Strike. *U.S. News and World Report* 109(9):20–24.

Bupp, I. C. 1979. The Nuclear Statement. In *Energy Future,* edited by Robert Stobaugh and Daniel Yergin, 108–35. New York: Random House.

Burtt, Benjamin P. 1973. Tests Prove You Can Save Fuel, Electricity. *Syracuse* (NY) *Herald Journal,* Nov. 26, 21.

Carter, Jimmy. 1990. America Needs a Policy to Cut Our Oil Habit. *Washington Post National Weekly Edition,* Aug. 22–26, 23–24.

Colglazier, William, Jr., and Rice, Michael. 1983. Media Coverage of Complex Technological Issues. In *Uncertain Power: The Struggle for a National Energy Policy,* edited by Dorothy S. Zinberg, 112–13. New York: Pergamon.

Davidson, Virginia. 1980. Charles Tennies, at 10, Showed Family How to Trim Heating Bills. *Milwaukee Journal,* Sept. 21, 7:2.

Dennis, Cynthia. 1981. Solar Window Unit Cuts Home Fuel Bills. *Milwaukee Journal,* Mar. 22, 7:3.

Farhar, Barbara C., Weis, Patricia, Unseld, Charles T., and Burns, Barbara A. 1979. *Public Opinion About Energy: A Literature Review.* Washington, D.C.: United States Department of Commerce, National Technical Information Service.

Ford Foundation. 1979. *Energy: The Next Twenty Years.* Cambridge, MA: Ballinger.

Griffin, Robert J. 1985. Media Use and Energy: A Panel Study of Education, Knowledge, and Conservation Behavior. Paper presented to International Communication Association Convention, May 15.

_____. 1989. Communication and the Adoption of Energy Conservation Measures by the Elderly. *Journal of Environmental Education* 20(4):19–28.

Hayes, Paul G. 1985. New Energy Crisis is Looming for US, Experts Warn Here. *Milwaukee Journal,* Oct. 23, 2:1.

_____. 1990. Shortsighted Notions Drive Energy Policy. *Milwaukee Journal,* Sept. 9, Jl, J3.

Honnold, Julie A., and Nelson, Lynn D. 1979. Support for Resource Conservation: a Prediction Model. *Social Problems* 27(2):220–34.

Hughes, Barry B., Rycroft, Robert W., Sylvan, Donald A., Trout, B. Thomas, and Hart, James E. 1985. *Energy in the Global Arena: Actors, Values, Policies, and Futures.* Durham, NC: Duke.

Kissinger, Meg. 1988. Energy Crisis Not Past for Poor, Study Says. *Milwaukee Journal,* June 15, B4.

Lambeth, Edmund B. 1978. Perceived Influence of the Press on Energy Policy Making. *Journalism Quarterly* 55(1):11–18, 72.

Landsberg, Hans H. et al. 1979. *Energy: The Next Twenty Years.* Cambridge, MA: Ballinger.

Leonardo Scholars. 1975. *Resources and Decisions.* Belmont, CA: Wadsworth.

Long, Robert E. 1989. *Energy and Conservation.* New York: H. W. Wilson.

Morris, Roger. 1976. Whatever Happened to the Natural Gas Crisis? *Columbia Journalism Review* 14(6):22–24, 51.

Murray, Allen E. 1985. My Turn: The Impending Energy Crisis. *Newsweek* 105(23):16.

Nuclear Energy Policy Study Group. 1977. *Nuclear Power Issues and Choices.* Cambridge, MA: Ballinger.

Quinn, Jane Bryant. 1987. Oil: Getting a Bet Down. *Newsweek.* 109(5):52.

Samuelson, Robert J. 1974. The Oil Companies and the Press. *Columbia Journalism Review* 12(5):13–20.

_____. 1990. Why We Should Stay in the Gulf. *Newsweek* 116(9):41.

Sandman, Peter M., and Paden, M. 1979. At Three Mile Island. *Columbia Journalism Review* 18(2):43–58.

Schurr, Sam J., Darmstadter, Joel, Ramsay, William, Perry, Harry, and Russell, Milton. 1979. *Energy in America's Future: The Choices Before Us: Resources for the Future.* Baltimore, MD: Johns Hopkins.

SNPA Bulletin. 1980. D.O.E. Criticizes Press Coverage of Energy Crisis. *Southern Newspaper Publishers Association,* Apr. 7, 1–2.

Stenson, Pat. 1983. Energy Answers. *Appleton* (WI) *Post-Crescent,* Mar. 6, D1.

Stern, Paul C., and Aronson, Elliot. 1984. *Energy Use: The Human Dimension.* New York: Freeman and Company.

Stobaugh, Robert, and Yergin, Daniel. 1979. *Energy Future.* New York: Random House.

U.S. Energy Information Administration. 1990. Consumption of Energy by End-Use Sector. *Monthly Energy Review.* 1990(2):21.

Wald, Matthew L. 1989. U.S. Progress in Energy Efficiency is Halting. *New York Times,* Feb. 27, 1, 27.

Warren, Anita. 1989. Kilowhat? The Sorry State of Energy Education. *Nuclear Industry,* Third Quarter, 35–40.

Wilhelms, David M. 1981. Age of Solar Energy Dawns on Tinkerer After Experiments. *Milwaukee Journal,* Jan. 11, 7:1.

Winett, Richard A., Leckliter, Donna, Chinn, E., and Stahl, Brian. 1984. Reducing Energy Consumption: The Long-Term Effects of a Single TV Program. *Journal of Communication* 34(3):37–51.

Yergin, Daniel. 1979a. No Quick Fix. *Columbia Journalism Review* 18(3):44.

_____. 1979b. Conservation: The Key Energy Source. In *Energy Future,* edited by Robert Stobaugh and Daniel Yergin, 216–33. New York: Random House.

Zentner, Rene D. 1976. Communication-The Real Energy Gap. *Journal of Energy and Development* 2(1):60–75.

Zinberg, Dorothy S. 1983. *Uncertain Power: The Struggle for a National Energy Policy.* New York: Pergamon Press.

This chapter was initiated by Griffin. Collaborator was Schoenfeld.

CHAPTER 12

The environment

BILL HEATH is the editor of the *News-Herald* in Marshfield (population 18,053), county seat of Wood County (population 72,799) Wisconsin. Bill is a long way from headline environmental disasters like Love Canal, but related issues are still an important part of his *News-Herald* agenda. In a recent year, Bill supervised forty-six stories on the problem of solid waste disposal alone. That amounts to nearly one a week. The following story shows how Bill interpreted the Marshfield solid waste situation in a background story that was part of a series nominated for an American Planning Association Award:

County ignores landfill needs

WOOD COUNTY slammed the door in the City of Marshfield's face this week.

Marshfield had requested that its proposed 103-acre landfill site in the Town of Rock be included in the county's Solid Waste Management Plan. Approval would have opened the state's purse for a feasibility study of the site.

Supervisors responded 22-14 against the plan.

Marshfield has an obligation to proceed—at least to find out if the selected site is acceptable. It has an investment in the property. Outside consultants studied 48 possible sites and determined that this property will work, and authorized an option to purchase on behalf of the city.

IT'S NO SECRET that some Town of Rock residents are upset about having a landfill as a neighbor.

But it doesn't matter where a landfill is placed—it is always going to generate that type of concern. Unfortunately, this area had a bad experience with a poorly run landfill in the Town of Cleveland—that created debris, rodent, and waste seepage problems. That site, however, has been closed.

With proper management a landfill can be a good neighbor. And when its life has ended, the site offers potential as a greenway park area or for other development.

THE REAL CONCERN about Wood County's refusal to look at Marshfield's plan is that the county really offers no alternatives.

Supervisors and planners have been searching for several years for acceptable sites to handle wastes. In recent years, they have been talking about developing sites at both ends of the county.

However, the county has offered little more than talk. As a result of its inaction, the City of Marshfield launched its own search and found a site. Meanwhile, the county has provided little help in answering a growing landfill need for its residents.

Some hope was advanced in recent weeks about burning wastes to generate power for an industrial plant in Plover. But that plan has been sidetracked, at least temporarily.

THERE ALSO HAS been talk about recycling efforts, but there is no market for many of today's discards. Eventually, we will probably see some small-scale recycling here.

But recycling and incineration will not answer our total waste needs.

Marshfield now hauls its wastes to Black River Falls. That is a costly and inconvenient trip. There is a need to have a dumping area closer to home.

Is the Town of Rock site perfect; can or will it be developed? A feasibility study could find some answers—about problems and costs. If it is acceptable, the site . . . eventually would have to be added to the county plan and it would have to gain use approval from the Department of Natural Resources.

THE TALK NOW seems to center on alternate sites—perhaps areas contiguous to the city of Marshfield. That would permit the city to annex the property and would diffuse the political ramifications that are present today.

Transportation and development costs are real considerations in this search. And attention must be paid to groundwater contamination and the other concerns that have been raised.

Wood County has an obligation to work with its municipalities to find sites and study their suitability, Mayor John Smith insists.

Bill Heath's story illustrates many of the key aspects of covering environmental issues that will be considered in this chapter:

in a complex called "the environment," a complex qualitatively different from the older "conservation" complex (Gans 1979).

• Whereas yesterday, the conservation/environment story was usually in the domain of agricultural, outdoor, science, or urban specialists, depending on the slant, today the environmental story can pop up on nearly any beat: capitol, courthouse, city hall, education, business, women's issues, finance, or health, to name several.

• Many public issues come together in the environmental arena. Urban affairs, rural affairs, government, economics, business, labor, education, recreation, consumer affairs, science and technology, energy—everything is connected to everything else.

• Only rarely does a national environmental issue not have a local angle.

• To generate complete information and interpret that information correctly, you must cultivate many sources of environmental news and share with your readers the history of any current development.

• More uncertainty than certainty surrounds the facts in almost every environmental situation.

• Every environmental reporter confronts a thicket of cost-benefit analyses.

• Environmental reporters must try to find the human element while writing about an increasingly complex world of data.

• Environmental events may provide news pegs, but your audience needs background information on underlying issues.

• Increasingly, media of any size have staff members who specialize at least part-time in covering environmental affairs, because many members of media audiences are actively seeking environmental information today (Grunig 1983).

Today's environmental reporter can be a busy person indeed. In a January 8, 1987 issue of the *Denver Post,* Lou Chapman had three major stories on pages 2 and 3B: "State Renews Interest in Unapproved Golden Dump," "Gravel Pit in Jefferson County Gets OK," and "Program to Protect States' Ground Water Given Final Approval."

Environmental problems are getting media attention all over the nation, especially in small communities. In the summer of 1988 the issue being covered for the *Cape Codder* of Yarmouth, Massachusetts, by Jan Welsh (1988) was the effect of a yacht club's dredging on sensitive salt marshes. In Greenbelt, Maryland, Mavis Fletcher (1988) was reporting on the fight against a new road plan by citizens trying to preserve green space in that Washington, D.C., suburb. A similar battle, between a developer and those trying to save a woodland in Mequon, Wisconsin, was on the beat of Mark Jaeger (1988) of the *News Graphic Pilot.*

Preserving the nation's water resources is a major concern, especially in growing urban areas. In Whitman, Massachusetts, demand from an influx of workers from booming Boston was outrunning the town's water supply (Neuringer 1988). Across the continent, San Diego curbed construction as the area's exploding population growth strained water resources

(Weisberg 1988). The importance of water as a public issue was suggested in the *Waukesha County Freeman*. The *Freeman,* located in a rapidly growing Milwaukee suburb, carried three articles about area water problems in a single issue (Cooper 1988a, 1988b: Kass 1988).

The background

Growing out of the antecedent conservation movement led by Presidents Theodore and Franklin D. Roosevelt in the 1900s and the 1930s, the environmental movement represented a growing public concern. Manifold threats to earth and human health posed by air and water pollution brought popular public protests in the 1960s that led in the 1970s to significant legislation at federal and state levels to protect the environment (Smith 1987).

"Earth Day" in April 1970 marked the development of public awareness. In the years since then, public support for environmental protection has remained strong even in the face of economic problems and a 1980s presidential administration that was not supportive of environmental controls (Gillroy and Shapiro 1986).

The face of environmental problems changes from time to time and from place to place. But underneath there are a set of basic concepts and big issues. The reporter must understand the concepts and report the issues, rather than focus only on the environmental crises that continuously arise in modern society.

Basic concepts

What basic ideas are implied by the term "environmental," particularly in contrast to yesterday's "conservation?" A panel of ecologists has distilled some key tenets (Schoenfeld 1983).

In locale—the fouled, clogged arteries of the city quite as much as scarred countryside. In scope—a comprehensive, interrelated humankind-environment-technology system. In focus—global environmental impacts of crisis proportions threatening the well-being of all humankind on an over-crowded planet. In content—tough ecological choices, not easy unilateral fixes. In strategy—long-range impact analyses and rational planning. In tactics—grass-roots participation in resource policy formation—in the streets and through institutional channels. In prospect—a necessary reliance on alternative sources of energy. In philosophy—a commitment to less destructive technologies and less consumptive lifestyles. In essence—a recognition of pervasive interdependencies, that everything is connected to everything else—what educator Jerome Perlinski has called "the principal intuition of the 20th century" (1975).

In covering the environment, the media have been introduced to, and in turn have introduced to the public, the language of ecology. Perhaps because the shortened "eco" has been a handy tool for newspaper headline writers, the term "ecology," after lying in the dictionary for more than one hundred years, now flits about in nearly everybody's vocabulary. What exactly is ecology, or more particularly, applied ecology? It is an "environmental" approach to "the system of interrelationships among society, economics, politics, and nature in the use and management of resources" (Gold 1978).

Big issues

A common journalistic mistake is simply to cover events—real or staged—and ignore underlying issues. The big environmental hazards, big trouble spots, and big causes have been identified by Resources for the Future (Brubaker 1972):

Big hazards—Toxic chemical wastes; radioactivity and related threats to gene pools; air pollution; water pollution and depletion—underground, wetland, aquatic, estuarine, marine; soil erosion; pesticides, additives, and other poisons; impacts on the global climate; forest, range, and wildlife degradation; encroachments on open spaces, natural beauty, and related amenities; precious resource depletion; inhospitable human settlements—urban, suburban, rural; noise, wastes, blight, sprawl; monocultures—the decline of diversity; cumulative effects on physical and mental health (Brubaker 1972).

Big trouble spots—Population trends; per-capita consumption; misuse of technology; food and fiber budget; industrial and household wastes; use of space—urban and open country; resource adequacy; transportation snarl; arms race; degradation of outdoor recreation areas; outer space and open sea policies (Brubaker 1972).

Big causes—Humankind's view of its place in nature; the growth syndrome; maldistributions of wealth; areas of scientific ignorance; governmental incapacities; antithetical cultures; inadequate public education; misdirected rewards and punishments; unilateral approaches; value system; velocity of change and growth in scale (Brubaker 1972).

Forefront issues in the '90s—Major items of unfinished environmental business in the 1990s include world overpopulation, global warming, tropical forest deforestation, the depletion of the ozone layer, acid rain, the handling of hazardous chemicals and nuclear materials, the creation of

EARTH CARE ISSUES IN THE '90S

In the *Earth Care Annual 1991,* National Wildlife Federation president Jay D. Hair comments on the most recent environmental issues:

In 1970 on the first Earth Day our challenges were immediate. We saw our lakes and streams dying, our land being sterilized with poisons, our air choked with toxic gas. The problems appeared at hand, the solution within reach. Now, a generation later, we are learning of the drastic consequences which turn rain to acid, strip our atmosphere of a vital shield of ozone and portend an epoch of planetary warming. As our resources are being stressed beyond their ability to meet even the minimum needs of a third of the world's people, global population growth continues at quantum intensity. Our problems remain immediate and at hand, but we now know they are global, too. As we look to the last decade of this century we are confronted by another prospect undreamed of a generation ago: We are entering an era when it is no longer considered naive to think of bending the metal of war into the implements of sustenance. A rendezvous between the environmental threat to global security and the means to meet it may be this generation's destiny.

JAY D. HAIR. 1991. Foreword. *Earth Care Annual 1991.*
Emmaus, Pa.: Rodale Press.

clean energy, protection of the ground water, an unprecedented loss of wild species, and protection of parks and scenic beauty.

Barry Commoner (1987) observes that since Earth Day in April 1970, "environmental issues have taken a permanent place in our political life." He adds that "we now know a good deal more about the state of the environment than we used to." In terms of actual improvements in environmental quality, however, the laws designed to eliminate air pollution, water pollution, toxic chemicals and wastes, with only a few notable exceptions (e.g., laws curbing lead pollution from automobile exhausts) have not been very effective. "In sum," he states, "there is a consistent explanation for the few instances of environmental success: they occur only when the relevant technologies of production are changed to eliminate the pollutant. If no such change is made, pollution continues unabated or, at best — if a control device is used — only slightly reduced."

Commoner also fears that some environmentalists have lost sight of the goals of the environmental movement. He comments that

> It seems that at least some environmental activists are moderately happy about their accomplishments. But such optimism does not necessarily respond to the original thrust of the environmental movement, which envisioned not an environment that was a little less polluted than it was in 1970, or holding its own against an expanding economy, but an environment free of mindless assaults on ecological processes. By this standard, the question is whether the movement's goal can be reached by the present spotty, gradual, and now diminishing course of environmental improvements or whether some different course must be followed.

Commoner takes national environmental groups to task for taking what he terms the "soft political road." A new grass-roots environmental movement has arisen as a result, he says. "This movement has arisen out of direct impact of environmental pollution on community life . . . For such groups, the front line of the battle against chemical pollution is not in Washington but in their own communities." Thus, whatever the national environmental agenda, there will be local angles on almost every issue.

The main point to remember in covering environmental issues is that far more uncertainty than certainty surrounds the facts in almost every environmental situation. Conservation Foundation editor Rice Odell points out that "uncertainty plagues scientific efforts to assess four major categories of environmental distress — pollution, resource scarcities, ecosystem functions, population." Policymakers may think the only way out of a dilemma is to call on the experts, but "this approach can quickly go bankrupt as people draw up lists of Nobel Prize winners on every side of an issue" (Odell 1982).

Jim Woolf, environmental reporter for the *Salt Lake Tribune,* agrees: "I can report that nuclear reactor waste is possible to be disposed of safely, or that nuclear reactor waste is impossible to be disposed of safely, depending on which scientist I quote. . . . Experts are not the unified mind of fact-knowers that they may pretend to be." His solution: use multiple sources (Schoenfeld 1983).

Reporters should also be aware that even apparently simple environmental problems are often complicated because of the conflicting interests involved. Susan B. Lane (1988) of the *Valley Advocate* in western Massachusetts looked into the problem of leaking gasoline tanks. Leaking underground storage tanks at service stations were contaminating community water supplies. The problem was enormous, with 35 percent of the buried tanks leaking in one survey. Lane, learning some geology as well as economics, discovered that in Massachusetts the problem was urgent. Shallow water tables kept the underground steel tanks wet, so the acidic soil quickly corroded them.

The solution, though expensive, seemed simple. Dig up the old single-wall tanks and put in double-wall tanks. The major oil companies are willing to pay the costs at their leased stations and could also afford the one million dollar liability policy that a new state law called for.

But Lane found that the apparent solution created its own problems. Independent service station operators, already struggling against the major oil firms, said the costs involved would put them out of business. Again, the major companies would pay their costs but only if the independent operator would give up control. The operators feared that the companies were only after the valuable real estate and would close the stations after digging up the old tanks. Their objections stalled action on a serious environmental problem. As in many environmental situations, the social, economic, and political problems have to be worked out first.

Key sources for environmental reporters

A fine newsletter that will help you cover environmental issues is *Environment Writer,* published monthly by the Environmental Health Center, a division of the National Safety Council in Washington, D.C. You can also keep up-to-date by joining the Society of Environmental Journalists (via the Scripps Howard News Service in Washington, D.C.). To cover the environment, you will have to cultivate many sources, most notably the following.

The media

In a recent survey, junior high and high school students rated television, magazines, and newspapers ahead of science classes and parents as sources of environmental information (Alaimo and Doran 1980). As an environmental reporter, you can learn a lot from the media, although you must exercise criticism and caution.

A recent analysis of the content of American general circulation magazines from 1966 through 1975 found that "in terms of holding a mirror to the environmental 'social current' of the decade, American magazine response was measurably adept." Accompanying this response was a remarkable eruption in numbers of new, specialized environmental periodicals (Schoenfeld 1983). Special interest publications may set the agenda for environmental concerns, because subjects often appear first in their columns, only to appear later in general interest media (Strodthoff, Hawkins, and Schoenfeld 1985).

A good way to keep track of national developments from a wide spectrum of viewpoints is to follow these publications: the monthly "Wildlife Digest" insert in *National Wildlife,* a report from Washington, D.C., that ranges far beyond wildlife concerns; the semimonthly *Outdoor News Bulletin,* which also is much broader than its name implies; the monthly *Environmental Action,* a bouncy, counterculture magazine; the *Conservation Foundation Letter,* a monthly objective essay on a current topic; *Environment,* a solid, semitechnical monthly that laypersons can understand without much difficulty; and the *Wall Street Journal* and *The Christian Science Monitor,* both of which have long track records of good environmental reporting, each with its own slant. In addition, almost every state has at least one environmental magazine or newsletter.

Government agencies

Perhaps nothing has so changed the face of environmental coverage in the mass media as has the requirement of the 1969 National Environmental Policy Act (NEPA) for the development of "environmental impact statements" on federally funded projects, accompanied by related requirements in many states. These statements can contain a variety of angles for in-depth reporting, because they assess the likely effects of a project on matters as diverse as air pollution and community services.

All three branches of government at all levels are sources of environmental information. Understandably, the resource management agencies of the executive branch are the most directly concerned. A fine source book is *Environmental Policy Implementation,* published by the North American Association for Environmental Education.

Federal, state, regional, and local bureaus of conservation, environmental protection, and land management traditionally have recognized what they typically call the information and education (I&E) function, and today they are giving it renewed emphasis. Not only do they try to explain regularly to the public how they are spending public funds, but they also attempt to set before the public an agenda for environmental action. To foster or keep pace with the environmental movement, the resource management agencies have broadened their communication efforts in both scope and depth. Yesterday their public messages were aimed primarily at boosting the particular roles of the various bureaus; today there is a growing acceptance of the particular interdependency of all conservation problems and programs and a recognition of the compelling need for broad public understanding of that interdependency.

Today, from the Environmental Protection Agency (EPA), for example, you can get national and regional monthly reports of problems and progress. Most state and local resource agencies are also prime sources of environmental news. However, as a reporter using I&E materials from any source you need to be cautious of agency promotional slants.

With respect to the legislative branch of government, congressional speeches and congressional hearings, duly recorded in the *Congressional Record*, often constitute environmental communication of the most basic kind. The official coverage of the emergence of the National Environmental Education Act, for example, became a primer of the environmental movement. Appropriate proceedings of the various state legislatures, likewise, can enter the literature of environmentalism. County board and city council documents are frequently devoted to environmental affairs.

Decisions by various courts add to public knowledge about environmental issues. Since 1970, as federal courts have interpreted the National Environmental Policy Act (NEPA), their decisions have expanded the concept of environmental quality and the impacts upon it. The United States Supreme Court is playing an increasingly important role in environmental law as disputes under statutes passed during the early 1970s reach the Court. State courts likewise render key environmental decisions, sometimes in classic language. An *Environmental Quality Index* issued annually by the National Wildlife Federation in Washington, D.C., is a useful reference for a diagnosis of environmental ills and trends in agency response.

Societies and organizations

It is difficult to imagine an environmental issue for which some environmental organization cannot serve as a source of background information. As a reporter, you will, of course, use due caution when using a special interest group as a source, because their selected battery of facts is frequently biased. Environmental organizations are varied indeed. Some date well back into the nineteenth century while others are as new or as ephemeral as today's headlines. Some are national, some regional, many local. Some are fiercely independent; others willingly form at least temporary alliances with related groups to attain common goals.

Some environmental organizations attend to a broad agenda of environmental concerns; others have very specific missions; still others, like the League of Women Voters, have acquired an interest in environmental issues along with a more general role. Some groups have a reputation for

MEET SARA

A boon to environmental reporting is a law Congress created in 1986—the "Emergency Planning and Community Right-to-Know Act," which was passed as Title III of the Superfund Amendments and Reauthorization Act (SARA). The press and the public can now get critical information on the use and storage of hazardous chemicals in their communities, including their locations and potential effects on people exposed to them.

The law was passed in reaction to the 1984 tragedy in Bhopal, India, where more than two thousand people were killed by the accidental release of a toxic chemical. "Hundreds of victims in Bhopal could have been spared their lives or injuries if they had known of the hazard around them and known how to respond," explained U.S. Senator Frank Lautenberg of New Jersey. "Many more lives could have been saved if a communications system had been in place to alert residents. . . . That is true of chemical releases in our country as well" (Environmental Health Center 1989).

SARA requires businesses and governmental agencies to give to state and local emergency planners detailed information about certain hazardous chemicals that they store or use locally. Some must also file annual reports on chemical releases. If any of a set of "extremely hazardous" chemicals is released, state and local emergency officials must be notified immediately. The press and public are guaranteed access to all of this information. In fact, the Environmental Protection Agency compiles information about chemical releases and makes it available through a national computerized database, the Toxic Release Inventory.

SARA also requires state and local governments to develop emergency plans based on information about chemicals in communities, including means of notifying the public of a toxic release. A focal point for this activity—and therefore a key resource for journalists—is the Local Emergency Planning Committee (LEPC), which includes representatives of government, emergency agencies, business, citizen groups, and the media. In some areas, reporters have not participated as members of the LEPC, due to a possible conflict of interest with newsgathering. In some cases, their places have been taken by others such as media business office personnel or journalism professors.

An excellent guide for reporters is the book *Chemicals, the Press, and the Public,* available from the Environmental Health Center (1989), a division of the National Safety Council in Washington, D.C. The book suggests unlimited story possibilities from SARA, including:

- the presence and release of toxic chemicals, locally and nationally;
- the environmental and health risks of hazardous chemicals;
- the extent of local and national community participation in community-based chemical risk management; and
- the extent of local and national industry participation and commitment to the goals of the law.

MEET SARA (continued)

"One thing is evident: Newspaper, TV, and radio audiences cannot be expected to understand an issue any better than the reporters
do," says Bud Ward, executive director of the Environmental Health
Center. "Indeed, the public depends on effective media coverage for
its information on environmental issues. And an informed public—
a citizenry actively involved in environmental management policies—is what makes environmental programs work in the first
place" (Environmental Health Center 1989).

supplying relatively balanced data on issues; other groups are openly propaganda mills, although most of them are less strident than they were a
decade ago.

For a comprehensive guide to national nongovernment agencies that
provide information on the environment, you can consult the *Directory of
National Environmental Organizations* (1987). State environmental agencies are listed in the *Directory of State Environmental Organizations*
(1985). Specifically developed to help journalists and others who are concerned with environmental problems is the *Health Detective's Handbook:
A Guide to the Investigation of Environmental Health Hazards by Nonprofessionals* (1985). Among the most helpful local organizations are likely to
be chapters of the Sierra Club, the Audubon Society, the National Wildlife
Federation, and an array of local, state, or regional groups of varying
longevity and purpose. You can probably get a current directory from your
state university extension office or from your state department of environmental protection. For example, the University of Wisconsin Extension's
directory of groups interested in environmental issues lists 64 statewide
groups with periodic newsletters and 251 substate groups.

The Scientists' Institute for Public Information (SIPI) has a Media
Resource Service that can help reporters cover technical aspects of environmental issues. The SIPI service has a toll-free phone number.

The National Wildlife Federation's *World Directory of Environmental
Organizations* (1985) lists more than 200 national and multistate environmental groups, and that is only the beginning. The country is full of environmental groups that work at state and local levels—from Save the
Tallgrass Prairie in Kansas and the Black Hills Alliance in the Dakotas to
the North Cascades Conservation Council in Washington. California has 45
separate groups working on local water issues alone. Nor is environmental

work any longer the exclusive province of environmental organizations. Today "environmentalism" covers everything from health and appropriate technology in the industrial work place, to organic gardening and preservation of agricultural land. Groups as diverse as the American Friends Service Committee; the Farm Labor Organizing Committee, in Ohio; Tom Hayden's Campaign for Economic Democracy; Nurses for Social Responsibility, in San Francisco; the Oil, Chemical and Atomic Workers' Union; the Machinists' Union; and the American Indian Movement carry on environmental work as part of broader programs.

The resource industries

For industry, environmental issues are often seen as economics versus ecology. Both management and labor have difficulties dealing with this conflict.

MANAGEMENT. The resource and related business industries have been in the conservation communication game for a long time via all manner of institutional advertisements, films, and manuals, although many of their messages admittedly are self-serving. The 1965–1970 era of growing public concern about excessive population, pollution, and pesticides caught business and industry by surprise. Editor William Houseman devoted an early issue of *Environment Monthly* to "the pitiful environmental showing of the public relations profession." In too many cases, the response of business was what commentator Lowell Klessig has called "successive levels of lying." National magazines came alive with corporate "image" advertising, proclaiming industry innocent of environmental degradation. Claims typically took two forms: first, the contention that industrial innocence had been retained; second, that innocence had been regained.

Enlightened industry could recapture some credibility as a source of environmental information. Two excellent ecological primers in early circulation were products of business public relations: Kaiser Aluminum's magnificently scripted and illustrated brochure on "Ecology, the Man-Made Planet," by Don Fabun; and the Bank of America's very solid environmental handbook, "Getting Down to Earth." Both contained reliable and straightforward information. But as a whole, industry still has a long way to go. For example, in a 1981 advertising campaign, Commonwealth Edison—proprietor of seven nuclear power units in the Chicago area—introduced readers to Kimberly Michelle Mayberry, who lived with her mother only "a holler away" from the towers of the Three Mile Island nuclear power plant in Pennsylvania. "Would Kimberly and countless others die before their time?" the copy writers asked. The answer, predictably, was no.

After a dexterous bit of pseudoscience, Commonwealth Edison concluded that the results of "long-term, scientifically sound studies" on the effects of low-level radiation are all the same: no excess leukemia or other cancers, no genetic damage. The Chicago Chapter of Physicians for Social Responsibility and the Citizens Against Nuclear Power contended that the company's information was incorrect.

Business leaders are interested in conserving energy and protecting the environment when they see an economic reward. Howard Geller of the American Council for an Energy-Efficient Economy estimates that business is investing one billion dollars annually to reduce energy consumed by the nation's office buildings and factories. For example, Lutheran General Hospital in Chicago bought new lighting fixtures. The lighting manufacturer profited and the hospital reduced its energy costs by 60 percent (Arndt 1988).

Overall, industry still sees many proposals by environmental groups as too costly. Appliance manufacturers persuaded President Ronald Reagan to veto legislation to set energy standards for appliances on the grounds that it would interfere with consumer choice in the marketplace. With gasoline more plentiful in the late 1980s, automobile manufacturers asked that fuel mileage requirements be eased. Although air pollution remained a serious problem, Vaughn L. Beals, chairman of the Harley-Davidson Company, continued to fight legislation to put emission controls on motorcycles (Doherty 1988).

Recently, however, the Conservation Foundation has reported "a new surge of public enthusiasm for environmental protection" (Odell 1986). The foundation credits the constant flow of information about environmental problems such as air and water pollution, pesticides, acid rain, and the ozone layer for the strong endorsement of environmental protection shown in public opinion polls. The Conservation Foundation said that, despite strong opposition, this public support has translated into substantial progress toward the goal of protecting the environment (Odell 1986).

LABOR. In the conflict between economics and ecology, organized labor may well hold the ultimate balance. If AFL-CIO (American Federation of Labor-Congress of Industrial Organization) unions were to negotiate for a clean environment as well as for wage and job security, the result could be climactic. To date, the rhetorical posture of AFL-CIO headquarters has been pro-environment. Labor leaders and their money have played key roles in environmental education. For example, you may think UAW stands for the United Auto Workers. It does, but it also stands for United Action for Clear Water, the Conservation and Resource Development Department of the UAW who lobby for passage of a Great Lakes protection act.

At the local level, however, the story of labor involvement in environmental issues is different, with unions often fronting for ill-conceived power plants and opposing legislation encouraging recycling of bottles. The local union's primary concern is short-term protection of members' jobs, whether they be building power plants or making bottles. Long-term social goals come later. As long as the most endangered species in America is the Detroit autoworker, labor's positive impact on environmental issues will be as tough to develop as it is pivotal to any kind of social and scientific entente on environmental affairs. More than in laboratories or legislatures, the coming sources of environmental information may be found in union halls. For example, the Coalition for Jobs and Energy in Washington state is made up not of proponents for nuclear power and lobbyists for utility companies, as its name implies, but of elements of Washington labor. The coalition, led by Tom Baker of Machinists' District Lodge 751 and Susan Levy of the Washington Federation of Teachers, is trying to reclaim economic issues from the conservative sloganeers. Its first step was to hurry to the state's registration office and appropriate the words "jobs" and "energy," which, members believe, underline their commitment to an energy strategy that combines community-based renewable resources with employment opportunities. Its next task will be to win support for a voter initiative which, if passed, would require a statewide vote before a consortium of utilities could issue public bonds to complete five nuclear plants. Coalition members see the financing of nuclear energy as a labor issue since they believe that rising nuclear energy costs could ultimately reduce the number of available jobs. Economic disruption is as much of a byproduct of nuclear power as environmental disruption is, they say.

Educational institutions

Professors and students helped shape the environmental movement, and now environmentalism is reshaping the university. The history of higher education may offer no more telling example of the interplay of life and learning in America. Barring English composition and math, few university subjects are being offered today in so many diverse ways and places, by such a mixture of colleges, departments, and faculty, as that complex of ecology, economics, energy, engineering, esthetics, and ethics known, precisely or not, as environmental studies. Scarcely a single campus is now without some gesture toward environmentalism. The more substantial enterprises represent a major departure in university focus and format toward multidisciplinary, multifunction, problem-oriented teaching, research, and outreach — making colleges and universities a prime source of environmental information. One study has shown that "environment" is considered a key element of the curriculum that journalism schools want or require their students to take (Griffin and Schoenfeld 1982).

Perhaps even more striking than the marriage of the university and the environmental movement has been the proliferation of educational materials to support environmental instruction in elementary and secondary schools. Prior to 1968, the subject of conservation was largely confined to the last chapter of the ninth-grade science text. Today, the problem faced by an alert teacher is that of digging out from under a deluge of study guides, field manuals, and film strips — all of them sources of environmental information.

The less formal educational institutions, such as libraries, museums, youth organizations, civic groups, and so on, are likewise the sources of stepped-up environmental information. Indeed, the environmental movement has brought about a revival of that special educational agency, the nature center. Various types of such centers are bringing a capsule view of Spaceship Earth to thousands of citizens around the country.

One of the most ubiquitous of informal, adult education activities in the United States is the agricultural extension service, epitomized by the "extension agent" in virtually every county seat in the country. Where once he or she was promoting pesticides, wetland drainage, sod busting, and other deleterious farm practices, today the county extension agent is starting to develop lines of communication with community conservation commissions, lake protection associations, and other public and private environmental groups; and he or she is being backstopped by an increasing array of environmental information materials emanating from land grant college departments. You can be placed on a mailing list for these materials.

Working the environmental beat

Perhaps nowhere in the coverage of social issues is balanced reporting more needed than on the environmental beat. The journalist must resist pressures for advocacy and sensationalism, as well as pressures to become too technical and dull. Good reporting principles, so often lost in covering major public issues, are required.

Cost-benefit analyses

As an environmental reporter, you must perform a sort of cost-benefit analysis — a tricky game. Debate over environmental programs is an intense political and philosophical dispute over how the government should make decisions that involve a jumble of trade-offs ranging from those that can be

THE COSTS OF PROGRESS

On April 25, 1985, the Baton Rouge, Louisiana, Morning Advocate *published a forty-page section on "Prosperity in Paradise — Louisiana's Chemical Legacy." The section evaluated the benefits and costs of Louisiana's petrochemical industry to Louisiana's citizens — prosperity and tax income vs. pollution and the highest lung cancer death rate in the nation.*

Bob Anderson, environmental editor for the Morning Advocate, *said the section "caused shock waves." Anderson has been reporting on the environment for seven years. He stresses the need to be fair to all sides to gain and maintain credibility. Apparently he is successful in doing this. Although he has been involved in some tough environmental controversies, he says, "oddly enough, my work has been honored by both environmental and industrial groups" (Anderson 1985).*

expressed in tangible, economic terms to those that defy objective measurement. For example, the economic cost of a scrubber to reduce sulfur-dioxide emissions from a power plant may be accurately pegged at $5 million, but what is the value of 100 people-years of protection from bronchitis, or of the 25 human lives prolonged for five years each as a result of the scrubber?

There are different ways to play the cost-benefit analysis game. At one extreme, all costs and benefits must be cast in dollars. At the other extreme, cost-benefit analysis can be defined so loosely that it includes virtually any qualitative method that organizes information on alternative courses of action or displays possible trade-off opportunities.

To provide a truly balanced picture to the public, the environmental reporter must see even the hidden factors. Suppose that by employing some form of cost-benefit analysis, federal and state governments and industry reach some kind of accord that will permit drilling for oil off a seacoast, provided certain environmental protection measures are met. Recent history suggests, however, that in the end, regulation involving everything from drinking water to public lands management tends to break down at the point of enforcement — Who is doing the policing, if anybody? Here is a fertile field for reporting and interpreting environmental issues—from Atlanta, Georgia, to Palouse, Washington.

One thing is clear: the cost-benefit debate—the clash between cost reason and moral perception—lies at the core of environmentalism. Environmental reporters will be up to their necks in it.

Dos and don'ts in covering the environment

Seven persons with quite divergent backgrounds met to share views on the state of the art of environmental reportage. The group consisted of the president of a power company, the publisher of a daily newspaper, a freelance author, the head of a regional environmental action group, the dean of a school of journalism, a journalism professor, and a newspaper reporter. Despite their varied perspectives, they reached remarkable agreement on what is good and what is bad in environmental coverage (Brier 1975):

SLOPPY REPORTING. "Reporters aren't asking for proof and documentation of some of the inflammatory statements made by parties to environmental conflicts."

"Pay no great heed to chambers of commerce; they're often wrong and their aims always short-term. Be wary of corporations and their spokesmen. On the surface they'll always make a good case. I said on the surface."

"Several times in the past year we have issued a press release. No one ever calls us for more information."

"We don't have an environmental-reporting problem; we have a reporting problem. Most newspapers continue to operate under the outdated journalistic convention that it is enough merely to sit back as passive observers and record events as they occur. . . . Instead of tying reporters to event assignments that require daily copy production, editors should be taking steps to free reporters to spend weeks, even months, if necessary, researching stories of crucial public concern."

ONE-SOURCE REPORTING. When covering an important hearing on a proposed power plant, "the (state) press used nothing except a news release [the company] circulated to the media before the meeting."

"When the State Power Company announced a $100,000 advertising campaign to counteract the [environmental action group], not one state bureau called the [group] to get a response."

CRISIS REPORTING. "There are indications that the press and specifically its environmental reporters are concentrating so diligently on certain subjects that other potential and even more serious problems are being slighted. It seems as if the press tends to react well to crisis situations, but I wonder if it is doing the best possible job in anticipating those crises."

"I think environmental reporting is crisis-oriented. We hear about news-peg events, but what about the rest of the time?"

BACKGROUNDING. "How much historical perspective has the press given coal development in [this state]? For example, what is the real economic story of [the eastern part of this state] since the 1920s, and what will be the effect of coal development in that context?"

"Newspapers have been among the leaders of a foolish parade. They have boosted their towns. They've endorsed efforts for factories and pay-rolls and what is falsely and euphemistically called an increase in the tax base. Now papers are beginning to wonder and question."

"The brute fact is that there are too many people on earth. . . . By and large the press hasn't tackled this problem. Soon it must bite the bullet."

"The story of [the environmental action group] is an excellent story in itself—a coalition of ranchers working with environmentalists. The story never has been told. The story isn't complicated, but it would take some leg work."

"I'd like to know a lot more about the decision makers on pollution issues. That means personality sketches in part—but mainly it means just basic reporting about them."

THE HUMAN ANGLE. "We have failed to give full consideration to the human environment and the socioeconomic environment. For example, we failed to consider the people who were hurt in our rush to eliminate the ill effects of DDT; we failed to give the sheepman adequate consideration in our zeal to protect the coyote."

"We do not want to jazz up environmental stories. We do not want to overwrite them, to inject false color into them."

"Too much environmental reporting is just plain dull. The interested reader may be able to glean the meaning out of a debate about the installation of an electrostatic precipitator or the increase in parts per million of a certain gas—but what about the average reader? What will the change mean in terms of smell? What will it mean in terms of fishing and hunting?"

"Take the (state) Board of Natural Resources. Who are those board members? What do they do for a living? What are they like? What are their views? Were they appointed because of their politics or because of their knowledge?"

"Environmental news is technical, so it's easy to fall into writing endless stories about each new pollution regulation, for example. I try to get lots of people in my stories. Not just bureaucrats. If I'm doing a story on sewage, I can go to [a city], where they have been operating a plant that turns sewage into lawn fertilizer, and interview a homeowner using it. The issues are complex. I try to strike a balance between getting all the information in and not losing too many readers."

INTELLECTUAL HONESTY. "Let us be careful when we identify the villains and scoundrels in the environmental battle. . . . There is quite a difference between a person who does something in a bad way and a person who is just no damn good. . . . Writing that builds an all-or-nothing image about an environmental issue probably will produce much more heat than light and contribute little toward building an understanding. . . . The role of newspersons has not changed: to describe choices as fairly as possible."

"Freedom of the press imposes responsibilities. It involves the obligation to report fairly, to recognize the perils of advocacy in politics, to investigate, to tell the people who the press serves."

BIG PICTURE. "Too often, stories are written with one point of view or a limited set of facts instead of showing how things relate to each other. I'd like to see more 'big picture' reporting—the kind that follows chains of events. . . . But you also have to convey a sense of immediacy and pertinence, usually by telling the story in human terms. . . . I try to find the human element while writing about an increasingly complex world of bewildering facts and figures. Every beat needs that, but the environment beat demands it."

In assessing the main problems and challenges facing environmental reporting, Friedman (1983) points out that both the short time available to research an article on complex environmental issues and the lack of background most general beat reporters have in regard to technological matters produce superficial coverage. The need for hard news pegs often results in coverage that lacks context and is overdramatized. She suggests that journalism students be required to take more science courses, that impartial groups sponsor professional workshops on environmental reporting, and that scientists become more willing to express themselves in the media.

Case studies: prize-winning environmental reporting

In recent years, environmental reporting has attracted awards from environmental and journalism organizations. These awards show that journalists in large and small communities can cover the environmental beat effectively.

WHAT THEY SAY ABOUT THE ENVIRONMENTAL BEAT

Gladwin Hill, New York Times: "The environmental movement is a bell that can't be unrung; the movement is probably the most extensive and profound event to hit the world since the Industrial Revolution."

Russell Delong, United Press: "The environmental establishment may turn out to be the single most powerful force shaping the lives of Americans for years to come."

Richard Anthony, Boston Globe: "Environmental protection, like issues such as health care and education, has become one of the lasting concerns of the public."

Andy Pasztor, Wall Street Journal: "The environmental movement is enjoying a national surge; its strategists have become remarkably astute in dealing with the press."

George Will, Washington Post: "Polls continually reveal a national consensus for governmental activism concerning environmental protection."

William Symonds, Fortune Magazine: "Washington is in the grip of a Green Giant, an environmental superlobby that is racking up victories in Congress which have been little short of sensational."

Michael J. Bennett, Washington D.C., public information person: "Environmentalism, in its fanatic form, fails to balance the risks, costs, and benefits of regulations with the need to build and sustain the economy. Now is the time to confront fanatic environmentalism and show it for what it is—a modern form of mass hysteria, a witch hunt in which industry is painted as the devil."

Jim Sibbison, Washington Monthly: "The truth of the matter is that official sources alone will never give you an accurate picture of an environmental agency's successes and failures. Take it from me. I used to be one."

Sharon Friedman, professor of journalism: "Journalism teachers and students need to realize that environmental reporting is a valid part of public affairs reporting. Public affairs reporting is a required course in most journalism schools, yet it frequently centers on courts, police, and city council meetings. Covering those aspects is necessary, but so is coverage of other elements of a community's existence. In these times of toxic dumps and polluted water supplies, environmental concerns must be prime among those elements."

National Wildlife Federation Award

California's Tuolumne River flows out of Yosemite National Park and drains approximately 1700 square miles before finding its way to the Pacific Ocean. Early in this century a number of dams were built along its 158-mile route to trap drinking water for San Francisco and provide irrigation water for the San Joaquin Valley. Three new hydroelectric dams were being planned for the river when President Carter recommended that the river's upper and middle reaches be designated as wild and scenic areas.

As a debate developed, Lynn Ludlow, reporter for the *San Francisco Examiner* and lecturer in journalism at San Francisco State University, proposed, researched, and wrote a five-part series on the Tuolumne to clarify the issues involved when decisions concerning water, land use, power, and the environment came into conflict. To understand the river's physical condition, and to acquaint himself with its natural environment, its human neighbors, and its current uses, Ludlow, accompanied by artist Don McCartney, spent two weeks backpacking downriver. Before the trip ended in Modesto at the Tuolumne's confluence with the San Joaquin River, it provided an opportunity for talking with planners, managers, and residents, while hiking through alpine meadows, boating across the Hetch Hetchy and New Don Pedro Reservoirs, helicoptering through Tuolumne Gorge, rafting over Clavey Falls, and canoeing the final, placid miles. "Ludlow's objective reporting on the river's history and the differing proposals for its future development gave his readers an opportunity to face the alternatives involved before a final decision was made," the National Wildlife Federation said in giving Ludlow a Conservation Communicator of the Year Award (National Wildlife Federation 1980).

Inland Daily Press Association Awards

Although a major daily newspaper may have more resources to offer, reporters for small-town dailies and weeklies can produce prize-winning stories on the environment. As a judge for the Inland Daily Press Association's annual reporting contest, Professor Clay Schoenfeld has seen many. He used them in classes at the Center for Environmental Communication and Education at the University of Wisconsin. Among the best (Schoenfeld 1985):

IONIA (MICHIGAN) *Sentinel-Standard*. For years, hundreds, perhaps thousands, of drums of wastes, many toxic, lay concealed at Ionia, a peril to the neighborhood. Local officials were slow to take action after erosion revealed some of the rusting drums. In a succession of carefully prepared articles, David C. Fritz, associated editor, reported developments in the toxic-waste inquiry. As a result of the articles, a driver who had taken part in dumping such wastes two decades earlier came forward and disclosed other sites. The articles aroused interest throughout the state, helping to alert communities to the long-range dangers of uncontrolled dumping.

PETOSKEY (MICHIGAN) *News-Review*. The paper dealt with the serious problem of environmental pollution by treating the subject at a personal level. Reporters Nancy Jarvis and Dianne Murray prepared a series on a contaminated well in Littlefield Township. The well, owned by Lillian and Jerry Belmer, contained several suspected carcinogens and was believed to be contaminated by the township's landfill. The water supply in a nearby lake was also potentially threatened. The *Petoskey News-Review* provided a valuable public service by bringing this matter to the attention of its readers.

LE MARS (IOWA) *Daily Sentinel*. Area farmers objected to the construction of a rural water system because of the possibility that the water would be contaminated by the chemical dump of a paint-manufacturing plant. While covering the long process of determining actual damage to local wells, the reporters from the *Sentinel* began informing the public about the scientific and legal aspects of the story. This often involved clearly translating technical information. The reporters also uncovered inconsistencies in the sampling techniques used to test the water and explained to readers the objections raised by scientists who disagreed with previous test reports. The *Sentinel* was the only paper to report on the deficiencies of the testing program and the financial fears of the paint company involved. The *Sentinel* provided its readers with an understanding of the issues in the controversy so that their input to the community project could be more informed.

WARREN (OHIO) *Tribune Chronicle*. Receiving a tip about trucks dumping fluids at a gravel pit, a reporter developed a network of sources that revealed widespread illegal brine dumping was contaminating the county's and state's ground and surface waters. As Gina Buccino reached these conclusions she staked out truckers, who threatened and then followed her. The reporter also unearthed another impropriety as she discovered that one of the suspect trucking companies was violating zoning regulations, and that tax appraisals of company properties were not being properly updated. As a result, the county prosecutor's office investigated the company. At the same time, the Environmental Protection Agency (EPA) closed the gravel pit in which industrial waste was being dumped and sought court injunctions against trucking company officials and against property owners who permitted dumping on their parcels.

BISMARCK (NORTH DAKOTA) *Tribune.* The paper undertook a massive effort to explain and to clarify a gigantic government project that had been underway for such a long time few people could even remember its origins. The huge Missouri River Diversion Project, called the Garrison Diversion, had been authorized by Congress in 1944, but was still far from completion in 1985. The paper devoted considerable resources—three reporters who produced more than fifty articles explaining all aspects of the project and the controversies that surrounded it. The articles ran four a day for two weeks, and offered compelling evidence that the newspaper had sorted through incredibly complicated history and detail to offer its readers a clearly written, organized, and visualized explanation of the project.

FRANKFORT (INDIANA) *Times.* Charges by a local farm couple that they and their animals were being poisoned by water pollution prompted a compelling series. The newspaper took the concerns of the couple seriously and spent three months interviewing officials and residents and digging through official documents. The well-written series expanded from the poignant story of the farm couple to the general problem of water pollution in the community, and it investigated the contribution of the sewage treatment plant, industrial wastes, and a sanitary landfill to the problem. The articles triggered an investigation by the state board of health into allegations of hazardous waste in the county's sanitary landfill.

COLUMBIA (MISSOURI) *Daily Tribune.* Reporter Chris Conway did an outstanding job in presenting the story and the controversy behind the construction of the nearly completed Harry S. Truman Dam on the Osage River near Warsaw, Missouri. He traced the history of the project from its conception in 1962 to recent protests concerning the dam and the problems to be expected below the dam when hydropower generation began. Conway discussed the potential of the dam, but more importantly, he also revealed the tremendous problems expected and the United States Corps of Engineers' complete ignorance and disregard for these problems despite sixteen years of work and expenditures of nearly one-half billion dollars in public funds. Conway's interviews and numerous quotes added to the interest and credibility of the article.

ELGIN (ILLINOIS) *Daily Courier-News.* When an "unknown substance" of a potentially dangerous nature was discovered on public property and public officials chose to keep quiet about its chemical makeup, the paper decided to do more than merely report the "non-news." It commissioned its own study of the water in a nearby river to be conducted by an independent environmental analytical laboratory. The results showed much higher levels of cyanide, phenol, and several metals downstream from the dumping site than occurred upstream. The paper's coverage clearly explained the problem, providing enough convincing data that foot-dragging local authorities were stimulated into faster action. The paper's effort included aerial photographs of the dumping site and other graphics to add to the impact of the series.

In summary

Most Americans now know that we have an "environmental problem" although they might have a vague understanding of its details. In mounting volume, the media have dramatized and disseminated information about the environment. Ecology is now commonly discussed from kindergarten through college. And public officials have preached protection of the environment almost to the point where it is not just the environment but the environmental issue that surrounds us. For example, interpreting the top problems facing the State of Washington Legislature in 1987, Bob Mertena wrote in the January 8, 1987, *Spokane* (WA) *Spokesman-Review:* "The Washington Legislature will once again tackle the problems of clean air, clear water, and a safe environment, and will shift emphasis from water cleanup to hazardous wastes" (Mertena 1987).

Changes in the environmental movement since it first flourished in the early 1970s have not altered its general direction. Ecology has risen from virtual political and media invisibility to continuing salience. As a nation, we will be involved throughout the next several decades in the complex and critical business of establishing through our institutions a national public policy on the environment. To the news media falls the responsibility of articulating environmental concern. To public officials falls the difficult but essential task of translating that environmental concern into authoritative policy. In order to investigate and interpret how and why environmental policies are enacted, it is clearly important for you as a reporter to know what policy alternatives are facing public officials, and to recognize that all policy choices of consequence involve a distribution of costs and benefits among a wide range of important interests (Schoenfeld 1983).

The challenge to environmental reporting in the decade ahead is one of facilitating a sober consideration of actions that will enhance environmental quality and energy conservation without jeopardizing human needs, and that will help meet human needs without jeopardizing the quality of the environment and the quantity of our energy resources.

References

Alaimo, Samuel J., and Doran, Rodney L. 1980. Students' Perceptions of Environmental Problems and Sources of Environmental Information. *Journal of Environmental Education* 12(1):17–21.

Anderson, Robert. 1985. Letter to author, July 12.

Arndt, Michael. 1988. Energy Misers, Your Day May Be Back. *Chicago Tribune,* Aug. 28, 7:3.

Baton Rouge Morning Advocate. 1985. Prosperity in Paradise. Apr. 25, Special Section.

Brier, Warren J. 1975. Environmental Reporting: A Symposium. *Montana Journalism Review* 18:20–34.

Brubaker, Sterling. 1972. *To Live on Earth.* New York: Mentor.

Commoner, Barry. 1987. A Reporter at Large: The Environment. *The New Yorker* 53(17):46–71.

Cooper, Geoffrey. 1988a. Homeowners Protest Cost of Water Line. *Waukesha County Freeman,* Aug. 20, 1.

———. 1988b. New Watering Rules Go Into Effect Tuesday. *Waukesha County Freeman,* Aug. 20, 1.

Directory of State Environmental Organizations. 1985. Washington, D.C. Environmental Law Institute.

———. 1987. St. Paul, MN. U.S. Environmental Directories.

Doherty, Chuck. 1988. Beals Speaks Harshly of Government Threat. *Milwaukee Sentinel,* Sept. 2, 5:2.

Environmental Health Center. 1989. *Chemicals, the Press, and the Public.* Washington, D.C.: Environmental Health Center.

Fletcher, Mavis. 1988. Boxwood Citizens Appalled by Road Changes Shown in New Master Plan. *Greenbelt News Review,* July 21, 1.

Friedman, Sharon M. 1983. Environmental Reporting: Problem Child of the Media. *Environment* 25(10):24–29.

Gans, Herbert J. 1979. *Deciding What's News.* New York: Pantheon, 19.

Gillroy, John M., and Shapiro, Robert Y. 1986. The Polls: Environmental Protection. *Public Opinion Quarterly* 50(2):270–279.

Gold, Roger E. 1978. Environmental Education Within the Institute of Agriculture and Natural Resources, University of Nebraska-Lincoln. In *Environmental Education in Action—II: Case Studies of Environmental Studies Programs in Colleges and Universities Today,* edited by Clay Schoenfeld and John Disinger. Columbus, Ohio: ERIC Clearinghouse for Science, Mathematics, and Environmental Education.

Griffin, Robert J., and Schoenfeld, Clay. 1982. Environmental Impact: University Programs in Journalism. *Journal of Environmental Education* 14(1):4–10.

Grunig, James E. 1983. Communication Behaviors and Attitudes of Environmental Publics: Two Studies. *Journalism Monographs,* 81.

Health Detective's Handbook: A Guide to the Investigation of Environmental Health Hazards by Nonprofessionals. 1985. Baltimore, MD. Johns Hopkins University Press.

Jaeger, Mark. 1988. Read Subdivision Fails in Mequon Vote. *News Graphic Pilot,* June 20, 1.

Kass, Mark L. 1988. City Agrees to Serve Town with Water. *Waukesha County Freeman,* Aug. 20, 3.

Lane, Susan B. 1988. Dealing with L.U.S.T. *Valley Advocate* (Hatfield, MA), July 18, 8.

Mertena, Bob. 1987. *Spokane* (WA) *Spokesman-Review,* Jan. 8, 1.

National Wildlife Federation. 1980. Awards Citation. Annual National Wildlife Federation Awards Dinner. Washington, D.C. Shoreham Hotel, March 21.

Neuringer, Felisa. 1988. Water Shortage Slows Expansion in Whitman. *Boston Globe,* July 16, 37.

Odell, Rice. 1982. Can Science Deal with Environmental Uncertainties? *Conservation Foundation Letter* (January), 2.

_____. 1986. Environmental Momentum Picks Up Again. *Conservation Foundation Letter* (November-December), 1.

Perlinski, Jerome. 1975. Positives and Negatives. In *Environmental Education Perspectives and Prospectives,* edited by Rudolph Schafer and John Disinger. Columbus, Ohio: ERIC Clearinghouse for Science, Mathematics, and Environmental Education.

Schoenfeld, Clay. 1969. What's New About Environmental Communication? *Journal of Environmental Education* 1(1):1–4.

_____. 1981. *The Environmental Communication Ecosystem.* Columbus, Ohio: ERIC Clearinghouse for Science, Mathematics, and Environmental Education, 31.

_____. 1983. The Environmental Movement as Reflected in the American Magazine. *Journalism Quarterly* 60(3):470–75.

_____. 1985. *Prize-Winning Environmental Communication Reporting.* Madison, WI.: Center for Environmental Communication and Education Programs.

Smith, Page. 1987. *Redeeming The Time.* New York: McGraw-Hill.

Strodthoff, Glenn G., Hawkins, Robert P., and Schoenfeld, Clay. 1985. Media Roles in a Social Movement: An Ideology Diffusion Model. *Journal of Communication* 35(2):134–53.

Weisberg, Lori. 1988. Results of Construction Curb Argued. *San Diego Union,* Apr. 24, B1.

Welsh, Jan. 1988. Allen Harbor Yacht Club Defends Disputed Expansion Plans As Safe. *Cape Codder* (Yarmouth, MA), July 15, 13.

World Directory of Environmental Organization. 1985. Washington, D.C.: National Wildlife Federation.

Worldwatch Institute. 1985. *State of the World.* Washington, D.C.: Worldwatch Institute.

This chapter was initiated by Schoenfeld. Collaborator was Griffin.

PART 5

Covering American life

In America, there are what an ecologist might term two principal "life zones": urban America and rural America. Over the years demographers have waffled over where one stops and the other begins, and indeed, on many a landscape today the line of demarcation is very fuzzy. Yet certain broad distinctions characterize each life zone, giving rise in each case to a cluster of pervasive public issues.

Urban America has a particular gestalt, the most common interpretations of which deal with pollution, crime, fiscal crises, freeways, depersonalization, and other handmaidens of high density. But there is another side to urban America that includes rich cultural amenities, an incredible diversity among people, and the acts of kindness — and hatred — that mark the contrast of the human condition, a tenuous balance between self-reliance and complete dependence on each other. Chapter 13, "Urban Issues," examines urban issues and how to report them.

In contrast, much of the face of rural

America still exhibits open space, dotted with picture-postcard villages. A country window can be a magic casement, opening on rocks and rills, woods and templed hills, fruited plains, foaming seas, and farmers performing that most ancient and honorable of annual rituals — bringing in the sheaves. Like the characters in Thornton Wilder's *Our Town,* rural Americans still have the opportunity to pay attention to things like birds, trees, plants, and the change of the seasons. But rural America, also has another side: it is increasingly becoming a mixture of agribusiness, high technology industry, urban sprawl, grinding poverty, ubiquitous interstate highways — and the strident messages of metropolitan media. Chapter 14, "Rural Issues," examines how to interpret rural life and rural change.

All of the issues we have discussed in this book are public issues. People, whether they live in the city or in the country, not only are affected by them but, at least in our political system, also shape them. They do so most often by getting involved in government. They elect to local, state, and national office officials who have the power to do something about the issues affecting the public. Because public issues ultimately are resolved through the electoral process, it is important for the public issues reporter to observe and interpret how the electoral process works. Chapter 15, "The Electoral Process," focuses on how that process can be analyzed as part of interpreting issues for the public.

CHAPTER 13

Urban issues

WHEN a developer proposed a major condominium project in the Wisconsin city of Glendale, the idea was greeted with emotions ranging from enthusiasm to dread. It set off a numbing succession of meetings, discussions, and public hearings. For reporter David Stewart, of the suburban weekly *Herald,* the issue provided an endless supply of material. His job each week was to fill the first three pages of the tabloid with news, a task made easier when public encounters filled with flaring emotions and quotable quotes took place week after week.

For six months, Stewart followed the issues in a detailed series of articles. Neighbors of the proposed development opposed the construction for fear that the three-story condominiums would destroy the residential character of the area. Other residents and a number of officials favored the development because of the addition to the tax base that it would create.

"The city council approval process seemed to take forever," Stewart recalls. "It was three steps forward, two steps back, for months. After awhile, my stories started to lose their zip — it was the same stuff over and over. I remember joking with my editor some times that he could just re-run articles that had been printed months ago" (Schoenfeld 1985).

The reporter was losing his sense of perspective, he admits. The condominium issue seemed to affect directly only a small, though vocal, minority of residents. What about the interests of the rest of the city? They were not being ignored, but they were receiving secondary treatment.

"I had a problem with cynicism, too," adds Stewart, who had been covering community politics for a few years. "After awhile, these problems all start looking alike. There's always a few noisy, emotional people who eventually give in to the will of the majority, and life goes on. The problem can be condominiums, or sewer projects, or roadwork — the process is essentially the same. When you've seen enough issues like that, with almost predictable results, the emotionalism of the minority seems pointless, or at least uninformed and silly" (Schoenfeld 1985).

Stewart decided to step back and try to gain an overview of the whole

345

issue — not only in Glendale, but throughout the state. Perhaps, he figured, questions of what was and what was not important could be clarified. He spoke at length to officials, developers, and residents, reviewed city records, and read whatever he could find on condominiums in general. One result of his effort was a full-page article that pointed out the historical highlights of the local issue, explained the arguments for both sides, and

THE NEW SUBURBAN AMERICA

If they are to keep up with the times in the 1990s, interpreters of urban issues will have to match their interest in the dynamics of the inner-city with coverage of that phenomenon, "the new suburban America that is changing the nation's character," as Associated Press reporter Rick Hampson wrote in a three-part series in 1990.

The conventional suburb was a custom-built bedroom community with no commercial life of its own, like Park Ridge north of Chicago, or a small town swallowed up by metropolitan sprawl, like Burnsville south of Minneapolis. The new suburb is a city created out of whole cloth on the outskirts of an old city, with its own gleaming office buildings, shopping malls, parking lots, art galleries, museums, theaters, concert halls, stadiums, and French restaurants.

Hampson took a concentrated look at Perimeter Center near Atlanta. He could just as well have examined Tyson's Corner in Maryland, Irvine in California, Irving in Texas, or dozens of other such developments that represent "the most rapid transformation of urban America in its history," as Hampson wrote.

He continued: "The typical American workplace is no longer an urban factory spewing pollution but a suburban office building spewing traffic."

Getting on top of this new America is a challenge for interpreters of urban issues — not to mention the circulation managers of their newspapers.

RICK HAMPSON. 1990. New Suburban America Changing Nation's Face. *Hagerstown* (MD) *Daily Mail,* Jan. 6, 1A, 6A.

placed the discussion in the context of condominium development in general.

But that was just the beginning. "I had sort of a journalistic rebirth," Stewart states. "I had done so much work—spoken to so many people—the community just suddenly became very interesting." Writing from a broader perspective, he says, made his follow-up condominium articles more thoughtful and insightful.

"I think I developed a better eye for detail," explains Stewart. "Where before every public hearing seemed the same as the one before, I now became much more aware of and fascinated by small, subtle statements and events which revealed a lot about human nature and the operations of the city" (Schoenfeld 1985).

The reporter found that the condominium issue, while immediately important to just a few people, actually touched nearly every activity in the city either directly or indirectly. With his newfound enthusiasm, Stewart had no trouble digging up news outside of the city council chambers. For example, a study of the tax base issue led to a number of articles about the delicate balance of aesthetic and economic interests that officials had to consider when zoning land for residential, educational, recreational, commercial, or industrial uses.

"One of my favorite stories, believe it or not, was about sewer allocations," Stewart says. "Whenever new construction was discussed, someone on the council would always ask about the sewer allocation situation. It was always dealt with quickly, so I hadn't given it much thought.

"But when I decided to investigate a bit more carefully, I found that not too may people understood the allocation system, and almost nobody was aware of the lobbying and maneuvering the city engineer and other officials had to confront each year" (Schoenfeld 1985).

The Glendale reporter's coverage of the condominium issue started out as event-oriented writing. He was simply waiting for things to happen at meetings and hearings. While the resulting articles were well-written, they did little more than tell what happened; they answered basic questions of who, what, when, and where. Later, the coverage became issue-oriented, and questions of why, what does it mean, and where are we headed were addressed. This emphasis on issues is an important element in public issues reporting.

One function of the news media in the diverse urban milieu is its fourth estate or watchdog role—to raise local problems to the level of conflict and discussion. To do so requires you to provide readers, listeners, and viewers with knowledge of, or acquaintance with, local problems. However, you must also provide them with knowledge about those issues—analytical or contextual information that gives the public a basis for comparisons, judgments, and decisions.

Urban journalism

Because of its broad perspective and its many subjects and approaches, defining urban journalism is quite difficult. Scholars and professionals alike have struggled with the elusive concept. It is the journalism of the urban environment. It is the reporting, investigating, and interpreting of all events influenced by the urban environment, as all-encompassing as that seems. It includes the issues that are discussed in this chapter. Urban journalism is a specialty in fact rather than in name at most large city newspapers (Hage et al. 1983).

Reporters should realize that these urban issues evolved through processes that have occurred over time. The problems of your city have to be put in perspective. At the start of their series on the urban problems in Madison, Wisconsin, reporters Bruce Webendorfer and Shanat Agajanian (1982) of the weekly *Isthmus* supplied their audience with this background:

> Let's broaden our view and see how central Madison's problems fit into the larger picture of the changing American city. We will see some disturbing implications about Madison's revitalization efforts, and some new possibilities.

> In broad outline, America's tale of urban woe is by now a familiar one. For the past 40 years, American cities have changed dramatically and continuously. Figuratively, and in some ways literally, the 1945 city represented a spike in the surrounding, settled landscape, with people, buildings and cultural activities piled right up in a small area, tapering off gradually as you moved away from the center.

> But much of that started to disappear decades ago, to the extent that one 1960 observer could comment wryly that "a central business district function is any function that has not yet left the CBD." Instead of piling up people and activities as its core the American city became a doughnut, with its center a gaping, widening hole.

> The reasons for the reversal are as familiar as they are numerous: the changing nature of American industry, cheap land at the urban fringe, cheap gas and cheap cars, and the enduring marketability of the single-family home.

> The process has been fueled by America's distrust of big cities and our peculiar notion of what a city should be. As a critic wrote a decade ago: "The American city, unlike the European city, has never been thought of as

a nucleus of civilization. The American city has been treated as a focus of economic activity—to put it bluntly, as a kind of service station."

In recent decades, to put it bluntly again, the suburbs have operated far more efficiently than the older centers in the production, distribution and sale of goods and services. The result in nearly every inner city has been decaying housing, empty shops and factories, an obsolete street system incapable of handling automobile traffic and a population increasingly made up of people who cannot afford to leave.

Urban issues

Urban issues relate to all areas of urban life. Many are issues that reporters have always considered important. Others have gained attention more recently and reflect more diverse ways of covering the urban scene. Particular issues involve dynamic, evolving conditions of the urban environment about which an urban society needs to be constantly and completely informed.

Urban power and urban politics

In any community, there exists a "power elite" which controls much of the decision making, yet which may be unlike and unrepresentative of the people it purports to represent. Some members of this group are elected public officials, yet others, banking and business leaders for example, are rarely in the public eye and never run for public office.

Sociologist David Bromley notes three basic ways of identifying and measuring the power held by various individuals in a city (Bromley 1977). You may find Bromley's detective techniques useful in finding the individuals who are most effective in governing and directing the community:

POSITIONAL METHOD. This method locates influential persons by analyzing power relationships. This approach assumes that people gain power by holding important positions in major institutions, both public and private. It is a quick and convenient method for identifying an influential person, but it often overlooks the fact that people are not always what they appear to be. Having power does not always require that a person hold a high-level position.

REPUTATIONAL METHOD. This technique relies on the assumption that powerful individuals are aware of other powerful individuals in the community. You start this procedure by compiling lists of leaders in civic, business, and government organizations, as well as of socially prominent and independently wealthy individuals. You then ask these people to provide their lists of powerful individuals in the community. Consensus distills a final list of important individuals, or key sources in the community.

DECISION-MAKING METHOD. This method is similar to the reputational approach, except that you categorize individuals according to community decisions into which they had input. This will provide you with representative "sectors" of issues. If you study the relative impact of those who participated in the decision-making process, you should be able to spot whose influence is greater than others.

Reporters seriously interested in identifying the truly powerful individuals in a community should not always assume those individuals to include the mayor, or the chairman of the board and chief executive officer of the city's largest corporation. By applying one or a combination of Bromley's detective methods, you should obtain a much clearer idea of who wields the most influence in each unique and changing community.

But do not expect it to be easy. Reporter John McCarron spent months developing background on the political and economic battles that blocked plans for redevelopment in some of Chicago's most blighted neighborhoods. Library research, interviews, a review of building permits, and even visits to neighborhood vacant lots were needed. The result was a series (McCarron 1988) that made Chicagoans aware of the politics of poverty and provoked serious and open public debate on the city's urban renewal policies (Devall and Strong 1988).

Social strife, social interaction, and the family

One of the most striking differences between rural and urban America is the complexity of social interactions that a city produces. A city, one group of urban scholars has observed, is a mosaic of social worlds arranged in confusing and seemingly incompatible patterns (Stone, Whelen, and Murin 1979). Yet, despite their diversity, the many parts of a city are socially and economically interdependent. A breakdown of one part of the system — for example, a rise in unemployment or growing dissent over segregation of minorities — can throw the urban system off balance by disrupting the social and economic fabric of relationships that form the true heart of the city. Such imbalance often manifests itself in urban unrest.

The major urban issues with which you will have to deal in the next decade include segregation, changes in the structure of families, and changes in urban demographics. Segregation of minority groups remains a critical issue. Levin called segregation the urban issue of the 1970s, and it may remain the urban issue of the future. Today this issue must be viewed in relation to all minority groups, in addition to those who are economically deprived. Ethnic, as well as racial, factors are taking on increasing importance. You will, as a reporter, have to cover the interaction of ethnic groups, as well as racial groups, with all other groups of society. You must evaluate public programs in terms of their effectiveness and potential in solving the problems of a wide range of minorities.

Urban segregation is no longer an issue in only the large urban centers. The issue moved to the suburbs along with the population shift from central cities. In 1988 the City Council of Yonkers, a New York City suburb, refused to obey a court order to allow one thousand low-income apartments in white areas. Court-ordered fines threatened to bankrupt the city. The New York State Emergency Financial Control Board, already providing emergency funds, had to take over Yonkers's finances. The controversy was reported in news media all over the nation (Tumulty 1988).

Smaller cities have also become increasingly concerned about crime. In Worcester, Massachusetts, where burglaries were increasing rapidly, the *Evening Gazette* devoted nearly a full page to advising its readers on home security systems (Blezard 1988). Joliet, Illinois, and Milwaukee, Wisconsin, are just two cities where police and neighborhood groups worked together to reduce the fear of gang intimidation (Gibson 1988, Merrifield 1988).

Historically, urbanization has led to changes in the structure of the family and a decline of its dominance in the lives of individuals and in society. In rural areas, at least in the past, family life focused on farming and agricultural production, which also provided a unifying force. In urban-industrial areas, members of families can become concerned with a much wider variety of occupations, as well as with the pursuit of the diversity of other interests that a city offers. The women's rights movement has brought about an increase in the variety of occupational roles that women can play outside of, or instead of, the traditional roles of wife and mother. In the next decades, the size of families may be decreased by changing societal values. The large family may no longer be useful, as it is for the traditional farm, or desirable, given the impact of the cost and availability of housing, the cost of raising a family, concern about overpopulation and crowding, and women's pursuits of alternative careers.

Changing urban demographics are another important social issue that can be studied by analyzing current census data. Population change within metropolitan areas, as well as between different areas and regions, will become increasingly important as urban areas compete intensely for federal and state aid in addition to political strength based on population. Beyond changing urban demographics are evolving urban life-styles that reflect new work schedules and conditions, and more emphasis on nonwork time.

Above all, author and social critic Michael Harrington (1988) says, it is in the nation's urban centers where the journalist will find great social change and the most significant public issues.

Urban development and decentralization

Urban development is certainly not a new issue, although a significant part of urban development—urban planning—is a new and expanding profession that is not without critics such as Jane Jacobs (1961). Urban developers disagree about how we should plan to use our valuable and often rare urban space, but nearly everyone agrees that it should be done carefully. In downtown Milwaukee, for example, there is a significant amount of undeveloped land on the coast of Lake Michigan. Numerous proposals for use of the land have been made, but it may be years before civic leaders decide what, if any, permanent or even long-term temporary usage should be permitted.

The news media's involvement in the planning process is necessary for obvious reasons: the city is built on public and private land, and decisions are made on behalf of the public by elected and appointed city and county officials. The public has a right to know what is going on when decisions are being made, not just after they are made.

Urban planning and design are guided by three main considerations, which constitute baseline issues for you on the urban-planning beat. The issues are (1) the formulation of a coherent scheme for the attainment of general goals such as community well-being, economic progress, and beautification of surroundings; (2) selection of the major elements in the physical attributes of the city—its streets, public buildings, transit lines, and parks; and (3) adoption of the legal, financial, and political means by which to construct the physical facilities and reach the goals that have been set (La Greca 1977).

So the specific issues confronting the city planner, as well as the reporter covering development of the city, can be summarized as follows:

- Planning that promotes urban diversity and choices for citizens
- Redevelopment and reutilization of land (urban renewal and beyond)
- Strategies for meeting planning goals
- Relocation and reestablishment of cities and urban areas
- Planning at the regional level, including multiple urban areas
- Rehabilitation of existing urban development
- Expansion and sprawl of the city
- Role of private consultants in city planning and development
- Financial interests in planning and development
- Increasing citizen involvement in the planning process

URBAN DEVELOPMENT: BENEFITS AND COSTS

To a larger extent than is true of many businesses, the profitability of a newspaper is tied to the growth and prosperity of the community in which it is located. When a community expands, a local supermarket cannot expect to keep its monopoly; another market moves in. The same can be said about service stations and real estate offices, even radio stations. But the result for the newspaper is likely to be more circulation and more advertising—not a new competitor. The temptation to ally a newspaper with whatever brings growth and income to a community has been fairly consistent in many communities. Perhaps in recent years the temptation has been easier to resist as a more sophisticated understanding of the financial and environmental costs of unplanned growth has begun to work its way into the editorial pages of American newspapers. Still, it remains difficult for the publishers of a paper not to get excited when a major industry, especially a "clean," electronics industry, chooses their town for a new plant. When I was on the *Columbian* in Vancouver, Wash., such a plant was announced for construction, in three phases, in our community. The company would start in an existing building, with modest employment, then build a larger interim facility while making plans for a giant plant for future construction on the edge of the city. The *Columbian* enthusiastically welcomed this new citizen to the community through its editorials. Just for fun, I also wrote a second editorial, a satirical one, suggesting that the new industry would disrupt the community, interfere with existing land use plans, and cost it a lot of money. I circulated the piece only among other newspaper executives, and we all laughed. The company was a good company. It did not pollute; it paid well; its employees participated extensively in community affairs. The interim plant was occupied, and the necessary rezoning and the building of new sewers and roads proceeded apace. Land values in the area of the proposed plant rose. Then suddenly the company announced that it was phasing out the type of equipment that it was making in Vancouver. The long-range plant would not be built, and the interim plant would be closed. The company left town, and the community was left with open sewer trenches, partly built roads, and empty positions on many community agencies.

If there is a lesson for public affairs writers here, it is probably that, in looking at economic as well as political issues, they need to cast a wary eye on what other members of the community may see only in black-and-white terms. Writers need to remind their readers, and local business and political leaders, that growth may carry a price that is not always immediately apparent.

KENNETH RYSTROM. (1983). *The Why, Who, and How of the Editorial Page.* Random House, New York.

• Advocacy, or special interest group representation in planning
• Limiting growth and restricting development in urban areas
• Planning that enhances the dynamics of nature in the city

Urban housing

Housing remains a significant urban problem. It is, therefore, a major issue you will face as an urban issues reporter. Rising interest rates have nudged many young adults out of the housing market entirely, forcing them to rent or to find creative, but not always desirable, means to finance a home. A spin-off of the phenomenon is increasing pressure for rental units, which results in higher rents and problems for low-income families. The cost of borrowing money has crippled the home construction industry, as well, and fewer homes are being built. The conversion of apartment complexes into condominiums to make more inexpensive housing available for purchase has also resulted in fewer rental units available and higher rents elsewhere for those displaced. All of this has led to important news stories that affect everyone in the urban milieu.

Another significant problem is posed by the number of substandard housing units in a city. Reducing the proportion of urban housing units classified as substandard is a major goal of government at all levels. The high cost of urban housing is affecting not only low-income groups. Businesses in Boston, New York, and Southern California are finding their workers cannot afford housing. Rohr Industries, an aerospace supplier, moved in 1988 from Southern California, where the median house price is three times the national median, to Arkansas. Motel 6 moved from Santa Barbara to Dallas because even new managers it tried to hire balked at a median house cost of $240,000 (Sharp 1988).

In one effort to counter the problem, the Greater Boston Real Estate Board offered a $10,000 prize to architects to design an inexpensive condominium (Hanafin 1988). Another organization trying to improve urban housing is Habitat for Humanity. It enlists volunteers—including former President Jimmy Carter and his wife—to renovate and build urban housing. Although such private efforts are laudable, the social problem is too huge for them to have much impact. In 1988 Habitat hoped to build or rehabilitate 120 homes in the 1200 miles between Maine and Georgia, an area with thousands of blighted urban blocks (Holmberg 1988). In Indiana, Laporte County's Habitat organization received a 1988 grant from the federal Neighborhood Assistance Program for just $25,000 to rehabilitate housing in that industrial area (*Post-Tribune* 1988).

Low-income groups have been hit hardest by the urban housing shortage. The United States Catholic Conference of Bishops said the lack of decent low-cost urban housing was creating a "national disgrace," widespread homelessness (National Catholic News Service 1988). The National Coalition for the Homeless in Washington, D.C., estimated there were 2.5 million homeless nationwide in 1987 (Farmer 1988). New York City and Los Angeles each have an estimated 50,000 homeless residents while even such smaller cities as Denver, Richmond, Milwaukee, and Portland, Oregon, have several thousand (Nelson 1987). Predictions are these numbers will rise as cities continue to demolish older housing to make way for new hotels, office buildings, and convention centers (Dunlap 1988).

The homeless represent a very visible urban problem. The older homeless may turn to begging while teenage runaways sell sex for survival (Beyette 1988). City residents become angry over what they perceive as a deterioration in the quality of their own lives and urban life in general whether it be New York City or Seattle (Butterfield 1988; Broom 1987).

Combining techniques of interviewing, polling, and participant observation, a team of reporters in Seattle spent six weeks investigating that city's homeless. The *Seattle Times* team found the city had two to three thousand homeless people living in cars, abandoned buildings, and on the pavement. Nearly 30 percent of the homeless were families who could not afford housing. Others were mentally ill men and women who left or were turned out of mental institutions and had no place to go. The homeless included a growing number of young people, runaways and drug addicts (Nelson 1987). They found, predictably, that people agree that there is a problem but not a solution (Shepard 1987).

Thus we come to our checklist of housing issues:
• Population growth
• Increasing housing costs
• Shortages of housing
• Finding low-cost housing for the poor
• Development and maintenance of effective housing projects
• Dealing with housing shortages and surpluses
• Stabilizing the rising costs of purchase and maintenance of housing, encouraging gentrification (the return of middle- and upper-class families to the inner city)
• Incumbent upgrading (improving the quality of housing without displacement)
• Slum clearance
• Relocation during housing improvement
• Condominium conversions
• Financial support for new housing starts
• Federal involvement in housing
• Slum clearance programs

- Housing welfare programs
- Housing standards for all citizens
- Lifestyles of urban residents and housing preferences
- Architecture and housing design: the civic image
- Urban sprawl and the individual housing unit versus multiple unit housing in the battle for urban space
- Integration of housing with business and industry
- Housing density and its psychological and physical effects
- Housing for a growing senior citizen population

Public health and welfare

The interweaving of urban issues is exemplified in the series written by *Milwaukee Journal* reporter Margo Huston on home health care for the elderly (Pearce and Street 1978). This series brought together two important concerns of a significant segment of the urban population by studying housing and medical care for senior citizens. Huston's (1976) series studied, as she put it, "the way we neglect our old people" in our urban centers. Spending several months researching her reports, Huston interviewed many elderly citizens who did not live in nursing homes but who were unable to care for themselves. Huston's reporting did not limit itself to the elderly; she studied private businesses and public agencies serving the elderly at home. The result? The Milwaukee area was exposed to a social problem it might not have known about. Not only was there reaction in the community, but government looked into its roles in the issue as well, and reviewed health care. Huston's efforts are a magnificent example of the type of urban reporting that looks at multiple issues in the investigative format and brings the issues to the public. For her work, she was awarded a Pulitzer Prize.

Maintenance of the public health, whether it be for the elderly or for the young, is generally a local government matter when not in the hands of individual health professionals or private institutions. Public welfare is similarly a local concern, and is administered at the local government level. While there has been an increase in federal government involvement in these matters in recent years, public health and welfare often remain the responsibility of local government in urban areas. This can put many urban communities in a difficult situation. In Wheeling, West Virginia, for example, the health of the community was threatened by inadequate sewage treatment facilities. But the economic condition of that Appalachian city made it impossible to raise local taxes (*Wheeling News Register* 1987).

While government does administer some health programs, the American health system is largely in private hands, and health care is poorly distributed. For example, individual doctors decide where and when they will practice and who their patients will be. When health care is provided by the government, the major concerns are for whom it will be provided and at what cost (La Greca 1977). For the poor in urban areas, La Greca notes, health care is simply out of the question in many cases because the families cannot afford insurance or per-service fees.

Reporters on the public health and welfare beat also face other concerns. Unemployment remains a significant urban problem, especially in industrial cities. Jobless persons place pressure on society at many points, not the least of which is on the city and county budgets. Urban areas especially are faced with large numbers of individuals who need medical and other services but cannot afford to pay for them (Spiegel 1988). Covering welfare issues means reporters must look at an increasingly complex program designed to assist those unable to assist themselves.

Economist James Heilbrun says these programs have "increased very rapidly since 1960, accounting for more and more of the gross national product. In recent years, this expansion has slowed, but these programs still require large amounts of public monies, particularly at the county and city levels" (Heilbrun 1981). Most aid is federal money, in that many of these programs were initiated by the Social Security Act of 1935, but the federal proportion varies according to the program. These programs are not always adequate to meet urban needs. Many inner-city hospitals find they do not provide the funds to administer health care for the rising number of indigent patients depending on them (Wilkerson 1988).

Once society has adopted the philosophy that it is responsible for the basic needs of persons unable to provide for themselves, policy for such social services must be determined. This process is a major concern of the urban affairs reporter. In a city, welfare is influenced by three factors: (1) the influences of suburbanization on welfare populations, programs, and resources; (2) changes in sponsorship, resources, and professional ideology in the larger national structure of social welfare; and (3) the changing role of the state and federal government in social welfare from the laissez-faire philosophy of the 1920s to the pervasiveness of social programs of the 1960s to the cuts made in programs in the 1980s.

Among the concerns you must report in the coming decade will be increasing dissatisfaction with the welfare system; development of a national welfare policy; financial problems of welfare systems; reform of welfare systems; the increase in the number of welfare programs at all levels; the corresponding increase in costs; and the economic and social problems of new, largely nonwhite, migrant groups, such as Latins, settling in inner cities and seeking public support.

The complexity of these inner-city problems should not be underestimated. For example, large numbers of the urban poor are functionally illiterate, unable to find jobs and unable to comprehend the programs that are developed to assist them (Fiske 1988). Some 85 percent of all urban juveniles who come before the courts are illiterate. Illiteracy is especially costly to minorities, with an estimated 44 percent of blacks and 56 percent of Hispanics being total, functional, or marginal illiterates (Ambrose and Taggart 1987).

In 1986 the *El Paso* (Texas) *Herald-Post* took its readers to the El Paso "where English is a foreign language" and where thousands of adults cannot read or write in any language (Carracino 1986a). *Herald-Post* reporter Theo Carracino introduced readers to the "humiliation, despair and defeat that serves as the illiterate's daily fare" (Carracino 1986b). The seriousness of the problem was illustrated when the *Herald-Post* launched its "Take 10" program—ten minutes of reading a day—to fight adult illiteracy. Shortly after the "Take 10" program started, one large corporate sponsor pulled out when it discovered that many of its employees lacked the basic skills needed to spend ten minutes reading (McQuaid 1986).

Transportation

Anthony La Greca argues convincingly that "the contemporary concern with urban transportation goes beyond the single dimension of energy supply and conservation. For the modern urbanite, transportation is means of access to the resources and services of the city. Any impingement on this needed transportation differentially affects the various social strata of the city" (La Greca 1977).

Interest in mass transportation is experiencing a comeback of sorts in urban areas, after it seemed to be nearly extinct in the middle of this century. Writer Eric Hirst traced the impact of America's love for the automobile on the decline of mass transit systems and increasing waste of fuel resources from 1950 to 1970. "As traffic shifted to cars," he wrote, "transit revenues declined, service and equipment worsened and the spiral continued. Because of higher costs and lower revenues, funds were not available for modernization, experimentation, and research" (Hirst 1973).

Although mass transit is more than twice as energy efficient as the automobile as a means of getting about in the city, we have strongly favored the automobile over use of mass transit. This has resulted in the use of more energy to transport ourselves within the city than has been used to transport passengers from city to city, or even to transport freight from city to city. When the 1973 oil embargo skyrocketed fuel prices, public and private interest in mass transit again were aroused. Yet, even with renewed interest, some mass transit systems are experiencing serious financial difficulties and employee strikes. In Massachusetts, for example, the "T" (metropolitan Boston's mass transit system) stopped running for a time when it ran out of funds and the legislature delayed a fiscal rescue package. Chicago's Regional Transit Authority has faced one financial crisis after another. Clearly, the leading issues in transportation in the coming decade are mass transportation and energy consumption for transportation, but public financial considerations must be placed right in line. Urban transit is heavily subsidized by government sources.

Mass transit is a growing concern. San Francisco opened its BART (Bay Area Rapid Transit) system in 1972 and Washington, D.C.'s METRO began operating in 1978. Both cities are planning to extend their lines. New York City and Chicago are expanding their old subway systems. Miami, Atlanta, and Morgantown, West Virginia, have monorail systems. But Philadelphia and other cities still use trolleys, seeing rapid rail systems such as San Francisco's BART and Washington's METRO as too expensive and too troubled.

Urban issues reporters need to be well versed about what kinds of transportation are appropriate for various urban transit needs. The answer may be a mixture of systems, not simple reliance on a single technology — be it automobile, bus, or subway — to solve transit problems. Traditional rapid-transit rail systems may be efficient in heavily traveled corridors of transportation in large cities, but they by no means are the answer to mass transit needs in all cities, or even in various parts of the same city. Other mass transit options, such as buses and the "light-rail," a modern descendent of the trolley, offer intermediate transportation alternatives. The automobile has contributed to urban congestion, pollution, and traffic problems. It seems that we must, in dealing with the transportation problem, learn to accommodate traffic, but at the same time institute and improve mass transit. However, dividing public priorities often hurts both areas, and slows solution of their problems. A checklist of the major urban transportation concerns includes:

• Financing mass transit systems
• Construction of technologically appropriate mass transit systems
• Reducing deleterious effects of the automobile, such as pollution and congestion, on the urban area
• Managing parking and land use for automobiles
• Continued development and financing of the railroad system
• Molding positive effects of transportation systems
• Continuing research and development of transportation systems for urban areas
• The increasing role of planning and concern for the future
• Cost and availability of energy for transportation
• Interdependence of transportation and land use

- Strikes and public transit labor problems
- Discovering new alternatives to transportation in urban areas
- Meeting public transit demands
- Financial stress in the transportation industry
- Stabilizing the rising cost of urban transportation

Case study: the urban transportation beat

Two years out of journalism school, Charlie Pluckhahn was a reporter on a typical mid-American daily newspaper, the *Dubuque* (Iowa) *Telegraph Herald*. This is his "true confession" of how he went about investigating the strange case of the city's one passenger train, which never ran on time but drew a government subsidy just the same. (Pluckhahn is now with the *Kansas City Star*.)

The tale of how "Amtrak: Often Late but Always Paid" was researched and written doesn't involve community passions, high adventure, or peril to the reporter who did the story. So this isn't a plot for a "Lou Grant" episode. But the Amtrak story and methods used to get it are probably typical of small-newspaper journalism, which is what most J-students will practice for the first few years out of college.

"Often late . . ." grew out of regular beat-style reporting on the subject. I say "beat-style" because when I wrote the stories the *Telegraph Herald* was changing from a beat arrangement to a more generalized system of covering the news, with reporters being assigned subjects or stories to cover from a wide variety of areas. So, I, the "Action Line" reporter, ended up covering Amtrak stories in the spring of 1981, while the transportation reporter was seeing his job shifting into that of a regional generalist. This proves a point which I think is true for just about all smaller papers: For all the talk about journalism specialties, reporters at my level cover a great variety of stories. In my case, it's meant everything from doing the Saturday night police beat to interrogating the president of a large corporation who flew 1,000 miles to see me. I don't know where else you can pick up experience and experiences like that.

Local Amtrak stories at the *Telegraph Herald* consisted of articles on the "Black Hawk" train. It ran between Dubuque and Chicago and was one of five trains whose government subsidies were split between the state of Illinois and Amtrak. Amtrak, of course, is a quasi-public corporation that gets a big subsidy from the federal government. It theoretically operates trains, but actually pays freight railroads to run its equipment on their routes. I was covering Amtrak news, along with several other stories in addition to my daily consumer help column, at the time that Illinois Gov. James Thompson decided to eliminate funding for the "Black Hawk," on the advice of officials in the state Department of Transportation.

The "Black Hawk" was of interest to readers for several reasons: It was government-supported; it was a transportation link; it was a train, with all the nostalgic feelings that engenders; and it was an easy and comfortable connection to Chicago, a city that has had close cultural and business links to Dubuque for over 100 years.

The "Black Hawk" had financial problems from day one (Valentine's Day, 1974). Ticket revenues never covered much more than a third of the train's costs. The biggest reason was time: In the 1950s, it took 2½ hours to get to Chicago by rail. In 1981 it took four—if the train wasn't late, which it often was. The four-hour scheduled running time made it difficult to get passengers to Chicago or back to Dubuque at convenient times of day, and delays and derailments made what service there was very unreliable. In addition, the train was plagued by equipment breakdowns due to an inferior locomotive often used, high maintenance and crew costs, and a lack of the promotional effort needed to attract new riders. Many of these problems had been hinted at in earlier coverage, especially that of on-time performance. The train's on-time record had dipped to less than 5 percent in the fall of 1980. That performance caused a drastic drop in ridership, precipitating the threat of a financial death blow.

Gov. Thompson's decision to eliminate the state subsidy from the 1982 budget made it desirable to examine these issues. The train was going to be cut, and readers would want to know why. My "Often Late but Always Paid" stories were intended to be more explanatory than investigative, and turned out pretty much that way. It wasn't necessary to piece this together by digging up primary information in files and the like; figures and explanations were willingly supplied by state government officials and a railroad spokeswoman.

It doesn't bother me that I didn't have to "investigate" the "Black Hawk." An investigative story is harder to get because the information isn't on the surface and doesn't come with a public official explaining it for you; but an explanatory story can be just as informative and have just as much impact. Still, the "Black Hawk" stories were complicated: There was the relationship among the state of Illinois, Amtrak, and the Illinois Central Gulf that had to be defined, trends and events to be explained and connected, and a mass of figures to be examined. Figures—percentages, totals, and the like—start to blur after a while, and the tendency is to discount the effect of errors by telling yourself that as long as the whole story makes sense, one number wrong won't matter.

Well, that's an impulse to be fought, if for no other reason than to save you the experience of having an editor look at you after you drop a few hundred thousand dollars off a figure five minutes before the story is set in type and say, "Charlie, sometimes you scare me." Also, steer clear of doing your own calculations. The "Often Late . . ." stories reported that for every $27.50 round-trip ticket from Dubuque to Chicago, the state and Amtrak each throw in about $37.50. I derived the $37.50 figure from my own math based on the fact that Black Hawk ticket revenues pay 26 percent of the train's expenses; the evenly-split state-federal subsidy accounts for 74 percent of revenues. I later learned that the state subsidy is calculated in a different and more accurate way and is $16 per passenger. Had I asked for one more number I could have found this out.

The first thing I did in preparing these stories was call Fred Wengenroth, who manages the state of Illinois' railroad bureau. I knew the basic issues, because I had covered the story for a few months before writing the series. Wengenroth was Illinois' train expert; he knew more about the "Black Hawk" than anyone else. Amtrak, the Illinois Central Gulf, and even those who opposed the policies of Wengenroth's department all referred me to him for answers to substantive questions. Luckily, Wengenroth turned out to be a talkative official with figures at his fingertips and no hesitancy to explain them. You can make a case that because his department wanted to change the status quo and drop a popular service that he HAD to be cooperative; whatever, he was a good source with accurate information.

Wengenroth had proved to be a reliable source for other stories, so I felt I could trust his figures. Of course I did some cross-checking and was on guard for anything that didn't make sense. The next step would have been to go to Springfield, Ill., to check state files, something there seemed no reason to do, let alone no time and money. After taking 1,500 words of notes from the first conversation with Wengenroth, the next step was to organize that information. This took time, because other stories and columns had to come first. So a couple weeks later I had a 2,000-word summary of the issues involved in the "Black Hawk" story and an idea of the questions I wanted to ask.

The summary was a new technique. I had done a long set of stories on a land development in the area a few months before. My master plan was less-defined and I had ended up chasing my tail. This time I was determined to be more organized. I took that summary to my city editor, who was expecting some ideas on the "Black Hawk" after I told him there was some fertile ground in it. He approved the explanation, and said that the main angle should be to go after the root cause of the train's on-time problem. I was to find out whether or not the Illinois Central Gulf had any financial incentive to run the train on time.

That 20 minutes was the only contact I had with the city editor on the stories until the day they were turned in. Then he ordered up a front-page summary that dramatized the incentive issue and I looked over his shoulder while he edited two of the four stories. The point is that on a small paper, editors don't hold your hand or tell you how to do a story. It varies from paper to paper, but the consensus I hear is that it's sink or swim once you start working. An editor who supervises five, 10, or even more reporters doesn't have the time to give you much more than tips and occasional criticism. You're on your own, which is better in the long run if you have the freedom to write with style and cover subjects fairly and accurately without bending to prejudices dictated by your publisher or managing editor.

After presenting the plan of action to the city editor, I went to work getting information I needed. I got facts, figures, and Illinois' position from Wengenroth (Amtrak referred me to him, too), quotes and analysis from groups trying to save the train, and some explanations for failures from the train crew and an ICG spokeswoman in Chicago.

It was the ICG spokeswoman who made the stories as important as they were. When I sat in her office in IC Plaza in Chicago, I could barely believe it as she admitted that ICG dispatchers had run freight trains ahead of the "Black Hawk" passengers in violation of company policy, that the company was bound to do so if no one was looking, and that ICG would rather not operate the train at all. Along with other facts and figures about the train's operation over the previous years, there was enough evidence to point a finger at the railroad for not operating the "Black Hawk" correctly and not being interested in doing so in the first place. True, these things had been explained to me by activists, passengers, and train crewmen on the way into Chicago for my interview with ICG. But it's one thing to attribute such statements to anonymous crewmen and others with an ax to grind and another to have them coming from the company's mouth.

ICG has been under so much criticism for its handling of passenger trains in other parts of the country that maybe it had decided to chuck the typical corporate mealy-mouthedness when it comes to failure. At any rate, the lesson is to not assume that a spokesperson, politician, or official will always evade a direct question. Sometimes they will answer yes when you ask them if they've been goofing off on the job.

Once I had the information I spent a few days writing 3,500 words—a main explanation, a story about crew pay, interviews with "Black Hawk" passengers and the Page One summary ordered at noon the Friday before the Sunday the stories ran. The main story was definitely the most difficult, with several interlocking trends and distinctions to be reported. So I gave it most of my attention, with the sidebars being much easier.

The accumulated effort resembled that which you'd put into a college term paper. At 5 p.m. Friday I felt like I'd been up all night (Schoenfeld 1988).

Pitfalls and preventives

There are at least two concerns in our varied reporting and editing approaches to covering urban issues. At times, there is great temptation for reporters and news organizations to "get behind" certain public improvement programs for the good of the community. This is a mass media phenomenon called "civic boosterism." A second area of concern is diagnosis of urban problems and potential urban problems before they become serious trouble for the metropolitan area. This approach is called "preventive journalism."

Civic boosterism

Over the years, newspapers have played a particular role in their urban environments—that of the booster (Street and Street 1978). Reporter Sean Devereaux described this kind of activity in Jacksonville, Florida (Devereaux 1976). In this case, the *Florida Times-Union,* owned by the Florida Public Company (Florida Publico), which in turn is owned by CSX Corporation, a merger of Seaboard Coastline Industries and Chessie Systems, Inc., became involved in what Devereaux says is an example of civic boosterism at its worst. The newspaper promoted a project to develop a new, floating, nuclear power industry centered in Jacksonville rather than in competing Portsmouth, Virginia. The newspaper ran 146 stories over an eleven-week period to support the project and to generate public interest in it. At the same time the newspaper chose to ignore the fact that heavy dredging and draining of a wildlife area near the city would be required in order to get the project in the city. Opponents of the plan were given little or no media access to express their side of the issue. Eventually the project was approved, but before it went very far in development, it was stopped when a major investor, Tenneco, dropped out. The project was slowed considerably, despite all the push by the *Times-Union,* and the city lost its wildlife area as well. In the end, Devereaux said, the newspaper's zeal to promote the city's industries produced imbalanced coverage and denied the public the chance to review all relevant issues.

Boosterism can take another form, that of the civic superlative. Cities are trumpeted as "Number One" by their newspapers, magazines, and radio and television stations, and other promotional outlets. While this is healthy to a degree, it often clouds issues and prevents journalists from taking a carefully distanced look at development and the true status of the city. Urban media expert Gene Burd says this form of boosterism is most prevalent in growing urban areas (Burd 1972). It often leaves the city without a serious analysis of its needs, of the effects of development, and of the aesthetics of growth—an important responsibility of the urban affairs journalist. For a while, city officials and news media managers alike were beaming as their Sunbelt cities grew in the 1970s, at the expense of Eastern and Midwestern industrial centers. Now, when it is perhaps too late, residents of Sunbelt cities are wondering if they can accommodate the expansion, or even if they want it.

Preventive journalism

Traditionally, journalists have paid attention to urban issues only after they have become divisive matters in the community. Journalists have usually taken the approach that all is well unless they see symptoms, or the permanent effects, of an illness.

Preventive journalism is an early warning system. It seeks to reorient reporting to look at issues and problems before they become crises in the community. You become a reporter who does not seek the obvious—what has already happened—but instead you become a "civic detective," looking for problems as they might occur or begin to occur.

The *San Francisco Chronicle,* in one example of preventive journalism, published a series on PCBs (polychlorinated biphenyls) in the everyday environment of the Bay Area and Northern California. PCBs are highly toxic synthetic substances used in a number of processes, including the manufacture of electrical transformers. PCBs have been linked to cancer and birth defects and their production was banned in the late 1970s (Commoner 1987). In a series of ten articles over four days, reporters Dale Champion and Anne Bancroft told how these chemicals existed within electrical equipment on power-line poles and in other similar gear in wide use. They told how this equipment leaked and at times exploded the chemicals into the environment. By publishing the series, the *Chronicle* said later, it hoped to warn the communities of the potential dangers which could continue to exist if the equipment remained in service. They wrote of citizens who tried to stop use of the equipment but received little publicity or heeding of their warnings. About the same time that the series was published, the Pacific Gas and Electric Power Company announced it would begin a program to remove the PCB-filled electrical capacitors from its poles. The day after the series concluded, a PCB capacitor exploded in Watsonville, California, hitting the home of the mayor of the community.

Even though some feel it came too late, the series provided good results. Consider what it accomplished: there might have been more such explosions, more property damage, and perhaps life endangered if the series had not been printed. This approach by the *Chronicle* helped produce a needed change in the community. Had the paper not taken the preventive approach, the series might not have been done, no one would have been cautioned, and PCBs would have remained on the poles.

In summary

Urban journalism and urban issues are ubiquitous terms that include a large number of salient issues and problems for you as a journalist. When you work as an urban issues reporter, you look at the unique urban environment from a news media perspective, and you utilize the detective tools of the reporter and editor.

As a reporter, you should always keep in mind that an urban area does not exist in isolation. For example, when reporter Richard Willing of the *Detroit News* examined Detroit's social and economic problems he found the city was part of a pattern of change that was affecting cities from New England to the Midwest. He talked with experts in urban sociology and to civic leaders, economists, politicians, public administrators, political activists, and residents of other cities from Boston to Milwaukee. A pattern finally emerged. He concluded that the problems fell into the following categories: demographic movement of large numbers of people was eroding large tax bases; geographic political boundaries were arbitrary rather than natural; race relations (racial antagonism remains high); housing (public housing had been a failure); schools (a "down-the-road" problem); and streets, public buildings, and basic services, the quality of which was deteriorating.

But Willing, after months of background reading and interviews, could see beyond existing patterns that were so discouraging to Detroit's citizens. He concluded his series with a final article on "How urban areas gird for rebound." Cities, including Detroit, were doing some things right, he reported. Downtown redevelopment had not only cleared up blighted areas but it had attracted white-collar industries to the area, and these industries in turn had attracted service businesses and new residents to the renewing city center. Willing had not only reported the problems of Detroit but had analyzed and interpreted the urban environment and found new patterns developing. The successful urban journalist can do no less.

References

Ambrose, Jay and Taggart, Kay. 1987. *A Testament from El Paso.* Cincinnati: Scripps-Howard, 3.

Beyette, Beverly. 1988. Teen Selling Sex for Survival. *Los Angeles Times Service,* Aug. 18.

Blezard, Robert C. 1988. Security Systems. *Worcester* (MA) *Telegram,* July 16, 31.

Bromley, David G. 1977. Power, Politics, and Decision Making. In *Contemporary Topics in Urban Sociology,* edited by Kent P. Schwirian et al. Morristown, NJ: General Learning Press.

Broom, Jack. 1987. People Who See the Homeless Most Often Are Least Sympathetic. In *On The Street: Seattle's Homeless,* A Times Special Report, *Seattle Times,* Mar. 17, 14.

Burd, Gene. 1972. The Civic Superlatives: 'We're Number One.' *Twin Cities Journalism Review* 1(2):3–5, 24–25, 32.

Butterfield, Fox. 1988. New Yorkers Turning Angry With More Beggars on Street. *New York Times,* July 29, A1.

Carracino, Theo M. 1986a. Gaining Confidence Through Reading. *El Paso Herald-Post,* Dec. 9, D1.

———. 1986b. Finding His Way. *El Paso Herald-Post,* Dec. 8, D1.

Commoner, Barry. 1987. A Reporter At Large: The Environment. *The New Yorker* 63(17):46–71.

Devall, Cheryl, and Strong, James. 1988. Not Against Development, Shiller Says. *Chicago Tribune,* Sept. 2, 2:1.

Devereaux, Sean. 1976. Boosters in the Newsroom: The Jacksonville Case. *Columbia Journalism Review* 14(5):36–47.

Dunlap, David W. 1988. From Dust to Demolition Rises New Times Square. *New York Times,* July 6, 18.

Farmer, Robin. 1988. Shelters Increase; Need Grows Faster. *Richmond Times-Dispatch,* July 31, A1.

Fiske, Edward B. 1988. Policy to Fight Adult Illiteracy Urged. *New York Times,* Sept. 9, Y11.

Gibson, Sharon. 1988. Merrill Park Residents Discuss Ways to Combat Gang Problem. *Milwaukee Community Journal,* June 8, 1.

Hage, George S., Dennis, Everette E., Ismach, Arnold H., and Hartgen, Stephen. 1983. *New Strategies for Public Affairs Reporting: Investigation, Interpretation, and Research.* 2d ed. Englewood Cliffs, NJ: Prentice-Hall.

Hanafin, Teresa M. 1988. A Challenge for Architects. *Boston Globe,* July 16, 37.

Harrington, Michael. 1988. *The Long-Distance Runner.* New York: Henry Holt & Company.

Heilbrun, James. 1981. *Urban Economics and Public Policy.* 2d ed. New York: St. Martin's Press.

Hirst, Eric. 1973. Transportation Energy Use and Conservation Potential. *Bulletin of the Atomic Scientists* 29(9):36–42.

Holmberg, Mark. 1988. Habitat Volunteers Are Building Houses and Hope. *Richmond Times-Dispatch,* July 31, B1.

Huston, Margo. 1976. I'll Never Leave My Home. Would You? *Milwaukee Journal,* Spectrum, Oct. 31, 1.

Jacobs, Jane. 1961. *The Death and Life of Great American Cities.* New York: Random House.

La Greca, Anthony J. 1977. Critical Urban Problems. In *Contemporary Topics in Urban Sociology,* edited by Kent P. Schwirian et al. Morristown, NJ: General Learning Press.

McCarron, John. 1988. Chicago on Hold: The New Politics of Poverty. *Chicago Tribune,* Aug. 28-Sept. 2.

McQuaid, E. Patrick. 1986. Phone Company Takes Close Look at Hispanic Dropout Rate. *El Paso Herald-Post,* Oct. 14, D1.

Merrifield, Bob. 1988. Joliet War On Gangs Reeling After Attack. *Chicago Tribune,* Aug. 21, 2:1.

National Catholic News Service. 1988. Plight of Homeless Noted. June 9.

Nelson, Robert T. 1987. Searching for a Solution. In *On The Street: Seattle's Homeless,* A Times Special Report, *Seattle Times,* Mar. 17, 15.

Pearce, Diana, and Street, David. 1978. Welfare in the Metropolitan Area. In *Handbook of Contemporary Urban Life,* edited by David Street et al. San Francisco: Jossey-Bass.

Post-Tribune (Gary, IN). 1988. Five Area Groups Receive Neighborhood Aid Grants. Aug. 1, C1.

Schoenfeld, Clay. 1985. David Stewart interview in author's files, Apr. 24.

_____. 1988. Charles Pluckhahn personal memoir in author's files, July 17.

Sharp, Kathleen. 1988. Firms Move As Housing Costs Rise. *New York Times,* July 31, 8:1.

Shepherd, Bob. 1987. Homeless, Helpless, Hopeless? In *On The Street: Seattle's Homeless,* A Times Special Report, *Seattle Times,* Mar. 17, 14.

Spiegel, Claire. 1988. Nation's Poor Overwhelming Trauma Centers. *Los Angeles Times Service,* July 27.

Stone, Clarence N., Whelen, Robert K., and Murin, William J. 1979. *Urban Policy and Politics in a Bureaucratic Age.* Englewood Cliffs, NJ: Prentice-Hall.

Street, David, and Street, W. Paul. 1978. Print Media in Urban Society. In *Handbook of Contemporary Urban Life,* edited by David Street et al. San Francisco: Jossey-Bass.

Tumulty, Karen. 1988. Housing Ruling Tears at Yonkers. *Milwaukee Journal,* Aug. 14, J1.

Webendorfer, Bruce, and Agajanian, Shanat. 1982. The Center Cannot Hold. (Madison, WI) *Isthmus,* June 6, 1, 17.

Wheeling News-Register. 1987. Decision Time for City Council. June 22, 3.

Wilkerson, Isabel. 1988. Small Inner-City Hospitals in U.S. Face Threat of Financial Failure. *New York Times,* Aug. 21, 1:1.

This chapter was initiated by Garrison. Collaborators were Griffin and Scotton.

CHAPTER 14

Rural issues

THE 1980s were the years our metropolitan media discovered — or rediscovered — rural America, their attention riveted by the imperiled economic situation of farmers. Even Hollywood dramatized the farmers' plight with the popular films *Country* and *Places in the Heart*. But rural issues have always been a staple on the agenda of small-city media, although at present they assume major proportions.

Rural America after the 1980s had become a heterogenous mixture of agriculture, industry, and urban sprawl, calling for interpretation at least as sophisticated as that given to urban issues. Some stories about rural issues have become prize winners.

Two examples:

When the Illinois State Legislature instituted a new tax assessment program basing farm values on "net income" instead of on conventional real-estate values, "the fuse was lighted for a tax time bomb that could cripple or severely curtail government services throughout Illinois." Reporter George Frazier (1984) of the *Shelbyville* (Illinois) *Daily Union* determined that "many officials are unaware of the looming crisis that could result in what has been described as 'a life and death' situation for local services." In a five-part series Frazier oriented rural and urban readers of the *Daily Union* to the varied dimensions of the problem.

Story No. 1 reviewed the 14 percent drop in assessed valuation throughout the state, the impact of which was "most severe in rural downstate counties which have small urban and industrial tax bases and depend on farmland taxes to fund county and township governments along with local services such as road, fire, park, and library districts and schools."

Story No. 2 discussed the million-plus dollars that Shelby County farmers would save in property taxes annually — and the resulting losses in property tax revenues faced by local schools.

Story No. 3 looked ahead to "a significant decline" in farmland assessments.

Story No. 4 was a background story explaining how "farmers have been caught in a squeeze between rising production and financing costs and declining prices for the crops—the squeeze reflected in a drop in overall profits and in the amount of local property taxes."

Story No. 5 was a wrap-up story giving the bottom line—that "the value of all property in Shelby County has dropped 10 percent this year, putting the County Board in a position of 'biting the bullet' over reduced services or increasing property tax rates."

Effectively linking rural concerns and urban concerns, the series won an Inland Daily Press Association Award.

Paul Jonas (1984), staff writer at the *Miles City* (Montana) *Star,* also won an Inland Daily Press Association Award for a series on massive soil erosion threats in the area.

Jonas led off his series with on-the-spot coverage of "plowout," turning grazing land into marginal cropland:

> Ground breaking of marginal cropland is increasing.
>
> A 76,000-acre spread of grazing land, the Crow Rock Ranch, will be plowed out in the next few weeks.
>
> A number of local ranchers are speaking out against the plowing. They complain about large landowners—often investment corporations—who can sometimes double grazing land market value by plowing it up for grain.
>
> Long-time ranchers are critical because the new landowners often use a minimum of soil conservation practices. The land-breakers rely on government programs to pull them through when the inevitable drought shrivels their yield below prescribed "disaster" levels.

In his next story, Jonas explained the financial incentives for plowing grazing land:

> Grazing land can double in value after it's broken.
>
> Local farm and ranch realtor Ed Kimball says grazing land valued at $100 to $125 an acre today could well sell for $250-$300 after conversion to wheat land, depending on its productivity.
>
> But many contend another reason large plowouts have increased in recent years is government price support programs and crop insurance subsidies offered through the U.S. Department of Agriculture to reduce financial risk.

Next, Jonas reviewed possible legislative and other legal remedies for plowout:

> Area conservation officials concerned with growing sodbusting activity in Montana rangelands say there are two ways to reduce plowouts.

The most practical one, they say, is Colorado Sen. Bill Armstrong's "sodbuster" bill, before Congress. The other is land-use regulations implemented by referendum at the county level.

Armstrong's bill would bar owners on highly erodible land from receiving federal subsidies.

Jonas enlivened his factual reporting with quotes from both sides of the issue:

Sand Springs rancher Bill Brown, Jr., has land in the Rock Springs area next to a large wheat farm broken in the early 1970s. After about five years, Brown says, his fence was covered by blowing dirt.

He built a second fence on top of the first about three years ago; that fence is now half-covered with wind-blown topsoil.

Brown says if adequate erosion practices aren't used at Crow Rock and other large areas of broken land, the land may eventually become useless, and taxpayers will end up paying reclamation costs.

"We don't want taxpayers financing headaches," Brown says.

Emmett Linnebur, about to plow up and plant Crow Rock Ranch, says he doesn't believe in stripcropping. He describes his breaking activities as "the art of making a living and keeping my kids in the country."

"If I don't [break it], there are five people behind me."

Linnebur says the government has no right to disrupt private land ownership.

"A guy is allowed to do with the ground what he wants," he says.

The background

As in the case of Shelby County, Illinois, and the Miles City, Montana, area, the rural issues beat today is one characterized not by placid pastoralism, but by mounting volatility. The long-standing trend of migration from rural areas to the cities was reversed in the mid-1970s. Although the number of people directly involved in agriculture has continued to decline slightly, the number of rural residents involved in industry and service occupations has increased, as has the number of people living in rural areas but working in nearby cities. Rural residents and their communities have lost what remained of their earlier isolation, and they now equal, and in many instances exceed, the characteristics of their urban neighbors in factors such as education and income (U.S. Census 1986).

With developments in technology and the growth of education in rural areas has come a change in the kinds of relationships that exist within rural communities and between these communities and the rest of the world. In many areas, towns have united into regional networks in an effort to solve

OK, SO DON'T HAVE A COW

One important role of the farm reporter is that of interpreting the inside of farming to urban readers. Agriculture beat reporter Mike Flaherty of the (Madison) Wisconsin State Journal *did that neatly on a bitter cold morning in January 1990. Here's his lead:*

OK, so it's 17 degrees below zero. It's rough starting cars. It's an unpleasant sprint from car to office.
Well, kwitcherbitchen. It could be worse.
You could be farming.
Worse yet, you could be dairy farming.
The normally serene starting point for those rows of cartoned milk and boxed butter on the grocery shelf turns into one ugly place when the mercury dips below zero.
"Oh, I just *loooveee* farming when it gets cold," said Jim O'Leary, Milton dairy farmer, as he scooped hot water over frozen water pipes in his barn Wednesday.

MIKE FLAHERTY. 1990. Farmers in a Deep Freeze. (Madison) *Wisconsin State Journal,* Jan. 18, 8B.

common problems that reach beyond individual communities. Increasing costs and a decline in the number of children have led to the formation of consolidated school districts in many areas, necessitating increased interaction between neighboring towns.

Additionally, the development of agriculture from a locally centered, small-market system to an international system of commodities, futures, and long-term marketing has increased the involvement of rural communities in the world outside. As Loris Jones, agriculture writer for the *Daily News-Idahonian* in Moscow, Idaho, put it: "Farming is, indeed, a changing world. The latest production technologies, changes in world trade, competition from the European Economic Community, increased foreign production, and changes in consumer demands put a lot of pressure on U.S. farmers" (Jones 1986).

Rural communities are also affected by the same social and economic changes that affect their urban neighbors. Low-income people who find urban living costs too high are moving to rural areas in Northern California. These rural counties find themselves staggering under the burden of state-mandated welfare and other services many of the newcomers require. Meanwhile, the tax revolt that produced Proposition 13 severely limits tax revenues. Robert W. Edkins, former editor of the *Record Searchlight* in the community of Redding, sees rural counties becoming "economic hostages of the state" (Bishop 1988).

Not all of the open country has experienced this boom in technology and education, and many rural areas still suffer from low income, poor education, and rural myopia. Generally, however, areas suited for large-scale agriculture, for high technology industry, or to serve as "bedroom" communities for urban areas have boomed. Areas that have remained static generally have done so because they lack one or more of the elements necessary to induce development, or because their residents actively oppose growth (Bradshaw and Blakeley 1979).

While world and national issues impinge pervasively on rural issues today, rural residents remain intensely interested in their neighbors. The audience for rural issues reporting is not just rural residents: an important objective is also to interpret rural developments for urban people. A large part of interpreting rural issues involves monitoring subtle trends rather than covering "events." Investigating rural issues requires checking with many sources, not just covering one or two conventional beats.

John Oslund, of the *Minneapolis Star,* applied these principles in developing his lead to a series on "Energy on the Farm." Oslund (1980) introduced his theme by linking the agriculture and energy beats and relating world issues to national issues:

> In a series of stories this week, *The Minneapolis Star* will take a look at how the energy situation affects the way U.S. Agriculture and agribusiness produce, process, and deliver the food we eat and export.
>
> Since World War II, the U.S. economy – and agriculture in particular – has been based on the assumption that there always would be cheap and abundant sources of energy. For U.S. farms, the research based on that assumption has resulted in increased mechanization and correspondingly increased production.
>
> But the expectation of unlimited, inexpensive energy evaporated in 1973 when the Organization of Petroleum Exporting Countries (OPEC) began driving the price of oil upward – from about $2 a barrel past $40 a barrel – and the United States and other oil-dependent countries have been struggling with the problem ever since.
>
> How will this affect U.S. agriculture?

But Oslund recognized the need to lend a local angle and human interest to his theme. So he led off his first story this way:

When Vincent Crowley, a Slayton, Minn., farmer, was breaking a young pair of Percheron draft horses, he took the most logical approach.

He parked his diesel tractor and put the 1,800-pound animals to work hauling silage and manure, and doing other chores.

Crowley, a dairy farmer, figures it costs him about $1 a day to feed the horses. (They eat the portion of the hay his cows don't.) Compare that to the $1 a day in electricity it takes to keep his tractor's diesel engine warm enough to start during the winter—not to mention the 25 gallons of fuel his horses *don't* burn each week for the same amount of work.

Buzz Christison raises pigs in southeastern Minnesota. Pigs have to be kept warm, and that takes a lot of energy—in this case LP gas (bottled gas). So Christison did some research, then designed and built an $800 solar barn for his intermediate-sized pigs. With LP gas at 62 cents a gallon, he figures the solar-heated barn will pay for itself in fuel savings within about three years.

Daryl Jorud is busy getting a wind-generator business off the ground. A good-sized farm in the northwestern part of Minnesota might use 100,000 kilowatt hours per year for a "typical" Minnesota home.

Jorud's company, Oak Ridge Wind Power of Underwood, Minn., will be turning out 45-foot rotors that sit atop 100-foot towers and "could very well generate 100,000 kilowatt hours of electricity annually."

Horses, solar heating, windmills. What's going on here? Are high energy costs driving farmers across the country back into the middle ages of technology? Will food costs soar any time OPEC ministers gather to turn the screws a little tighter?

Oslund talked directly to *Star* readers about real Minnesota people wrestling with a current public issue that had national implications. He did not simply cover a single event; rather, he wove together several trends into a coherent whole.

Rural issues: sources and strategies

Rural areas are not immune to the types of public issues that confront urban areas. Crime, politics, economics, the gamut of social problems—all are present in small communities and open country. But there are important issues that are distinctive to rural affairs. We outline them briefly here and suggest reporting tactics.

Conflicting land and water use pressures

America's frontier dream of limitless land and water, ripe for exploitation irrespective of damage to productive or environmental values, is passing. The emerging view of land emphasizes long-term land management over immediate gain and gives priority where possible to adapting and reusing existing development rather than abandoning and replacing it.

Fundamental changes at work today on the American landscape underscore the need for a view of land that can guide growth and development while protecting resources at the same time. People are settling in greater numbers in small towns and rural areas. Timber companies are harvesting the last available old-growth timber on private lands in the Northwest and must look increasingly to young forests regenerating on land from which timber has already been harvested.

Community leaders and government officials will find themselves challenged through the 1990s by the need to accommodate such forces. They will have to find ways to balance multiple public objectives and respect the great differences in a country as diverse as the United States. They will need to improve the ways in which conservation and development goals are pursued.

Reporters of rural issues can seek to identify, examine, and interpret practical approaches to land and water management. Three key questions demand answers: whither rural resources? what price soil conservation? and what are the key questions facing water resources?

WHITHER RURAL RESOURCES? Rural America today faces pressures that may reduce the productivity of land and transform the landscape. Small towns and rural areas are growing again after decades of decline. Many rural communities are unaccustomed to dealing with growth and the new demands for roads, police and fire protection, planning, and other public services.

The uses of soil, water, energy, timber, and mineral resources also have emerged as important issues in rural America. Soil losses have increased since the grain export boom of the early 1970s brought new land into production. Runoff from agricultural lands continues to pollute rural waterways. The need for new energy and mineral development is competing for land and water with agriculture and other traditional rural activities. The scattering of new housing and other development through the countryside threatens open space and wildlife habitat. How will rural Americans — local and state officials, landowners and citizens' groups, resource users, and others — meet the challenges posed by these emerging problems? Public affairs reporters will be keeping track.

WHAT PRICE SOIL CONSERVATION? Many Americans remember vivid images of the dust bowl days in the 1930s — droughts and windstorms, soil blown halfway across the country from the Great Plains to the Atlantic Ocean, carloads of displaced farmers migrating to California and other places in the West. They may remember, too, that the federal government tried through the Soil Conservation Service, established in 1935, to stop the loss of essential soil resources. For many Americans, the problem of soil erosion seemed under control.

Unfortunately, it persists. The surge in demand for agricultural exports in the early 1970s caused farmers to plant more acres and abandon many soil conservation practices. Indeed, the loss of fertile topsoil remains one of the major environmental problems in America today.

Although significant erosion is found only on a small proportion of the nation's total cropland, some of the most critical erosion problems occur in areas of high agricultural production—the Corn Belt, the Texas High Plains, the Mississippi Delta, and the Palouse region in Idaho and Washington. For years, cheap energy, extensive irrigation, and increasing amounts of fertilizers kept crop yields high, masking the effects of erosion. Today, awareness is spreading that if the loss of fertile topsoil is not reduced to tolerable levels through conservation methods, future crop yields may decline, and the serious problems caused by pesticides, fertilizers, and sediment washed off farmlands into America's waterways will continue unabated.

How much erosion is occurring? Where? How much is too much? How does it affect crop yields? Why does the problem persist? How can soil conservation programs be improved? Seeking answers to such questions can stimulate the interpretation of a crucial rural issue for both city and country audiences. For example, a drastic decline in the amount of available farmland and alarming rates of soil erosion in Dane County, Wisconsin, led the (Madison) *Wisconsin State Journal* to conclude in 1981 that the land was a threatened resource. For eight days that October, the *State Journal* presented a picture of land use and abuse in the county and the state (Bjorkland 1981).

During the 1970s, development in Dane County swallowed 20,000 acres of farmland. Families migrated into the rural, unincorporated areas, hoping to escape the city for the Shangri-La of the country. Instead, they often found other former city folk: about 40 percent of the dwelling units in the towns were built during that decade. At the same time, cropland was eroding at an average rate of 7.6 tons an acre each year. As much as 50 tons of soil per acre were washing away each year on some county land. A look at history, as well as conversations with farmers, landowners, land experts, and politicians, led to a conclusion that the poor economy had perhaps given officials the time they needed to sort out the problems and begin working on solutions.

Four years later, the *State Journal* (Bjorkland 1985) took a second look with a series of articles introduced as follows:

Today: We begin with a report on a typical area in Dane County, the town of Westport.

Monday: Soil erosion problems caused by the town of Westport's largest landowner, and a second look at a farm where saving the soil is not a top priority.

Tuesday: Trempeauleau County in Western Wisconsin is the showcase for the state's reorganized soil conservation program.

Wednesday: The state's Farmland Preservation Act: is it working?

Thursday: Dane County looks to computers for the answer, while Westport shows the way.

Friday: City aldermen soon may have a zoning fight on their hands.

WHAT ARE THE KEY QUESTIONS FACING WATER RESOURCES? Historically, U.S. water problems have been considered in terms of physical characteristics, such as flooding, drought, water pollution, irrigation supply, municipal supply, waste treatment, or groundwater depletion. For example, the *World Press Review* (1983) reported in 1983 that "nowhere is the problem more pressing than in North America, where the amount of water available for every person is dwindling at an alarming rate. Shortfalls are due not only to increasing population but also to the loss of usable water as industrial chemicals continue to pollute, as acid rain continues to fall, and as major underground sources of water for cities and agriculture dry up."

While such statements are useful in focusing attention on the problem, they typically miss two very critical dimensions that are essential to the solution of the nation's water problems.

First, where is the problem located? Each physical problem is a local problem for some part of the country. For example, the United States consumes less than 3 percent of the water that falls within its borders. Apparently, the nation has a surplus of water. In fact, some parts of the country are experiencing severe water shortages, while other areas do have a surplus, enough sometimes to inundate fields, streets, and homes. The "coming water crisis" may be acid rain in Vermont, saltwater intrusion in Florida, groundwater depletion in the Texas High Plains, surface water depletion in Arizona, water distribution in California, navigation in Missouri, municipal water supply in South Dakota, and flooding in Mississippi.

Secondly, who should be responsible for solving the problem? The federal system, with its checks and balances, was intended to provide protection for states and individuals, protection against power amassed in a central government. States traditionally have had a key responsibility for allocation and management of the water within the borders. Agricultural interests have traditionally had the strongest voice about how water was managed in rural areas but new economic forces are demanding a larger share of this essential commodity. The clash over water use is a major issue in Montana, where tourism is now the third largest industry. As the water situation deteriorated in the drought of 1988, tourism operators asked that huge irrigation projects be shut down because they were draining prime fish habitats. They pointed out that out-of-state fishermen spend one hundred million dollars annually in Montana (*New York Times* 1988).

In the past decade, however, the balance between states and the federal government has been altered. The fiscal capability of the federal government to construct water development projects led to the assumption that this was the federal government's role. The net result was great uncertainty over whose place it was to solve water problems. This uncertainty over proper federal-state roles has hampered the solution of water problems.

Do the states have the ability to undertake the task? Will they assume the responsibility? Do they have the authority? Will they be accountable for their actions?

The long-established system of prior appropriation in the West is increasingly being adapted to such emerging water demands as instream flow uses of water for fish and recreation, on one extreme, and energy development, on the other. In the East, where states have relied traditionally on the common law riparian doctrine, new forms of water permits are being developed to accommodate increasingly consumptive water uses (Council of Environmental Quality 1983).

But a federal role will always be there, as will local concern, if not capability. Covering water resources issues may at times dominate the attention of public issues reporters covering the rural beat today.

Farming and ranching

For most rural areas, an important aspect of local life and economy is agriculture. In the past one hundred years, farming in the United States has changed drastically, as have the communities that service it.

Timely issues that hold the key to future American agricultural productivity include soil productivity, water availability, climatic change, international policies, dependence on fossil fuels, competition for agricultural lands, and crop monoculture. [An excellent overview of these can be found in *The Future of American Agriculture as a Strategic Resource* (Batie and Healy 1980).]

Traditionally, farming in the United States has been a family enterprise with families managing relatively small farms. That has changed, however, as farming equipment and methods have become more large-scale and more efficient. The large, flat, wheat fields stretching from Texas to the Dakotas and into Washington, the corn fields of Illinois, Indiana, and Iowa, and the vegetable farms of southern California and Florida (as well as other areas) lend themselves to large-scale farming. With investments in equipment running into the hundreds of thousands of dollars, it is financially more feasible in these areas to farm large tracts of land. (For example, in wheat-farming areas, one thousand acres is considered a minimal amount of land to be farmed.)

In areas where the terrain does not lend itself to large-scale farming (such as the Northeast, the upper Midwest, and parts of the South), farming has developed into a high-value crop venture. Instead of growing crops that require large sections of land in order to be profitable, farmers have turned to types of farming that require much less area to be profitable, such as dairying and truck farming.

Regardless of the terrain, the scale of farming necessary to survive financially has increased continually over the past twenty years. Many of the farmers still working smaller farms have taken up farming as a part-time venture, supplementing their income by working in local towns.

No matter what the size of the farming enterprise, the marketing of farm products is the same—large-scale. Agriculture is no longer a matter of taking a truckload of produce to the local town and selling it. Agriculture has truly become agribusiness, and marketing of farm produce is tied to nationwide, and frequently to international, markets.

For example, much of the corn grown in Iowa and Illinois is sold to foreign customers such as Japan and Europe. Over 80 percent of the wheat grown in the winter wheat area of Washington is exported to the same countries, and even the rice grown in Arkansas and Louisiana finds its way to the Far East. The marketing of farm produce has become a matter of speculation with commodities markets rivaling the stock market as a target of investors and speculators.

Additionally, the late 1970s saw in influx of foreign investment in American farmland. Japanese and European industrialists as well as oil-rich investors from the Middle East bought thousands of acres of prime farmland in Illinois and other states as investments, in many cases outbidding American buyers and eventually forcing states to consider limitations on the amount of foreign investment they would allow in the state.

One observer stated that "there is considerable evidence that agriculture in the advanced industrial society is being integrated out of the fabric of the local community life into a network of large corporate agribusiness organizations. As a result, decisions making huge differences in the lives of the community residents are made afar, not locally" (Bradshaw and Blakely 1979). The situation may not be quite that far advanced in many areas, but a key resource for many American farm families today is their lawyer, who draws up the papers for incorporating the family farm.

Covering agriculture is a multilevel enterprise. In addition to reporting the local conditions, markets, and concerns, those must be related to regional, national, and even international trends.

Local coverage involves such aspects as weather conditions, crop forecasts, local marketing trends, innovations, and local farmers as successful businesspeople. Additionally, local coverage of agriculture reaches beyond the farming community and into the local business community. Success of the local farmers portends success for local merchants who supply the farmers with both agricultural and nonagricultural goods.

Regional coverage is important because farmers do not define their area of concern by geographic boundaries but rather by agricultural ones. Their interest stretches as far as their kind of farming stretches—wheat farmers in Texas are interested in crop and weather conditions throughout the entire Midwest, because the success of crops in Kansas and the Dakotas will have an impact on the marketing of their own crops.

National issues, similarly, are part of the coverage, but generally the attention paid to national and international factors is limited somewhat to those concerns that have particular impact on the local farmers. For example, a government order stopping wheat sales to foreign markets would be of interest to the wheat growing areas, but a change in the government tobacco subsidy programs probably would not be of interest (at least not enough to warrant coverage).

Part of the importance of intensive coverage of agriculture in agricultural areas is to inform not only the farmers but the nonagricultural portion of the community as well. If agriculture is a large part of the community's economic picture, most of the people in the community will want to know what is happening. Additionally, part of the small-town concern for each other will still exist, and an interest in agriculture will exist simply because friends and neighbors are involved in it.

Keep in mind that many people in any rural community are involved indirectly in farming. Public issues in agriculture may well lie off the farm. The meat packing industry, for example, employs thousands of workers who live in rural settings surrounding its plants. A major public issue here is on-the-job safety. Tom Knudson (1984) of the *Des Moines Register* discovered that farming is an extremely dangerous occupation, with five times the death rate of other occupations. Ironically, government statistics show that the meat packing industry, often the major source of alternative employment in farming areas, is the most dangerous industry in the nation for workers (Glaberson 1988).

SOURCES. There are three major kinds of sources of agriculture information in most communities: government agencies, specialized organizations, and the farmers and business people involved in agribusiness. All three are increasingly supported by computer-based agricultural information services.

Most agricultural centers, particularly county and other government seats, will have offices of the United States Department of Agriculture (USDA) and its subdivisions. These offices are available to help farmers with agricultural problems as well as to help them through the maze of bureaucratic red tape and regulation. The Agricultural Stabilization and Conservation Service (ASCS), the Soil Conservation Service (SCS), the Farm Home Administration (FmHA) and others, depending upon the section of the country, are prime sources of government reports, surveys, and other information. In fact, many newspapers make it a policy to run regular columns written by the local USDA representatives.

States where agriculture is important will also have well-developed state agencies that are useful sources of information. Most inspection and licensing within a state is conducted by the state department of agriculture or department of health. There are also state agricultural financing and assistance agencies. But for the most part, much of the agricultural assistance and information service is left to the federal agencies.

One warning about the use of government sources: official reports will often need a good deal of translating before they will make sense to the average reader.

A second major source of agricultural news is the specialized organizations and people who can provide information on local agricultural concerns.

One of the foremost of these is the state university extension network. Land grant universities are required to provide agricultural research and information and other assistance to farmers within the state. Most states, particularly those heavily involved in agriculture, have a network of extension offices. Local extension agents are expected to be knowledgeable on local conditions and problems, and equally important, they have direct access to the university's main campus for more detailed information.

Farmers' organizations are another specialized source of information. Since the beginnings of the Grange over one hundred years ago, farmers have been active in organizing. Though much of the organizing at that time was in protest over low prices, the roles of today's farm organizations vary. Purchasing and marketing cooperatives aimed at providing a united marketing front, lobbying organizations directed at influencing local and national leaders, and other associations have been formed by virtually every kind of farmer. Cattle producers, dairy producers, pork producers, wheat growers, corn growers, and others all maintain organizations in areas where those forms of agriculture are important. Most of these groups have paid administrators who are responsible for gathering and having on hand information on marketing, legislation, economics, weather, and whatever else will affect the farmer and the specific crops. These organizations exist on the local, state, and national levels.

The third major source of agricultural information is the local farmer. As noted earlier, farming has become a technology-intensive and education-intensive venture, and there are farmers in virtually every community who will be able to supply much information. Frequently, they will be officers in local and state organizations and can provide access to the organizations mentioned earlier. Other times they will simply be modern, informed businesspeople, as will the agriculture supply businesspeople of the community.

MONITORING. An important note on the coverage of agriculture is that unlike many public issues, agriculture does not produce meetings that can

HARVEST OF HARM

Tom Knudson, Iowa City bureau reporter for Iowa's Des Moines Register, *talked to individual farmers to document the hazards of farming. He had to. No government agency compiles case histories of the maimed, the sick, and the dead on America's farms. He found no farm organization eager to publicize the fact that farmers were five times more likely to die from on-the-job accidents than workers in other industries. Knudson's six-part series, "Harvest of Harm," ran in the* Register *from September 16 through 23, 1984, and began with this lead: "Agriculture set another record last year. But this record wasn't measured in bushels per acre or dollars per pound. And it wasn't something to be proud of, for agriculture became the most hazardous occupation in America."*

Knudson's "Harvest of Harm" series won the 1985 Pulitzer Prize for national reporting.

tip off reporters. Much of the coverage of agriculture involves a continuous process of marketing trends, changing weather, and a varying economy. Occasionally an incident such as the passage of a piece of legislation will arise as a "news peg," but for the most part, covering agriculture involves monitoring the field and being aware of subtle shifts in trends and circumstances.

Recent studies indicate the mass media devote considerable time and space to reporting on agricultural markets, at least in terms of listing the prices of commodities. Interpretation is less common, appearing only in 14 percent of daily newspapers and 35 percent of radio and television stations. Yet audiences report having trouble "making sense out of raw figures" (Fett 1983). Interpretation of supply, demand, and price information would seem to be a challenge for news media seeking to cover rural affairs adequately. Studies (e.g., Bowes et al. 1978) suggest several "rules" for effective interpretation of increasingly technical agribusiness information:

- Decide exactly what it is you want to get across.
- Use plenty of examples, analogies, general rules, and exceptions to general rules.
- Be explicit.
- Use as little complicated terminology as possible.
- Use shorter sentences and words.
- Introduce, intersperse, and end your material with something other than hard data.
- Use tables and graphs to improve comprehension, especially in stories involving agricultural economics.
- Indicate practical applications.

An example of applying these rules is Bert Caldwell's story in the Spokane *Spokesman-Review* on the state of Washington's Family Farmer Bankruptcy Act. Faced with interpreting a very complicated law, Caldwell (1986) fell back on a time-tested technique stating that the law is complicated, and its principal feature can best be explained with an example:

Assume that a farmer bought land worth $200,000 six years ago. The land subsequently dropped in value to $100,000. Even though the farmer's mortgage is still almost $200,000, under Chapter 12 the Bankruptcy Court judge can set the amount owed at $100,000 — the current value of the land.

That helps the farmer stay in business.

A common flaw in agricultural reporting is the story that lapses into technical jargon to the confusion of urban audiences—and likely of some rural audiences as well. For example, a *Pullman* (Washington) *Herald* story led off this way:

> The Palouse Conservation District was awarded a grant of $127,000 in Referendum 39 funds by the Washington State Department of Ecology (D.O.E.).
>
> The purpose of the project is to demonstrate and evaluate the effectiveness of no-till seeding on 10,000 acres over a five-year period in the South Palouse River watershed.

How many readers could define "Conservation District," "Referendum 39," or "no-till seeding?" Later, the story referred just as cryptically to a "Public Law 566 project." These terms could easily have been explained.

SPECIAL PAGES FOR AGRICULTURE

News media in agricultural areas periodically devote special pages to agricultural issues. For example, an issue of the Moscow, Idaho Idahonian *carried stories with the following headlines:*

UI Computer System Helps Egyptian Agriculture

PIK, Prices, Weather Combine to Cut Crop Yields

Farmers Union Leader Rips Lowered Loan Rate

Russia, China Deals Smell Sweet to Farmers

Grain Harvest Starting Slowly for Pullman-Moscow Farmers

Exports Alone Can't Solve Farmers' Problems

Old MacDonald Gets a Turn in Classroom

UI Crop Specialist Earns World Honor

Local FmHA Office Closed Friday

Livestock Markets

Weathervane

Forestry

The United States and Canada lead all other continents and regions in the production of wood products. In the United States alone, approximately half a billion acres of land are rated as commercial forest — land capable of producing commercial wood products. Two-thirds of these lands are privately owned. So, while the importance of forestry to newsroom agenda will vary considerably from region to region, as a rural affairs reporter you will at least occasionally pay attention to forest management and cropping issues in your circulation area, if only because "forestry" includes acres and acres of small farm woodlots scattered across the country.

One recurring forestry issue revolves around the concept of multiple use, the idea that forests can and should provide a variety of uses other than the provision of timber products. These other uses include grazing, wildlife habitat, recreation, soil conservation, and watershed protection. Competition among uses can become intense, particularly on public lands. Another recurring forestry issue revolves around the two basic systems of cutting now in use in forests managed for timber: selective cutting and clear-cutting. Each has its economic, ecological, and esthetic strengths and weaknesses. A third perennial forest management issue relates to means and methods of forest protection. Prevention and suppression of wildfires enjoys public acclaim; utilizing prescribed burning as a forest management tool does not. Using wide-spectrum, persistent pesticides to attack forest insect pests is highly controversial. Then there is the perennial debate over whether, in fact, we face a timber famine; and if so, whether we can continue to export forest products while opening more public forest lands to harvest. Finally, there is debate on what to do about the millions of small unproductive forests. Leave them alone, try to coax more output from them, or try to force their owners to carry out more intensive forestry? How important is it that these many woodlots turn out more output per acre in the future than they have in the past? How, if at all, can their noncommercial values — watershed and recreation, particularly — be enhanced and the owners of such forests be reasonably rewarded?

For background on local angles to such issues, a good place to start is with the extension specialist in the forestry department of the nearest land grant university, or with a district forest ranger.

Federal land management

Young reporters unfamiliar with American land history are often amazed to discover the extent of public land ownership in a country that puts such stress on free enterprise and the private ownership of property.

The federal government of the United States is and always has been the largest single proprietor of land in the country. Today about one-third of our total land area is federally owned. This large-scale federal ownership of land is usually not in major conflict with the dominant ideology of private enterprise, for the federal lands are used by individuals and businesses, and the products of the federal lands are gleaned largely through private efforts.

Because of regional differences in land history, ecology, and economics, the amount of land in federal ownership varies widely from state to state. All but a nubbin of Alaska is federal land; all but a nubbin of Maine is not. Virginia is 8.5 percent federally owned; Nevada 85 percent. Naturally, the amount of federal land in an area will affect the reporting of rural issues, but even a small unit of federal land in a state can produce a running story. For example, the relatively tiny federal Horicon Wildlife Refuge in mid-Wisconsin is the site for an annual battle among farmers, hunters, birdwatchers, the local tourism industry, legislators, biologists, and bureaucrats over United States Fish and Wildlife Service (F&WS) management practices.

Table 14.1. Uncle Sam as Landlord

	Percentage of state land owned by U.S. government	Federal holdings in millions of acres
Alaska	89.4	333.4
Nevada	86.1	60.5
Idaho	63.8	33.8
Utah	63.6	33.5
Oregon	53.4	32.3
Wyoming	48.6	30.3
California	46.6	46.7
Arizona	44.0	32.0
Colorado	35.5	23.6
New Mexico	33.2	25.9

Source: *Time,* Aug. 13, 1982, p. 52.

While the F&WS, the Bureau of Reclamation, the Corps of Engineers, and the Department of Defense manage significant amounts of specialized federal lands, the three principal federal land management agencies—in order of territory—are the Bureau of Land Management, the National Park Service in the Department of Interior, and the United States Forest Service in the Department of Agriculture. While each has a somewhat different form of regional organization, each will be represented by a district office. Those offices should be your haunts as a rural issues reporter.

Particularly in the West, squabbling between federal and state governments over the use and management of the nation's public lands provides a running story. Many issues come to a boil in many places. Disputes occur over the relative emphasis on development and environmental protection for Alaska's public lands; over the disposal of nuclear and hazardous wastes; over deployment of strategic weapons; and over an endless series of problems related to development: water allocation, timber production, cattle grazing, mining, wilderness designation, off-road vehicle use, other recreation activities, environmental protection, and wildlife.

Lumber companies are permitted to log in the national public forests, provided they adhere to the sustained-yield system of cutting the timber, the idea being to replace the lumber by careful replanting and care. Timber cutting in the public forests has increased greatly since 1950, because replanting and tree thinning often permit lumber companies to harvest more.

Each year the secretary of the interior rents one hundred million acres of public grasslands to ranchers for grazing. The ranchers pay a nominal amount per animal per acre per month. While this practice is meant to subsidize small ranches, much of the federal rangeland is taken over by large ranches, whose owners lobby vigorously to keep the rent of rangeland low. While the government sets aside some of its revenues from renting rangeland for reseeding it, the range has been deteriorating since the First World War, because the amount of grazing exceeds the capacity of the forage to regenerate itself. Range rehabilitation work is far behind schedule, and grazing continues to be permitted in areas designated as part of the National Wilderness Preservation System.

Sociologist Marion Clawson notes that "land use in the United States is controlled or influenced by public action" (Clawson 1973). Investigating and interpreting federal land use policies is a key to comprehensive coverage of the rural beat. Important questions include: What values do the public lands provide? How much land should the federal government own? How much should be turned over to private interests or to state and local governments? What management objectives should guide federal land managers? How should decisions regarding the use of public lands be made? (Conservation Foundation 1983).

TOUCHING ALL THE BASES. Threading the way through conflicting private and federal land management jurisdictions and practices is a constant challenge for rural issues reporters, particularly in the West. Covering a planned timber sale that was to have impact on a national park, a wilderness area, private lands, environmentalists, hunters, and taxpayers, as well as the United States Forest Service, *Billings* (Montana) *Gazette* staffers attempted to touch all the bases (Nell 1983):

The Forest Service is working with private landowners in a unique timber sale to clearcut 223 acres of timber one mile from both Yellowstone National Park and the Absaroka-Beartooth Wilderness area.

The timber cuts will be in two sections, one 188 acres in size and the other 35 acres, both located about five miles northwest of Gardiner in prime grizzly bear country.

The arrangement of a combined public-private timber sale is a first for the Gallatin Forest.

Of the 223 acres involved in the 3.8 million board feet sale, 43.5 acres of public land will be cleared. The rest is owned by three private entities.

Two road sections will be built, one almost a mile and the other about a half-mile, at a combined cost of $25,000.

"Whether or not we're involved, they may choose to do it anyway," explained Forest Supervisor John Drake, referring to the private landowners who could not be denied access by the agency for their timber plans.

The private landowners want to harvest the thick, mature lodgepole pine before it gets killed by the spreading mountain pine beetle epidemic, explained Jim Wiebush, timber specialist on the Gardiner ranger district.

The area is comprised of several 20-acre sections of private land in patented mining claims laced between public land. After reviewing the access problems and the common desire to harvest the timber, Wiebush said the coordinated effort seemed to be the best approach to lessen the number of roads and insure a minimum impact on wildlife.

Although the proposed clearcut is only one mile from the park boundary, it lies over a ridge and will be out of view of both the park and the town of Gardiner.

Most of the area is in critical grizzly bear habitat, but the agency's wildlife experts have determined that harvesting the trees will provide more forage for the endangered bear.

The roads that would be built and improved for the project will also be used by elk hunters who use the Palmer Creek trailhead for access to the wilderness to reach the Hell-Roaring Drainage, Wiebush said. A parking lot will be built at the end of the road.

Wiebush said the area "is pretty well roaded up; so we're really not opening up additional access, just providing access that's suitable."

This story has one major flaw: it reads like a public relations announcement for the Gallatin Forest. Other sources who should have been consulted and other questions that should have been asked include:

• The Forest Service Regional Headquarters — "Is the taxpayer cost of road-building and sale administration defensible?"
• Private landowners — "Why don't you selective-cut instead of clearcut?"

• The superintendent of Yellowstone Park — "Does the clear-cut threaten Park area integrity?"

• The Montana Department of Fish, Wildlife, and Parks — "Does the clear-cut really benefit endangered grizzly bears? Can the Hell-Roaring elk herd stand the added hunting pressure?"

• The County Highway Department — "Will existing county roads in the area support added logging truck traffic?"

• The Bozeman Chapter of the Sierra Club — "What's your view of the project? Isn't it currently illegal to clear-cut adjacent to a wilderness boundary?"

• The Montana Environmental Council — "Did the Forest Service submit an environmental impact statement for public review?"

• The Bozeman, Montana, Chamber of Commerce — "What's the estimated value of the timber sale? How will the project contribute to the economy?"

• The U.S. Fish and Wildlife Service — "How does the clear-cut fit with the federal Grizzly Bear Recovery Plan?"

• The Montana State University College of Agriculture — "Is the stepped-up timber harvest a sign of the federal government's new emphasis on the commercialization of forest lands?"

For example, in doing a somewhat similar story on land use conflicts in northern Idaho, *Spokane* (Washington) *Spokesman-Review* reporter Jeff Sher (1983) interviewed two Idaho Fish and Game Commission biologists, a United States Forest Service supervisor, a local environmentalist, two federal Fish and Wildlife Service agents, two Forest Service district rangers, two mining company officials, a ski resort operator, a county commissioner, a local attorney, two ranchers, and a logger.

Community dynamics

Throughout the past decade, cities, towns, and rural counties across the country have struggled with the problems of growth and decline. The litany of land use problems is a familiar one. It includes the scattering of new housing and other development through the countryside; the attendant demands for roads, schools, police and fire protection, planning, and other public services; the loss of farmlands, timberlands, wildlife habitats, and other productive resource lands; blighted neighborhoods; and so on. Some communities, especially in the South and West, are unaccustomed after decades of little change to coping with intense pressures from population growth and new development. Other communities are the sites of essential but highly unpopular facilities, such as hazardous waste repositories. Still other places must learn how to encourage growth and new development where it is needed. Despite recent land use innovations, including growth controls, fiscal and environmental impact analyses, and resource-based planning, these problems persist.

Inevitably, the use of land stirs conflict and controversy. Governments face these challenges at a time when concern about public spending and regulation has prompted reexamination of existing land use laws and programs and reduced the funds available for administering them. How will these programs fare? What is needed to be done? How will decision makers weigh the difficult choices and trade-offs inherent in managing land resources to meet the demands and expectations of a changing society (Conservation Foundation 1983)?

The possibilities of community growth and progress have always mesmerized rural areas. Initially, the concept was growth at all costs. The more industry a community could attract, went the thinking, the better it was for the town. Every town in the Midwest had visions of being the next Chicago or Minneapolis. That idea has changed, however, and with it the attitudes of many smaller communities toward growth. Today communities seeking to grow usually are careful about what kinds of development they seek, and the growth they do allow is often carefully planned.

Growth can have a variety of effects on small rural communities. The acquisition of a high technology industry, such as an electronics assembly plant, can create new jobs for the area, allowing many young people, who otherwise would leave, a chance to remain; but too large an addition can produce an influx of large numbers of new residents necessitating increased housing and service facilities. The wrong kind of industrial addition can lead to problems of pollution and noise, affecting the quality of life within a town. Businesspeople are also leery of new ventures that will compete directly with established concerns in the community (Weber and Howell 1982).

The addition of a new business can have effects on many aspects of the community. In 1972, the Wurlitzer Piano and Organ Company, of DeKalb, Illinois, decided to build a factory in Logan, a rather remote college community in northern Utah. The factory meant an additional 450 jobs for the community, as well as increased tax and income revenue. Wurlitzer placed the factory in Logan because at the time the savings realized from the cheaper labor in Logan outweighed the extra transportation costs from the remote area. With the surge in energy prices in the mid 1970s and early 1980s, however, as well as the depressed economy, the company decided to close its factory. This sent a ripple effect through Logan and the surrounding area. A decision made in Illinois cost the Logan community 450 jobs and added more people to an already tight job market. Additionally, it removed over $5 million in payroll from the local economy, not to mention the taxes paid by the company and the sales taxes paid by the employees. Local businesses, additionally, felt the effects. Lumber companies with contracts to supply hardware materials lost as much as $5000 per month in business. Other suppliers suffered, too.

SOURCES. The sources available for reporting on community growth vary greatly from community to community. Some areas employ regional or local planning officials, people who have been hired to coordinate the overall growth and development of an area. Such persons generally appear in areas of anticipated long-term, extensive, controllable growth. Other sources of information on community development issues are frequently less reliable and more likely to be biased in some way. These sources must be used carefully. The most obvious source of information is the local chamber of commerce or businessperson's association. Since the chamber of commerce's primary duty is to promote the community, it is the most likely place in most communities to find information about potential development. Because it is, however, charged with promoting the community, the information gained is usually tilted toward the positive and may obscure the negative aspects of proposed development.

City officials are another prime source of information about community development. Many kinds of development require licensing or other permission from city councils or commissions, county commissions, or zoning boards of some sort, and prospective developers are required to provide these boards with certain information. Like a chamber of commerce, however, government officials are not necessarily impartial in their assessment of community progress. Personal concerns and involvements may color the information they provide.

The source of the growth is also a possible source of information. A new industry locating in the community or a new residential development can provide much information, but obviously, these sources are likely to be even more biased than the sources mentioned above. No company representative will tell a reporter that a new factory is going to pollute the local river and drain community services.

Perhaps the best method of dealing with the inevitable bias of information is to seek out opposing voices on the issue. Attempt to find people within the community who oppose the development or project. Frequently, they will have gathered and be willing to release the negative information that a chamber of commerce will not. The most important thing about reporting community development is that its effects generally go beyond the

HOW TO REPORT RURAL ISSUES

Charles McDowell, a journalist with a major urban paper, the Richmond Times-Dispatch, *and PBS's nationally broadcast "Washington Week in Review," provides the following strategy for covering rural issues:*

1. Find the issue and research it. Information is abundant at the land grant colleges, state governments, extension services, and so on.
2. Get the essence of the story straight by researching it and consulting experts.
3. Then take your information to real people—farmers, storekeepers, and so on, and talk to them about it.
4. Then what you write will be about real people—anecdotal, with a setting and a feel, but loaded with the research and the experts' information.
5. Remember, this system works for many kinds of stories.

CHARLES McDOWELL of the *Richmond Times-Dispatch* and PBS's "Washington Week in Review." August 25, 1983. Personal correspondence with authors.

obvious ones of economic cost and benefit, so investigating proposed growth means you must do more than look at jobs, payroll, and the number of newcomers expected.

If you are a reporter covering the potential impact of shale oil development on a rural community in the West, for example, you have to go beyond economic and demographic considerations to the more elusive, complex impacts on the social fabric—crime rates, community cohesion, sense of place, sense of personal worth, family structure, organizations, and so on. Sociologist Stan Albrecht points out that "while it is important to ask how many people will be brought into the community and what kinds of facilities and services will be required to meet their needs, you have to recognize that the impacts on the social systems of the community can be of far greater magnitude than the impacts on the sewer system" (Odell 1982). If you are initially confused by the alphabet of federal agencies associated with a rural area, the computer can help. The Federal Assistance Programs Retrieval System (FAPRS, pronounced "fappers") is a directory to which communities and individuals may refer in order to obtain information about programs under which they might obtain federal assistance.

Ask the computer a question or questions and you will receive a handy printout. You can file your search request at the local county extension office. For example, if you wanted to know what federal program or programs might help a community plan and build a better sewage treatment plant, abate soil erosion, provide public housing, or move to higher ground from a flood plain area, you could ask FAPRS.

Case studies: interpreting diverse rural affairs

Eagle County, Colorado, is a microcosm of today's rural America. At the western end of the county is the traditional ranching country that is associated with the West. Many of the people who live there are second, third, and fourth generation members of ranching families that settled the area in the late 1800s. The eastern half of the county is the new—new money, new people, and a new form of life. The Vail ski resort, founded in 1958, and its later neighbor, Beaver Creek, draw skiers from around the world. They boast a wealth of celebrity residents including former President Gerald Ford. In the middle of the county is the county seat, Eagle, in itself a microcosm. Its population includes longtime residents, newcomers from the city who moved to the mountains for a quiet, small-town life, and speculators who look at the Vail boom as only the beginning. The population includes local businesspeople who are satisfied with their small but profitable enterprises, as well as those who face only marginal success with their businesses and are looking for a stronger financial base. Added to this mix are a number of people who make a living working in Vail but seek cheaper housing in Eagle and its sister town, Gypsum.

Reporting in this environment requires a broad background and the flexibility to handle a variety of stories. In addition to the typical crime, accident, and local government stories, there are local and regional stories that require extensive research and the tying together of a myriad of items. In one recent summer, editor Steve Berta and reporter Rick Karlin were faced with two massive stories that reached from Eagle to Denver, St. Louis, and Washington, D.C.

The impact of growth

Berta's story was Adam's Rib, a ski resort to be built in the mountains fifteen miles south of town by a St. Louis corporation, HBE. Originally, the plan called for thirteen separate villages, connected by a monorail, with skiing facilities for seven thousand skiers a day. The cost was an estimated half a billion dollars. A Final Environmental Impact Statement (FEIS) was issued by the United States Forest Service in the summer of 1982. By then the project had been toned down to one village and no monorail, but the builders still planned on seven thousand skiers a day. The Forest Service gave permission for usage of only part of the public lands requested — enough for five thousand skiers per day, but that opened the door for the start of development.

It was just the beginning:

The new resort was expected to impact on the local water situation. Water would be required by the resort, and the original plan called for treated sewer water to be returned to Brush Creek, the source of Eagle's water, upstream from the Eagle water plant. The highway to the resort would have to be converted from a two-lane country road to a four-lane highway — at a cost of $25 million. Housing for the hundreds of construction workers needed for the project would put an additional strain on the already tight situation in Eagle. The HBE Corporation asked the county to enlarge its airport to accommodate large jets. Quick access to the resort was considered essential to its success. The county as a whole would foot the bill, and many ranchers saw little benefit in it for them.

Differences of opinion added to the complexity of covering the situation. In Eagle, some businesspeople did not want growth, and others did; some people wanted to maintain the small-town (1000 people) atmosphere and others wanted to profit from the growth. Many of the smaller landowners in the area had not been able to make a living through farming and saw a quick chance for wealth in the possibility of selling their land at highly inflated prices for housing and commercial development. The contention was so great that it led to an attempt on the part of the developers to recall three members of the city council who were antigrowth. For Berta, covering the debate meant dealing with local citizens, leaders, nonleaders, businesspeople, county government officials (the county commission had the final approval on the resort), and state and federal government agencies. He became an expert on Forest Service land use policy and state water and land use laws. He became an expert on state municipal government laws (he already had some experience in that from covering a recall election in his previous job in Rifle, Colorado), and he was forced to become an expert in ski resort regulations.

The need for water

In all, the *Eagle Valley Enterprise* used hundreds of inches to cover the long-running dispute. Over the six-plus years that passed between the proposal and the FEIS the paper ran two special sections and many other articles. It was up to Berta to understand and report what was happening. While Berta was caught up in the ski controversy he could get little help from reporter Karlin, who was tied up with another local controversy that stretched beyond the county line—water. The arid nature of much of the West makes water a precious commodity. Development is impossible without it.

Karlin's story was Homestake II, a plan to build a reservoir in Eagle County to serve the Front Range communities of Aurora and Colorado Springs. The Eastern Slope communities from Ft. Collins to Colorado Springs were faced with large populations and limited water supplies. The Western Slope has few people but abundant water. The controversy was over whether the western communities should "give their water" to Denver and its suburbs and, if not, what legal rights these communities had to the water. Also being argued was where the reservoir would be built and how the water would get to the Eastern Slope. One proposal, the cheapest for the cities interested in acquiring the water, called for building a pipeline through the Holy Cross Wilderness Area. This brought nonlocal environmentalists and naturalists into the dispute.

As with the Adam's Rib situation, Karlin was faced with manifold agencies, meetings, interest groups, and considerations. The municipal governments of the Eastern Slope communities, the county governments on both sides of the mountains, regional government agencies including a number of Western Slope counties, special-use boards set up to deal with the situation, and state and federal officials all were involved. Property rights, water rights, the rights of cities within a state, and more were open to discussion in the controversy. Karlin spent countless hours in meetings and at workshops listening to the problems being discussed, and he contacted dozens of sources in an attempt to determine the impact of the various proposals. His political science background stood him in good stead in understanding the myriad bureaucracies he faced, but he felt he could have used a law degree to make better sense of the controversy (Schoenfeld 1988).

Hints for covering rural affairs

1. Don't underestimate the residents of rural communities; they have the same interests and concerns and are just as well educated as the people in urban areas.

2. In general, rural residents will have more knowledge of and interest in local matters than urban residents. Commu-

nity residents will tend to be closer interpersonally, so covering controversy and conflict will be more difficult. Coverage will require an objective, balanced approach.

3. Most rural communities will be a mixture of longtime traditional residents and newcomers, and they will view the community from different perspectives.

4. Don't assume that the division between traditional residents of the community and the newcomers will be clear. There will be longtime residents of the community who favor development as well as those who oppose it, and the same holds true for newcomers.

5. Various levels of governmental agencies will be involved in rural areas, with county officials being more important than municipal officials in many cases.

6. Agriculture has become a multibillion dollar business. The days of the family farm and local marketing of produce have markedly declined.

7. Local farmers are a viable source of agricultural information in terms of production, marketing, and innovations.

8. University extension service personnel are also good sources of local information, as well as accesses to land grant university campus experts.

In summary

Recent years have seen an increasing interest in the nonurban aspects of the United States. How we use our land has become an issue of as much interest to city dwellers as it is to those in the country. Agriculture, one of our biggest industries, has undergone tremendous changes in recent decades as events ranging from the collapse of farm land prices to a record drought have brought the not-so-pastoral reality of farm life home to the urban resident.

In addition, controversies over the use of natural resources have sparked furious debate. The question over the designation of vast tracts of range and timber land is wilderness areas has caused controversy in many western states. The West has also become embroiled in battles over the distribution of water. Booming metropolitan areas such as Denver, Phoenix, and Los Angeles are seeking to divert water from sparsely populated areas that have their own needs for this essential resource.

In the East, acid rain, strip mining, and the migration of people from the cities to the ever-expanding suburbs are but a few major rural concerns.

In fact, rapid growth of suburban and new urban areas has changed the character of rural areas in all parts of the country.

All of these developments and others have led to a new importance for rural affairs in the lives of Americans. The controversies are crossing city/country lines and are also crossing state and regional boundaries.

Most significant rural affairs issues are long-term matters. Covering these issues requires reporters to have a breadth of knowledge about history, agricultural economics, local government and other subjects. The journalist covering rural affairs frequently finds the process tedious and complicated but, nonetheless, vital.

References

Batie, Sandra S., and Healy, Robert G. 1980. *The Future of American Agriculture as a Strategic Resource.* Washington: Conservation Foundation.

Bishop, Katherine. 1988. Rural Counties Are Still Gasping From California's Tax Revolt. *New York Times,* Aug. 18, A10.

Bjorkland, Robert. 1981. (Madison) *Wisconsin State Journal,* Oct. 3–10.

———. 1985. (Madison) *Wisconsin State Journal,* Apr. 3–5.

Bowes, John E., Stamm, Keith R., Jackson, Kenneth M., and Moore, Jeff. 1978. *Communication of Technical Information to Lay Audiences.* Seattle: Communication Research Center, School of Communication, University of Washington.

Bradshaw, Ted K., and Blakeley, Edward J. 1979. *Rural Communities in Advanced Industrial Society.* New York: Praeger.

Caldwell, Bert. 1986. Help for Farmers, Hurt for Lenders? *Spokesman-Review* (Spokane, WA), Dec. 31, A12.

Clawson, Marion. 1973. *Land for Americans.* Chicago: Rand McNally, 133.

Council on Environmental Quality. 1983. Annual Report. Washington, D.C.: Government Printing Office, 163–64.

Fett, John. 1983. Market and Outlook Information Disseminated by U.S. Daily Newspapers, Farm Magazines, Radio and Television. Paper presented at national meeting on agricultural information, July 17–21. Madison, Wisconsin.

Frazier, George. 1984. *Shelbyville* (Illinois) *Daily Union,* May 13–18.

Glaberson, William. 1988. Safety Remains Elusive at Morrell. *New York Times,* Aug. 21, 3:1.

Jonas, Paul. 1984. *Miles City* (Montana) *Star,* July 9–11.

Jones, Loris. 1986. Palouse Farmers Must Face 1987 With More of The Same Kind of Toughness. *Moscow Daily News-Idahonian,* Dec. 31, 9.

Knudson, Tom. 1984. Harvest of Harm. *Des Moines Register,* Sept. 16–23.

Nell, William. 1983. Cooperative Clearcut Is First of Its Kind In Gallatin Forest. *Billings* (Montana) *Gazette,* Aug. 3.

New York Times. 1988. Drought Hurts Tourism As Well As Ranchers and Farmers. Aug. 18, A10.

Odell, Rice. 1982. In Can Science Deal with Environmental Uncertainties? *Conservation Foundation Newsletter* (January):8.

Oslund, John. 1980. Energy on the Farm. *Minneapolis Star,* Dec. 22–24.

Schoenfeld, Clay. 1988. Steve Berta and Rick Karlin personal memoir in author's files, March 3.

Sher, Jeff. 1983. Where the Grizzly Roams Free. *Spokane* (Washington) *Spokesman-Review,* June 20.

U.S. Census Bureau. 1986. Farm Population of the United States. Current Population Reports, Series P-27, No. 10. Washington, D.C.: U.S. Government Printing Office.

Weber, Bruce A., and Howell, Robert E. (Eds.) 1982. *Coping with Rapid Growth in Rural Communities.* Boulder, CO: Westview Press.

World Press Review. 1983. The Coming Water Crisis. 30(2):28–29.

This chapter was initiated by Cassady. Collaborator was Schoenfeld.

CHAPTER 15

The electoral process

S TAFF MEMBERS of the *Longview* (Washington) *Daily News* (circulation 27,000) had won the Pulitzer Prize for local news coverage in 1981 for their reporting of the eruption of Mount St. Helens. One factor that undoubtedly contributed to the winning of the award was the 100 percent commitment of the *News* reporting staff to the telling of the St. Helens story. City editor David Connelly found, to his surprise, that all eleven reporters could be working on the volcano story, and still get out the regular day-to-day news. A second factor in the *News*'s success was the emphasis on telling about Mount St. Helens events in terms of personalities and impact on people.

Consequently, when the next general election approached, Connelly asked himself why the *News* could not take the same all-out, personalized approach to politics. The result was a meticulous plan to provide more coverage, and more interesting coverage, to the political campaign. Emphasis was placed on letting readers know that the candidates not only had political opinions but had distinguishing personalities and characteristics. Connelly said he planned the coverage with the conviction that voters make up their minds about candidates on the basis of how they feel about the candidates' personalities as much as whether they agree with their politics.

As a result, when reporter Laurie Smith (1982) wrote about Jack Shero, who was challenging an incumbent county commissioner, she noted that when Shero had a job with the state in Olympia, he preferred to keep his home in Castle Rock — "a grey house with window boxes full of geraniums — and commute 100 miles a day." The story, noting that Shero had been outspoken in his criticism of the incumbent commissioner, reported that "more than once during the campaign he has made strong statements and later phoned the newspaper, hoping to soften his words before they appeared in print."

In a roundup campaign story the day before the election, reporter Jack Darnton (1982) recounted that "Jack Shero has tilted at every windmill in sight — the *Daily News,* turncoat Democrats he calls 'lower than a whale's belly' and even Republican Van Youngquist's good-looking daughters as he struggles to defeat the well-entrenched Cowlitz County commissioner."

The *News*'s campaign coverage suggests several points about reporting politics:

• Elections can, and should, be reported in terms of both personalities and issues, with personalized material perhaps serving to put readers in a frame of mind in which they become receptive to discussion of issues.

• The reporting of elections need not be limited to a reporter specifically identified as the political writer. Other staff members may be able to make candidates and politics seem real to readers in a manner that is different from traditional political reporting.

• Newspapers may be the major source of information that many voters have about local and regional campaigns. During the weeks before an election, providing coverage of candidates and issues may be one of the most important functions served by all news media.

• Even small- to medium-sized media can muster substantial resources for covering an election campaign if staff members consider that coverage important and exploit the perspectives of geography and history.

Elections today

Every two years Americans vote twice, in a primary and then in a general election, on state and national candidates. In states that have the initiative and referendum, voters are likely to be asked to cast their ballot on issues ranging from school construction bonds to legalization of marijuana. In between those biennial elections, many communities hold elections for local candidates. Although Americans may participate in more elections than almost anyone else in the world, they also turn out in fewer numbers. While about 80 percent of eligible voters turn out in most developed democracies, the turnout in a presidential election in the United States rarely reaches 60 percent. In most other elections it hovers near 40 percent (Alters 1988).

This low turnout, combined with a parallel decline in voters' attachment to political parties, has caused concern among political writers, government officials, and political scientists. "Participation makes people feel they have a voice," says political scientist G. Bingham Powell. "Countries with lower voter turnout tend to have more citizen turmoil, more voter discontent" (Alters 1988). Burt Neuborne (1988), former legal director for the American Civil Liberties Union, says of voting: "It's the hope of changing things without violence."

With the help of census data, you can discover who votes and who

INTERPRETING POLITICAL TRENDS

*Deciphering trends is an essential part of interpretive report-
ing. At the start of the decade of the 1990s, Michael Barone
of* U.S. News and World Report *discussed how voters would
interact with the political system in "The Age of Indifference." His lead began:*

In a world where millions are enthusiastically turning to democratic
politics, Americans are increasingly turning away from it. The trend
could intensify during the next decade, with most American politicians slugging it out before mostly indifferent audiences. Yet this
indifference should not be taken as a sign that the political system
has failed. To the contrary, Americans are mostly satisfied with the
direction of the economy and foreign policy and with their leaders.
Polls in the last five years have shown little anxiety over the central
issues of foreign policy and the economy. . . .

*Barone later predicted that, in politics, "apathy will reign,
with continued low voter turnout. It will be sound-bite politics in which candidates concentrate, as Bush did with steely
discipline in 1988, on the few pivotal occasions when large
numbers of voters were watching, such as during conventions
and debates."*

Other trends that Barone observed include:

- Government activism is not being rejected by voters, but it will
  continue to move into the domain of local and state governments.
- Neither major political party will have a lock on the electorate.
- Americans are looking for pride in their country and ways to
  pull their diverse nation together.
- Rather than flashy, charismatic leaders, Americans will prefer
  politicians who are competent managers.
- "Student activists" will be out of favor with the public,
  "smoother activists" in.
- "Hard-line cold-warriors" will be out, "managers of military
  cuts" will be in.

*Barone cautioned that these trends could easily change if
major events (for example, war or economic collapse) intervene, and that existing tensions in the country can also alter
what he foresees. Most Americans, he said, "continue to be
troubled by the homeless on their streets and the festering
problems of the urban underclass. These lingering problems
may well dominate the nation's agenda in the next decade."*

MICHAEL BARONE. The Age of Indifference. *U.S. News and World Report,* Dec. 25,
1989/Jan. 1, 1990, 30–33.

does not in any community. Nationally, voter turnout is particularly low among the young, the poor and the uneducated. This nonvoting pattern has had a profound effect on our entire political system, according to one recent study. The authors, Francis Fox Piven and Richard A. Cloward, argue that devices such as voter registration represent a deliberate attempt to disenfranchise the poor (Piven and Cloward 1988). "If nonvoting were spread equally across the board, we wouldn't be so worried," said Cloward (Muro 1988).

The media regularly campaign to increase voter turnout. Registration requirements, voting hours, and polling places are listed. Editorials call on voters to participate in the democratic process. The *Boston Globe* decided to go beyond this in 1988. In its Sunday Focus section, the *Globe* asked, "If Half of Us Don't Vote, Are We a Democracy?" (Muro 1988). It then went on in four pages of text, maps, and charts to explain to its readers how restrictive voter registration has created a national embarrassment (Ribadeneira 1988).

Another reason for low voter turnout seems to be ineffective political parties (Muro 1988). Increasingly, political battles are being waged through the media instead of through political parties. In many ways the media have taken over the function of political parties by informing voters, encouraging voting, and helping to select candidates.

Yet the picture is not as dismal as it may seem. Americans, at least many of them, never have been strong party members. The drafters of the Constitution and the authors of the *Federalist Papers* had wanted to avoid the development of partisan factions altogether. The parties that did develop were never as tightly organized nor as ideologically strict as parties in many other nations. During most of our history, at both state and national levels, two major, politically amorphous parties have dominated elections. Why the electorate has not splintered into more, and more tightly controlled, parties is not entirely clear, but one reason may be the election of state and national legislators from single-member districts. In a single-member district a party must appeal to a broad enough range of voters to obtain a majority of the votes in the district. Consequently, candidates and parties tend to define issues in broad terms, to obscure rather than to define issues clearly.

Yet voters do make an impact, and elections can make a difference. One political scientist (Pomper 1980) who examined state elections, party platforms, and relationships between minority voting and minority rights in the South concluded that elections "do largely meet the standards of meaningful popular decisions; true voter influence exists." He found that the two parties do compete freely at the national level and in most states. No party or administration can control the means of communication, and voters usually are offered fairly simple choices in electing officials. He concluded that in the vast majority of cases, elections are conducted honestly.

The electoral process should not be judged completely by the splashy, expensive, and often negative campaigns waged for president, governor, and U.S. senator. In fact, other, less flamboyant elections may have greater effects on people's lives. Men and women who are elected to the state legislature determine how much money will be spent to educate the children of a state. Those elected to a city council decide whether a service station will be constructed next to a single-family residential area. Elections at these levels usually are conducted without a lot of money or a lot of hoopla.

The nation's politics also should not be judged solely by elections. Politics is a year-round process. Only when the election is over do legislators vote on school budgets and city councils on zoning. With elections coming at least every two years, candidates and would-be candidates never stop trying to win votes.

THE MEDIA AND MAIN STREET

Decision-making structures in small towns and suburbs are not yet as complicated as they are in big cities and in Washington; and that leaves more room for the amateur. Washington politics, on the other hand, is largely a spectator sport. We follow the fortunes of national political gladiators much as we do the ups and downs of the Phillies and the Kansas City Royals. Local politics is more like sand-lot baseball, because it offers anyone the chance to come out and give it a try, and it guarantees everyone a turn at bat. People who never in their lives said anything in public may show up one night at a town board meeting and discover in themselves reserves of eloquence and practical wisdom that they never knew they possessed. There is something good, and human, and quintessentially American about that. The townships of America are the one area where the popular participation of "plain people" still has a chance to take root. But whether it grows or withers may depend on how much attention and dignity it is accorded by those who bring us the news.

GEORGE McKENNA. 1982. Toward Better Coverage of Local Politics. *Mass Communication Review.* Vol. 9, Nos. 2,3. Spring and Fall. 34.

One final point might be made about the supposed decline in political participation. In one sense, participation simply has taken a different form. Political scientist James Q. Wilson has contended that never have so many Americans participated in politics. Instead of working through parties, or merely voting, they are working through other organizations, notably special interest groups, and they are working through them year-round, not just at election time (Wilson 1983). This means that the job of the political writer also has changed. Instead of being a seasonal assignment, the coverage of politics never stops.

The role of political parties

Political parties generally are thought to perform at least three roles: (1) recruitment of leadership positions; (2) representation and integration of group interests; and (3) control and direction of government.

The power of parties in the selection of leaders has been hampered by the creation of nonpartisan political offices, especially at local levels; by presidential primaries and caucuses; by limitations on campaign spending and contributions; and by the increased role of the mass media. When candidates were selected by party leaders, the leaders had an opportunity to pick persons who represented the party's philosophy. Now a virtual unknown, such as Jimmy Carter, can win a vote in an Iowa caucus and sweep on to win the Democratic nomination for president. Legislation that limits campaign contributions has restricted funds flowing through the parties, while other legislation has encouraged the passing of contributions through political action committees (PACs) directly to candidates. In deciding which candidates they will cover and which aspects of the campaign they will emphasize, the media, especially in primaries, may do more than the parties to determine who the major candidates will be.

Activity of single-issue, special interest groups has increased. In many instances, these groups do not work through political parties. Groups as powerful as the National Rifle Association, the American Medical Association, organized labor, antiabortion forces, or retired citizens have little need to work through the parties. With a more volatile electorate and the growth of interest groups, the parties have lost much of their ability to bring voters together and keep them together.

Some political forecasters have predicted that the country may be in for a long period in which no party holds the presidency and controls both houses of Congress for an extended period of time. Similar splits have occurred commonly within states, and are likely to occur in many communities as well. Here, too, we need to look beneath the surface of politics. For many sessions of Congress, Democrats were nominally in control, but power lay largely with a coalition of Republicans and conservative, mostly southern, Democrats. Similar coalitions exist in some states. In many counties and communities, the party affiliations of officeholders mean little. As a political reporter, you must look beneath party labels to see who really is directly controlling government. Urban-rural or growth–no-growth divisions may be more important than party divisions.

The role of elections

The principal roles of elections are to allow voters to select representatives who will make policy decisions on their behalf and to hold those who have made decisions responsible for their actions. Elections allow voters to throw out "the bad guys" and put in "the good guys." The alternatives are not always clear-cut. Voters are often faced with so many election decisions that many of them do not know for whom or for what they are voting. Some of their decisions may seem inconsistent. Voters in 1982 elected a strong majority of Democrats to the House of Representatives but left the Republicans in control of the Senate. California voters elected a Republican governor but boosted Democratic majorities in both legislative houses. How does a political reporter make sense of this?

How does a political reporter make sense of the many other races on the ballot? A poll of California voters taken before the 1982 election found that only 30 percent of them could name the person who represented them in Congress. If they are not even acquainted with the name of this person, what is likely to be the extent of their knowledge as they proceed down the ballot, at the state level, from governor to lieutenant governor, secretary of state, treasurer, controller, attorney general, and state superintendent? In some states, voters would also elect a land commissioner, a utility commissioner, a tax commissioner, and judges. At the county level, the absence of party labels may make decisions even more difficult for voters. Yet anyone who has watched the political scene for very long knows that elections can make a difference. It becomes the responsibility of the political reporter to help provide the information and the insight that is necessary if voters are to have a chance of understanding what they are being asked to decide.

The role of voters

How a reporter covers an election and political affairs in general may depend on how he or she views the voters. Political scientists, such as Pomper and Lederer (1980), talk about three types of voters. One is the "philosophical citizen," who decides primarily on a rational analysis of policy questions. But most voters probably decide more on the basis of issues that are of immediate interest to them—job situations, prices, concern over crime. The reporter who confines election coverage solely to broad policy issues will not be giving most voters what they need to make decisions.

Another type of voter is the "manipulated subject," whose vote is largely determined by group membership, party affiliation, religion, ethnic group, or geographic location. This concept, which suggests that what goes on in a campaign makes little difference to the voter, probably was more valid in the past than it is today.

Voters now are more likely to be what are called "protective meddlers." These voters may not exhibit much interest in politics most of the time. But, when issues of major concern arise or political leaders seem to be ignoring the wishes of the electorate, the voters will intervene—meddle—to make their impact felt. As interests and influences change during and between elections, the allegiances of these voters are also likely to change. In such circumstances, opportunities for meaningful political reporting would seem much greater with voters who are issue-oriented and who can be activated by a lively campaign than with those whose political opinions are largely determined by their socioeconomic and family backgrounds.

The role of the media

How reporters cover an election also will depend on how they see the role of the mass media in general, and their own medium in particular. In the days of the Federalists and the anti-Federalists, and to a lesser extent even until the Civil War, reporters tended to cover politics from a partisan point of view. A newspaper was allied with one political party or the other, or at least it supported one party. Subscribers expected to see their newspaper cover the news from their point of view. Even after party ties began to be broken, in most communities multiple papers still continued to exist and to represent different political points of view.

During much of this time it was assumed that papers had a substantial influence on voters. Then, especially in the 1930s, during the era of Franklin D. Roosevelt, when the country went Democratic but the publishers remained Republican, doubts began to arise. Communications theorists began to discount the previously held bullet, or hypodermic needle, theory concerning the effect of the media. Voters were not reacting as though the press was shooting opinions and interpretations directly into their political thought processes.

Out of the 1940s and 1950s came another attempt to explain the influence of the media: the two-step flow theory. According to this idea, the media pass information and opinion to an elite group of leaders, who in turn pass the word on to friends, neighbors, and associates. Other studies seemed to show that voter behavior could be accounted for largely by family and socioeconomic background and by psychological defense mechanisms. This "limited effects" theory left little room for influence by the media, outside of reinforcing beliefs people already held.

More recently, it appears that the media can be powerful when it comes to matters such as conveying political information, and less powerful in influencing opinions and behavior. The media, says Jeffres (1986), "are not blunt instruments used to influence the electorate at will, but rather complex vehicles that have some direct and some indirect impact. . . . The emerging perspective of political effects that seems most consistent with current knowledge is a contingency model which recognizes the direct impact of media as well as the individual differences and influence felt through other sources."

One trend in research is to examine the ways in which people learn about political and other news from the mass media. "Mass media messages are not imprinted on the minds of audiences in the precise manner in which they are offered," states Doris Graber (1988). "Rather, audiences condense the offerings in their own ways, select aspects of interest, and integrate them into their own thinking." People organize information by creating general mental frameworks called "schemata," Graber says, and these schemata guide the ways in which people pay attention to and absorb new information from the news media. Often, this means ignoring the flood of details about news events and seeking instead a more general understanding. "Political information processing could be facilitated if newspeople learned to cast information into formats that closely matched those used by audiences for storing information," Graber states. It is difficult, she says, for journalists to know what kinds of information people need to fill-out their schemata, and how to present that information so it helps people learn. "To meet the audience's needs more fully," Graber recommends, "newspeople will have to engage increasingly in scientific audience analysis, as advertisers, political campaign consultants, and other marketing professionals are already doing."

Another trend has been to see the media as agenda-setters for the public. The agenda-setting model proposes that the more the media stress certain issues, the more the public comes to see those issues as important, as issues worth thinking about (McCombs and Shaw 1972). Issues that become salient can influence the way in which voters evaluate the performance of people in public office. In describing this media "priming" effect, Iyengar and Kinder (1987) state that:

Priming presumes that when evaluating complex political phenomena, people do not take into account all that they know—they cannot, even if they are motivated. Instead, they consider what comes to mind, those bits and pieces of political memory that are accessible. Television news, we suppose, might be a powerful determinant of what springs to mind and what is forgotten or ignored. Through priming (drawing attention to some aspects of political life at the expense of others) television news might help to set the terms by which political judgments are reached and political choices made.

Our results support this claim handsomely. When primed by television news stories that focus on national defense, people judge the president largely by how well he has provided, as they see it, for the nation's defense; when primed by stories about inflation, people evaluate the president by how he has managed, in their view, to keep prices down; and so on.

CONTRIBUTING TO THE ELECTORAL PROCESS IN RAY COUNTY, MISSOURI

Since the electorate of Ray County, Missouri, is overwhelmingly Democratic and has elected a Republican to local office only once in the twentieth century, primary balloting in August every even-numbered year is of fundamental importance in filling public offices. This situation makes elections revolve around the personalities of candidates rather than around their party labels (as long as they are Democrats), and since several candidates generally run for the nomination, the task of the voter in making an informed decision is much more difficult than in a two-party, two-candidate contest.

Accordingly, the *Richmond Daily News* produces comprehensive special election editions before the Democratic primaries. All candidates are asked to respond to identical questionnaires for each office. Their answers, their pictures, sample ballots, and political advertising go in a special supplement distributed as part of the *Daily News* shortly before the primary election. These special editions are among the largest single editions the paper publishes.

The election editions are distributed to every house in the county, subscriber or not, and have resulted in larger voter turnouts and an informed electorate. Many primary candidates, even losers, have commended *Daily News* publisher Howard Hill for his initiative. The primary election editions have won an Inland Daily Press Association Award for Distinguished Local Government News.

This research certainly has implications for journalists, since the way news media stress certain issues is based on a myriad of journalistic decisions regarding whether stories are covered and, if so, how much attention they will be given. Some news coverage reflects the need to "routinize" the gathering and processing of news (Tuchman 1978) and, perhaps, the deep ideological beliefs of journalists, such as the value of democracy, moderate capitalism, individualism, and the values of small American communities (Gans 1979). Journalists need to examine more carefully the ways in which these gatekeeping forces affect their coverage of news and the ways in which news is presented to audiences.

During the election campaign

Many election stories are determined by the campaign itself, by the actions of the candidates, and by events that are planned or unplanned. Candidates schedule speeches, barnstorming tours, debates, and press conferences. They issue handouts and leak rumors. Various groups may sponsor candidate forums, where candidates make two-minute presentations. These may serve to help call attention to an election, but unless all candidates focus on one or two issues, these sessions usually are not very informative. Much of what takes place routinely during campaigns provides only the most simplistic information about what really is going on in the political arena. To provide readers and listeners with what they need for intelligent decision making, reporters need to exert initiative and to dig out stories on their own.

Comparison of issues

One service a reporter can perform for readers and listeners is to seek out candidates' stands on key issues and present them in a conveniently understood form. This obviously is more easily done in print than in broadcast. Some communications research suggests, not surprisingly, that readers understand more quickly and remember longer when the stands of candidates are presented issue by issue, so that they can be compared, than when all of the stands of each candidate are listed together (Bybee 1980). In spite of the "bombast of 30-second television commercials and the barrage of accusations about each other," *Sacramento Bee* reporter Jeff Rabin (1982) discovered, by digging, that the candidates for California governor actually were talking about issues. He then proceeded to itemize for readers the candidates' stands on the economy and jobs, taxes, housing, agriculture and water, crime, handgun control, education, welfare, energy, and abortion. He explained the position of both candidates on one issue before he moved on to the next issue.

Finding the issues is not easy. Political advisors admit they prefer their candidates to stick with themes and slogans that sound good but mean very little (Katz 1988). Reporters have to get behind the ideology if they are going to report on public issues.

Explanation of issues

Complex issues, especially ballot propositions, require more attention than a quick summary of candidate positions. Again, writers and editors have the choice of whether to write a separate article on each side of the issue or to combine the arguments into a single story. If supporters of each side are asked to write an article expressing their positions, a brief article summarizing the positions might accompany the opposing pieces. Readers will probably get a better idea of the arguments if they are all presented in a single article written by a neutral party, the political reporter. One of the more elaborate efforts to explain ballot propositions was made by the *Los Angeles Times* (1982). In a table that took up half a page, the *Times* summarized each of the fifteen propositions on the 1982 California ballot, then explained what would happen if each passed, and listed the major proponents and opponents.

Campaign finances

Information about campaign financing is an important area that needs coverage during and after the campaign. Many states require periodic, detailed reporting of contributions and expenditures. Sometimes these reports can provide the basis for stories that show whether a candidate is trying to buy the election by outspending his or her opponents. The reports also show which interest groups and individuals are supporting the candidates.

Large amounts of money are involved, particularly in races for federal offices. The National Conservative Political Action Committee had the highest outlay during 1983–1984. Its spending topped $19 million. It costs an estimated $25 million to win the presidential nomination of either party with television eating up the lion's share (Martin 1988). Some of the money, by the way, about $9.2 million in 1988, comes from individual taxpayers who checked the box on their tax returns authorizing one dollar for funding presidential campaigns (Tackett 1988).

The high cost of television advertising is having an impact on the nation's political profile. Wisconsin Congressman James Moody was considered a strong candidate to succeed Senator William Proxmire, who retired from the United States Senate in 1988. But Moody dropped out of the Democratic primary after Herb Kohl, a business magnate, spent $500,000, most of it on television advertising, in a single month of primary campaigning (Rix 1988). Kohl later won the senatorial election.

Charges and countercharges

As an election approaches, charges and countercharges, innuendoes, and downright nastiness almost invariably increase. When voters resist their calmer appeals, candidates seem to forget early vows to keep the campaign clean and impersonal. Even if the candidates keep their cool, their professional and amateur supporters may be under less compulsion to do so. Consequently, preelection stories may be filled with slanderous accusations.

Such accusations, which often surface first as rumors, increasingly involve alleged character flaws in a candidate. Rumors of alcohol abuse or sexual indiscretions, formerly ignored by the media, are now considered legitimate public issues. Reporters and editors find them difficult to deal with. As *Atlanta Journal and Constitution* editor William Kovach told a seminar on "Evaluating Candidates," just investigating the rumor is likely to create a story (Goodwin 1987).

It is possible for a reporter to do something constructive about charges and countercharges. You can identify specific charges that have been made, then explain what the facts seem to be. You will be doing the electorate a service by bringing some perspective to the campaign hyperbole.

There are risks, however, in reporting campaign charges. One case, which arose out of the 1982 Minnesota gubernatorial campaign, provides a dramatic example of the risks for the journalist. Reporters from two newspapers, the *Minneapolis Star Tribune* and the *St. Paul Pioneer Press Dispatch,* accepted information from a staff worker for one candidate. They agreed to keep secret the source of the information, which involved a twelve-year-old shoplifting charge. The two papers not only printed the story but also named the source, with the *Star Tribune* denouncing him for attempting dirty campaign tricks. The source sued and won a $700,000 court judgment on the grounds that the reporters and their papers had broken their promise to keep his name a secret (Scardino 1988).

There are plenty of potential stories involving questionable activities by candidates and office holders. The public deserves to have them investigated. However, an opposition candidate is always a risky source and waiting until the last weeks of a campaign to look into them adds to the danger. Edward A. Achorn, writing for the *Middlesex News,* dug up his own information early in the 1988 election year. He looked into fund raising (Achorn

1988a), speaking fees (Achorn 1988b), and nepotism (Achorn 1988c) among area congressmen up for reelection. His series revealed there was plenty to write about in all three areas. His use of public records and interviews rather than secret sources contributed to a thorough, well-balanced series that fully informed the voters well before election day.

Predictions of turnout

On the eve of an election, a standard news story quotes a county elections official or state secretary of state predicting the turnout of voters. Aside from simply calling attention to a coming election, these stories usually serve little purpose, except to get the forecaster's name in the paper or on the air. Sometimes that official's name is on the ballot.

Public opinion polls

Public opinion polls are a popular source of political news during a campaign. Undoubtedly, interest in the latest standings grows out of the horse-racelike aspects of the campaign, but polls can have more than just an informational effect. If a candidate seems to be moving ahead of or catching up with an opponent, the perception of momentum may motivate some voters to jump on the bandwagon. A candidate's standing in the polls, especially early in the campaign, can provide the basis on which potential contributors make decisions to offer support.

National polls, such as Gallup and Harris, can be subscribed to by media. In some states, polls such as Mervin Field's California Poll are available. A number of large newspapers, including the *New York Times,* the *Los Angeles Times,* the *Des Moines Register,* and the *Minneapolis Tribune,* have their own polling organizations. Until recently, most polling, whether by a newspaper staff, broadcast station, or professional organization, was limited to major media. But a survey in 1978 found growing use of polls in medium- and small- as well as large-sized papers and stations. Overall, 37 percent of the papers that responded had conducted polls on which to base news stories. The researchers concluded that "small circulation need not be a bar to polling," but they also expressed some concern about the quality of some polls, especially those conducted by newsroom staff members (Rippey 1980).

Several publications readily available to newspeople can provide help in planning, carrying out, and analyzing polls. One very useful book is *Precision Journalism* by Philip Meyer (1983). The secret to carrying out a credible poll lies in selecting the persons to be interviewed. They must be selected on a strictly random basis if the poll's results are to be valid.

Meyer's book has a convenient chart that shows how many people, selected randomly, need to be polled in communities of varying sizes to assure a margin of error of 5 percent or less, in either direction, in 19 out of 20 times. The number ranges from 278 for a community of 1000 up to 384 for a community, or a nation, of any size. Of course, if you start breaking your sample into subgroups, then the listed size is required for each subgroup to obtain the same degree of accuracy.

Just as important as the preparation of the polls is the reporting of them. Readers need to be told exactly what the poll does and does not say. Professional pollsters generally agree that, to be credible, a published report needs to explain who sponsored or financed the poll, how many people were interviewed, how they were selected, and within what range of accuracy the poll is judged to be. (See the section on surveys in Chapter 2.)

After the election

Some of the easiest, and some of the hardest, stories for a political writer are those that follow an election. The easy ones include those that simply quote the winners and losers and the instant analyzers. The losers offer excuses and accusations; the winners take pride and offer promises; the analysts usually disagree with each other. The hard, creative part for the political writer involves looking behind these predictable and usually meaningless responses to find out what really went on in an election. The votes are in and counted, but what do they mean?

Exit interviews

Increased polling also has come in the form of exit interviews in which voters are asked how they voted and why. In terms of predicting the outcome of an election, these are of value principally to broadcasters, who rush to the airwaves as soon as, or before, the polls are closed. But exit interviews can provide more information about who voted for whom and why than can the actual (and anonymous) ballots. Exit interviews can also, however, provide misleading results. Samples gathered at a limited number of polling places tend not to be truly random; furthermore, certain types of voters may be more reluctant than others to respond truthfully to face-to-face questions.

Explanation of the outcome

Political writers probably have the most fun explaining to readers what the election means: who were the real winners and why did they win? Writers with good memories, or carefully kept files, can put an election into context with previous elections and other political events.

Voting patterns by precinct, county, or state can show where candidates and issues ran strong or weak, especially if the reporter has information from previous elections for comparison. It is relatively easy, for example, to look at precinct returns and report that a particular candidate did well in urban areas but poorly in less populated areas. It requires more work to determine whether a candidate or a political party may have done better or worse than in a previous election. Election returns and precinct maps usually can be obtained from county and state elections offices, but the work of processing and comparing thousands of figures must be done by the political reporter.

Nonpartisan local races also can yield worthwhile data when analyzed. A study of the impact of a local citizens' group on the municipal affairs of Redlands, California, provides an example. In 1978, a group of citizens, calling themselves the Friends of Redlands, organized because of concern about unrestricted growth in the community. They put a limited-growth initiative on the ballot that year, and it was approved by 70 percent of those voting. Local observers had speculated that this group presented a new political force in city affairs. An analysis of the precincts in which the initiative had received the greatest percentages of votes revealed a pattern that was substantially different from voting patterns of the immediately preceding city council election, as well as from the voting on state and national issues and races that had appeared on the same ballot with the initiative. A year and a half later, at the next council election, the precincts that had been strongly for the initiative were lined up almost uniformly in support of two council candidates who had associated themselves with the Friends of Redlands. Two years after that, however, those precincts were split primarily among three candidates. The one who had the closest ties to the Friends did not make the council. Additional analysis would be required to determine whether the Friends had spent its political force or whether, with two of its members on the council and one of them mayor, the group had merely been resting on its laurels, waiting for a bigger fight in the future (Rystrom 1982).

Campaign spending

Postelection stories can be based on campaign spending. You can even establish cost-per-unit figures (for example, the amount spent per voter) as

CHEROKEE, IOWA DAILY TIMES

Political contests oftentimes become a blur in a voter's mind because there is no personal contact with candidates and no point of reference in day-to-day living. In an effort to bring about that contact and to have candidates answer concerns of local people, the Cherokee *(Iowa)* Daily Times *initiated a series of public meetings that went beyond the usual forum approach.*

The Times *sponsored four sessions with candidates and arranged that the candidates would answer questions posed by panels of representative citizens and then by members of the audience. There were two objectives: to provide personal exposure between candidates and voters in a nonpolitical setting and, through extensive reporting of the sessions, to provide readers with an understanding of issues of importance to their neighbors.*

Interviews by author with Ruby Peterson and Marvin Wilmes of the *Cherokee Daily Times.* August 24, 1988.

well as comparative figures on total expenditures, total broadcasting advertising, amounts spent on consultants, and other expenditures. Breakdowns can include percentages of contributions from union funds, professional organizations, business and industry, conservation groups, political groups, and banks, savings and loans, and insurance companies.

Unresolved or future issues

One type of story that is often worthwhile attempts to explain what issues, if any, were resolved in an election, in the approval or rejection of a ballot measure, or in the approval or rejection of a candidate, a party, or a political philosophy. A somewhat related story attempts to look forward to the issues that were not resolved or that were raised by the election. Often, this type of story looks to the challenges that await an incoming governor or newly constituted county board or state legislature. Closely related to that story is one that looks at what outgoing officeholders are doing or might do with their powers before they are replaced by the winners.

Between elections

After an election, much of the political interest that has been centered around the electoral process shifts back to the branches of government. Competition between political parties and among interest groups moves to the city councils, county commissions, state and federal legislative bodies, and executive offices. Consequently, much of the political reporting becomes the responsibility of reporters who cover those agencies. Still, the electoral process never ceases. For the political reporter, opportunities for keeping readers informed about the electoral process still abound.

Political party news

In spite of being partly eclipsed by the media and interest groups, the political parties remain good sources of news between elections. After an election, questions about leadership often are raised at all levels of the party. Jockeying begins for position among potential candidates in the next election. Parties that have lost may be looking for new faces. Parties that have won may also be looking for people to carry out the wishes of a new set of elected officials or to replace party leaders who may have received government jobs from the winning candidates. After its 1984 loss in the presidential election, the Democratic party went through a period of introspection and regrouping to prepare for the next campaign. The Republican party leaders also began looking ahead, knowing that President Reagan was in his last term of office and that a new nominee would have to be selected.

Some of this intraparty selection process takes place out of the sight of the public, and perhaps out of the sight of most party members. But a political writer with good contacts should be able to find and tell the story.

Caucuses and conventions

Some leadership decisions are made in precinct and county caucuses that are open to the public, or at least to party members. These can make good copy, although they generally are not well attended unless a controversial issue or candidacy is involved. One purpose of the caucus in some states is to select delegates to caucuses or conventions at the next higher political level. Precincts may select delegates for county meetings; counties may select delegates to the congressional district or state level.

Because of the growth in presidential primaries, a large number of delegates to national conventions are selected directly by the voters. Following the 1980 convention, however, the Democratic party decided to reserve a substantial minority of convention seats for party leaders and officeholders. Some of these are selected through the convention process. The Democrats also have been holding national conventions in the even-numbered years between the presidential elections, and some states also have formal or informal party sessions between major elections. Sometimes these meetings provide a more thorough airing of issues than the presidential-year conventions because party leaders are less concerned about preserving an image of party unity.

Reapportionment and redistricting

A political matter that touches the electoral process directly is the twin issue of reapportionment and redistricting. Every ten years, seats in the United States House of Representatives are reapportioned among the states to reflect population shifts. This allocation of seats largely has become a matter of applying a formula. But after the reapportionment, battles occur in many states over how the new district lines will be drawn. Similar battles are waged over the redrawing of state legislative district lines. The drawing of boundaries can affect not only the fates of individual legislators but also the relative legislative strengths of the major parties for an entire decade. Computers allow fine shading of boundaries to favor one party, or even one candidate.

In some states a neutral commission has been assigned the task of drawing district lines, but party leaders and legislators generally have been reluctant to give up the power to draw the lines. The details of redistricting

STORY ANGLES FOR THE ELECTORAL PROCESS

DURING A CAMPAIGN
A look at candidates
A comparison of issues
Explanation of issues
Campaign finances
Notable races
Campaign strategy
Minor candidates and parties
Speculation about the election
Charges and countercharges
Predictions of turnout
Public opinion polls

AFTER AN ELECTION
Exit interviews
Explanation of the outcome
Analysis of the voting
Campaign spending
Unresolved or future issues

BETWEEN ELECTIONS
Political parties
Caucuses and conventions
Reapportionment and
   redistricting

can be so complicated that only the map drawers know why they put a line in one place instead of another. Sometimes blatant political purposes are involved: a favorite legislator is given a district with lots of friendly voters, or an out-of-favor legislator is matched with a heavy majority of voters of the opposite party.

Politicians often try to use redistricting to hold off the social and economic changes that population shifts bring. Legislators in Virginia, which is still experiencing rapid urbanization and a heavy influx of new residents to counties adjacent to Washington, D.C., tried to do this after the 1980 census. Various legislative redistricting plans were invalidated by federal courts or vetoed by Governor John N. Dalton. The United States Justice Department became heavily involved because Virginia was seen as having a history of racial discrimination in voting practices. "They just had a horrible mess," said one Virginia state senator (Ruberry 1988a).

The situation in the 1990s may not be as politically contentious in Virginia. In some areas of the country, however, every new census serves as what one Washington journalist termed "a rough outline for profound change" (Ruberry 1988b). Politicians and others seeing their interests threatened are bound to resist the change. With good contacts, a journalist ought to be able to find sources who can explain the public issues involved, and perhaps even point out the crafty details.

Some less than desirable practices

Unfortunately, not all types of political reporting merit commendation to young journalists. Political reporting, in fact, has been criticized for exhibiting some of the same characteristics as present-day political campaigning: too much concern with personalities, images, sensation, controversy, trivialities, and the "horse race."

Personalities and images

In their attempts to look for something that listeners and readers can relate to easily, reporters sometimes exaggerate the perspective of human interest at the expense of significant issues. Nothing makes better television footage than the candidate displaying a strong personality in an unusual setting. In illustrating how the presidential campaign had become image-oriented, *Los Angeles Times* writer Robert Scheer described a scene in Waco, Texas, in 1980, in which President Carter was "happily waving his gifts of 'stomping boots' in the air and going on about how he would use them 'to stomp Republicans on November fourth' and to walk through the 'horse manure' they have been spreading." The television people, with their minicams clicking, loved it. "The President's men knew they would," Scheer wrote. The scene would play well on the evening news. Concerning such activities, a Carter aide was quoted as saying, "We do media events — we do television events. We stage these things because we know that the reality is that there's going to be an evening news tonight and they are budgeted for a Carter spot and a Reagan spot and, if we give them pictures on a subject we think is good for us politically, they're likely to cover it" (Scheer 1980). Responsible journalists do not fall for such tactics.

Campaign politics

Even when a candidate makes an issue-oriented speech, the press may choose to focus on the candidate's image or the possible political effects of the speech, not the speech itself. Bernard Weinraub of the *New York Times* noted a speech by Senator Edward M. Kennedy early in the 1980 presidential campaign in which he called for gasoline rationing and wage controls and attacked President Carter's foreign policy. These proposals represented major departures from a program supported by a president of his own party. Yet, Weinraub wrote, "that evening, the three television networks led their shows with the candidate's speech but focused less on Mr. Kennedy's specific proposals than on the potential effect of the speech and whether it would salvage his campaign" (Weinraub 1980). Audiences deserve more comprehensive reporting.

Focusing on the negative

Reporters also are accused of looking for the negative in covering candidates. The publicizing of errors became a theme in the 1980 and 1984 presidential campaigns of Ronald Reagan. At one point during a debate during the primaries, Reagan, smarting from accusations of using incorrect figures, pulled out of his coat pocket a United Press International (UPI) story that he said vindicated him on one set of figures concerning unemployment. A UPI story published later in the campaign concluded that "an examination of some of the criticism suggests Reagan has sometimes been faulted wrongly, even pettily, by the news media for 'mistakes' that anyone else might consider an honest expression of opinion." The story noted that on one occasion Reagan was criticized for saying that the Statue of Liberty was "looking on" the festivities whereas she actually was facing out to the ocean (United Press International 1980).

New angle every day

Reporters sometimes feel pressure to come up with a new story angle every day. Even though candidates may stress issues day after day as they campaign, they may have a hard time getting their messages through to voters. To reporters, the messages are old ones. They already have reported them. Today they want to report something different, so they turn to minor issues, personalities, and anything else that seems new and different. Most readers and listeners are not paying enough attention to need a new tidbit every day.

Pack journalism

Another disease to which political reporters are susceptible is "pack journalism," reporting and emphasizing an element of a campaign because other reporters are doing so. One might expect that reporters would try to make their stories distinctive, reporting aspects that other reporters were not reporting. But pressures work the other way sometimes. If reporters are not covering what their competitors are covering, editors want to know why. This tendency was vividly illustrated, and decried, by Timothy Crouse in *The Boys on the Bus,* an account of the 1972 presidential campaign. Reporters were found to have watched to see what the Associated Press and the *New York Times* reported (Crouse 1973).

It is true that most persons see no more than one newspaper during a day or no more than one network news program, so they are not likely to be as aware of pack journalism as reporters, editors, producers, and campaign people are. But this lack of awareness should not relieve reporters of doing their own evaluating of news, and if necessary standing up to editors and producers who want to know why they do not have a story on the hot topic of the day. Stories on less popular subjects today may serve to broaden the general campaign discussion by encouraging other reporters to turn to those subjects on subsequent days.

Hints for covering politics

The political process is in constant flux and the requirements of good reporting dictate that you keep checking on activities between elections, even though it may seem that not much is happening. Some suggestions that may help during and between campaigns:

1. Every community has political enthusiasts who can be solid sources when there seemingly is a lull in party business.

Periodic checks with them will help keep you up to date although the information may not bring an immediate story. Most of them like to talk politics and appreciate an audience.

2. Government actions, whether in state or national capitals or at the city hall, often have political overtones. Stories that explain the political angles can be valuable for listeners or readers, but the possibilities often are overlooked by reporters.

3. Colleges and universities can offer a rich source of expertise that can give more body to your stories. Political scientists and economists in particular should be cultivated as sources who can provide knowledge in depth.

4. Do not ignore minor party leaders and candidates. Their chances of success may be minimal, but audiences should have a chance to learn about them and their views.

5. Be cautious about treating political polling results as a basis for sweeping conclusions. The polls are guides to public thinking and should be considered as such. Results can change during a campaign. Be especially wary of polls conducted by political parties, candidates, and special interest groups.

In summary

The mass media do not constitute a branch of government. The media play no legally prescribed role in elections and election campaigns. Yet the media probably have become the major mechanism linking candidates and voters. If the media do not carry the political messages to the voters, most of the messages will not get through. So, whether the media perform adequately or not, they serve as a common carrier in the election process.

Because the clamor of competing voices is likely to create as much confusion as understanding among voters, the media have the responsibility to help make sense out of the confusion. Reporters can dig beneath the rhetoric of the campaign to provide interpretation and insight into issues. They can play an investigative role when the regular political institutions fail to tell the public about matters it has a right to know about. Reporters, and the media in general, can play the role of watchdog, letting politicians, in and out of government, know that their words and actions are being watched and reported to the public. Finally, the media must be viewed as a political force, however imperfect they may be. To a large extent, the media determine which candidates and which issues receive the most attention. To a considerable extent, they create or at least affect the atmosphere in which elections take place. They may not have the power to influence directly how substantial numbers of citizens cast their votes, but the manner in which they report the campaign can have a great deal to do with the attitudes of those citizens when they cast their votes.

References

Achorn, Edward C. 1988a. Some Lawmakers PAC in Special Interest Dollars. *Middlesex News* (Framingham, MA), July 12, 1A.
_____. 1988b. Some Congressmen Find Talk Isn't Cheap. *Middlesex News* (Framingham, MA), July 13, 1A.
_____. 1988c. Capitol Hill Hiring Often All in the Family. *Middlesex News* (Framingham, MA), July 14, 1A.
Alters, Diane. 1988. Why Americans Don't Vote. *Boston Globe,* July 17, 67.
Bybee, Carl R. 1980. Facilitating Decision-Making Through News Story Organization. *Journalism Quarterly* 57(4):624–30.
Clarke, Peter, and Fredin, Eric. 1978. Newspaper, Television and Political Reasoning. *Public Opinion Quarterly* 42(1):142–60.
Comstock, George, Chaffee, Steven, Katzman, Nathan, McCombs, Maxwell, and Roberts, Donald. 1978. *Television and Human Behavior.* New York: Columbia University.
Crouse, Timothy. 1973. *The Boys on the Bus.* New York: Ballantine Books.
Darnton, Jack. 1982. Election Campaign Winds Up Rowdy, Raspy and Relevant. *Longview* (WA) *Daily News,* Nov. 1, A1.
Gans, Herbert J. 1979. *Deciding What's News.* New York: Vintage Books.
Goodwin, Doris Kearns. 1987. Evaluating Candidates: Standards and Responsibilities. In *Covering the Candidates.* Reston, VA: American Press Institute. 27–51.
Graber, Doris A. 1988. *Processing the News: How People Tame the Information Tide.* Second edition. New York: Longman.
Iyengar, Shanto, and Kinder, Donald R. 1987. *News That Matters.* Chicago: University of Chicago Press.
Jeffres, Leo W. 1986. *Mass Media: Processes and Effects.* Prospect Heights, Ill.: Waveland.
Katz, Jeffrey L. 1988. Finding Just the Right Words: GOP, Advisers Seek Themes for the Fall. *The Milwaukee Journal,* Aug. 18, A7.
Los Angeles Times. 1982. Proposition on the Nov. 2 Ballot. Nov. 1, A3.
McCombs, Maxwell E., and Shaw, Donald. 1972. The Agenda-Setting Function of the Mass Media. *Public Opinion Quarterly,* 36:176–87.
Martin, John Frederick. 1988. The Curse of Campaign Fund Raising. *New York Times,* July 11, A17.
Meyer, Philip. 1983. *Precision Journalism.* Bloomington: Indiana University.
Muro, Mark. 1988. If Half of Us Don't Vote, Are We a Democracy? *Boston Globe,* July 17, 68.
Neuborne, Burt. 1988. Disenfranchising the Poor. *Civil Liberties.* no. 364 (Spring/Summer): 10.
Piven, Frances Fox, and Cloward, Richard. A. 1988. *Why Americans Don't Vote.* New York: Pantheon.
Pomper, Gerald M. 1980. *Party Renewal in America.* New York: Praeger.

Pomper, Gerald M., with Lederer, Susan S. 1980. *Elections in America,* 2d ed. New York: Longman.

Rabin, Jeff. 1982. Governor's Race: Major Issues Divide Deukmejian, Bradley. *Sacramento* (CA) *Bee,* Oct. 29, A8.

Ribadeneira, Diego. 1988. Get The People Registered, Chances Are They'll Vote. *Boston Globe,* July 17, 69.

Rippey, John N. 1980. Use of Polls as a Reporting Tool. *Journalism Quarterly,* 57(4):642–46, 721.

Rix, Paul A. 1988. Democratic Showdown. *Shepherd Express* (Milwaukee, WI), Aug. 18, 1.

Ruberry, William. 1988a. District Mapping Fights of '80s Called 'Nightmare.' *Richmond Times-Dispatch,* July 31, B6.

_____. 1988b. 1991 Redistricting Could Mark Big Changes. *Richmond Times-Dispatch,* July 31, B1.

Rystrom, Kenneth. 1982. Friends of Redlands: Participatory Democracy. Unpublished manuscript.

Scardino, Albert. 1988. When the Press Breaks a Promise. *New York Times,* July 17, E3.

Scheer, Robert. 1980. TV Reshapes Coverage of Candidates. *Los Angeles Times,* Nov. 1, E1.

Smith, Laurie. 1982. Jack Shero Knows County From His Youth, Jobs. *Longview* (WA) *Daily News,* Oct. 30, B1.

Tackett, Michael. 1988. Wondering What Our $1 Is Funding? *Chicago Tribune,* Aug. 16, A10.

Tuchman, Gaye. 1978. *Making News: A Study in the Construction of Reality.* New York: Free Press.

United Press International. 1980. Reagan: "I Don't See Where That's A Gaff To Say That." *Redlands* (CA) *Daily Facts,* Sept. 17, 1.

Weinraub, Bernard. 1980. Students of Campaign News Find Hard Issues Neglected. *New York Times,* Apr. 30, A26.

Wilson, James Q. 1983. The American Presidency. Lecture. University of Redlands. Nov. 6.

This chapter was initiated by Rystrom. Collaborators were Molen, Scotton, and Griffin.

INDEX